RED GUIDES

BUYING A PROPERTY

France

2005

Merricks Media Ltd

THE UK'S NO.1 PUBLISHER FOR BUYING PROPERTY ABROAD

Trisha Mason
Founder and MD of VEF

Nobody has helped more people buy property in France than VEF

"At VEF, our service helps you find the house of your dreams in France, and then guides you through the process of buying. We have been helping people buy in France for 17 years and have created 1000s of happy and secure home-owners.

For all types of property, new or old, for all budgets, £10,000 to £2 million, VEF is the only place you need to go.

For the best service, from choosing your region and finding your house to receiving the keys in the notaire's office, VEF is the one to help you.

Just ask the 10,000 we've helped already!"

Trisha Mason, founder and MD of VEF

BUYING A PROPERTY IN

France
2005

EDITOR
Justin Postlethwaite

Merricks Media Ltd

THE UK'S NO.1 PUBLISHER FOR BUYING PROPERTY ABROAD

BUYING A PROPERTY IN
France 2005

THE ULTIMATE GUIDE TO BUYING, SELLING AND LETTING IN FRANCE

Compiled, edited and designed by **Merricks Media Ltd**, 3 & 4 Riverside Court, Lower Bristol Road, Bath, BA2 3DZ. Tel: 01225 786800
redguides@merricksmedia.co.uk www.redguides.co.uk

Managing Director Lisa Doerr
Group Editor Ali Stewart
Managing Editor Daphne Razazan
Editor Justin Postlethwaite
Senior Researcher Leaonne Hall
Researcher Helen Hill
Chief Sub Editor Victoria Crumpton
Art Director Jon Billington
Art Editor Nigel Morrison
Design Hayley Liddle, Jess Wright
Production Manager Graham Prichard
Sales Director Nick Hemburrow
General Sales Manager Keith Burnell
Sales Executives Barney Pearson, Lucy Owen
Advertisement Design Becky Hamblin
Contributors Andrew Ashwin, Steve Bradley, Lisa McGee, Mary Richards, Adam Waring, Mark Wheatley

is a trademark of **Merricks Media Ltd**

Cover image © **Duranti/www.wallis.fr** Regional maps by Jamie Symonds © **Merricks Media Ltd** 2004. France Touring Map © **Michelin et Cie**
Illustrations by Felix Packer © **Merricks Media Ltd** 2004. All rights reserved.

Printed and bound in Spain by P&R GRAFIS Fuengirola

Copyright © 2004 **Merricks Media Ltd**
ISBN 1-905049-09-9 British Library Cataloguing in Publication Data.
A catalogue record for this book is available from the British Library.

Welcome

JUSTIN POSTLETHWAITE

Justin Postlethwaite's passion for France began with school twinning exchanges to a small Normandy town. A degree in French was then followed by a spell living in Pau and many, many holidays and journalism trips all around France. He is now Editor of *French Magazine*, Britain's leading resource for fellow lovers of the French lifestyle.

"We've scoured the country and talked to leading agents to find the best places in which to buy in 2005"

WHY DO SO MANY OF US DREAM OF BUYING A HOME IN France? It could simply be that property is much cheaper there than in the UK – have you *seen* what you can snap up for £50,000 in Limousin? Clearly, such great value is a key factor, but there are many other compelling reasons: the laidback lifestyle, traditional values, rich cultural heritage, beautiful countryside, not to mention fantastic food and wine.

2005 will be a great year to buy in France. Improved access to and around France will make life easier for visitors and homeowners. Budget airlines will take flight to more regional airports, the impressive TGV infrastructure will expand and the spectacular Millau viaduct on the A75 will open up the South of France to a new generation of road users.

And then there are the hotspots. We've scoured the country and talked to leading agents to find the best places in which to buy in 2005. We've also got the best financial and legal advice to guide you through the process from start to finish. And we've compiled a comprehensive price matrix to help you find the right property in the right place at the right price.

Buying a Property in France 2005 is the UK's most authoritative guide to the current French property scene. If you are thinking of buying a property in France, whether as a new family home, a retirement bolthole, a *maison secondaire*, a holiday apartment or as an investment opportunity, this publication will serve as your buying bible.

I hope that we can play a small part in helping you realise the dream of a new life in France.

Bonne chance!

Justin

Justin Postlethwaite, Editor

INTRODUCTION

Contents

■ OVERVIEW

*Check out our regional and touring maps
of France, and see how to use this book*

■ BUYER'S GUIDE

*Look here for all the information you
need for buying a house in France*

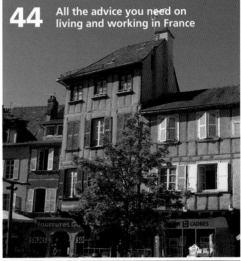

44 All the advice you need on living and working in France

114 Fancy buying a place in 'Gay Paris'? Take a look at our hotspots

REAL-LIFE CASE STUDIES

We did it!...

*Read our real-life case studies of people
who have bought properties and
relocated to France*

PROPERTY GUIDES

■ REGIONAL PROFILES AND PRICE GUIDES

A guide to all the regions, prices and hotspots in France

France has some of Europe's most spectacular scenery and ski resorts **211**

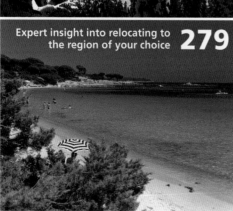

Expert insight into relocating to the region of your choice **279**

■ BUYER'S REFERENCE

All the facts, figures and contact details you need in an easy-to-read directory

Map of featured regions

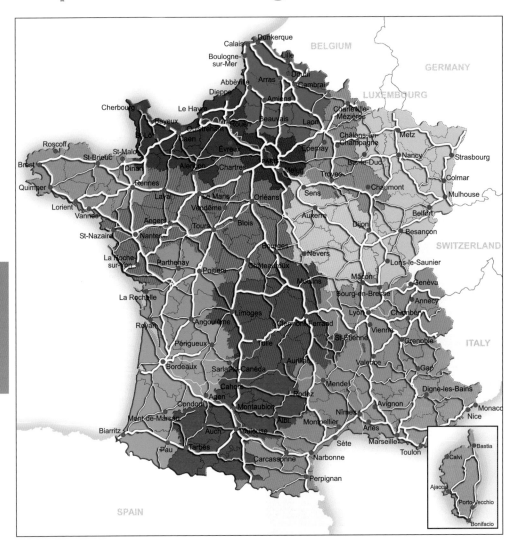

- Since the Middle Ages, 4,000 châteaux and stately homes have been built in Brittany
- Normandy has 362,000 hectares of forest, 600km of coastline and 14,000km of rivers
- Lille, in Nord Pas-de-Calais, was European City of Culture in 2004
- Île-de-France is home to more English-speaking expatriates than any other region
- Champagne-Ardenne is famous for its medieval castles and churches
- The Alsace is renowned for its pretty medieval villages and half-timbered houses

- Le Mans, in the Loire, is home to the famous 24-hour race
- Burgundy has more Michelin-starred restaurants than any other region
- Poitou-Charentes is the home of Cognac brandy
- One third of Limousin is covered by forest
- Rhône-Alpes contains the world's largest skiing area.
- The Aquitaine coastline is famous for its oysters
- The Midi-Pyrénées is the largest geographical region
- Languedoc-Roussillon has the fastest projected population growth of any region
- The region of Provence is famous for its lavender

Touring map of France

MICHELIN

TOURING MAP

POPULATION

- The total population of France currently stands at 60.4 million
- The population is growing at a rate of 0.39% per year, and has increased by 2.9 million in the last 10 years
- The median age in France is 38.6 years
- The most populous metropolitan area is around Paris, with a population of 2.2 million
- Population growth in rural areas is outpacing that of urban areas

GEOGRAPHY

- France covers 547,030 sq km in total
- The total length of France's borders is 6,316km, of which 3,427km is coastline
- France is bordered by Spain, Andorra, Italy, Monaco, Switzerland, Germany, Luxembourg and Belgium
- The terrain of France mostly consists of rolling hills in the North and West, with mountain ranges in the South and East
- The highest point in France is Mont Blanc at 4,807m
- The lowest point in France is the Rhône river delta at -2m

CLIMATE

- Northwest and Midwest France have an oceanic climate, with mild winters, cool summers and frequent rain
- Inland France has a continental climate with cold winters, hot summers and medium rainfall
- The mountain ranges have very cold, snowy winters and hot but often wet summers
- The South coast has a Mediterranean climate, with mild winters and hot dry summers
- The French climate is one of the most temperate in Europe

ECONOMY

- The current economic slowdown and inflexible budget have pushed the 2003 deficit to 4% of the GDP, above the EU's 3% debt limit
- Unemployment currently stands at 9.7% and has risen every year since 2001
- There has been recent movement towards privatisation of many large companies
- A dynamic service sector accounts for an increasingly large share of economic activity (71.5%) and is responsible for nearly all recent job creation

Buyer's Guide

JUSTIN POSTLETHWAITE

BUYER'S GUIDE

Economy 2005

Political and economic policies and trends, as well as less predictable global events, have had an impact on the tourism and property markets. The repercussions have affected the French economy…

A CENTRE-RIGHT GOVERNMENT LED BY PRIME Minister Jean-Pierre Raffarin returned to power in May 2002 after five years of Socialist rule, with plans to roll out reforms aimed at liberalising the economy, promoting competitiveness and intensifying the appeal of France to foreign investors.

John Howell gained his LLB from Bristol University in 1971. He then moved to Leeds where he took his articles, becoming a solicitor in 1975. John practised as a general private solicitor, a public prosecutor and a tribunal chairman.

Economic reform

Some steps have already been taken but some of the major structural reforms – including the privatisation of the huge French public sector companies such as Air France – have yet to be completed.

Over a five year period the government aims to reduce income tax by 30 per cent. It has also shown signs of a commitment to reforming pensions and the public sector, in particular calling a halt to public sector spending.

The practical achievements have been a lot less impressive, with the French still having amongst the highest level of overall taxation in Europe. Depending on the view you take on 'tax', i.e. social charges and social security payments, the overall

"Over a five year period the government aims to reduce income tax by 30 per cent."

level of taxation in France in 2003 (the latest year for which statistics are available) lay somewhere between 43.8 and 51 per cent of GDP. This compares with about 40-41 per cent for Great Britain.

The French government's budget deficit far exceeds euro rules (over four per cent for 2003 and looking like it will increase for 2004). This compares, of course, to the target of three per cent laid down in Maastricht. At least France has a lower deficit than America, which is currently running at six per cent. France also has

Despite recent reports, the French property market is thriving due to low interest rates

long-term liabilities in certain public enterprises, along with unsustainable pension commitments. The intention to solve this by privatising the huge public utility companies was thwarted by the poor state of the stock market, hence this strategy was postponed.

Another major worry in the French economy is the highly protected status of the French workforce. Many industries complain that the much vaunted 35 hour week and minimum five weeks holiday are a crippling expense and proposals are underway to alter some of these commitments.

The French national health service, although recognised as being superb, is also unaffordable in its present state. Such is the political delicacy of reforms to either workers' rights or the health service that change could take some time.

State of the French economy

In common with most other western economies, France has recently experienced peaks and troughs.

Its important tourist sector has bounced back from the post 9/11 trauma which saw a 50 per cent reduction in tourism in Paris. Even tourism from the United States has picked up substantially as confidence in air travel has improved.

In the real estate sector there has been much activity buoyed by continuing low interest rates (mortgages are still available from 2.75 per cent variable) and much interest from overseas, including Britain and the United States. Property prices continue to rise in key locations such as central Paris (about 14 per cent in the third/fourth and sixth arrondissements – the Marais and the posh parts of the left bank). We have also seen substantial price rises in the old favourites such as the Côte d'Azur and, buoyed by external demand, in Charentes and on the southeast coast of France.

A deterrent to inward investment – particularly from the United States – has been the huge drop in value of the dollar against the euro. From a situation where a dollar bought 1.3 euros we see a euro now buying 1.3 dollars.

Other negative indicators within the economy in 2004 included continued high unemployment.

The effect of world events

Last year, of course, was dominated by the war on Iraq and it's too early to say what the impact of this will be as far as the French economy is concerned. France has traditionally had strong ties in the Middle East and much will depend upon the proposed January elections and the new government in Baghdad.

Population shifts

While there is a huge strain on the French government's coffers – as a result of a high percentage of its population now at pensionable age – many

The wine industry is fundamental to the economy

British nationals are also choosing to move to France and retire. Well who can blame them? They foresee the benefits of more clement weather, an unrivalled health service and an altogether higher standard of living. France offers the British more for their hard earned cash: value for money in property, quality food and fine wine – even the cheapest wine is fine for cooking, and it's all to be found on the doorstep.

As more of us, whatever our age, succumb to the charm of French country life, certain enclaves have become what some describe as 'ghettos'. And this is not solely in the regions traditionally popular with British buyers, such as Provence in the South of France and Dordogne in the Southwest, where there are so many homeowners from the UK that villages have their own cricket team. A positive rush on buying a dream home in France has led to British buyers moving en masse to certain areas that were once rather overlooked, such as Gard, which lies to the west of Provence in the increasingly popular Languedoc-Roussillon. ●

∎ **CONTACTS**
Blevins Franks, Financial Management Ltd
Barbican House, 26-34 Old Street, London
EC1V 9QQ, Tel; 0207 336 1116
www.blevinsfranks.com

BUYER'S GUIDE

The French property market

France has always been popular with foreign property investors but the last three years have seen unprecedented growth

THE FRENCH PROPERTY MARKET IS EXPERIENCING A fascinating time. In the three years from 2002 to 2004, the number of buyers entering the market each year has doubled.

Think France...

The fascination with France and love of French life is growing at the same time as generations of Britons are becoming disenchanted with life in the UK. The consequences are obvious: thousands of British people are now buying in France and many more of them are planning to move there full-time.

As well as discontentment with the UK, the market is also being driven by the factors that have always driven it: lower property prices in France; easy and affordable accessibility; a better climate; and a love of the French way of life. Think wine, think food, think space, think coast, think mountains, think art, think culture, think national pride, think regional diversity... think France.

The question everybody wants to ask is what happens in 2005? Well, the access to France continues to improve with more flights and more developments from Eurostar. France's road network is already good and is being improved, providing more autoroutes linking more places and reducing travelling time from port of entry to final destination. The climate, alas, will always be better and warmer than that of the UK.

"Property prices have increased in France, so you are now getting a little less property for your money than at the same time last year"

Property prices have increased across most areas of France so you are now getting a little less property for your money than you were at the same time last year. However, as house prices in the UK have increased at the same rate or more (excepting the southeast at the very end of 2004), the difference between what you get for your money in France and in the UK is still substantial. You are likely to be able to buy a bigger or a better, or a cheaper (or all three!) property in France than in the UK. As for the widespread disenchantment with UK life, there seems no sign of a change.

Property prices in 2005

It seems therefore that the property market in France is set for another busy year in 2005 but how exactly will it pan out?

Paul Owen is Sales and Marketing Director at VEF French Property, and is regularly quoted throughout the media as the leading market commentator. He has had articles published in the national press, and made several appearances on national television

It is safe to predict that prices will continue to rise in 2005 across most areas of France in which overseas buyers have an interest. Do remember that point as part of the equation: overseas buyers affect the market enormously as, traditionally, the French do not buy and sell property to the extent that the British do. For this reason, conditions in the UK particularly will have an impact on the market in France.

The end of 2004 saw a 'slowing' in the UK property market, particularly in the southeast. There seemed very little substance to the concerns of buyers as interest rates, though raised, remained low and few expect them to rise above 5 per cent. At the same time, employment has remained high. Worries that the price of crude oil would feed down to every country's economy had dissipated by the end of October. The market was talked down by the people, by the media, but there was nothing of substance to take it down to serious levels. Whilst few expect the UK market to surge ahead in 2005, it can be expected to remain stable and, once the media stop talking it down, the UK buyers will again kick into life.

Once they start buying (expected to be early in 2005), many of the vendors will be buying in France. Driven on, as ever, by the lower property prices, the change of life and the change of location, UK buyers will be pouring over to France and into its properties. So what will they be looking for? And will they get it?

Few UK buyers are looking for French city life; it's the countryside they seek or the quaint French village or the sleepy hamlet. Five years ago, many buyers wanted to buy a run-down property in rural France

BUYERS GUIDE

and invest time, money and love into its renovation. Over the course of 2004, a higher number of people began to put this route to bed, preferring to buy a property that had already been renovated. They still wanted a character property but without the hard work to deliver it themselves!

This move away from 'do-it-yourself' is further illustrated by another huge change in the French property market that is expected to continue through 2005: new build property. Fifty per cent of new-build property buyers in 2004 were buying purely for investment. Making the most of the government-sponsored leaseback scheme, investors receive a guaranteed rental income whilst expecting good capital appreciation for their holiday home purchases.

The new-build market

The other 50 per cent of new-build property buyers are motivated by a hassle-free holiday property that can make them some money to cover costs when they are not using it themselves. With more and more developments being offered across France in 2005, the new-build market will clearly feature strongly in the plans of the UK buyer of French property.

Returning to the traditional French re-sale market, the trend for renovated properties rather than tumble-down shacks will affect the price movements for 2005. In the preceding three years, some of the largest price increases had been for properties in need of renovation in quiet, rural spots in France such as Limousin and Poitou-Charentes. It was not unusual to see the value of a renovation property double in three years. This type of property will always be popular but, with the buyer now demanding more properties with renovation work done, the renovated character property in rural France is set for substantial price increases in 2005.

Looking forward to the next year in French property, it is genuinely hard to see anything other than a busy 12 months. There are still many buyers who love France, who like the UK a little less than they used to and who are willing to make substantial changes to their lives or significant adjustments to the way in which they invest their money. More of them will look to new-build properties as a vehicle for investment but the long-standing British love affair with the French countryside and its character properties will continue to blossom.

Renovation properties have seen the greatest price appreciation

Those who took the French property plunge in the last few years, whether new-build or re-sale, have seen the value of their asset in France increase substantially. Their money has worked well for them but, for most, there is much more to it than that. They have bought into a new way of life, whether that is a more relaxed day-to-day existence by moving to France or a deep enjoyment of all things French when they are able to visit their holiday home in Gallic paradise a few times a year.

Think France

If there is one conclusion, one lesson to be learned from the last few years to help you decide if 2005 is the year to buy in France, it is simple: yes!

The longer you wait to make a decision, the less you are going to get for your money, and the less time you will have to enjoy your home in France or, indeed, to make money on it. ●

■ CONTACTS

VEF (UK) Ltd, Ground Floor City Reach,
5 Greenwich View Place, Millharbour,
London E14 9NN
Tel: 020 7515 8660
Fax: 020 7515 5070
URL: www.vefuk.com

BECKY HAMBLIN

BUYER'S GUIDE

Buying and Selling

In 2005, France is very much a seller's market. So once you have found that dream property, it's essential that you act fast

NEW TRANSPORT LINKS HAVE CONTRIBUTED TO THE rising popularity of key regional areas, especially those with holiday letting potential, making France very much a seller's market in 2005. So once you have found that dream property, it's essential to move quickly to begin the purchase process.

David Franks is the Chief Executive of Blevins Franks and is an accomplished and experienced practitioner in both UK and overseas taxation. Published in a number of leading taxation works he can be contacted at Blevins Franks on 0207 336 1111.

Overview

Over the past year, changes in air travel to France have had a significant impact on both buyers and sellers of French property. These changes, particularly the operations of budget airlines in responding to the need for improved and more affordable access to French regions, affected how, and how often, people travel to France. New routes came on stream, while the apparently ephemeral nature of others has resulted in some of last year's potential hotspots turning into this year's has-beens.

In 2002 and 2003, there was a great deal of excitement over the introduction of budget flight routes into parts of France that other airlines had not previously serviced. It was widely believed that these routes would open up areas little known to tourists and house hunters, and that property in these areas could prove a wise purchase, either for personal use or as an investment. However, anyone who rushed to buy in areas now easily accessible from other European countries may be regretting that decision, and buyers should bear in mind that choosing a location because it is served by a less-established route is not always prudent. Low-fare routes such as London Stansted to Strasbourg or Bordeaux have been discontinued, either because they proved unprofitable or because courts ruled that incentive payments to encourage budget airlines to fly into these airports were illegal. If more routes are terminated this year, it will prevent you making the most of your French home, and may also make it more difficult to rent out.

Terrestrial travel routes could also affect the buying and selling of property in 2005. Although still only on the drawing board, the official go-ahead has been given to extending the TGV rail service from Paris through Provence and the Côte d'Azur. High-speed rail connections to Europe's towns and cities will no doubt add extra cachet to properties near new TGV destinations in this southeastern corner of France. It's not all good news though: work on the tracks and indeed, the tracks themselves, may not be too appealing to those living in or renting property nearby.

In France today, apart from travel considerations, it is very much a seller's market. So much so that properties, especially in areas popular with foreign buyers looking to invest, are frequently sold within hours of them appearing on the market, sometimes even before there has been time to print particulars. This has made finding an apartment in the resorts popular with international skiers – in the Savoie and Haute-Savoie *départements* of the French Alps, for example – exceedingly difficult.

"In France today, apart from travel considerations, it is very much a seller's market, especially in areas popular with foreign buyers"

It should be particularly easy in 2004 for vendors to find a buyer through agents – whether estate agents in the UK, or French agents, immobiliers and *notaires* – with a web presence and an international outlook. Well-targeted advertising opportunities in the classified sections of specialist magazines and national newspapers, both in France and abroad, are increasingly available for sellers who can advertise directly or through the agents who are marketing the property. Sellers can also advertise their property directly on websites dedicated to overseas properties. Alongside the development of marketing opportunities on and off-line, there is a growth in French property fairs in and outside France.

The increasing number of publications and websites advertising French property makes it easier both for owners to find buyers and for buyers to find their ideal home, especially if they are searching from far afield. Surprisingly, perhaps, less than half the 600,000

CRT TOULOUSE MIDI-PYRÉNÉES

Relocating to France can be lead to a relaxing lifestyle, especially if you secure the right advice

annual property sales are handled by estate agents, with the remainder arranged either privately or by the notarial profession.

Whether you choose to buy through an estate agent or not, with properties changing hands as swiftly as they are at the moment, you could find yourself pressurised into buying without checking on the property and its area thoroughly. If you do need to proceed rapidly with a sale in order not to miss what you believe is a perfect opportunity, make sure you do so subject to a contract. The contract should be one that provides you with the opportunity to 'get out' if you discover problems after you have signed and handed over your deposit.

Capital gains tax on property

The declaration of capital gains on French property was simplified in 2005, off-loading the burden of declaration from the vendor. From 1st January 2004, the *notaire* in charge of the sale became responsible on behalf of the client for progressing the calculation and payment of capital gains tax during the registration of the sale.

The calculation itself was simplified by the granting of a fixed allowance of 15 per cent on the sale price, to take into account potential renovation works that may have been carried out on the property. There is now no capital gains tax levied on a property that has been owned for 15 years or more, instead of the 22 years previously. After the fifth year, capital gains have been reduced by 10 per cent for every complete year, instead of using the *coefficient d'érosion monétaire* (monetary depreciation coefficient).

Other changes to the regime include the exemption of property under 15,000 euros from this tax, and a

fixed reduction of 1,000 euros on the total capital gains due. The vendor is also now taxed at the time that the buyer transfers the balance of the purchase price to them, with the tax payable being taken from the sum transferred, instead of waiting more than a year to pay when the income tax for that tax year is due.

Rental income

Any rental income received for a French property is liable to French income tax, whenever it might have been paid. Mortgage interest arising from a loan charged against the French property is tax deductible, along with costs directly attributable to the letting. Your own travel costs are not normally allowable.

Succession taxes

On death, France can charge succession tax. A married couple may be able to avoid this by planning the asset in joint names and entering into a community marriage contract.

Succession law

France gives the children of a deceased parent the right to receive up to 75 per cent of the estate, even against assets in joint names. For children of the same marriage, the community marriage contract overrides the children's rights, but it is not effective against claims of children from a different union.

Ownership structure

Beware suggestions to place the ownership into a corporation, including an SCI (Société Civile Immobilière, or French Private Limited Company). This can lead to unnecessary tax costs in the UK under the 'benefits in kind' rules. ●

The lettings market

Renting out a holiday home or second property can be a profitable business if you get it right. Read on for advice on letting in France

LETTING RESIDENTIAL PROPERTY CAN involve a mixture of both short and long-term lets. If you are questioning whether you should purchase a holiday home in France because you will not be able to make use of it, it may be worth considering letting out your home to other holiday-makers.

There are a number of rental options that the would-be landlord can weigh up. Depending on type and area, residential properties can be rented as short-term (for holidays or business trips) or long-term lets.

The length of the holiday letting season differs greatly from region to region. There are also areas in France that have two distinct seasons, bringing landlords rental returns over more weeks of the year. The Provençal Alps, for instance, attract skiers in the winter and outdoor enthusiasts in the summer, many of whom will book holiday accommodation.

If you buy in a city, you may be able to let to travelling businessmen and holidaymakers for short periods, and in addition, find tenants looking for long-term lets. As a general rule, cities yield the best rents and number of prospective tenants for long-term lets.

Finding tenants

Owners of French property have a range of options when it comes to finding tenants and managing. If you choose to let privately you can place an advertisement in a specialist publication with lettings advertisements in France, and in the home country of your target audience, or on specialist websites. In France, local papers have listings sections of properties for rent. To advertise holiday lets to a foreign audience, place an advertisement in publications distributed in the relevant countries.

If you prefer to relinquish the responsibility of marketing your property yourself you can, for a certain percentage of the rent, do it through a local estate agency or holiday-lettings specialist, or, in the case of new-builds especially, a management company that services the entire building or complex. Tourist offices also market holiday properties. For details of your local or regional tourist office, contact Maison de la France in France or overseas (see Directory of contacts p318).

"It is essential that if you are going to be letting directly to tenants, you have a contract that complies with French law drawn up by an experienced lawyer which contains clauses protecting your interests"

Managing lets

Overseeing the cleaning and changeover days of properties let for short periods can be difficult to manage from a distance, though not impossible. Some holiday home owners find they can rely on their clients to leave the property in a good state and simply send a key to them, though help can usually be hired in most of France's towns and villages. A local job centre, or *agence nationale pour l'emploi*, can be good source of help.

Any intermediary who lets a property for commercial or residential use must, by law, be licensed to do so, and anyone engaging a letting agent, or *agent locataire*, should ensure that both their own rights and obligations, and those of the agent, are clearly defined in a written agreement.

A letting agent will probably have standard tenancy agreements, but these can contain clauses that are disadvantageous to the landlord. If you are presented with such an agreement, consider asking an independent legal advisor to review it, even if it has been translated into your own language. If you are letting directly to tenants, you should have an agreement drawn up by an experienced lawyer. This should contain the necessary clauses to protect you as the landlord, and a schedule of the condition of the property (*état de lieux*), and it should be signed by the parties concerned before the tenant moves in. This agreement must comply with French laws. The rights and obligations of landlords (*bailleurs*), and their tenants (*locataires*) will in most cases be governed by French law.

Before any contract becomes binding, make sure you communicate your terms and conditions clearly to your tenant.

If you do not do so, you could face not only a claim for a refund, but also for damages for additional expenses incurred. Your terms and conditions should cover subjects such as your payment terms (including the amount of your deposit); booking cancellations in the case of holiday rentals; circumstances for which you will not be liable; and the correct complaints procedure. These terms and conditions must, of course, comply with the law governing the letting of a property.

Great care should be taken when advertising your property. If you are letting to British clients, for example, the UK Trade Descriptions Act 1968 makes it a criminal offence to knowingly or 'recklessly' misrepresent a property to clients. Under the Consumer Protection Act 1987 it is also a criminal offence for a business to mislead clients about prices, as well as accommodation, facilities and services.

Despite the potential pitfalls, it is common practice to let a property on an informal basis, with only a verbal or a loosely worded written agreement. This is often the case when homes are rented out for short periods to holiday-makers. When a property is let without a formal contract, the tenancy will, however, be governed by the French Civil Code, which offers landlords limited protection in the event of a dispute with the tenant. It is important to note that, whatever form the agreement has taken, if a tenant who has been renting on a short-term basis does decide to stay beyond the end of the letting period, it may be difficult to force their eviction if they do not have a permanent home elsewhere, if the property is unfurnished, or if the letting period exceeds three months.

In some cases, the property must be registered with the local authorities and comply with standards and regulations set by them. When renting out a property that you use for holidays, or that is your main residence, you should also ensure that your insurance policy covers damage caused by tenants, and injuries caused to tenants on the premises.

Letting as a business

According to the French Commercial Code, a landlord is considered a tradesman if the property is owned in the name of a commercial company, or if it is classed as commercial rather than residential. The latter would apply if, for example, the lease (bail) is taken on by a company or an individual operating a business on the premises, or if the property contains more than five furnished self-contained rooms or units available for let throughout the holiday season or for longer periods. In

these circumstances, the landlord must register with the local Chamber of Commerce within two months of starting to trade.

To run a property as a hotel you must register the business at the local chamber of commerce and obtain a licence to run it. The property must first be inspected by a number of administrative bodies to ensure that the establishment complies with safety and hygiene standards.

One disadvantage of being classified as a tradesman is that when any of your properties are sold, the sale can attract a transfer registration duty of 4.8 per cent. There are ways of structuring ownership to avoid this, however, by buying through a civil company that does not engage in commercial activities itself, for example. If you buy a commercial property, or *fonds de commerce*, this rate of registration tax is payable if the property is up to 23,000 euros in value, or 15 euros and a rate of 4.8 per cent if the value exceeds 23,000 euros.

To run a business in France, a number of documents must be filled in annually. Your local tax office, or *chambre des métiers*, and chamber of commerce should be able to help talk you through these.

Finance

If the letting of a property does not constitute a business in the eyes of the local authorities, both profits and losses from lettings must be reported on the normal French income tax return, Cerfa 2042. The tax applicable to French rental income is not the standard income tax. Residents should submit the form to the local tax office, and non-residents to the *Centre des impôts des non-résidents* in Paris (see Directory of contacts p318) before 30th April each year following the French tax year, which runs from 1st January to 31st December. French rental income must be declared in France, even if disclosed to the tax authorities in the country of tax residency. A double tax treaty with countries such as Britain means France still has the principal right to tax – the French tax paid is simply set aside against any UK tax liability arising from the same source. ●

AVERAGE WEEKLY RENTAL PRICES

	1-bed	2-bed	3-bed	4-bed	5-bed
Brittany	€425 (£293)	€510 (£260)	€610 (£424)	€783 (£544)	€1200 (£833)
Normandy	€363 (£252)	€505 (£351)	€650 (£451)	€853 (£592)	€1200 (£833)
Île-de-France	€745 (£517)	€1338 (£929)	€1985 (£1378)	€2305 (£1601)	€2940 (£2042)
The Loire	€395 (£274)	€923 (£641)	€728 (£505)	€1013 (£703)	€1210 (£480)
Aquitaine	€385 (£267)	€623 (£432)	€813 (£564)	€1085 (£753)	€1350 (£938)
Côte d'Azur	€490 (£693)	€693 (£481)	€1065 (£740)	€1468 (£1019)	€1878 (£1304)

Choosing your home

Once you've found your perfect piece of France, it's important not to let your heart rule your head, and think about septic tanks instead

MANY OF THE POTENTIAL PITFALLS INVOLVED IN buying a French property can be avoided by not rushing into a purchase, seeking independent advice, and having the building thoroughly checked over by a qualified surveyor. This section is essential reading for anyone considering making that all-important purchase this year.

David Franks is the Chief Executive of Blevins Franks and is an accomplished and experienced practitioner in both UK and overseas taxation. Published in a number of leading taxation works he can be contacted at Blevins Franks on 020 7336 1111.

Overview

Foreign purchasers can all too easily be persuaded to sign a sales contract before properly protecting their interests, and to buy what they assume will be a dream home without calculating the full cost of repair or renovation work.

Involving both an independent legal advisor and a qualified buildings surveyor, although still not common practice in France, is highly recommended as a way of avoiding setbacks.

If you are considering buying a home in France but cannot quite afford your dream property, you could group together with like-minded friends or families to make the purchase attainable. If you do consider this option – sensible if you do not anticipate spending more than a handful of weeks there each year – it is wise to seek advice on how best to structure the purchase of the property.

An increasingly popular option is to use a civil company, or *société civile immobilière* (SCI), to buy the property. Be aware that owning through an SCI can

It is recommended you use a qualified lawyer

HEADLANDS INTERNATIONAL

incur extra legal costs at the outset, as well as accounting costs and substantial amounts of paperwork each year, but it can make ownership more manageable by simplifying the disposal of shares in the property without recourse to a *notaire*, and by saving owners a great deal in inheritance tax.

"If you cannot quite afford your dream property, you could always group together with like-minded friends or families to make the purchase attainable"

Another way to make a holiday property more affordable is to participate in a leaseback scheme. These are set up by developers, who pass on government tax breaks in the form of a TVA (French VAT) rebate to the buyers and who manage the property as a rental investment for a number of years; the VAT rebate is currently 19.6 per cent. But also, provided they keep it on for a certain period (typically nine years), users can enjoy the property for several weeks of the year and earn a guaranteed net return on their investment of between three and seven per cent. In addition, the owners' holiday home and changeover days are managed in their absence.

Although these schemes are generally only available in the main tourist areas, if the development has been awarded *résidence de tourisme* (tourist class) status, they can be found in a great variety of French regions, from Île-de-France to the Midi-Pyrénées.

Buyer beware

If you are planning to buy a home in the country, you should also be aware of some of the current issues involving rural properties that may not be pointed out

JUSTIN POSTLETHWAITE

Ensuring your rural home has proper drainage facilities is essential and required by law

during your search. One such issue is foul drainage. By law, all homes must either be on mains drainage or have a self-maintaining septic tank system by 2006, when a new inspectorate will have been set up. Even if a property already has a septic tank in place, it may not necessarily comply with these incoming regulations. If the property you are considering does not have an approved drainage system, you need to take into consideration the cost and time required to have one installed.

An approved *fosse septique* (septic tank) can cost between €3,500 and €4,500 and, on top of that, you will need to set money aside for the installation. There is another cost to take into account which, although it is minimal by comparison, is one more addition to the mounting cost of the purchase. If there is neither a proper septic tank in place, nor mains drainage, and the local *commune* has not already carried out a general survey of the area, the buyer will also be required to have an *étude du sol* (soil test) carried out by a registered inspection service, which will state exactly how and where a septic tank can be installed.

This test should be carried out before completion of the property purchase, and will add approximately €400 to your costs. Local town halls can help by pointing buyers in the right direction. Anyone installing a septic tank must now follow the guidelines provided by this type of report, or by the survey for the area. As work progresses, the local water authorities will need to inspect the site to ensure that it complies with regulations.

While not everyone will need to improve their drainage system immediately, the new regulations will have an immediate impact if you need to obtain planning permission for any alterations to a property. Applications for planning permission will only be accepted if your property either has a foul drainage system that complies with these new regulations, or if there is the means to connect to a mains system or sufficient land to accommodate a new septic tank.

Barn conversions are another problem area since legislation – brought in to protect agricultural buildings – came into place in 2000. As a result of this legislation, local planning offices are being much stricter about planning applications, and the worst case scenario is that you could find yourself buying a heap of bricks in a field that you are unable to turn into a home. The only way you can be confident of being able to convert an agricultural building into a house is to ensure that a *certificat d'urbanisme* (planning permission certificate) is in place before you purchase the property.

Buyers need to also be aware of new legislation concerning swimming pools, in order to avoid incurring hefty fines and curtailed lettings. Since 1 January 2004, properties wth newly built private swimming pools have been required to have a fence or similar device to enclose the pool as a safety feature. This also applies to all rental properties with pools, even those that were built *before* the 2004 deadline. However, with *private* pools built before 1 January 2004, owners have until 1 January 2006, to take the appropriate security measures. ●

DUTY-FREE COMMISSION FEES

■ Commission fees are a potential hidden cost that you need to take steps to avoid paying duties on when buying a French property through an estate agent.

■ Check that, where the agent's fee appears in the sales contract, it is accompanied by a note explaining that this figure is the commission paid to the estate agent. Should a phrase such as 'commission de l'agence immobilière à la charge de l'acquéreur' appear, you need only pay duties on the price the vendor receives, saving a significant amount of money.

■ On a property sale of €1,908,000, including a six per cent agency commission of €108,000, not paying duties on the commission would save €5,280.

French transport in 2005

New developments in France's cutting-edge transport infrastructure are set to make getting to and around the country even easier

TGV overview

With a state-of-the-art transport infrastructure that includes the fast TGV train network linking Paris to Britain and Brussels and cutting a definite artery from the North to the South of France, it's no surprise that France continues to look forward to faster, easier links within its transport infrastructure.

The existing TGV network links the capital to Lyon and Marseille, and services Bordeaux by its route to Vendôme. Eurostar runs a weekly, direct summer service from London to Avignon (launched in 2002) between July and September.

New TGV links

Both relocators and buyers-to-let will be excited by the forthcoming plans to improve all forms of transportation into and within France. The most significant developments for house hunters/holders in France must surely be the planned routes due for completion in the next couple of years, including a link between Paris and Metz, bringing the Champagne-Ardenne closer for UK travellers. Antwerp's link to Amsterdam in the Netherlands, in 2005, will open up possibilities for those wanting to commute to Belgium from Lille, and new track on the Channel Tunnel rail link between Britain and France is due to be constructed in 2007.

By 2020, France's TGV routes are set to include a

Phase 2 of the Channel Tunnel is set for 2007

EUROSTAR

new easterly route to Strasbourg, stopping at Reims, Metz and Nancy en route. A new branch of track to the east from Brussels will link to Köln in Germany, providing fantastic links for relocators hoping to work in Brussels and Germany. This will also open up a potential lettings market in Köln.

Channel Tunnel developments

The second phase of construction on the Channel Tunnel Rail Link (CTRL 2) is underway and due for completion in 2007 (the first phase of the 74 kilometre new line – CTRL 1 – from the channel entrance into Kent was opened by Tony Blair in 2003), and has already cut the journey time to Paris by 20 minutes. Designed to give Eurostar double the capacity it has had at peak journey times, CTRL 2 should reduce journey times from London to Brussels by 15 minutes, decreasing the time to around two hours.

Road and rail developments

Following the update to the Paris metro service via the 'Meteor' project – named after the city's 'Est-Ouest Rapide' project, Line 14, which runs between Gare de Lyon and Châtelet – alternative transportation for up to 8,000 passengers an hour has been provided since December 2003.

Recent additions to the road network include the arterial A20 from Paris, which cuts a link through the heart of France to the Midi-Pyrénées, and has recently opened up the South.

The A28 Rouen to Alençon should now be completed and this is going to be a really important road for anyone travelling from the Benelux or Great Britain to the West of France or Spain.

The last remaining portion of the A34 Reims to Charleville-Mézières was completed in 2004. This means that there is now a four-lane road from Reims to the A4 in Belgium (a road connecting Brussels to Luxembourg).

To be completed this year, the A75 route extending from Paris to the Languedoc will make Béziers a logistic centre for industry and commerce. Elsewhere, more motorways are planned for the Clermont-Ferrand area of Limousin and the Auvergne district.

On the A89, the last remaining part between Bordeaux and Brive-la-Gaillarde (and the A20 motorway) is scheduled to be ready in June 2005. The 16km stretch from Brive to St Germáin is due for completion in 2007.

New air routes

Perhaps the biggest concern for relocators who depend on cheap and speedy flights to any of the 16 areas currently serviced by budget airline, Ryanair, is its threat to suspend flights to airports that do not prove cost-effective.

However, the bad news for potential relocators to more off-the-beaten track parts of France has to be the airline's lost legal fight to sustain subsidised airport payments from Strasbourg's publicly owned airport. Ryanair's Stansted to Strasbourg route ceased in September 2003. The airline has cancelled services to Belgium's Charleroi airport and could be pushed into dropping services to airports that no longer prove profitable. Last year, Ryanair axed all flights to Brest, Clermont-Ferrand and Reims. However, the airline opened new routes from Luton to Dinard and Nîmes.

Last year, BMI Baby introduced routes to Bordeaux (from East Midlands and Manchester) and Paris from Manchester. However, the flights from Manchester are currently suspended.

Bargain flight operator Flybe's routes to France expanded widely in 2004 with new routes to Brest (from Birmingham, Southampton and Exeter), Chambéry (from Birmingham and Southampton) and Cherbourg (from Southampton). Flybe plans to fly to "a number of French regional airports" from Liverpool during 2005.

Twice-daily flights to Berlin from Paris Orly via easyJet have been operating since May 25 2004, and new routes between Berlin and Nice are set to take off. Flights from Gatwick to Marseille and Toulouse began on 26th October 2003. EasyJet will begin flying to the Alpine ski resort of Grenoble in Eastern France from London Stansted on 5th January 2005.

During 2004, Thomson Fly started flights from Coventry to Lyon and Nice. The company has announced that it will be operating flights from Bournemouth from March 2005. Destinations have yet to be confirmed, but there is a possibility of flights to France.

Limousin and Auvergne are set to become more accessible thanks to a new airport that's planned for the town of Brive – although it's not due to be built until 2021. British Airways franchise GB Airways offers flights from £69 return to Montpellier and Nantes from London Gatwick, and the airline has recently added a weekly service to Corsica, with fares starting at £129.

New sea routes/developments

P&O Ferries' cross-Channel services to Le Havre, Caen and Cherbourg from Portsmouth, and Cherbourg-Rosslare, are expected to end in early 2005. P&O also plans to cut the number of sailings between Dover and Calais by early 2005. Brittany Ferries are hoping to provide an

BRITTANY FERRIES

There is a lot of competition and many new ideas for ferry services across the Channel

alternative service between Portsmouth and Le Havre. No new routes are planned for Condor Ferries, which only launched its Poole to Saint Malo service in 2003.

Hoverspeed reintroduced its Dover-Calais route in 2004, and with a fleet of three Seacats, provides up to 15 return sailings daily, with a crossing time of just one hour. Norfolkline, the Dover/Dunkirk passenger ferry operator, has introduced a price freeze on a range of fares for travel until 31st December 2005.

On 19 May 2004, Speed Ferries launched its Dover/Boulogne service via its new catamaran vessel, SpeedOne, which is able to transport 200 cars and 800 passengers to Boulogne across the Dover strait in 50 minutes.

SeaFrance is building a sister ship for the 2004 award-winning SeaFrance Rodin. When SeaFrance Berlioz is brought into service in spring 2005, SeaFrance will be the only ship owner operating two brand-new ships between Calais and Dover – the world's largest passenger terminals. These ferries have been specially designed for the Calais/Dover route. They will be the quickest vessels on the route, making the journey in only 50 minutes, and they will be able to carry 700 cars or 120 trucks, and 1,900 passengers each.

In addition, residents in Boulogne are set to benefit from a new 320-boat mooring development, which is due to be installed as part of the new Boulogne harbour revamp. ●

Steps to buying...

Beautiful France offers something for everyone, and more and more people from the UK are buying homes in Europe's third largest country

CFT TOULOUSE-MIDI-PYRÉNÉES

BUYING A PROPERTY ABROAD IS NOT A decision to be taken lightly, nor is it a decision that should be made on impulse, even when the turnover of properties in your area of choice is swift. Buying a house you fall in love with at the end of a holiday, for example, can be a recipe for disaster. In a foreign country in particular, there are legal, cost and other practical issues that you must take into consideration before embarking on house purchase.

One of the first questions to ask yourself is how much you can really afford to spend. When you know how much you can raise, consider the purchasing costs, then set yourself a realistic price limit. Once you've set your budget, you will know whether you should be looking for a stone *fermette* (a small farmhouse), a town house or a much grander *manoir* (a manor house).

In some regions, a manor house can cost the same as a farmhouse does in others. By taking a look at property in areas you may not have considered before, simply because your travels have not taken you there yet or because it is not an area that people tend to talk about, you can open up your options. This is particularly important in today's climate, as budget flight routes and high-speed train links have made areas that were once inconceivable to visit for a long weekend, for example, easily accessible from the UK.

STEP 1: *Finding the right property*

Buying a home abroad can be an emotive business, but it's important that buyers are practical when choosing a property. An isolated farmhouse can be perfect for escaping the bustle of city life, but if you need medical assistance close at hand, or would like neighbours to look after your property when you are away, you should think of buying somewhere within easy reach of other households and village amenities. You should also spend time getting to know the locality properly, seeing it in winter as well as summer if possible, before you take the plunge. If, for instance, you find your dream location off-season, it may be spoilt by hordes of tourists in the summer and, although in summer it appears an idyll, winter gales may make it feel inhospitable.

There are several different routes buyers can follow to find their dream French home. You can simply trail around the region of your choice, hunting out *à vendre* (for sale) signs and looking in the windows of *agents immobiliers* (estate agents) and *notaires* (public notaries), but you don't have to rely on this method to track down your dream home. A good way to start is by searching through specialist magazines and websites, as well as attending the growing number of overseas property fairs held outside France.

It may be even more convenient to work with a property search agent, or 'homefinder'. Based in France or even the UK, they can cut the legwork out of finding your property and present a select range of properties for you to view. These could be on the books of local estate agents, selected from forthcoming auctions or even private sales.

Whichever intermediary you choose, at some point you will have to organise a trip to France to arrange viewings of your shortlist of properties. Narrow the final list down as much as you can before you go. The details intermediaries provide on French properties are rarely as exhaustive as the particulars produced by UK agents. Quite often, for example, details such as room measurements or fixtures and fittings will not be included unless you ask, so make sure you request extensive details and see as many pictures of the properties as possible before taking time to visit them.

New-builds

While foreigners moving to France or looking for a holiday home there are often keen to find a charming period house, building a home in the right location can prove to be good value and a practical alternative. Many French families opt to buy a plot of land on which to have a house built, as in France building land is cheaper and more readily available than in other countries, particularly in the countryside.

When it comes to buying a home, the French tend to consider practicalities and convenience before heritage issues and new homes can provide more comfort from day one, and be more conveniently located for schools and workplaces than the traditional rural buildings that were typically inhabited a century or more ago.

A newly built home is often easier to look after – a particularly important consideration if it is to be let out – and is usually much less expensive to buy. For this reason, new-builds can also make a sensible holiday rental investment, although there is a significant disadvantage to buying a property under five years old that is being sold for the first time: VAT, or TVA as it is known in France, is normally charged on the sale, but there is a way of avoiding it. A new property leased back immediately to the developers, who then rent the property to holiday-makers over a period of about nine years, is exempt from VAT if the property is held for at least 20 years. Owners can

expect to earn a net return of around six per cent, as well as save on the initial cost of their purchase. Leaseback schemes are only found in areas popular with tourists, and are only available if the property is accepted as tourist standard by the local authorities. This is a government initiative to encourage the development of tourist accommodation (this is not a second home but very much an investment in a building similar to a hotel), as tourism is a key contributor to France's economy. Tax breaks are given to developers building tourist accommodation, and the VAT refund is passed on to buyers, to encourage them to participate in the scheme.

If you are interested in new-builds and are considering buying a building plot on which to have a home built, plots of land, or *parcelles*, can be found through estate agents or specialist publications and internet sites such as www.terrain-a-batir.com and www.frenchland.com. Should you choose this option, it is best to scrutinise the *plan local d'urbanisme* held at the local town hall and the related coefficient *d'occupation des sols*. Used in combination, these can confirm whether or not the land can be built on and should provide a reasonably accurate picture of the size of building that could be constructed there. In any case you need to have in the preliminary contract a clause allowing you to pull out if the planning permission is not granted. Note also that the granting

"Foreign buyers are not always aware of the local market prices of property, and can run the risk of paying inflated prices"

Fix the exchange rate and avoid fluctuation

TOBY POCOCK; WWW.VIEWSPAIN.COM

WHO TO BUY A FRENCH HOME FROM

Every town in France should have at least one estate agent and there is an increasing number of UK-based agents specialising in French properties who have a network of French agents providing them with local knowledge and property details. These agents understand the needs of foreign buyers, and, of course, they offer an English-speaking service, which makes buying considerably easier. All French estate agents should have a *carte professionelle*, proving that they have the correct professional qualifications and are backed by a financial guarantee and professional liability insurance, and also that they are members of a regulatory body such as the Fédération nationale des agents immobiliers et mandataires, or FNAIM.

Estate agents' fees are normally included in the sale price, so buyers do not usually have to worry about raising extra money to pay them. Mortgage providers usually lend only a percentage of the actual sale price and do not take additional costs into consideration. However, if an estate agent's commission is included in the price, the buyer may end up paying purchase duties on this fee as well as on the property itself.

To avoid paying more duties than necessary, ensure the contract includes the statement *'commission de l'agence immobilier à la charge de l'acquéreur'* (agent's commission paid for by the buyer). For a list of estate agents in France, contact the FNAIM (see Directory of Contacts on page 346).

of planning permission will depend on access to roads and utilities. (See also Building a New Home.)

STEP 2: *The survey*

Foreign buyers are not always aware of the local market prices of property, and can run the risk of paying inflated prices. A valuation by a local valuer, or *expert immobilier*, can help avoid this. They can also help estimate the cost of any renovation work to make the property habitable or to simply improve the living space.

Even an *expert immobilier* will not, however, provide a full structural survey. The survey, or expertise, that they carry out is, in effect, more like a valuation. The closest equivalent to a British structural survey is an *évaluation structurale*. The French do not have a professional equivalent to the British chartered building surveyor. They usually either turn to an *architecte* (an architect), who will normally provide only a very brief report on the condition of a building, or they rely on testimonies from local tradesmen, or artisans, to gauge a property's state of repair. Be careful when looking for an older property, as age often brings problems. An older property may have been left for years without proper maintenance, for example, perhaps because it was part of an inheritance and not subsequently lived in. Others may never have been connected to mains electricity or had proper sewerage.

The cost of renovating and connecting utilities can be onerous, and should be borne in mind when thinking about buying an old French building. One of the best ways to obtain a structural survey can be to instruct one of the growing number of properly qualified British building surveyors or architects who now live in France; or who will travel across the Channel, to carry out such surveys.

British buyers of French property should also note the need to check certain details that would not necessarily require checking when buying a property in the UK. If a property is made up of a collection of buildings, for instance, it should be determined whether or not all the buildings are actually included in the sale. Boundaries can often be blurred too, especially if land has been split up into several *parcelles*, or if a wood obscures part of one of these. They can be checked against a *plan cadastral*, the official record of site boundaries, although this can sometimes be out of date.

A land surveyor, or *géomètre*, can help verify such details. There is no legal protection in France allowing purchasers to pull out from the preliminary contract if the survey is not satisfactory; it is necessary to ask for such a clause up front, as soon as the offer is made.

STEP 3: *Managing your euros*

As a rule of thumb, to roughly calculate the total cost of buying a French property, add another 10 per cent on top of the actual purchase price. In reality, however, the total can be much higher than this. One of the main costs is the sales commission, which is normally about five or six per cent but, particularly in the case of less expensive properties, can reach up to 20 per cent. You must therefore check whether or not the fee is included in the advertised price and also whether VAT has been added. Phrases like '*toutes taxes comprises*' or '*TVA comprise*' should indicate that this fee has been included.

Although it is sometimes the vendor who pays the agent's commission, the buyer is always responsible for paying the conveyancing fees to the *notaire*. The *notaire*'s fees are fixed by law, and are a percentage based on a sliding scale, depending on the purchase price of the property. They can range from around

three per cent for a property less than five years old to about 10 per cent for a property more than five years old. If two *notaires* are appointed, one by the buyer and one by the vendor, this does not increase the fee paid, as it is simply divided between them.

On top of their own fee, the *notaires* will collect various duties and fees, including stamp and transfer duties, land registry fees, taxes and disbursements. When a mortgage is taken out on a property, there will also be a charge payable to the *notaire* that is usually between one and three per cent of the mortgage value. This is for registering the charge of the lender with the relevant land registry, or *conservation des hypothèques*.

Exchange rate fluctuations can potentially increase the cost of financing if a borrower is converting sterling to make payments on a euro mortgage. However, fixing the exchange rate through a currency specialist over a long period of time can give the borrower peace of mind. If the property is being bought for cash, it can also be a good idea to fix the exchange rate at the beginning of the purchase process, so that the actual price of the property will not increase unexpectedly due to exchange rate fluctuations before the completion date.

Not everyone bears in mind from the outset that one of the biggest costs of buying an older property is renovation work. A would-be buyer may spot a derelict building in a field, for instance, and think it's a bargain, without giving due consideration to how much it will actually cost to restore. This can be at least as much as the price of the building itself and to prevent a dream home turning into a renovation project that was never completed, the potential buyer must calculate all the outlays before proceeding with a sale. To gain a realistic estimate of this cost, buyers should consider obtaining estimates (*devis*) from local builders before signing a contract. This is still, however, merely an approximate price for the work and materials.

Financing

In recent years, it has become much easier for non-residents to raise a mortgage, or *prêt immobilier*, on a home in France. There are two basic ways to do this: by remortgaging a property in the UK in sterling with a UK lender or by taking out a euro mortgage with a French bank against the French property – since British and French banks cannot take first legal

Ensure you always get independent legal advice

charge on a property outside their own countries, they do not offer mortgages on properties in any country apart from their own.

Although there can be a substantial initial exchange rate fee to pay when money is raised in a currency other than the euro, remortgaging in sterling can protect the British buyer against the effect of future exchange rate fluctuations on their repayments. Taking out a mortgage in euros on a French property will always, on the other hand, reflect the true euro value of the property, and the bank will have the first legal charge on the actual property being financed. The cost of the mortgage can also potentially be offset against any income received from letting the property.

There are many French lenders for overseas buyers to choose from if a mortgage is to be raised on a property in France, but one of the most interesting propositions today is offered by the French branches of UK banks. All the paperwork can be supplied in English, for instance, and although the mortgage will be in euros, the monthly payments can be made in sterling, straight from a British bank account. You also need to be aware that a French bank usually asks for a life policy to be taken out on the life of the borrower, which requires both a medical and a blood test.

Repayment mortgages, or *prêts amortissables*, are most commonly offered by French banks to foreign buyers because they have been traditionally favoured above interest-only mortgages and endowment policies by the French. British buyers are usually lent money by a French lender for between five and 20 years. Rates can be fixed (*à taux fixe*), or variable (*à taux variable*). There are likely to be early redemption charges payable on the former, but not on the latter.

"In recent years, it has become much easier for non-residents to raise a mortgage, or prêt immobolier, *on a home in France"*

STEPS TO BUYING

FINANCE TIPS

1. If you declare the income you receive from letting a property in France to the tax authorities in the country where you are resident, France still retains principle taxation rights on French sourced income.

This is the case no matter where both landlord and tenant reside, or where and in which currency the rent is paid.

2. French tax authorities may tax up to three years in arrears, and usually add interest and penalty charges on late tax returns.

3. When lettings qualify as a business for the purposes of French taxation, the method used to determine the taxable income depends on the level of annual turnover from the preceding year.

4. One, the 'simplified regime' (*régime simplifié*), is relatively straightforward, while the other, the 'normal regime' (*régime normal*), requires the preparation of detailed accounts and involves compliance formalities similar to those of a company liable to French corporation tax.

5. Some rentals may be subject to TVA, and there are also local taxes that can be levied on leases.

6. Although the supply of food, telephone and other services to self-catering accommodation is subject to TVA at the standard rate, when an establishment provides accommodation on a full-board or half-board basis, TVA can be reduced. Other financial incentives to landlords come in the form of grants. In some French *départements*, owners can obtain grants from local authorities for the conversion of homes into rental accommodation. Contact the administrative offices of the local state representative, or *préfecture*, for further information.

French variable rates are linked to the EURIBOR (Euro Interbank Offered Rate), and for foreign buyers this is usually fixed for a period of 12 months, mainly for convenience. One main difference between UK and French variable interest rates is that, whereas in the UK the monthly payments are likely to fluctuate regularly, in France the rates tend to stay stable, and it is only the term of the loan that changes according to the EURIBOR rate change.

A deposit of at least 20 per cent of the price of the property is usually required, and it is generally true that the higher the deposit, the better the interest rate. French lenders are usually obliged to prove that the borrower can afford the repayments, so they often insist that the monthly payments for all the borrower's mortgages and other fixed outgoings should not exceed 30 to 35 per cent of their income.

Even if properties financed by a residential mortgage are to be let out for part of the year, lenders will not usually take into consideration the potential rental income when assessing the loan request. Neither will they lend money to cover the costs of buying a property, though subject to the approval of relevant estimates from builders or developers, mortgages can cover the cost of renovation or construction work.

Note that once a mortgage offer is received, the borrower must wait at least 10 days, but no longer than 30, before signing and accepting it. This is in order to comply with French financial legislation. On the acceptance of a French mortgage offer, an arrangement fee of between one and two per cent of the loan value will usually be payable. Borrowers are also obliged to take out a life insurance policy so that, in the event of death or disability, the outstanding loan value will be repaid.

French banks pay the sum of money being lent directly to the *notaire*. The portion covering renovation or construction costs, however, is paid directly to the contractor on presentation of invoices (duly authorised for payment by the customer) and after the customer's personal contribution has been paid. As a general rule, you should allow two months between the receipt of the completed mortgage application and the mortgage offer.

STEP 4: *The legal process*

The French legal system can be a minefield for foreign buyers. Never does the expression 'take independent advice' ring more true than in the case of buying a property abroad. There are numerous pitfalls that the unsuspecting buyer can encounter when buying a home in France and there are also ways that a legal advisor can help the buyer best structure their purchase.

A French property can either be purchased by individuals, in single, joint or multiple names, or through a French property-holding company, a *société civile immobilière* (SCI), whose shares are held by the buyers. Although an SCI can cost between £1,000 and £3,500 to set up, and annual accounts must be prepared for the company, this purchase structure should be considered in many cases, as it can have tax advantages and make it easier for owners to dispose of their share of the property. It can also overcome some of the restrictions of France's succession law. French law dictates that upon the death of a homeowner, the property is divided up equally between the surviving spouse and any children. Shares in a company, however, are easier to distribute than immovable property, thus enabling better management of inheritance and property transferring. The transfer of shares can be done under English law if you are domiciled in the UK on your death but it is still submitted to French tax law.

STEP 5: *Protecting your interests*

The *notaire* who oversees the sale of a property is primarily concerned with registering the sale, ensuring that the conveyancing is carried out according to the law and collecting the relevant taxes on behalf of the government. Although they are perfectly qualified to provide legal advice, *notaires* are not acting on behalf of either side so, to make sure that you are bound by favourable terms, it would be best to either employ a separate *notaire* in France or to employ a British lawyer familiar with conveyancing law in France from the very start of the legal process. There are quite a few UK-based solicitors who specialise in the buying and selling of French property and it's worth seeking them out.

Not only can solicitors working on behalf of the buyer draw up any necessary get-out clauses in the contract, they can also advise on the best way to structure the purchase according to personal circumstances and recommend ways of minimising the effect of French inheritance law. The latter should be considered a long time before the conveyance is signed.

Special *assur'titre* insurance policies can be taken out to insure the title of a property against unknown title defects, such as unforeseen claims by third parties and the violation of planning regulations by former owners, as well as mistakes on behalf of the *notaire*. This policy gives the buyer protection against any costs or damages that may follow as a result of any claims from third parties or subsequent owners. Such policies are being offered increasingly by estate agents as part of their service, and are a good complement to the advice of an independent solicitor.

STEP 6: *Contracts*

In France when you buy a property you will be very quickly asked to sign a preliminary contract. A contract, known as a '*compromis de vente*', a '*promesse de vente*' or a '*sous-seing privé*', is entered into early on in the process, and this commits the vendor and buyer

NOTAIRES

Much of the property sold in France is still offered through *notaires*, who were the principal source of French property before estate agents set up in business. *Notaires* are highly trained lawyers who oversee the purchase, and their sales commission will not normally be included in the price.

Properties sold through *notaires* can often be more reasonably priced than those sold through estate agents, as the latter are usually more aware of market trends. For details of regional *notaires*, contact Notaires de France. (See Directory of Contacts on page 346.)

to a deal they will conclude with a deed of sale, or conveyance. The agreement is normally drawn up either by an estate agent or a *notaire* and then handed to the *notaire* who will be overseeing the completion of the sale together with the deposit to conduct the sale.

Unless special arrangements have been made, the conveyancing on the sale will be conducted by the *notaire* appointed by the seller of the property. The buyer may, if he wishes, appoint his own notary to protect his interests. The contract gives the details of the parties and the property, and the price and the completion date when the signing of the final deed of sale takes place. It will also include details of the notary or notaries overseeing the transaction and of where the deed that completes the conveyancing, the *acte de vente* – sometimes referred to as the '*acte authentique*' or even the '*acte authentique de vente*' – will be signed. At this stage, a deposit of 10 per cent of the purchase price is paid by the buyer to the *notaire* or the estate agent, backed by a financial guarantee and a professional liability insurance. Under no circumstances whatsoever should money be paid directly to the vendor at this or any other point in the process, nor should the buyer agree to any side payments, or *dessous la table*.

There is a seven-day 'cooling-off' period from the day after the buyer receives a copy of the contract, countersigned by the vendor. During this period, the buyer can withdraw from the sale and not be liable for any penalties. If the buyer withdraws from the purchase after this cooling-off period, however, they will probably lose their deposit and may be liable for penalties. If a penalty clause is included in the contract, it will stipulate the amount payable in case of withdrawal. Should the vendor withdraw, the deposit

"There is a seven-day 'cooling-off' period from the day after the buyer receives a copy of the contract, counter-signed by the vendor"

10 TIPS FOR BUYERS

1. Cast your net wider than the areas you already know.

2. Ask for detailed descriptions of properties before you view them, to help you cut down on wasted trips.

3. Do not buy simply on impulse – this is a major purchase that could have any number of hidden costs.

4. Visit the area in all seasons, if possible.

5. Rent in the locality if you can, to get to know the area before you buy.

6. Introduce yourself to the neighbours to get to know them and the neighbourhood before you commit yourself to a property.

7. Be prepared to negotiate the asking price, engaging a local *géomètre*, or valuer, to offer an independent opinion.

8. Seek independent legal advice before signing any contract and handing over any money, and consider instructing your own *notaire* who can oversee the sale alongside the *notaire* instructed by the vendor – there is no extra cost for this service.

9. Instruct a qualified buildings surveyor to provide a full survey and estimate the cost of any necessary repairs or building work.

10. Plan the move to the property as carefully as the purchase itself.

will normally be refunded and the vendor must pay any damages stipulated in the contract. These damage payments will have to be settled in a court action.

If the contract contains what are called '*clauses suspensives*' (get-out clauses), which lay out conditions to be met during the sale process, the buyer may, in some circumstances, be able to withdraw from the purchase without the risk of losing the deposit and having to pay penalties. The sale can be made conditional upon a number of factors, such as the offer of a mortgage, the absence of rights of way across the property, or a *droit de préemption* (right of pre-emption) that gives a local authority, land commission or another third party the right to buy the property or its land.

In the case of properties whose construction has not yet been completed, a *contrat de réservation* precedes the conveyance. The contract should preferably provide a full description of the property to be built, an approximate surface area or *surface habitable*, a floor plan and a proposed date for the completion of the construction. When this contract is signed, the buyer will need to pay the developer a non-interest-bearing deposit, or *réservation*, of up to five per cent. If construction is due to be completed within a year of

signing the contract, the deposit cannot exceed five per cent; or two per cent if within two years. No deposit is payable if the construction is not due for completion within two years.

STEP 7: *Completing the sale*

When all the procedural formalities have been concluded, the notary will summon the parties to his office for the signing of the final deed. The formalities usually take between two and three months. The completion date in the contract will be postponed automatically by the notary if any part of the administrative process remains outstanding. This should be borne in mind by the buyers, who should not make any travel arrangements until the notary has given them a date. The notary will ask for the balance of the purchase money and the costs to be sent direct to his bank. This process can often take up to two weeks, so buyers are advised to pursue this as soon as they are given instructions by the *notaire* to do so.

Many buyers complete the purchase by proxy using a power of attorney drawn up by the notary. Indeed, it is common practice for a member of the notary's staff to be appointed to sign the final deed on the buyer's behalf.

After completion, the notary will stamp and register the title deed which can take about six months. A certified copy of the purchase deed, or *expédition de vente*, is then sent to the notary by the land registry who usually keep it on behalf of the buyer. This is the only evidence of ownership available. There are no title deeds. If a buyer requires evidence of his ownership, he can ask the notary for declaration to this effect (*une attestation de vente*).

On completion of the purchase of an unfinished property, ownership of the land and incomplete construction (if building work has begun) passes to the buyer, though proprietorship of the rest of the building is only transferred as works proceed. In contrast to completed buildings, the balance of the purchase price is payable in instalments as construction progresses; a 30 per cent payment is usually requested on the signing of the conveyance as foundations have to be laid down for legal completion to take place. Further staged instalments are then payable on completion of the foundations, on the building being made watertight and on completion of the building work. A final payment is made when the property has been inspected by the buyer, who is in agreement that there are no faults with the construction.

HOW TO BUY THROUGH A DEVELOPER

It's quite common in France to buy a property before it is completed – a *vente en l'état futur d'achèvement* – from a developer, or *promoteur constructeur*. This can be an apartment in a building, a villa, a town house on an estate, or a *lotissement*. French developers buy land, obtain planning permission and then try to attract buyers. You can obtain details of developers through the Fédération nationale des promoteurs constructeurs (for more information, see Directory of Contacts on page 346).

Joining a user group You can purchase a share in a new *multipropriété* or an existing one – resales do become available – set up by a group of individuals or a specialist company. Check out publications or newspaper sections advertising French property for announcements of the sale of shares in *multipropriétés*, or contact specialists like Owner Groups Company (www.ownergroups.com).

Buying at auction Auctions can be a source of real bargains, as here properties are often sold as a result of inheritance disputes or mortgage defaults, and consequently are priced keenly for a swift sale. At an auction, or *vente aux enchères*, a notary must usually bid on behalf of the buyer.

Written authorisation, in the form of a mandate to bid up to a certain value, must be given to the notary or *avocat* before they attend the sale. Be prepared also to pay 20 per cent of the highest price you are prepared to bid to them in advance. The balance of a successful bid must be paid between one and three months after the sale date. Note that there is no prospect of including get-out clauses in the sale agreement, so care must be taken to examine carefully the property and details such as third party rights of way over it, and in addition, any loans should be in place before the sale. Auction details will appear in local newspapers, in national publications such as the bi-monthly *Le Journal des Enchères* and *Les Ventes aux Enchères des Notaires*, and on websites like www.encheres-paris.com and www.ventes-judiciaires.com. Both estate agents and *notaires* should also have details of properties up for auction in their area.

Buying direct Homes in France can also be bought direct from the owner. Private sales are advertised in specialist magazines and on websites based in France itself and in many other countries. If you buy from an owner, do not be pressurised into handing over a deposit to the owner themselves. There may be no guarantee that they will return it if either party withdraws from the sale for valid reasons. Deposits should be handled by the *notaire* in charge of overseeing the sale. It is also preferable not to hand over any deposit without seeking independent advice, as it may prove to be non-refundable.

STEPS TO BUYING

STEP 8: *Moving in*

The new owners of a French property are only allowed to take possession of it officially when the sale has been completed by the *notaire*. If the property is vacant, it may be possible to arrange an earlier removal date but solely for the purpose of installing furniture. Once the moving-in date is set, almost as much planning can be required at this stage as for the purchase itself.

After completion, the buyer will need to start paying for utilities that are connected, as well as for local services like rubbish collection. A *notaire* or estate agent will often help with this. Water is supplied by a range of private companies in France. When a property is not connected, an application should be made to the local supplier. New owners also have to contact Electricité de France (EDF) and Gaz de France (GDF) to read the meters and to change the name on the accounts. A connection charge is usually payable, as is a deposit if the owner is a non-resident. Mains gas is not always provided in rural areas, where inhabitants usually rely instead on cylinder gas.

Homeowners are also legally obliged to take out a third-party liability insurance policy on their property. A *notaire* will ask to see some proof that the buyer has adequate insurance cover from the day they take ownership of the property. The vendor's insurance can simply be transferred into the new owner's name. This can be part of a multi-risk household insurance policy, or *assurance multirisques habitation*, which includes contents and buildings insurance. Contents and buildings insurance policies specific to holiday homes may be preferable for those who only intend to visit the property from time to time.

Although it is possible to pay utility bills and insurance premiums from across the Channel, if the French home is not going to be used as a main residence, it can be more convenient to pay by direct debit, or *prélèvement automatique*, from a French bank account. Not only does it simplify the process, but it also avoids supplies being cut off simply because letters and cheques never reached their destination. Opening a French bank account is easier now than it has ever been. Help is usually on hand as part of the service from estate agents, homefinders and even solicitors involved in the purchase, and today banks in

France even have English-speaking branches, and non-resident as well as resident bank accounts. The main difference between the two is that non-resident bank accounts offer no overdraft facilities.

There are no restrictions on the importing of most furniture and other household goods into France by an EU citizen, provided they are for personal use. However, the movement of antiques in and out of the UK can be more complicated than other items, and proof of their origin should be kept ready to be produced when they are moved between countries.

These days, thanks to a new 'pet passport' scheme, pets are much freer to move between the UK and other European Union countries, without the need for quarantine periods. To enter France, they must have a current Anti-Rabies Vaccination Certificate, and to get back into the UK they will need a pet passport and a microchip.

STEP 9: *Taxation*

A foreign homeowner only usually becomes a resident of France when they spend more than 183 days in the country, or if their permanent home is there. Even if they are not a tax resident, apart from the taxes paid to the *notaire* at the time of the property purchase, owners of French homes may also be liable at some time or another to pay a range of other taxes.

Both the tax offices of France and the country in which a foreign national resides will be interested in their annual income from activities in France, which could range from simply the interest from a French bank account to rental income from a French property. If this is above an official threshold, an annual declaration of income in France must be made. In theory, a tax resident of France could be liable for both French and UK taxes.

Fortunately for tax residents of both countries, there is a double tax treaty between France and the UK, which protects most British nationals with property in France from paying tax twice. Anyone planning to move permanently from the UK to France would be advised to notify the British tax authorities before leaving, and provide them with proof of new employment and property details.

It is also important to note that direct taxes are not deducted by means of a PAYE system in France. Instead, they are paid in the year following the tax

"If you buy a new apartment under construction, you should be protected from the developer going bankrupt"

year in question, which runs from January 1 to December 31. This is done either in three or 10 instalments, and taxation is always on a self-assessment basis. Residents' taxes are collected by the Direction générale des impôts, which is organised on a national and a regional level, while non-residents deal with the Centre des impôts des non-résidents in Paris. A tax return form, a *déclaration des revenus*, can be obtained from the local tax office, or *centre des impôts*, which can also help the uninitiated fill out their forms.

Property taxes

Based on the average rental value of a property, there are two types of local tax payable by individuals. The *taxe foncière* is a property ownership tax paid by the owner, whether a resident in France or not; while the *taxe d'habitation* is a residential tax paid by the occupiers, who may or may not be the owners. Both are paid in the year following the rental period. Retired residents may be exempt from paying these taxes, as may owners of new houses.

Income tax

Income tax, or *impôt sur le revenu des personnes physiques* (IRPP), is levied on 'earned' income, and depends on the total level of income. There are, however, a number of allowances from which you can get tax relief. A tax on investment or 'unearned' income tax, named the *impôt sur les revenus de capitaux*, is payable on property and investment income, as well as interest paid on bank accounts. There is also a separate rental income tax called the *contribution sur les revenus locatifs*, which is levied on gross rental income.

Wealth tax

A wealth tax called the *impôt de solidarité sur la fortune* is levied on net assets held in France valued above a certain threshold, and can include property, a car and bank balances. Wealth tax can be minimised if you buy a property through an SCI and the net worth of the property can be reduced by way of debt.

Capital gains tax and social charges

There is no tax on any gain made from the sale of a principal home, but capital gains tax, or the *impôt sur les plus-values*, is levied on the profits of the sale of other property, as well as shares, subject to certain allowances. Non-residents do not, however, pay CSG (generalised social contributions) or CRDS (repayment of the social debt contribution).

CRT TOULOUSE-MIDI-PYRENEES

See as much of France as possible before buying

Inheritance tax

French inheritance law, which governs inheritance tax, and death and estate duties, decides who inherits a person's assets. It is probably quite unlike anything that a British buyer will ever have encountered previously. In theory, inheritance tax is paid on the global assets of a French tax resident.

The beneficiaries pay inheritance taxes, depending on how closely they are related to the deceased. Inheritance tax is payable on any French property owned by a non-resident.

There are several ways in which you can minimise an inheritance tax bill, however, and careful planning at the time of the house purchase is crucial. In certain circumstances, for example, changes to a marriage contract can help, as can buying through a property-holding company or SCI, of which the owners are the shareholders.

Be aware that you should be very careful with an SCI as the shareholder's heirs will have to pay French inheritance taxes. Usually the law of the country in which the property is located is applicable.

If, however, the property is owned by an SCI, the applicable law will be that of the deceased's last country of residence, as it is not immovable property, which is always subject to French inheritance civil law. Again, this needs to be borne in mind.

Clause tontine

To benefit the surviving spouse, provisions can also be made in the French will of an owner to ensure that their husband or wife receives a lifetime interest in the property (*usufruit*) on their death.

One of the most popular methods that couples opt for, however, is to put a clause called a '*clause tontine*' in the conveyance, which, in effect, suspends the ownership of the entire property until one or other of them dies. However, this does not make the property exempt from taxation.

STEP 10: *Renovations and building works*

If you buy a property with a view to making alterations, you should check for any planning restrictions that may affect any building plans you have. A certificate showing planning permission, a *certificat d'urbanisme*, will provide precise details of the rules regarding the potential development of an individual property. Each area has an official maximum planning density, the *coéfficient d'occupation des sols*, and some areas have no-build zones. Contact your local town hall for these. Buyers should also be aware that not all buildings can be improved and turned into gîtes. Some buildings may be too small in the first place to do so. The maximum size for which smaller buildings can be increased should be checked under the planning regulations.

Some minor works require no formalities, but even before building a swimming pool, you may need to fill in a form called a *déclaration des travaux* at your local *mairie*. In the case of more extensive alterations to a French property, both planning permission and a building permit, called a *permis de construire*, must be applied for through the local *mairie*.

Once the application has been considered by the *mairie*, it is forwarded on to the local planning office, and following approval it is then passed back to the *mairie* for a final sign-off. The whole process usually takes approximately two months. Applications can be made by the owners themselves or a surveyor, unless the net surface area to be built upon exceeds 170 square metres, in which case it should be made by an architect who is a member of the *Ordre des architectes*. A listed historical building, or a building that is situated near one, will also require review by an *architecte des bâtiments de France*. The majority of planning applications in France also require an environmental declaration providing an assessment of the impact of the proposals on the local area. An architect will usually organise this for you.

It may be tempting to try to carry out renovation work without recourse to builders or architects, but anyone renovating or adding to a historic building must be competent in the use of the local wood and stone, and understand the regulations governing the use of building material in the area. French builders are not renowned for their punctuality, but they are known to do a good job. The local *chambre des métiers* (chamber of trade) can supply details of builders registered in the area.

Some British homeowners are more comfortable employing British builders, even though they will probably not be as knowledgeable about the local materials and planning regulations. There are plenty of British builders who live in France or will travel to France to work. It is essential, however, to check that the work of British builders, electricians, plumbers and other tradesmen complies with French standards.

When the owner cannot be on site to supervise the project, employing an architect or surveyor, French or British, to see the project through can end up saving you money as well as time. However you decide the project should be managed, when work has been completed, the owner will need to obtain a certificate, or *certificat de conformité*, proving that it complies with the planning permission. All new building works come with a 10-year guarantee from the contractor who has carried out that work, provided that they are properly registered with the French authorities. The guarantee will be backed by the contractor's professional insurance.

What is rarely guaranteed, however, is the actual cost of the work itself. Estimates form the basis of a fixed price deal if the builder carrying out the works signs an estimate endorsed with the words '*prix global au forfeit*'. This binds them to completing the job for the price shown. Completion dates can also be hard to guarantee, but again there is a way to help fix the date. By inserting a few more words on the paperwork, such as '*le délai d'achèvement des travaux sera le 31 juillet 2005*' (building work will be completed on July 31 2005), the builder will feel obliged to stick to that date. A penalty clause can also be included in the agreement, such as '*avec une pénalité de 20 euros par jour de retard*', in which case if completion is delayed, the bill will be reduced by 20 euros for each day the work is delayed.

A nationwide organisation called the Conseil d'architecture, d'urbanisme et de l'environnement (CAUE), which has local branches in all of France's regions, can offer advice on renovating or extending traditional buildings. It is also well worth checking with a *mairie* to discover if the local council provides grants for restoring buildings in the area. Some offer particular help to anyone converting buildings into holiday accommodation, as part of a drive to attract tourism into the regions. The larger gîte rental companies are also known to offer money for this purpose, with the proviso that the agency will have the right to let out the property afterwards.

Building a new home

If you buy a home to be constructed by a developer, they will oversee the construction of your new home, and your choice of architectural style may be limited

HEADLANDS INTERNATIONAL

Secure a binding estimate from your builder

by the designs drawn up for that particular development. If you are not buying from a developer, you can choose between hiring an architect to draw up plans or buying a ready-made plan from the builder you engage to construct it. If you choose the former option – which will give you the greatest scope for influencing the style of the building according to your personal tastes – you can either oversee the building of the property yourself, or engage a *maître d'œuvre* to do so. In any case, you will usually be expected to pay the cost in stages over the course of the construction.

In France, if you buy a new apartment or villa under construction which forms part of a development, you should be protected by the *code de la construction* (construction law) from the developer being made bankrupt during its construction, and from other possible pitfalls. By law, when the keys to your newly built home are handed over, there will be a one-month guarantee against obvious structural defects and a 10-year warranty against latent defects affecting the structure of the building. There will also be a two-year warranty against defects in equipment in the building, such as central heating.

Maintaining your property

When owners are away, they often turn to neighbours to help look after their property. Having someone clean the property and tend the garden in their absence makes visiting even more enjoyable.

Specialist companies can also offer property checks, sending someone round regularly to see if there has been any damage to it and to check if any pipes are leaking, for example. ●

STEPS TO BUYING

"Finance your dream."

or How to acquire property in France.

You're interested in buying property or a home in France? If so, we are the ideal partner you've been looking for. Who could be better placed than Entenial - the leading French financial institution specializing in real-estate and asset financing - to offer you the help you need to make your dream come true?

Our most heartfelt wish is to be able to say:
"Welcome to your new home!" So, don't hesitate any longer! It's easy to make contact and start getting better acquainted…

We'll design a financing solution perfectly tailored to your resources and your desires, and guide you with a sure hand through the legal labyrinth of buying property in France.

For mortgages tailored to your future home in France, send us an e.mail at:

international@entenial.com

Entenial

We did it!

BUYING A BUSINESS

David Barnes and his family moved from Devon to Poitou-Charentes to run a hotel

Meet the buyer...

David Barnes

Age: 58

Job: David runs a hotel and leisure complex

Where: Moved from Devon to Les Granges in St-Jean-d'Angély near La Rochelle in 1993

Contact: Tel: 08717 174 274 or +33 5 46 59 77 41; email: holidays @lesgranges.com; www.lesgranges.com

David thinks the best thing about living in France is being able to eat outdoors when you want

TWELVE YEARS AGO, DAVID BARNES AND HIS family moved to Poitou-Charentes to run a *gîte* complex – Les Granges, in St-Jean-d'Angély – and are now well-settled into French life. They tell us about their *nouvelle vie*.

They started looking in France after seeing the bargain prices of property there, and 1993 they'd found Les Granges, a ruined farm with outbuildings in Charente-Maritime.

Now, with a settled *gîte* business and two kids taking the French squash scene by storm, David tells us about his experiences…

Q: The decision to move your family to France is a pretty big one, so did it take a lot of thought?
A: Not really. We'd decided – over a curry! – to move on and set up a similar business to our country house hotel, but without the hassles of running the restaurant and the bar. When we realised that Devon country properties were beyond our reach, I suggested France and Jane said 'why not?'.

Q: Why did you decide on this particular area?
A: It was the best compromise between hours of sunshine per year against hours travelled by car, allied to its proximity to really good beaches and interesting, well-known towns, such as La Rochelle.

Q: How did you go about finding a property suitable for what you needed?
A: It was too easy! We spent a week here in October 1992, having booked appointments with local estate agents, and found Les Granges on the fifth day.

Q: What kind of home is it?
A: It was originally a rundown, working dairy farm with numerous 17th-century barns, set in nearly four hectares of land above the river Boutonne, on the opposite bank to the medieval town of St-Jean-d'Angély. Now it consists of our large three-bedroom farmhouse (with two bathrooms, drawing room, dining room, library, two kitchens and patio), 16 luxury *gîtes* (with a total of 101 beds), an outdoor pool, an indoor pool with jacuzzi and sauna, a squash club and a huge sports, leisure and crafts centre with bar, restaurant, games room, function room, gym, covered tennis court and changing rooms.

Q: What did you originally pay for the property?
A: In 1992 we got it for just £100,000.

Q: And how much do you think it's worth now?
A: I would say over £3 million.

Q: You've had to do a lot of work to the property though, haven't you?
A: For the first three years we 'camped' in the

grounds while we worked on the first nine *gîte* conversions. We'd have gone bankrupt if we hadn't.

Q: Any major set-backs along the way?
A: The most serious down was Jane's accident: she fell out of a hot-air balloon on to a high tension cable of 200,000 kilowatts, an accident that left her hospitalised with severe injuries and left two villages without electricity for 24 hours! Certainly an eventful month, that one!

"We are currently putting together the finishing touches to plans for our new 13 million euro residential development"

Q: What plans do you have for the land?
A: After finally getting our three hectare field re-zoned, we are currently putting the finishing touches to plans for a 13 million euro residential development just the other side of the river Boutonne, which will have 72 luxury houses and a huge communal swimming pool.

Q: What kind of accommodation will the new development have?
A: Rather than building pastiche copies of traditional Charentais houses, we set out to design and build a development suited to a beautiful rural setting, but in tune with tomorrow's needs. We are really excited by the initial plans: ultra-modern labour and energy saving houses with the latest technology, including rooftop patios with provision for a hot tub and powerful telescopes for star-gazing! All the houses are wirelessly connected with high-speed internet connections and cable TV.

Q: Was it easy to settle into French life?
A: It was hard work initially, but we made an effort to integrate. I became president of the Charente-Maritime Squash Association and I am currently on the committee that oversees the St-Jean-d'Angély tourist office. And we all now have dual nationality.

Q: And how about the kids?
A: To be honest, Sarah was too young to notice and Jonathan was too busy trying to converse in French with his new friends to worry about anything else.

Q: Tell us about their squash exploits
A: I used to play squash twice a week in England so before leaving the UK I bought a second-hand prefabricated court and assembled it in one of our barns. As a result my children began to play, and

The Barnes' hotel was originally a rundown, working dairy farm with many barns

some years later I'm very proud of their achievements: Sarah became French National Champion (girls under-13s) in 2004. Jonathan was a member of the National Junior Team (boys under-15s) and won a bronze medal at the European Junior Squash Championships in Stuttgart 2002. He once again represented France (boys under 17s) at the same championships in 2004. Sarah is currently ranked #3 in Europe (girls under 15s) while Jonathan has reached the top 20 adult players in France at the age of 16! Even the old man reached the finals of the French Open Veterans (over 55s) in 2001!

Q: How have you all managed with the language barrier?
A: It's been easy enough but again, it was hard work initially.

Q: What's the best thing about living here?
A: Space and time to spend as a family and being able to enjoy meals outdoors

Q: Any downsides?
A: I miss my Wadworths 6X bitter, but I smuggle cans of it in from time to time. And I miss English pubs… for their atmosphere more than for the booze!

Q: How easy was it to set up the business?
A: It's been an expensive learning curve and we are still learning, but it's almost automatic now.

Q: What advice would you offer to any readers intending to make a similar move?
A: Make sure you learn some rudimentary French before you arrive, and make sure that you've done your sums with your pessimistic hat on. ●

Living in France 2005

All the information you need for living and working in France, from work permits and visas, to healthcare and collecting your pension

CARTE DE SÉJOUR CHECKLIST
(Resident's permit)

EU nationals will typically be asked to produce the following documents to obtain a *carte de séjour*:

- Valid passport
- Birth certificate or a marriage certificate
- Proof of accommodation
- Proof that you pay contributions to the French state health insurance scheme, or have medical insurance that will cover you until you join it
- Three passport photographs
- Proof of employment or receipt of a state pension, or proof of enrolment with a French university

Work permits and visas

EU nationals are no longer required to apply for a resident's permit (*carte/titre de séjour*) after living or working in the country for more than three months. You must, however, hold some other form of ID (with proof of address) from your home country. For residents from the UK, this is a passport and a document, such as a utilities bill, displaying your address.

However, many French officials are not yet familiar with how to apply the new law, so in some instances, for the time being at least, it may be easier to obtain a *carte de séjour*. If, for example, you apply for a job or set up a business, you may still be asked for a *carte de séjour* because traditionally this permit has served as an ID card and as proof of a right to work.

Anyone working in France, either as an employee or self-employed, must be registered with the social security organisations (*caisses*), that cover their particular occupation and pay contributions to the relevant *caisses*.

Tax

A foreign homeowner usually becomes a resident of France when they spend more than 183 days in the country. If they spend less than 183 days, they could still be classed as 'resident' if they practise their profession or have a permanent home in France. Non-residents must pay tax if they have income from a rental property or a French employer.

If you own a property in France and stay for over 183 days you become an official resident

JUSTIN POSTLETHWAITE

Both the tax offices of France and the UK will need to be notified of French annual income – this could include interest from a bank account or rent from a property. If this is above an official threshold you must make an annual declaration of income.

In theory, a tax resident of France could be liable for both French and UK taxes, but a double tax treaty between France and the UK protects British nationals owning French property from paying tax twice. Anyone planning a permanent move should tell the British tax authorities and pass on new employment and property details.

Income is collected on 'earned' income, and depends on the income level. A number of allowances exist. A tax on investment or 'unearned, income tax, is payable on property and investment income, as well as interest paid on bank accounts. A separate rental income tax is levied on gross rental income.

French inheritance law, which governs inheritance tax, and death and estate duties, decides who inherits a person's assets. In theory, inheritance tax is paid on the global assets of a French tax resident. The beneficiaries pay a percentage of their inheritance, depending on the value of the estate and how closely they are related. Inheritance tax will also be due on any French property owned by a non-resident.

Healthcare

In 2000, the World Health Organization voted the French healthcare system the best in the world. If you are an EU national and only visit your French home for short periods, you will need to present a valid E111 form to receive emergency medical treatment when in France. The form can be obtained from post offices in the UK. If you reside for periods of more than three months and are not working, you may be entitled to the same treatment and benefits as French nationals, up to a certain time limit. After this period, to cover much of the cost of your future medical treatment, you may be able to start contributing voluntarily to the state health insurance scheme or you will have to take out private medical insurance. Once you are employed in France, your employers will register you with the social security and will automatically pay contributions to the state health insurance scheme. While making these payments, the scheme will cover most of your healthcare costs. The same applies if you are self-employed and paying contributions to the *caisse*.

If you are retiring in France and receive a state pension from another EU country, that country will usually pay for your healthcare. Form E121 will let you register for free healthcare in France. If you also receive a French state pension, though, you will be treated as a French pensioner and France's health insurance scheme will cover all healthcare costs. If you will not be working in France, but are not yet eligible for a state pension, complete form E106 to obtain medical cover for up to two years. After this, you could pay voluntary contributions or take out private insurance.

British nationals can contact the Department of Social Security (DSS) for further information. In France, your local health insurance or social security office can give you forms and advice.

Even when someone is living in France and has joined the state health insurance scheme, unless they fall into the 'low income' bracket or are suffering from a serious illness, the full cost of any treatment is not usually borne by the state health service. Consultations, treatments and prescriptions are usually paid for upfront, before being reimbursed, in full or in part, by the relevant health insurance *caisse*. This applies unless treatment is carried out in an approved hospital, in which case the state will pay 80 percent of the cost of the treatment directly to the hospital. You

Help is readily available if you are looking for work in France

"A double tax treaty between France and the UK protects British nationals owning French property from paying tax twice"

BUYER'S GUIDE

"Any foreign child living in France has the right to join the French education system and attend the local state school"

must then pay the balance and any fixed daily hospital charge. You don't have to register with a particular GP and can visit any doctor or dentist of your choice, although fees can vary greatly. Details of local hospitals and practitioners can be obtained from a gendarmerie or by dialling 15 on any French telephone. Your local social security office can provide a list of the doctors who charge the official social security rate.

Education

Any foreign child living in France has the right to join the French education system and can attend a local state school, a private school or one of the many bilingual schools – both state-run and private – depending on which establishment best suits their needs. Between the ages of three and five, children can join an *école maternelle* (a nursery). All six to 16-year-olds must first attend an *école primaire* (a primary school), then a *collège* (a secondary school). The last two years are spent at a *lycée*, where students can choose to either study for a *baccalauréat,* or for vocational qualifications.

The French state education system has an excellent reputation, but if children have a poor command of the French language when they arrive in the country, they may be better off at a bilingual school rather than a local state school. Each region has one or sometimes two *académies* (education districts), managed by a *rectorat* (local education authority), which can provide details of all the different schools and universities based in their locality.

Insurance

Homeowners are legally obliged to take out third-party liability insurance on their property. The vendor's insurance can be transferred into the new owner's name. This can be part of a multi-risk household insurance policy which includes contents and buildings insurance. Contents and insurance policies specific to holiday homes may be preferable for those who only intend to visit the property from time to time.

All cars in France must have at least third-party insurance cover. Proof of insurance must be kept with the car at all times.

Don't gamble on insurance...

Securing a driving licence

Citizens of EU countries are permitted to drive within France on the driving licence issued by their country of origin. UK licence holders moving to France should note that the DVLA do not permit foreign addresses on UK licences. When you notify them that you have a foreign address they'll send you an application form for a French licence. If you commit a driving offence in France that results in penalty points, you will have to change your licence to a French one.

If you do wish to apply for a French driving licence you should contact your local *Préfecture*. You will need to provide a valid current licence, proof of domicile, two passport-sized photographs, and the fee, in the form of *timbres fiscales*. By law you must have your driving licence with you at all times while driving.

Securing a job

Looking for a job in France is much the same as in the UK. You can send speculative letters to companies of interest or apply for vacancies published in the French press or online. There are also numerous temporary

JUSTIN POSTLETHWAITE

It is the law in France that you must carry your licence with you when driving any vehicle

employment agencies, recruitment centres and vocational guidance centres, as well as employment services to help you in your search for work. If already in France, you could try www.parisfranceguide.com or the *Agence National Pour l'Emploi* (ANPE) at www.anpe.fr. If job-hunting from Britain you should take a look at the Recruitment and Employment Federation, www.rec.uk.com, and www.ukworksearch.com. Alternatively, try a European agency such as European Employment Services (EURES).

Making a will

British wills are recognised in France, but they are much more costly to implement. As such, it's always advisable to draw up a French will. This should be done in consultation with a lawyer. Leaving no will at all can cause complications and great expense for your heirs.

Pet travel checklist

■ When exporting cats and dogs from Britain under the Pet Travel Scheme (PETS), you must ensure that they are microchipped and vaccinated against rabies. The rabies vaccine must be given at least 30 days prior to departure to allow time for immunity to develop. Once a blood test confirms a sufficient level of rabies antibodies, the microchipped pet qualifies for a British Pet Passport.
■ After your pet has lived in France for three months, it's regarded as a resident and must comply with French laws.
■ For re-entry to the UK, check your pet for ticks and tapeworms one to two days before travelling. This can be done by a vet who will then issue you with the relevant certificate. You must sign a declaration stating that your pet hasn't been outside any PETS qualifying countries within

PET CHECKLIST

■ Your pet must be vaccinated against rabies

■ You are required to secure a PETS certificate, essentially a 'Pet Passport'

■ Your pet must be microchipped – this will be done by your vet

■ Your pet is required to undergo a blood test to clear it of carrying any rabies antibodies

COMMUNICATIONS

Mobile phones Most foreigners in France use their British mobile, but substitute their UK sim card for a French one. It is then possible to operate on a 'Pay as you go' tariff, purchasing a *mobicarte* (top up card) from any *tabac* or supermarket, thus avoiding a contract and billing system for which you need a permanent address.

Internet France's main internet service provider is www.wanadoo.fr. They provide free software for internet connection but you do have to pay through your phone bill for time online. This is only a few euros per minute but these can accumulate. There are various deals on offer through telecom providers (France Télécom) which can be faster and cheaper.

Postal services *La poste* (the French post office; www.laposte.net) is easily recognisable due to its yellow and blue colouring. Not only does it function as your traditional post office, you can also pay your bills, receive your welfare payments and also open a bank account of sorts.

the previous six months. If your pet doesn't meet these requirements it must spend six months in quarantine.

■ For more exotic pets, check with the French authorities, as special certificates may be needed or importation may not be permitted at all.

Retirement and pensions

Anyone moving to France to retire should inform their social security office a few weeks before their departure date, so that they can set the necessary administrative arrangements in motion. You can still receive a state pension from one country if you retire to another, but you must make sure you that you pass on details of any new bank account.

   If you work in France before you retire there, and have made contributions to the French state pension scheme, you will probably be entitled to receive a French state pension in addition to one from any other country you have lived and worked in. The level of state pension you receive will depend on how long you contributed to the pension scheme of that particular country. In France, on reaching retirement age you should contact the *Caisse Nationale d'Assurance Vieillesse* (CNAV). The overseas branch of the UK's Department of Social Security can provide information about pensions for British citizens moving abroad.

Utilities

Most French home utilities are state run, which makes getting connected a fairly simple process. The majority of France's power (supplied by *Electricité de France*, or EDF) comes from nuclear reactors and hydro-electric plants, and is among the cheapest in Europe. Hence, most home heating and appliances run on electricity. Contact your local EDF office to arrange connection. You'll need proof of home ownership and another form of identity. Mains gas is supplied by *Gaz de France* (GDF) and is part of EDF.

Each region has one or two education districts which will provide details of schools in your area

JUSTIN POSTLETHWAITE

Both utilities are usually billed together.

Water is privatized and supplied by *Générale des Eaux*. It's expensive, but costs vary depending on the region you live in. Mains drainage is much more expensive than the septic tanks that many rural homes rely upon. Contact your local water company to set up a new account and have the meter read before moving in.

For telephone connection, visit your local *France Télécom* office with ID and proof of your address. You will be charged a call-out and connection fee.

Voting

All EU citizens resident in France are legally entitled to vote in certain French elections, specifically the local (municipal) elections and European elections. You will need a voter registration card and an identity document.

Finding a job in France is much the same as in England

Marriage

France is different to the UK in that only civil weddings are legally recognised. Religious ceremonies have no legal standing, so if you want to marry in a French church you will also have to have a civil ceremony elsewhere. Alternatively, you could have a civil marriage in Britain followed by a religious wedding in France.

At least one of the partners to be married must reside in the place where the wedding will be held for at least 40 days before the wedding. After 30 days, you must display the marriage banns at the town hall (*mairie*) for ten days.

British nationals don't lose their nationality when they marry. Equally, marriage to a French citizen does not automatically grant you French citizenship. To acquire French nationality upon marrying a French citizen you must sign a declaration before a French consul or magistrate. This will grant you dual nationality.

Renovations and building works

If you buy a property with a view to making alterations, you should check for any planning restrictions that may affect your plans. A certificate showing planning permission will provide precise details of the rules regarding the potential development of a property.

Some minor works require no formalities, but for more extensive alterations, both planning permission and a building permit must be applied for through the local *mairie*.

Once the application has been considered it's forwarded to the local planning office, and once approved is passed back to the *mairie* to be signed

INTERESTING FACTS

■ The average retirement age in France is 60 compared with 65 in the UK

■ French workers are entitled to 47 days holiday compared with an average of 28 days in the UK

■ The average working day in France is under 8 hours, whereas UK workers average 8.7 hours a day

■ Costs in the UK are 13% more expensive than France

■ The French enjoy an average disposable income of £22,668, £1,739 less than the UK, but the French save 15.8% of that income compared with 5% in the UK

BUYER'S GUIDE

Short cuts to
France *and* Spain

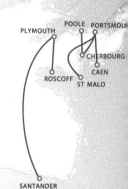

Save miles of driving <u>and</u> up to 33% on fares

Wherever you're heading to in France or Spain, there's a Brittany Ferries route to save you miles of unnecessary driving. And if you join our Property Owners Travel Club you'll save up to **33% on ferry travel** and benefit from special on-board savings, and even discounts for your friends. What's more, the savings start the minute you call, with no points to collect, and no strings attached. **So join now and start saving.**

New for 2005

High speed service from Portsmouth to Cherbourg
High speed service from Portsmouth to Caen
Additional cruise ferry capacity from Plymouth to Roscoff

For further information call **0870 908 9520**

PLYMOUTH
POOLE PORTSMOU
CHERBOURG
ROSCOFF CAEN
ST MALO
SANTANDER

JUSTIN POSTLETHWAITE

The French love their food, and market throughout France offer an abundance of fresh produce

off. The process takes about two months. Applications can be made by the owners or through either a *notaire* or a surveyor, unless the net surface area to be built upon exceeds 170 square metres, whereby it should be made by a member of the Ordre des Architectes. A listed building must be reviewed by an *architecte des bâtiments de France*. Most planning applications also require an environmental declaration that assesses the likely impact of the proposals on the surrounding area.

Anyone renovating a historic building must be competent in the use of the local building materials, and understand the regulations governing their use. The local chamber of trade can supply details of registered builders in the area. If you prefer to employ British builders, it is important to remember that they probably won't be as knowledgeable about local materials and regulations, and always check that their work complies with French standards.

If you cannot personally supervise the project, employing an architect or surveyor can save time and money. Once the work is completed, you must obtain a certificate to prove that it complies with planning permission.

Most residential building works come with a 10-year guarantee, but the actual cost of the work itself is rarely guaranteed. Estimates form the basis of a fixed price deal if the builder signs an estimate endorsed with the words '*prix global au forfeit*'. This binds them to completing the job for the price shown.

For advice on renovating traditional buildings contact the *Conseil d'Architecture, d'Urbanisme et de l'Environnement* (CAUE), which has branches throughout France. You should also check whether the local council provides grants for restoring buildings in the area. Some councils will offer help to anyone converting buildings into holiday accommodation. ●

"If you cannot personally supervise the project, employing an architect or surveyor can save you time and money "

We did it!

BUYING TO RENOVATE

Claire and John Bussell purchased a run-down mill in Vendée in the summer of 1999

Meet the buyer...

John and Claire Bussell with their children Jack (7), William (5) and Oliver (18 months)

Where: South Vendée, about an hour from the coast

When the Bussells stumbled across Vendée, they knew they had found the location for their dream

WHEN THE BUSSELLS DECIDED TO RELOCATE TO France, they planned on moving to the Loire Valley. But when they stumbled across the beautiful landscape and rustic houses of Vendée, they knew they had found their ideal location. They purchased their property in 1999 for £140,000, and today it's valued at £600,000. The property required complete renovation and the Bushells restored it using reclaimed materials. In doing so they earned the admiration of the community and, as a result, the house was showcased by the Maisons du Pays, a society for the preservation and restoration of local, historic properties, as an example of sensitive workmanship in keeping with traditional methods.

Q: Is this the first restoration project you have undertaken?
A: No, we seem to be in the habit of finding dilapidated properties! We already had a string of renovations under our belts, including several jobs for clients, and we're not afraid of the challenge and hard work it takes to restore these properties to their former glory

Q: What is your occupation in France?
A: I am a registered artisan in Vendée, and my restoration business, established in 1999, which specialises in one-off, original restorations, has gone from strength to strength. I now have a growing customer base and increasing recognition for my work in the local area. Claire loves to find original fittings and pieces of furniture, so we were ideally qualified to undertake the renovation of the mill.

Q: When did you purchase your property?
A: We purchased the mill in 1999 in a tumbledown state and it has been our most ambitious project to date. Built in 1573, the mill was originally owned by, and named after, the Chevalier de Darot. But it was referred to locally as Moulin Garot, as it has connections with the Vendéen wars when it was used as a garrison. We were keen to retain the place's sense of history, while at the same time making it a more habitable living space.

Q: What drew you to the property?
A: The previous owners had been unable to sell the house for over two years as prospective buyers had been discouraged by its overgrown wilderness. Claire thought it was like the castle in *Sleeping Beauty*! We came across and instantly fell in love with its rural charms. It had everything we wanted. It was large enough to bring up our family while living the idyllic lifestyle that we had always dreamed about. It may have taken us three years, but we now have our dream home.

Q: How did you go about renovating the mill?
A: Our first tasks were outside, and there was as much

to do outside as in. We have about four acres of ground and we had to set to work on the garden, cutting back years of growth to allow light and air back into the property. Next, we had to clear the driveway, which involved hacking through 500 metres of undergrowth to allow cars and, more importantly, heating fuel deliveries to get through to the site. We also needed to fence off the steeper parts of the river bank to ensure the children's safety.

> "Our watchwords were 'cosy' and 'rustic', and I think we have managed to stay faithful to that in each room"

We wanted to cause as little disturbance to the natural surroundings as possible, so the fences were designed to blend in. We did this by coppicing hazel branches to form 'living' hedges alongside the river. The garden now couldn't be further removed from the overgrown wilderness we were faced with when we first moved in. We have red squirrels in our trees as well as kingfishers, wild ducks and moorhens that nest on our river outside the kitchen windows. It is a paradise for our three boys, who can now recognise a bird simply from hearing its song.

Q: What about renovating the inside? Was it hard to adhere to the original design of the house?
A: Inside, things were less chaotic, but still in need of some urgent attention in order to make it habitable. Our watchwords were 'cosy' and 'rustic', and I think we managed to stay faithful to that in each room. On the whole, the main structure of the house was pretty strong, but we urgently needed bedrooms upstairs and a sanitation system, so we set about creating four bedrooms, a bathroom and a shower room from scratch.

The biggest task involved turning the old *bergerie* (sheep fold) next to the main house into an enormous kitchen and living space.The entire building was falling down and needed a new roof, floors and windows as well as plumbing and electricity. It meant knocking through from the main house to create a doorway; through walls over a metre thick! The rest of the house simply needed careful cosmetic attention to enhance its natural rustic features, and as it was all structurally sound, there was little actual building work to do, so the focus was on finding suitably authentic fixtures and fittings.

Q: How hard was it to find original fittings and fixtures?
A: As we preferred the rustic look, Claire scoured around for individual items from reclaimed sources and

The Bussells are now preparing to open up their home to paying guests

brocantes (flea markets). We were lucky to have some beautiful fireplaces and original floors that we cleaned and restored alongside rustic furniture and old fabrics,. As lovers of traditional style, we feel more comfortable when surrounded by things that look as if they can really tell a story.

Q: How are you finding life in the Vendée?
A: Well, it's been three years since we moved into our home and we've settled into rural life and are now preparing to open up our home to guests. We will be offering accommodation, along with freshly cooked meals made with local produce and home-grown vegetables. We want to share the tranquillity we have experienced at Moulin Garot with others. We all feel very comfortable in our new home and our ten-year experience of French living has been an enjoyable voyage of discovery. We are all looking forward to the next ten! ●

Top tips

1. For decorating and furnishings, visit local vides greniers (car boot sales) where you can find some one-off pieces at very affordable prices.

2. With branches all over western France, VM Matériaux is a great place to buy building supplies such as plasterboard, wood and cement.

3. The most important piece of advice Claire and John can offer is to learn the language, as it makes everything much simpler and more enjoyable. Also, it helps to get involved with the local community.

4. Having young children can help with the integration process and shouldn't put families off moving abroad. "Our two eldest boys are bilingual and happily settled into the French education system," Claire says.

We did it!

RETIRING TO FRANCE

Enamoured with France, Pam and Mike Brazier retired to their *fermette* in Chevagny-sur-Guye

Meet the buyer...

Pam and Mike Brazier

Age: "Old enough to be retired!"
Job: Retired primary school head-teacher (Pam) and secondary school teacher (Mike)
Where: Moved from Pinner, Middlesex to Burgundy in 1995

When the Braziers bought this *fermette* they transformed it from a run-down ruin

PAM AND MIKE BRAZIER'S LOVE AFFAIR WITH France began a long time ago on family holidays during the 1980s. They bought their first holiday home soon after in Chevagny-sur-Guye, and this peaceful Burgundian village seemed like the ideal destination when they took early retirement in 1995.

Q: When and why did you move to Burgundy?
A: We moved from Pinner, Middlesex to Burgundy in May 1995. But long before that, we had bought our first French property in this same village, back in 1981. We used to spend family holidays in Spain and it wasn't until we met a family from Cluny that we discovered the delights of Burgundy.

Q: How did you find your first property?
A: In Burgundy, we found the local people good-humoured, kind and proud of their history, and they seemed to us to have it all: wonderful food, magnificent wines, beautiful scenery and a pleasing climate. With two days to go before our return journey, we decided to visit the *notaire* with a view to a possible purchase.

There were several brochures in varying colours, each one containing details of properties ranging from ruins to châteaux. We stuck with the ruins and found five houses in varying states of disrepair. We visited four properties, all quite pretty but unsuitable for varying reasons. The last call was at Chevagny-sur-Guye, and we knew as soon as we saw the house that we would buy it.

Q: Can you describe it?
A: It was quite a small place. A short flight of stone steps led up to the front door and inside there were only two rooms. However, the rooms were quite large and there would be space for a staircase. The roof area was a good size, too.

Q: When and why did you decide to settle here more permanently?
A: When we were discussing our mutual early retirements, it seemed logical to consider France as a place to put down our roots. We felt that retiring and then staying put in the same place we had lived all our lives would be pointless. Why not take a new turn in life and do something challenging like actually living with the French!

But our holiday home in Burgundy wasn't big enough, nor did it have a garden, so it was time to move to a bigger place. One weekend in Pinner, we received a phone call from friends in France saying there was an ancient *fermette* (small farmhouse) for sale in the village and asking if we were interested.

Q: Did you have much work to do?
A: The *fermette* was in a sorry state at first and could

hardly be seen due to the brambles and trees all over and around it. It has taken us years to renovate. However, while we were toiling away, we did have the other house to run back to for a hot shower and all the comforts of home. We had agreed to give this move out to Burgundy a year, during which time we could get the feel of the place, and find out first-hand the difference between visiting for holidays and actually residing here.

Q: How did the locals react to your arrival in the village?
A: We were the only English there at first, and people from other villages had heard of the rather eccentric *étrangers* who had arrived from England. Time passed and we renovated the little house, putting in stairs so that we could make two more rooms upstairs. It was unheard of then to have bedrooms upstairs. The neighbours turned out in droves to look at our new staircase, and to marvel at a second-hand sink that we had fitted in the kitchen.

We became a source of interest, and we were only too happy to have folks in to see what we were doing. We got used to the life of the village and the 'bush telegraph' was amazing. We knew that we had really arrived when the locals finally included us when they had a bit of gossip to share or spread!

Q: Do you feel part of the community now?
A: Yes, we do. Despite having the rest of our family back in the UK, we are still very happy here. A comment from our deputy mayor made it all worthwhile when she was introducing us to some of her friends from Paris: "These are the English who are resident here. We have adopted them." Right from the start, we felt part of this little community.

Q: Did you encounter any problems?
A: Our first small house was without mains drainage so we had to have a septic tank in the cellar and pipes running down to the garden at the foot of the lane. The work was done while we were back in England and when we returned everything was working well. The only snag was that the bill was twice as much as the original quote. The plumber was apologetic and explained that the extra cost was due to the difficulty of laying the pipes underground. We began to panic. Our budget was tight and we had no extra money to cope with this bill.

The plumber took us to the mayor who gave us a glass or two of wine while he pondered on the problem. He decided that, as the lane was a public 'road', the commune ought to pay the excess. Our relief knew no bounds. In just 20 minutes, a decision had been made and our worries were over. The mayor sent us on our way with more wine and a friendly handshake.

Pam and Mike's holiday home in Burgundy was too small to move into permanently

Q: How have you coped with the language?
A: Our French has improved and our efforts have caused a lot of amusement, but we have made good progress. Nobody spoke English at the beginning and it was a learning curve for us. We had no option but to communicate and so we did, often with a little mime thrown in for good measure!

We have a good social-life with other English couples scattered around the area, and with our French friends here. Our own children are adults with their own families back in the UK, but all our grandchildren have been to Chevagny-sur-Guye and we hope that will continue for many years to come. They will certainly be here for our wedding anniversary party in 2007. We are planning to invite the entire village as well as our family and friends from the UK. That should certainly be an event to remember: our very own *entente cordiale*.

Q: Do you have any advice for readers?
A: The mayor of our village is a great character; it is wise to get such an exalted figure on your side. I am happy to report that we are on kissing terms, so nothing can go wrong. Always ask the mayor's permission to do almost anything. When we built a garage, we had to submit drawings for approval of this and the colour of the roof tiles!

Over the years, I have come to realise that you have to accept and respect the ways and traditions of the local people if you want to live among them, and you must adapt to those ways yourself. ●

JUSTIN POSTLETHWAITE

Property Guide

We've travelled the length and breadth of France to reveal the up-and-coming areas and hottest property prospects

PROPERTY GUIDE

How to use this book

The guide's three sections – the Buyer's Guide, Property Guide and Buyer's Reference – cover every aspect of finding and buying a home in France, providing a wealth of expert advice

Hotspots

Our experts have identified the key 94 places in which to buy property in France. For the purposes of this guide, a hotspot is classified as a place that's desirable both for its investment potential and quality of life, and that defines the property price bracket of both itself and the surrounding area.

Part One: Buyer's Guide

This section offers the latest facts and information about the financial and legal process of buying a property in France. It includes a number of articles written by our panel of experts (see page 317) and a comprehensive Steps to Buying chapter, which takes you through every stage of the French conveyancing system, from appointing a lawyer, right the way through to completing a purchase.

A section on Living and Working provides detailed advice on visas and taxes, as well as information about the French healthcare and education systems, along with practical information on renovating a property.

Part Two: Property Guide

Divided into 15 regional chapters, the Property Guide offers up-to-the-minute information about the current performance of each region's property market, with comparative price charts and profiles of the hotspots, as well as illustrated property price guides highlighting the types of homes available in each area.

Regional Profiles

An introduction to each region, including general information on the area and its main attractions, the state of the economy and housing market, and the main social groups living there and buying into it. In addition to these general profiles, we go the extra mile with in-depth sections that focus on the ever-popular Gascony, Charente and Dordogne areas that continue to be of special interest to British buyers.

Property Price Chart

An at-a-glance snapshot of property values in the region, the price chart provides average sale prices for two, three, four and five-bedroom properties in each hotspot, wherever available. The prices are averaged from the most recent sales prices achieved – supplied to us by a panel of property market specialists.

These will not always tally directly with the average property price listed in the hotspots profiles and key facts boxes, because the latter figures are the median property prices, averaged from sales of houses over last year (2004) as a whole.

Regional Maps

For each listed region a map of the area is provided. A number on the map marks the location of each hotspot mentioned in the chapter, which corresponds to the number next to that hotspot's profile. Major ports, airports, roads and rivers are also marked.

In these real-life case studies, UK citizens who have bought properties in France tell their tales

All the important regional facts about the areas of France that are attracting house hunters

Hotspot Profiles

This section provides information on the cultural, economic and architectural identity of each hotspot, its popular residential areas and the dominant social groups. The profiles give an idea of the central focus of a community, and highlight the main characteristics of the hotspot.

Hotspot Key Facts

These handy key fact panels detail each hotspot's pros and cons, population, airports, local taxes, rental market, and the nearest medical centres and schools. In some cases we have been rigorously selective, for reasons of space.

For each hotspot's rental market there is an indication of average rental prices both long and short term, depending on the nature of the market. If this is short term, details are provided regarding which seasons of the year you can expect to be able to let out your property. The 'Pros' and 'Cons' of each hotspot have been compiled in association with our panel of market experts, and include information, as appropriate, on employment prospects, potential tenants and current price trends.

Regional Price Guides

The regional price guides give a flavour of the type of property available in each area. They are not intended to be used as a sales brochure, as, given the fast-moving nature of the French property market, it is impossible to include properties that are still available to be purchased. However, they do offer comparisons between each region, for both prices and a wide range of architectural styles. The properties are divided into price bands which vary according to the nature of the market and the type of property on sale within each region.

The price of each property is in euros and the agent's three-letter code, e.g., LAT, for Latitudes, is listed at the top of the property details; these codes can be cross-referenced to the alphabetical list of agent names and contact details with their codes in the Index of Agents (page 330).

The next line details the town/area, followed by a brief description of the property and underneath, the price in £ sterling.

A selection of symbols indicates number of bedrooms, whether the property has a garden, if it's situated in a town, city or country location, its proximity to a main road and whether there is parking, followed by a brief description or number.

These symbols are:

Bedrooms: 🛏 followed by a number.

Garden: ❀ with the size in square metres, or a description, e.g. 'large garden'.

Near shops/amenities: 🏪 followed by a brief description of the distance from the property, or with the assumption that they are within five miles.

Near a road: 🛣 followed by a brief description of the location.

Parking: 🏠 followed by a brief description of what is available, either a carport, room for parking, or garage.

Part Three: Buyer's Reference

The Buyer's Reference offers useful information and contacts to help you at each stage of buying a property.

Price Matrices

To enable you to calculate potential outlay and rental return, there are three price matrices offering a clear comparison between all the hotspots. The House Price matrix (see page 302) lists average 'for sale' prices for two to six-bedroomed properties, while the Apartments matrix (see page 306) offers prices for one to four-bedroomed apartments. The Lettings matrix (see page 309) similarly covers all the hotspots and gives the average weekly figures you can expect to achieve for a one to five-bedroomed property. Compiled from extensive research at the time of going to print, these prices reflect the current market situation.

Directory of Useful Contacts

A listing of professionals and organisations, from architects and estate agents to lawyers, with addresses, telephone numbers and website details.

Index to Agents and Index

All the contact details for the estate agents featured in the Price Guides are listed on page 330, while a comprehensive general index begins on page 332. ●

HOW TO USE THIS BOOK

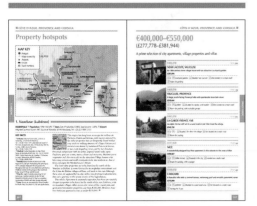

The Hotspots and Price Guides tell you where to look to buy, and how much to expect to pay

Brittany

Gulf Stream currents, historic Dinan, and Neolithic sites

JUSTIN POSTLETHWAITE

FACT BOX 2005

■ **Population** 2,906,197
■ **Migration** 78,737
■ **Unemployment** 52,591
■ **Median house price** €111,400
■ **House price increase** Since 2002, house prices
in Brittany have increased by 6.8%

Price Guide

■ BRITTANY

GETTING THERE

AIR Brittany can be reached easily by air and its main airports are Brest, Nantes and Rennes. **Ryanair** (0871 246 0000; www.ryanair.com) flies directly to Dinard and Brest from London Stansted, while **Aurigny Air** (0148 182 2886; www.aurignyair.com) offers direct flights to Dinard from Guernsey and Jersey, and via Guernsey from Manchester, East Midlands, Bristol, Stansted, Gatwick and Southampton. **Air France** (0845 084 5111; www.airfrance.co.uk) flies to Nantes, then on into Brittany.
SEA Ferries travel frequently into the ports of Saint-Mâlo and Roscoff. **Brittany Ferries** (0870 366 5333; www.brittany-ferries.com) sails between Portsmouth and Saint-Mâlo, and between Plymouth and Roscoff. **Condor Ferries** (0845 345 2000; www.condorferries.com) sails from Poole and Weymouth to Saint-Mâlo.
ROAD In general, the best way of getting around Brittany is by road. The autoroute N12/N165 offers easy access into Brittany, running along the coast and on to Rennes. Travelling across Brittany's more isolated areas can prove to be much slower. There are autoroutes from Normandy and the Loire that run into Brittany, as well as the A11 from Paris.
COACH Brittany has an extensive local bus network, but services are infrequent. An express coach service operates from outside the terminal building to the central rail station in Saint-Mâlo. **Eurolines** (0870 514 3219; www.eurolines.com) operates services from the UK to Brest, Lorient, Quimper, Rennes, Roscoff, Saint-Mâlo and Vannes.
RAIL Brittany has a good rail network that follows the coast, although the interior has only a limited number of stations. The high-speed TGV runs direct from Paris and Lille into Rennes, and across to Brest and Quimper, and there is a good local train service. The **Eurostar** runs from London Waterloo to Paris, and from there it is possible to get a connection to Dinan. For information, contact **Rail Europe** (0870 830 2008; www.raileurope.co.uk).

Area profile

BRITTANY SITS ON THE WESTERN OUTCROP OF FRANCE, A REGION isolated both geographically and, in many respects, culturally, from the rest of the country – the ancient local Breton language is still practised and taught in certain areas. The rocky coastline stretches for over 1,000 kilometres; the northern half faces the English Channel and the southern section is swept by the Atlantic in the Bay of Biscay. Gulf Stream currents brush the coast ensuring the region enjoys a very clement climate.

The region's capital is Rennes, a handsome university city with a picturesque old quarter and a wealth of good restaurants and museums. Even more outstanding is the small medieval city of Dinan, home to some stunning half-timbered buildings which date back to the 15th century. Travel 15 miles north of Dinan and you reach Brittany's northern coast, and the seaside towns of Saint-Mâlo and Dinard. While the latter is a rather brash resort, Saint-Mâlo is lively yet austere, and it has a busy ferry port.

At Brittany's western point lies Brest, a city which had to be virtually rebuilt after heavy German bombing in the Second World War. It has a rich maritime history, and it is home to France's largest naval facility as well as Océanopolis, the biggest open-air aquarium in Europe. Inland, Brittany is much quieter although there is much to explore, including a number of Neolithic sites, ancient castles, regional parks and great forests.

The region's cuisine is dominated by fish, with oyster and mussel dishes being a particular speciality. Dark wheat crêpes and biscuits are very popular here, too.

The economy and housing market
Brittany is France's main agricultural producer and it has a strong livestock industry. At a local level, the government encourages new industries, and Rennes has now developed its motor trade, while Brest has a thriving engineering and electronics industry. Tourism is still a vital business in

Brittany's cuisine is largely dominated by delicious seafood

JUSTIN POSTLETHWAITE

PROFILE

Brittany, and the fishing industry remains active in various ports. Brittany remains one the most popular destinations in France, with the average property costing between £80,000 and £130,000. The market remains buoyant, and has always attracted buyers seeking cheap properties to renovate, a trend which is inevitably leading to a dearth of renovation projects. This, combined with an increase in the average budget of British buyers, has served to increase prices in the areas of demand.

Property is most expensive along the Gulf of Morbihan, where £175,000 will buy you a fairly modern property. Affordable family property tends to be located on the border between the Côtes d'Armor and Morbihan *départements*, which are experiencing more demand, especially as there are plenty of properties to choose from. The region offers warm winds washing up the Gulf of Morbihan, creating mild winters and a Mediterranean climate. This is an ideal location for those seeking a certain Côte d'Azur decadence and glamour.

With the French dominating the market in the Gulf of Morbihan and recently inundating the Saint-Mâlo area, prices have risen here, too. Despite these increases, Brittany is still cheaper than most areas in France, and few foreign buyers apply for a mortgage when buying in the region.

Brittany does not experience a great demand for new developments and newly built properties, although the demand for modern properties is increasing in the south, and some developments have sprung up. In recent years, the transport network has improved with the introduction of new rail and road links, and this has led to the development of previously isolated areas and of industrial projects within Brittany.

With most points in Brittany only one hour from the coast the beach is still accessible, but property is generally cheaper inland, where there are more renovation properties on the market. Most British people seeking property on the south coast are buying around the Baud area, just inland of Lorient and the band of expensive properties situated on the south coast, while Finistère's west coast offers some bargains in undiscovered areas.

The triangle of Dinard, Dinan and Saint-Mâlo is convenient for those who desire easy and regular access to Britain. Finistère is frequently chosen by those who love nature, and seek more than just sea and sand.

Social groups

Traditionally, Brittany is the home of the British family holiday and it has an abundance of small villages within easy reach of the coast, ideal for a family holiday home. The region has been given the nickname 'Little Britain' by the French because of its popularity with the British who are looking for a holiday home or permanent residence. ●

> *"Brittany is a region that is isolated both geographically and, in many respects, culturally from the rest of France – the Breton language is still practised"*

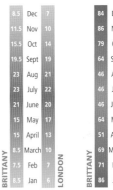

Average monthly temperature °C (Celsius)

Average monthly rainfall mm (millimetres)

AVERAGE HOUSE SALE PRICES

Hotspot	2-bed	3-bed	4-bed	5-bed+
Dinard, Dinan & St Mâlo	€110K (£76K)	€153K (£106K)	€233K (£162K)	€295K (£205K)
Lorient	€118K (£82K)	€185K (£129K)	€254K (£176K)	€269K (£187K)
Golfe du Morbihan	€147K (£102K)	€199K (£138K)	€275K (£191K)	€445K (£309K)
Brest	€114K (£79K)	€142K (£99K)	€198K (£138K)	€254K (£176K)
Quimper	€103K (£72K)	€119K (£82K)	€167K (£116K)	€250K (£174K)
Guingamp	€82K (£57K)	€117K (£81K)	€189K (£131K)	€258K (£179K)
Rennes	€106K (£74K)	€162K (£112K)	€194K (£135K)	€237K (£165K)

Property hotspots

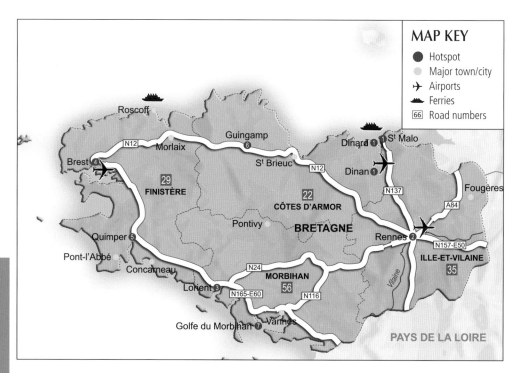

1. Dinard, Dinan, Saint-Malo

ESSENTIALS ■ **Population** 1999: 75,821 ■ **Taxes** Taxe d'habitation: 9.28%, Taxe foncière: 10.79%
■ **Airport** Dinard/Pleurtuit/Saint-Malo Airport, L'Aérodrome, 35730 Pleurtuit, Tel: +33 2 99 46 18 46, Fax: +33 2 99 88 17 85

KEY FACTS

■ **Schools** Rectorat de l'Académie de Rennes, 96 rue d'Antrain, 35044 Rennes Cedex, Tel: +33 2 99 28 78 78, Fax: +33 2 99 28 77 72
■ **Medical** Hospitalier de Saint-Malo, 1 rue Marne, 35400 Saint-Malo, Tel: +33 2 99 21 21 21
■ **Rentals** The rental season lasts from April to September, with winter seeing long-term rents
■ Properties in the area make for a good rental investment ■ Proximity to the coast and good access keeps this rental market healthy ■ Rental prices vary between €300 and €1,000 per week
■ **Pros** Many Britons are choosing to buy their second home here and it is a very popular area ■ Exceptionally easy to get to, the area is good for commuters and second home buyers
■ **Cons** Easy access for the UK market also results in high property prices ■ Owners of properties on Brittany's northern coast experience a climate that is colder and damper than that of southern Brittany ■ International schools are in short supply and many families send their children to a French-speaking school.

All located on Brittany's northern coastline, the seaside towns of Saint-Malo, Dinard and Dinan are popular with both British and French property buyers. The large city of Saint-Malo and its old walled Intra Muros has a lively feel, with a citadel, marinas, restaurants and nightlife. Dinard boasts a casino, sea water therapy centre, antique shops, art galleries and a superb sandy beach with beautiful panoramic views over the Rance estuary. Dinan has been dubbed Brittany's most evocative town, its timbered houses making it a striking example of medieval architecture. The central region celebrates its local culture and traditions, with several schools still teaching the Breton language. Sea views are breathtaking, with high cliffs, islands and rockpools named after their shapes and colours.

The best value homes are found in inland Brittany, throughout the Argoat, where the woods and heathland dotted alongside picturesque villages are graced with traditional granite and slate-roofed cottages, although many properties are in need of renovation. This is a popular area where many Britons choose to buy their second homes, but increased Parisian interest has raised property prices, as has the ease of access between Brittany and Britain. Small renovation projects start at about €40,000, and you can buy a large stone house for €200,000. ●

2. Rennes

ESSENTIALS ■ **Population** 1999: 212,494 ■ **Taxes** Taxe d'habitation: 7.19%, Taxe foncière: 7.54%
■ **Airport** Rennes Saint-Jacques Airport, Avenue Joseph Le Brix, 35136 Saint-Jacques-de-la-Lande, Tel: +33 2 99 29 60 00

The capital of Brittany and a university city, Rennes has a distinctly cosmopolitan air compared to other cities in Brittany. Although you will find stylish squares and perfect medieval houses with pointed façades overlooking the streets, this is the business centre and market hub for the Breton region. Gutted by a fire in 1720, Rennes was then redesigned by Parisian architects, giving the impression in some parts that you are in Paris and not in Brittany. Nonetheless, the Place des Lices, just one of the four squares which dominate the city architecturally, provides useful navigational references for the visitor. The square itself is lined by fine medieval houses, their crooked beams and oriel windows stretching high over the market stalls. The architectural interest of the Place des Lices is enhanced by the two *halles* in the middle of the square.

As the road network in the area is good, purchasing a cheaper property in the countryside surrounding the city is recommended. Property prices within Rennes itself can be very steep, as local agents deal primarily with the local French market. Two-bedroom homes cost around €105,000; add an extra €10,000 for three bedrooms. The average price of a four-bedroom home is just under €200,000. A classic six-bedroom, stone-built house can be bought for about €260,000. ●

KEY FACTS

■ **Schools** Rectorat de l'Académie de Rennes, 96 rue d'Antrain, 35044 Rennes Cedex, Tel: +33 2 99 28 78 78, Fax: +33 2 99 28 77 72 ■ **Medical** Centre Hospitalier Guillaume Régnier, 108 avenue Gén Leclerc, 35000 Rennes, Tel: +33 2 99 33 39 00
■ **Rentals** Long-term lets can be the best rental option ■ Rennes is too far inland and too industrialised to appeal to the holiday market ■ Rennes is primarily a French-dominated city
■ **Pros** Voted among the top 12 best places to live in France ■ Rennes is easily accessible by ferry and by air, and is well served by the autoroute ■ There are many services and amenities in the area and it is particularly geared for those relocating to work in France ■ The biggest city in Brittany
■ **Cons** As Brittany's capital, Rennes commands some of the highest prices in the region ■ This area is not popular with international holiday or second home buyers, and is mainly a local market.

3. Lorient

ESSENTIALS ■ **Population** 1999: 61,844 ■ **Taxes** Taxe d'habitation: 7.22%, Taxe foncière: 10.82%
■ **Airport** Aéroport de Lann Bihoue, Lorient, 56270, Tel: + 33 3 14 90 44 44, Fax: + 33 3 14 90 63 28

Situated in the region of Morbihan and located on an immense natural harbour, Lorient is the second largest fishing port in France. During the 18th century, the French East India Companies were founded here, importing spices and salt into Lorient. Badly damaged during World War II, the town is functional rather than pretty, yet it has a delightful market, a very good beach at Larmor Plage, and a good number of restaurants serving the excellent local country fare. Lorient hosts the Inter-Celtic Festival, held for 10 days from the first Friday to the second Sunday in August. Over a quarter of a million people from Celtic countries attend more than 150 different shows.

Property in Lorient itself can cost up to three times more than in areas just 20 minutes from town. As most people buy slightly further inland from Lorient, where property is cheaper, demand and quick turnover in this area can make it difficult to secure a property. Dominated by the French market, the area is expensive, and a two-bedroom apartment overlooking the marina costs around €260,000. Some estate agents tend to try and deal only with French buyers, and over the last couple of years prices have increased significantly, as has demand. The Baud area, behind the southern coast, experiences more demand due to cheaper prices and more property availability. ●

KEY FACTS

■ **Schools** Rectorat de l'Académie de Rennes, 96 rue d'Antrain, 35044 Rennes Cedex, Tel: +33 2 99 28 7 878, Fax: +33 2 99 28 77 72 ■ **Medical** Centre Hospitalier de Bretagne Sud, 27 rue Doct Lettry, 56100 Lorient, Tel: +33 2 97 64 90 00
■ **Rentals** If you can afford to pay the high prices, you are guaranteed excellent rental income, especially from the French market ■ Property is expensive and there are few bargains on the south coast, with the majority of properties being modern and habitable ■ Parisians have flooded the rental market on the Breton coast
■ **Pros** The port is home to one of Brittany's most renowned festivals, the Inter-Celtic festival ■ Ideally located for those who want to be on the seafront ■ Foreign interest, particularly from British buyers, is high in this area
■ **Cons** Lorient itself is not the most dynamic town on the south coast ■ Most people buy inland from Lorient where property is cheaper ■ Property is in very short supply in Lorient.

HOTSPOTS

4. Brest

ESSENTIALS ■ **Population** 1999: 156,210 ■ **Taxes** Taxe d'habitation: 7.31%, Taxe foncière: 7.95%
■ **Airport** Brest Airport, 29490 Guipavas, Tel: +33 2 98 32 01 00

KEY FACTS

■ **Schools** The only international school in the region is located in Rennes, which is 249 km from Brest ■ Rectorat de l'Académie de Rennes, 96 rue d'Antrain, 35044 Rennes Cedex, Tel: +33 2 99 28 78 78, Fax: +33 2 99 28 77 72
■ **Medical** Centre Hospitalier Universitaire, 5 avenue Foch, 29200 Brest, Tel: +33 2 98 22 33 33
■ **Rentals** Inclement weather prevents Brest from being a popular tourist and rental area ■ Foreigners generally are not interested in Brest and the Finistère département
■ **Pros** Located on a natural harbour, it is one of France's most important ports, with a very rich maritime history ■ The rugged landscape of the area is excellent for nature lovers and activities
■ A strong employment area, excellent for relocation
■ **Cons** This is not an area with a strong foreign property market ■ Brest's post-war architecture gives the city a rather bleak appearance ■ Brest lacks greenery, a result of the high winds that plague the city ■ Despite being located on the coast, Brest has no beaches ■ Rainfall is much higher here than in other parts of France.

Brest is a university city and seaport, located in the far northwest of Brittany. It boasts a rich maritime history and is France's premier naval facility. The river divides the city by flowing between the two hills upon which the city perches. Brest dates from Roman times when a settlement was established around 50BC. During World War II, Brest was continuously bombed to prevent the Germans from using it as a submarine base. When liberated in 1944, the city was devastated beyond recognition and the architecture of the post-war city is in places raw and bleak. There have been attempts to make the centre more verdant, but as Brest experiences the heaviest rainfall in France, it has proved too windswept to respond. One remaining treasure is the 12th-century château, which is now a naval museum. Another major attraction is the futuristic Océanopolis, renowned for being the biggest open-air aquarium of its kind in Europe.

Brest offers a wide assortment of restaurants along rue Jean-Jaurès, while to the north, Place Guérin is the centre of the *student quartier*, Saint-Martin. There is no British enclave or strong foreign property market here. The closer you buy to the city, the more expensive the property. For a luxury six-bedroom house with sea views, expect to pay around €300,000; two-bedroom homes average at around €115,000. ●

5. Quimper

ESSENTIALS ■ **Population** 1999: 63,238 ■ **Taxes** Taxe d'habitation: 7.31%, Taxe foncière: 7.95%
■ **Airport** Quimper Cornouaille Airport, Kermaduit, 29700 Pluguffan, Tel: +33 2 98 94 30 30

KEY FACTS

■ **Schools** Rectorat de l'Académie de Rennes, 96 rue d'Antrain, 35044 Rennes Cedex, Tel: +33 2 99 28 78 78, Fax: +33 2 99 28 77 72
■ **Medical** Cornouaille Centre Hospitalier, 14 avenue Yves Thépot, 29000 Quimper, Tel: +33 2 98 52 60 60
■ **Rentals** Quimper is popular with the French, and rental prices are higher than elsewhere in Brittany ■ Up-and-coming Pays Bigouden and Pont l'Abbé generate good rental income ■ It is difficult to attract the foreign market to such an expensive area
■ **Pros** Quimper is Brittany's oldest city and was once the capital, maintaining a traditional Breton character ■ Quimper is easily accessible, with its own airport, and is located on the motorway and rail network ■ The town is within easy reach of the sea
■ **Cons** Property is extremely expensive around Quimper and the surrounding coastline ■ More of a holiday and rentals market than a permanent home-buyers' market.

Split in two by the Odet river and surrounded by seven hills, Quimper is the ancient capital of the Cornouaille coast and head of the *département* of Finistère, where Breton traditions are still very much alive. Featuring decorative footbridges and lined by rows of trees, lights and colourful hanging flower baskets, Quimper is well placed for exploring inland towns and villages, and offers quick access to the area's spectacular beaches.

A must-see is the Gothic 12th-century Cathédrale Saint-Corentin, named after Quimper's first bishop. Dominating the skyline, the cathedral was constructed between the 13th and 16th centuries. Walk directly to the old town from the cathedral's front to see cobbled squares, the Musée Départemental Breton and the charming narrow streets, teeming with half-timbered houses and the celebrated crêperies. In the Middle Ages, each street of the *vieux quartier* was devoted to a single trade and each still bears the names of its original trade.

Property is very expensive around Quimper and the surrounding coastline, and this is primarily a French market, with foreign buyers reluctant to meet the prices. In the countryside within 20 minutes of Quimper, you could buy a stone and slate property to renovate for approximately €75,000. ●

6. Guingamp

ESSENTIALS ■ **Population** 1999: 8,830 ■ **Taxes** Taxe d'habitation: 9.28%, Taxe foncière: 10.79%
■ **Airport** Dinard/Pleurtuit/Saint-Malo Airport, L'Aérodrome, 35730 Pleurtuit, Tel: +33 2 99 46 18 46, Fax: +33 2 99 88 17 85

Not far from the Côtes d'Armor, on Brittany's rugged north coast, Guingamp is an attractive historic town of alleyways and cobbled streets. The town's university ensures a youthful atmosphere with plenty of nightlife and bars, while the Place du Centre is traffic-free. La Plomée is surrounded by fine old houses and hotels with wood and slate façades. The three-turreted Basilica of Notre-Dame-de-Bon-Secours dates back to the 13th century, and each year on the first Saturday in July, it finds itself encircled by the annual Celtic festival, known as a *pardon*. This fête has a candlelit night procession and bonfires, and a traditional dance festival performed by children. In August, the Fête de la Saint Loup continues for a week, during which there is folk-dancing in the streets. On the outskirts of town, the Warenghem Breton whisky distillery is interesting to visit: try one of the apple-based specialities, such as *pomig* (an apple liqueur).

Central Brittany offers some of the best bargains in the region, and is also the ideal place to look for properties suitable for renovation. Although there is demand for properties in this area, they remain cheaper than they would be on the coast, or in a slightly more upmarket area such as the Golfe du Morbihan. Two-bedroom stone properties cost around €80,000; add another €100,000 for four beds. ●

KEY FACTS

■ **Schools** Rectorat de l'Académie de Rennes, 96 rue d'Antrain, 35044 Rennes Cedex, Tel: +33 2 99 28 78 78, Fax: +33 2 99 28 77 72 ■ **Medical** Hôpital de Guingamp, 17 rue Armor, 22200 Pabu, Tel: +33 2 96 44 56 56 ■ **Rentals** The Saint-Brieuc area, Côte de Granit Rose and Ile de Bréhat are more popular for rentals and generate a fair amount of interest from tourists ■ There is a guaranteed rental season from April to September ■ Weekly rental income for a two-bedroom property averages from €293 in low season to €450 in peak season ■ **Pros** Guingamp is near the stunningly attractive Côtes d'Armor coast ■ Modern Guingamp has a football team in France's first division ■ There is a good demand for property, which is slightly cheaper here than coastal properties ■ **Cons** Guingamp is not an easily accessible area ■ This is not a coastal area, making it less attractive for those seeking to rent property.

7. Golfe du Morbihan

ESSENTIALS ■ **Population** 1999: 32,988 ■ **Taxes** Taxe d'habitation: 7.22%, Taxe foncière: 10.82% ■ **Airport** Rennes Saint-Jacques Airport, avenue Joseph Le Brix, 35136 Saint-Jacques-de-la-Lande, Tel: +33 2 99 29 60 00

The Gulf of Morbihan in southern Brittany enjoys its own balmy microclimate and is an ideal place for nautical activities, beachcombing or walking along the many miles of coastal paths. It is dotted with hundreds of small islands, the largest being Île aux Moines, which has sub-tropical vegetation and a pretty fishing village. Although many islands are privately owned retreats, you can visit most of the bay by boat. Surrounded by the Gulf's inlets and islands, the historic town of Vannes enjoys a superb location, and has a wealth of exquisitely preserved buildings, particularly its classic half-timbered houses and medieval market square. Carnac, an elegant summer resort on the bay of Quiberon, offers low-rise villas and apartments, not unlike the Côte d'Azur. Famed for its megalithic monuments, the town also has a prehistoric museum and delightful pine-fringed beaches.

The whole of the Gulf of Morbihan is extremely expensive, especially if you are intending to let your property. Again, this area is dominated by the French market. A four-bedroom house in the centre of Vannes can be found for €275,000. If you prefer the seclusion of a Gulf of Morbihan village, a one-bedroom country cottage close to the sea can be bought for under €80,000. This is generally the most exclusive area in Brittany. ●

KEY FACTS

■ **Schools** Rectorat de l'Académie de Rennes, 96 rue d'Antrain, 35044 Rennes Cedex, Tel: +33 2 99 28 78 78, Fax: +33 2 99 28 77 72 ■ **Medical** Centre Hospitalier Bretagne Atlantique, 20 boulevard Gén Maurice Guillaudot, 56000 Vannes, Tel: +33 2 97 01 41 41 ■ **Rentals** This is the most popular area in Brittany with British buyers ■ The warm climate of the Gulf of Morbihan guarantees the buyer the longest rental season in Brittany ■ The region's stunning coastline ensures a strong interest from holiday-makers ■ **Pros** Areas such as Vannes and Carnac are extremely popular ■ This stretch of coastline offers a Mediterranean-style climate together with a healthy standard of living ■ **Cons** The whole of the Gulf of Morbihan is extremely expensive ■ This is primarily a French market, with foreign buyers purchasing further inland ■ The coast can become overcrowded in the busy summer months ■ Prices are creeping up almost to Mediterranean levels.

HOTSPOTS

USEFUL CONTACTS

PRÉFECTURE
**Préfecture de la Région
de Bretagne**
3 Avenue de la Préfecture,
35026 Rennes
Tel: +33 299 02 10 35
Fax: +33 299 02 10 15
www.bretagne.pref.
gouv.fr

Préfecture-Côtes d'Armor
1 Place du Général de Gaulle
BP 2370
22023 Saint-Brieuc Cedex
(France)
Tel: +33 296 62 44 22
Fax: +33 296 62 05 75
www.cotes-darmor.pref.
gouv.fr

Préfecture – Finistere
42 Boulevard Dupleix
29320 Quimper Cedex (France)
Tel: +33 298 76 29 29
Fax: +33 298 52 09 47
www.finistere.pref.gouv.fr
Email: courrier@finistere.
pref.gouv.fr

LEGAL
Chambre des Notaires
D'Ille-et-Vilaine
2 Mail Anne-Catherine
CS 54337
35043 Rennes Cedex
Tel: +33 299 65 23 24
Fax: +33 299 65 23 20
www.chambre-ile-et-
vilaine.notaires.fr

**Chambre des Notaires
du Finistère**
38 Bis Boulevard Dupleix
B.P. 1135
29101 Quimper Cedex
Tel: +33 298 53 18 55
Fax: +33 298 52 19 07
www.chambre-
finistere.notaires.fr

**Chambre des Notaires des
Côtes d'Armor**
27 Rue Saint-Benoît
B.P. 218
22002 Saint-Brieuc Cedex
Tel: +33 296 68 30 90
Fax: +33 296 68 30 91
www.chambre-cotes-
armor.notaires.fr

**Chambre des Notaires
du Morbihan**
20 Rue des Halles
56000 Vannes
Tel: +33 297 47 19 97
Fax: +33 297 47 54 31
www.chambre-
morbihan.notaires.fr

FINANCE
**Direction Régionale des
Impôts de l'Ouest**
6 Rue Jean Guéhenno
CS 14208
35042 Rennes Cedex
Tel: +33 299 87 18 30
Fax: +33 299 63 28 90

BUILDING AND PLANNING
**Chambre Régionale
des Métiers de Bretagne**
2 Cours des Alliés
35029 Rennes Cedex
Tel: +33 299 65 32 00
Fax: +33 299 65 32 59
www.apcm.com

Caue du Morbihan
13 Bis Rue Olivier de Clisson
56000 Vannes
Tel: +33 297 54 17 35
Fax: +33 2 97 47 89 52
Email: caue56@wanadoo.fr

Caue des Côtes d'Armor
29 Rue des Promenades
22000 Saint-Brieuc
Tel: +33 296 61 51 97
Fax: +33 296 52 01 70

Email: caue22@
wanadoo.fr

EDUCATION
**Rectorat de l'Académie
de Rennes**
96 Rue d'Antrain
35705 Rennes
Tel: +33 223 21 77 77
Fax: +33 299 28 77 72
www.ac-rennes.fr

HEALTH
**Caisse Primaire d'Assurance
Maladie de Bretagne**
236r Chateaugiron
35000 Rennes
Tel: +33 299 26 74 74
Fax: +33 299 29 45 74
www.cpam-rennes.fr

**CPAM des Côtes
d'Armor**
106 Boulevard Hoche
BP 64
22024 Saint-Brieuc
Tel: +33 820 904 179
Fax: +33 296 94 52 40

CPAM du Nord-Finistère
Rue de Savoie
29282 Brest Cedex
Tel: +33 820 904 198
Fax: +33 298 34 53 89
www.cpam-brest.fr

CPAM du Sud-Finistère
Cité du Guerlac'h
BP 515
29192 Quimper Cedex
Tel: +33 820 90 41 99
Fax: +33 298 95 67 13

CPAM du Morbihan
37 Boulevard de la Paix
BP 321
56018 Vannes Cedex
Tel: +33 820 90 41 49
Fax: +33 297 01 54 14
www.cpam56.fr

MSA du Finistère
3 Rue Hervé de Guébriant
29412 Landerneau Cedex
Tel: +33 2 98 85 79 34
www.msa29.fr

Brittany is known for its maritime culture

JUSTIN POSTLETHWAITE

€10,000–€100,000
(£6,944–£69,444)

This is a great place to start for bargain hunters with an eye for potential

€12,958   CODE JOS

LA-GRÉE-ST-LAURENT, MORBIHAN

A small semi-detached cottage with 2 rooms. Requires total renovation
£8,999

🛏 1 ❀ – 🏞 *Situated in a small hamlet* 🛣 *Not located on a main road*
🏠 *Room for parking*

€28,109   CODE BRE

NEAR DINAN

A former stone and earth stable to renovate. A great opportunity
£19,520

🛏 – ❀ *7,500m² 🏞 Situated near the town of Dinan* 🛣 *Not located on a main road*
🏠 *Room for parking*

€47,587   CODE BRE

NEAR DINAN

A 1914 stone house with a slate roof. In need of complete renovation
£33,047

🛏 1 ❀ *400m² 🏞 Situated in a quiet hamlet* 🛣 *Not located on a main road*
🏠 *Room for parking*

€68,450   CODE JOS

HELLÉAN, MORBIHAN

A delightful mid-terrace cottage in the centre of Helléan. Has potential
£47,535

🛏 3 ❀ *Garden to the rear 🏞 Situated in the village centre* 🛣 *Not located on a main road* 🏠 *Room for parking*

€70,481   CODE BRE

BRITTANY

A stone-built property with a slate roof and a loft for conversion
£48,945

🛏 2 ❀ *No garden 🏞 Situated on the village square* 🛣 *Not located on a main road* 🏠 *Room for parking, with a garage*

€100,000–€200,000
(£69,444–£138,889)

A selection of larger renovation projects and small habitable homes

€104,518   CODE BRE

NEAR LAMBALLE

A superb stone farmhouse in beautiful countryside with plenty of room for renovation
£72,582

🛏 2 🏵 With a garden 🏞 Situated in a quiet rural area 🛣 Not located on a main road 🏠 Room for parking

€105,037   CODE JOS

COËT-BUGAT, MORBIHAN

A stone-built cottage with first-floor storeroom. Includes a second stone building
£72,942

🛏 2 🏵 Garden at rear 🏞 Situated in the village centre 🛣 Not located on a main road 🏠 Room for parking

€111,000   CODE LAT

NEAR GUINGAMP, CÔTES D'ARMOR

A pretty stone farmhouse with a garage in a lovely area of countryside
£77,083

🛏 2 🏵 2,500m² 🏞 Situated in a peaceful region 🛣 Not located on a main road 🏠 Room for parking, with a garage

€112,350   CODE LAT

NEAR ST-BRIEUC, CÔTES D'ARMOR

An unusual single-storey stone house with land; in need of some renovation
£78,021

🛏 2 🏵 3,000m² 🏞 Situated just outside the village 🛣 Not located on a main road 🏠 Room for parking

€123,043   CODE BRE

NEAR DINAN

A partly-renovated stone house with a garden and an attic for conversion
£85,446

🛏 2 🏵 238m² 🏞 Situated near the town of Dinan 🛣 Not located on a main road 🏠 Room for parking

€129,300 CODE LAT

TRÉDARZEC, CÔTES D'ARMOR

A habitable spacious stone house with quality fittings. Just 4 km from the sea

£89,792

3 | 391m² | Situated close to shops and schools | Located on a main road

Room for parking, with a garage

€150,000 CODE FRA

NEAR CORLAY, CÔTES D'ARMOR

A charming property in central Brittany that has been tastefully renovated

£104,167

3 | 1,435m² | Nestled in a quiet hamlet | Not located on a main road

Room for parking

€162,945 CODE FRA

PLOËRMEL, MORBIHAN

A modern detached house set within a good-sized enclosed garden

£113,156

3 | 700m² | Situated 5 minutes from town centre | Not located on a main road | Room for parking

---

€175,725 CODE FRA

NEAR VANNES, MORBIHAN

A lovely stone-built house with a slate roof. Great views from the back garden

£122,031

3 | 1,700m² | Situated in a very pretty village | Not located on a main road

Room for parking, with a large garage

€177,000 CODE FRA

NEAR PAIMPOL, CÔTES D'ARMOR

A delightful L-shaped property, consisting of 2 houses linked by a conservatory

£122,917

5 | 1,334m² | Situated in a peaceful cul-de-sac | Not located on a main road

Room for parking, with a garage

€186,375 CODE FRA

NEAR JOSSELIN, MORBIHAN

A superb house with established gardens and an independent barbecue patio

£129,427

5 | 1,281m² | Situated in village with amenities | Not located on a main road | Room for parking, with a double garage

€200,000–€300,000
(£138,889–£208,333)

For this sort of money you can expect plenty of bedrooms and large grounds

€205,260   CODE FRA

NEAR BONNEMAIN, CHÂTEAUNEUF-D'ILLE-ET-VILAINE
A pretty stone-built house in a quiet area on the outskirts of town
£142,541

🛏 4   🌳 800m²   Situated on the outskirts of town   Not located on a main road   Room for parking

€208,434   CODE JOS

JOSSELIN, MORBIHAN
A traditional townhouse comprising 5 studios and 3 single-bedroomed flats
£144,745

🛏 8   🌳 –   Situated in a quiet hamlet   Located on a main road   Room for parking

€209,479   CODE JOS

TAUPONT, MORBIHAN
A detached stone house with outbuildings, including a workshop and 2 garages
£145,471

🛏 4   🌳 1,000m²   Situated in a quiet hamlet   Not located on a main road   Room for parking, with 2 garages

€214,210   CODE FRA

NEAR CARHAIX-PLOUGUER, FINISTÈRE
A completely renovated 19th-century stone cottage with land and outbuildings
£148,757

🛏 4   🌳 10,000m²   Situated in national parkland   Not located on a main road   Room for parking

€223,265   CODE JOS

MOHON, MORBIHAN
A detached house with a pool and a second large building in need of renovation
£155,045

🛏 3   🌳 2,600m²   Situated in a quiet hamlet   Not located on a main road   Room for parking, with a garage

PRICE GUIDE

€240,484   CODE JOS

MÉNÉAC, MORBIHAN

A detached stone house in substantial grounds with outbuildings and a barn

£167,002

4 | 30,000m² | *Situated in beautiful countryside* | *Not located on a main road* | *Room for parking*

€241,874   CODE JOS

NEAR LIZIO, MORBIHAN

A detached stone cottage just outside the pretty village of Lizio

£167,968

4 | 1,080m² | *Situated just outside the village* | *Not located on a main road* | *Room for parking*

€242,045   CODE FRA

NEAR MONCONTOUR, CÔTES D'ARMOR

This house is in great condition and has additional space to create further bedrooms

£168,086

7 | *Large garden at rear* | *Situated in a quiet hamlet* | *Not located on a main road* | *Room for parking, with a garage*

€261,500   CODE FRA

NEAR JUGON-LES-LACS, CÔTES D'ARMOR

A wonderful house in beautiful countryside with a spacious conservatory

£181,597

4 | *With a garden* | *Situated near the village* | *Not located on a main road* | *Room for parking, with a garage*

€264,385   CODE JOS

LA-CROIX-HELLÉAN, MORBIHAN

These 2 recently-renovated stone houses offer spacious living and room for expansion

£183,600

6 | *With land* | *Situated in the village centre* | *Not located on a main road* | *Room for parking*

€286,809   CODE JOS

JOSSELIN, MORBIHAN

This townhouse is currently used as a B&B and is situated close to the canal

£199,172

4 | *Garden at rear* | *Situated in the village centre* | *Located on a main road* | *Room for parking*

PRICE GUIDE

€300,000–€400,000
(£208,333–£277,778)

A selection of large well-restored properties in idyllic locations

€302,043   CODE LAT

NEAR LANNION, CÔTES D'ARMOR
A completely restored 19th-century stone house with a convertible outbuilding
£209,752

🛏 3   ❀ 1,750m²   🏞 Situated in quiet rural area   🚧 Not located on a main road   🏠 Room for parking, with a garage

€302,185   CODE FRA

CHÂTEAUNEUF-D'ILLE-ET-VILAINE
A superb fully restored 16th-century farmhouse with 2 outbuildings
£209,850

🛏 4   ❀ With a garden   🏞 Situated in the village centre   🚧 Not located on a main road   🏠 Room for parking

€341,250   CODE FRA

NEAR GUINGAMP, CÔTES D'ARMOR
This house is bursting with character. We thought the Addams Family lived in the US!
£236,979

🛏 8   ❀ 1,100m²   🏞 Situated in the village centre   🚧 Located on a main road   🏠 Room for parking, with a garage

€359,658   CODE FRA

NEAR PLOËRMEL, MORBIHAN
This large neo-Breton house is built on 3 levels with stunning views of the nearby lake
£249,762

🛏 6   ❀ 2,000m²   🏞 Situated in a small hamlet   🚧 Not located on a main road   🏠 Room for parking, with a double garage

€395,200   CODE LAT

NEAR ST-BRIEUC, CÔTES D'ARMOR
An attractive farmhouse with large outbuildings set in substantial grounds
£274,444

🛏 4   ❀ 25,000m²   🏞 Situated just outside the village   🚧 Not located on a main road   🏠 Room for parking

€400,000+
(£277,778+)

These properties are perfect for those wanting to start a business in the region

€404,920   CODE FRA
NEAR VANNES, MORBIHAN
A beautifully renovated 5-bedroomed house plus 2 gîtes and apartments
£281,194

🛏 5 ❀ 7,500m² 🖼 Situated near the village 🗾 Not located on a main road 🏠 Room for parking

€411,000   CODE JOS
GUÉGON, MORBIHAN
A group of buildings including a manor for renovation, 2 converted gîtes and a stable
£285,416

🛏 13 ❀ 50,000m² 🖼 Situated in beautiful countryside 🗾 Not located on a main road 🏠 Room for parking

€430,500   CODE FRA
NEAR VANNES, MORBIHAN
An elegant neo-Breton house with swimming pool and beautiful landscaped gardens
£298,958

🛏 5 ❀ 11,300m² 🖼 Situated in a quiet location 🗾 Not located on a main road 🏠 Room for parking

€508,800   CODE FRA
NEAR VANNES, MORBIHAN
A lovely property with a number of outbuildings, suitable as a gîte complex
£353,333

🛏 5 ❀ 24,000m² 🖼 Situated just outside the village 🗾 Not located on a main road 🏠 Room for parking

€761,250   CODE FRA
NEAR JOSSELIN, MORBIHAN
A large successful gîte complex with a swimming pool, set in substantial grounds
£528,645

🛏 – ❀ 30,000m² 🖼 Situated in a peaceful location 🗾 Not located on a main road 🏠 Room for parking

PRICE GUIDE

Normandy

Coastal resorts, Mont-Saint-Michel and English-style countryside

COMTÉ RÉGIONAL DE NORMANDIE

Profile **80 ■**

Hotspots **82 ■**

FACT BOX 2005

- ■ **Population** 3,202,385 (+2.4% from 1990) Basse-Normandie: 1,422,193, Haute-Normandie: 1,780,192
- ■ **Foreign residents** 68,887
Basse-Normandie: 20,608, Haute-Normandie: 48,279
- ■ **Migration** 122,436 international migrants
- ■ **Unemployment** 76,882
- ■ **Median house price** €145,500
- ■ **House price increase** In Basse-Normandie prices have increased by 10.8% since 2002, and Haute-Normandie has experienced appreciation of 7.1%

Price Guide

€20,000 − €100,000	**88 ■**
€100,000 − €200,000	**89 ■**
€200,000 − €350,000	**90 ■**
€350,000+	**93 ■**

GETTING THERE

AIR Air France (0845 0845 111; www.airfrance.co.uk) flies directly from Heathrow into Caen airport, while Caen's Carpiquet airport (Tel: +33 231 71 20 10) and Cherbourg's Maupertus (Tel: +33 233 88 57 60) handle domestic and some international flights. The closest airport outside Normandy is Dinard (Tel: +33 299 46 18 46) which receives **Ryanair** (08712 460 000; www.ryanair.com) flights from Luton. **Aurigny** (01481 822 886; www.aurigny.com) flies to Dinard from Bristol, Bournemouth, East Midlands, Gatwick, Stansted and Manchester.
SEA Brittany Ferries (0870 366 5333; www.brittany-ferries.com) sails to Caen-Ouistreham from Portsmouth and from Poole to Cherbourg. **Transmanche Ferries** (0800 917 1201; www.transmancheferries.com) operates from Newhaven to Dieppe, while **Hoverspeed Fast Ferries** (0870 240 8070; www.hoverspeed.co.uk) sails from Newhaven to Dieppe, and from Portsmouth to Le Havre. Services from Portsmouth to Le Havre and Cherbourg are operated by **P&O** (0870 520 2020; www.poferries.com).
ROAD The A28/29 offers quick and direct access from Calais to the whole of Normandy, joining the A13 motorway, which runs west through Caen, and ends in Paris. The A16 runs from Calais to Rouen, while the D100 runs down the Manche peninsula to Avranches. Main roads link the ports of Dieppe, Le Havre, Caen and Cherbourg.
COACH Eurolines (0870 514 3219; www.eurolines.com) travels from the UK to Caen, Cherbourg, Dieppe and Rouen.
RAIL The TGV rail network runs throughout Normandy linking Cherbourg, Bayeux, Caen, Evreux, Le Havre and Rouen, then continuing to Paris. The **Eurostar** (0870 518 6186; www.eurostar.com) arrives at Lille Europe train station, and from there TGV services operate to Rouen. From Paris there are regular services to Le Havre, Dieppe, Caen, Rouen, Cherbourg and Bayeux. Contact **Rail Europe** (0870 584 8848; www.raileurope.co.uk) for more details.

Area profile

NORMANDY TAKES ITS NAME FROM THE NORSEMEN WHO ARRIVED uninvited from Scandinavia in the 9th century, and it was from here that William the Conquerer crossed the English Channel to crush the English forces in the Battle of Hastings in 1066.

Home to fashionable resort towns on the coast, Normandy is characterised inland by verdant, pastoral farmland, which, unusually for France, has miles of hedgerows that separate the fields. Indeed, the landscape is often likened to England. The capital is Caen, a university city that suffered terrible bombing in the Second World War. A couple of outstanding Romanesque abbeys survived and the modern, pedestrianised centre is pleasant enough. Rouen was also heavily damaged in the war but it has been superbly restored; the Gothic cathedral and plethora of half-timbered houses are particularly impressive.

Normandy's most fashionable resort is Deauville, an expensive weekend playground for wealthy Parisians. Its seafront is lined with Victorian beach huts and the wide, sandy beaches are very popular in the summer months. Deauville's twin town, Trouville, on the eastern bank of the River Touques, is less exclusive but has some fine fish restaurants along the waterfront. Other popular resorts include Honfleur, Fécamp and Dieppe, the latter being particularly popular with English visitors because of its ferry port.

Normandy is also home to Mont-Saint-Michel, a small island that houses one of the most impressive and spectacular abbeys in Europe. The region's other major tourist attraction is the 900-year-old Bayeux Tapestry at Bayeux's magnificent cathedral, which depicts the Battle of Hastings.

Normandy's rich pastures and wealth of apple orchards exert a strong influence on the local cuisine. Cheese is a speciality, *Camembert* and *Brie* in particular. Cider is a popular tipple, as is the apple brandy *Calvados*, named after one of Normandy's *départements*.

The economy and housing market

Normandy prospers from its production of meat, milk, butter, cheese and cider apples, with 45 per cent of Upper Normandy and 30 per cent of Lower Normandy given over to arable land. The coastline boasts more

Honfleur has been attracting artists since the 19th century

COMTE RÉGIONAL DE NORMANDIE

than 50 ports, and the region is renowned for its cuisine, producing many speciality seafood dishes. The dairy industry has suffered of late at the hands of EU regulations, with many small dairy farms being forced to close, impacting on much of inland Normandy. Recent years have seen diversification into light industry and agri-foodstuffs, while Upper Normandy specialises in petro-chemicals and car manufacturing, though the region retains its agricultural character.

Normandy has long been a favourite destination of the British buyer, and it continues to offer something for everyone. Glamorous and glitzy resorts can be found in Deauville, Trouville and Honfleur, while the Manche peninsula offers traditionally French family resorts. Deauville and Trouville are both expensive, with wealthy Parisians driving prices up. The best bargains can be found in the Orne department, where towns and cities, relatively undiscovered by the foreign market, offer cheap property. The areas near Rouen and Caen experience high prices, trading primarily to the French market, and high rates of turnover make property a good investment. The Manche peninsula yields a glut of affordable properties, with attractive countryside, proximity to the sea and a buoyant rental market. The area around Dieppe makes for a good rental investment too, offering affordable property and excellent access routes.

Normandy is popular with commuters who live in France and work in the UK, or own weekend homes here, aided by the convenience and ease of the transport system centred around Cherbourg, Dieppe and Caen. Avranches in the Manche peninsula is the ideal location for a family home, being affordable, close to the sea and surrounded by countryside.

In recent years, Normandy has mopped up the overflow of property seekers who have been priced out of neighbouring Brittany, but the region has now begun experiencing a certain amount of market saturation.

Social groups

Overseas buyers have been targeting Normandy because of its easy access and abundance of cheap property. Two-thirds of foreign buyers are British, with concentrations around the expensive port resorts, though higher prices have driven many property seekers inland.

The closer you get to Paris, the steeper the prices, and cheaper areas such as Orne have seen a resultant explosion of interest and prices. The Seine-Maritime attracts high demand from London buyers, as commuters seek easy access to the UK. Prices rose almost 14 per cent in the first three quarters of 2004, and as demand continues to grow, they are expected to rise a further 20 to 25 per cent in the next few years, making cheap properties increasingly rare. ●

"Normandy's interior is characterised by verdant, pastoral farmland, which, unusually for France, has many miles of hedgerows that separate the fields"

Average monthly temperature °C (Celsius)

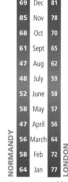

Average monthly rainfall mm (millimetres)

AVERAGE HOUSE SALE PRICES

Hotspot	2-bed	3-bed	4-bed	5-bed+
Deauville	€194K (£135K)	€275K (£191K)	€350K (£243K)	€528K (£366K)
Trouville	€158K (£110K)	€213K (£148K)	€423K (£293K)	€391K (£272K)
Honfleur	€186K (£129K)	€209K (£145K)	€305K (£209K)	€408K (£283K)
Rouen	€136K (£94K)	€144K (£100K)	€240K (£167K)	€369K (£256K)
Caen	€133K (£92K)	€179K (£124K)	€258K (£179K)	€401K (£279K)
Avranches	€100K (£69K)	€141K (£99K)	€195K (£135K)	€279K (£194K)
Dieppe	$112K (£78K)	$185K (£129K)	$167K (£116K)	$356 (£247K)

Property hotspots

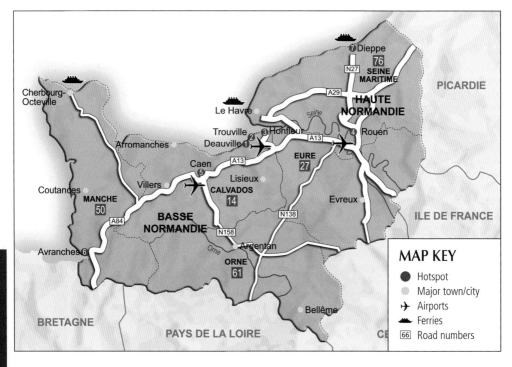

MAP KEY
- ● Hotspot
- ◉ Major town/city
- ✈ Airports
- ⛴ Ferries
- 66 Road numbers

1. Deauville

ESSENTIALS ■ **Population** 4,300 ■ **Taxes** Taxe d'habitation: 5.37%, Taxe foncière: 11.88% ■ **Airport** Aéroport de Deauville Saint Gatien, 14130 Saint-Gatien-des-Bois, Tel: +33 231 65 65 65

KEY FACTS

■ **Schools** Contact the Rectorat de l'Académie de Caen, 168 rue Caponière, BP 6184, 14061 Caen Cedex, Tel: +33 231 30 15 00 for advice on education in the region
■ **Medical** Hôpital de Trouville, 20 rue Soeurs Hôpital, 14360 Trouville-sur-Mer, +33 231 81 84 84
■ **Rentals** In such an expensive area it is difficult to make your money back through rentals ■ The British are reluctant to pay the high prices charged for apartments and villas, but the French market is more willing to pay a premium ■ A two-bedroom property rents at an average of €430 a week
■ **Pros** Located on the Côte Fleurie, Deauville is known as the 'Cannes of the North' and the 'Riviera of Normandy' ■ Deauville's own airport makes it easily accessible and the port of Caen is nearby
■ **Cons** A slightly pretentious resort which is extortionately expensive, commanding prices on a level with the Cote d'Azur ■ A two-bedroom property costs upwards of €194,000 ■ This is primarily a market flooded by the French ■ There is an immensely rapid turnover of property.

Close to Paris and known as the '21st *arrondissement*', fashionable Deauville attracts the affluent weekend crowd and Parisian purchasing power has caused prices to soar. Frequented by film stars, millionaires and royals alike, this resort is full of glamour and glitz. With a picturesque port, wide sandy beaches and historic wooden walkways, such as the Promenade des Planches, Deauville is an authentically preserved village of Norman half-timbered architecture. Each year Deauville plays host to the International Festival of American Cinema, and the seafront is lined with Victorian-style beach huts named after Hollywood movie stars, past and present. There is also a casino and golf course, and the race track is one of the town's social hubs. Visit the Wednesday to Saturday market, which sells a wide range of regional specialities including seafood, cheeses, cider and *calvados*. A 10–minute drive inland from Deauville will take you into the Calvados region, boasting some Normandy's most beautiful countryside.

Deauville's coastal situation pushes property prices up, due to the sea views. If you seek a sea view, expect to pay at least €170,000 for a one-bedroom apartment compared to prices of around €73,000 in the town's backstreets. A four–bedroom home, just two minutes from the centre, will cost around €350,000. ●

HOTSPOTS

2. Trouville

ESSENTIALS ■ **Population** 6,500 ■ **Taxes** Taxe d'habitation: 5.37%, Taxe foncière: 11.88% ■ **Airport** Aéroport de Deauville Saint Gatien, 14130 Saint-Gatien-des-Bois, Tel: +33 231 65 65 65

Separated from its 'twin' resort Deauville by the estuary of the river Touques, the fishing port of Trouville can be reached in five minutes by ferryboat. A smart, but more modest relation in terms of the glamour and social calendar of the season, Trouville is arguably more authentic and family-friendly, and has a native population that makes it livelier out of season. It has an excellent beach, sports facilities, fish market and Planche promenade. Other interesting places to visit include its Napoleon III extravagant casino, Aquarium Vivarium de Trouville and Villa Montebello, Napoleon's old summer residence which holds regular art exhibitions.

British and Norman history has long been interwoven, and it was the British in the 19th century, along with painters such as Turner, who made the Normandy coast fashionable. French painters too, from Delacroix to the Impressionists and the Fauves, were inspired by the clear light of the coast and created many wonderful seascapes.

The love affair continues, but these days the British are reluctant to pay the average price tag of £150,000 to buy in Trouville. As property here is sold essentially to the French market – the area is popular with people who commute to Caen, Paris and Rennes – it carries a premium, but you can still find a three-bedroom home for €200,000. ●

KEY FACTS

■ **Schools** Contact the Rectorat de l'Académie de Caen, 168 rue Caponière, BP 6184, 14061 Caen Cedex, Tel: +33 231 30 15 00 for advice on education in the region
■ **Medical** Hôpital de Trouville, 20 rue Soeurs Hôpital, 14360 Trouville-sur-Mer, +33 231 81 84 84
■ **Rentals** Trouville, as Deauville, is servicing the French rental market ■ Rental demand comes from Parisians and the cities of Caen and Rennes ■ The British are unwilling to pay the high rental prices the area commands ■ A two-bedroom property will rent at an average of €485 per week
■ **Pros** Selling property to the native market should be easy in this popular resort ■ A typical French resort, Trouville has a lovely beach and down-to-earth diversions
■ **Cons** Trouville property is expensive and carries a premium ■ The area is frequented by people commuting to Caen, Paris and Rennes ■ Despite the exclusive nature of the area, some describe it as unmemorable and pretentious ■ Property is expensive and a four-bedroom house will cost an average of €423,000.

3. Honfleur

ESSENTIALS ■ **Population** 12,738 ■ **Taxes** Taxe d'habitation: 5.37%, Taxe foncière: 11.88% ■ **Airport** Aéroport de Caen, Carpiquet, 14000 Caen, Tel: +33 231 71 20 10

Honfleur's charms are hard to resist, as it remains picturesque with an unspoilt ambiance, while continuing to be a busy, working port. The Vieux Bassin or inner harbour is the hub, frequented these days by fishermen, yacht owners, painters and tourists, rather than the explorers and corsairs of yesteryear. The tall, irregular houses that flank the harbour contain bars, eateries, antique shops and galleries, which become crowded in season.

Miraculously still standing in the market square is the Église Sainte-Catherine, the 'temporary' Gothic church built of oak by shipwrights, to celebrate the departure of the English at the end of the Hundred Years War. The original farm (Ferme Saint-Siméon), where local artist Boudin and friends met to drink cider and later formed the Impressionist movement, is now a very expensive hotel, and the Boudin museum displays some of the fine paintings and pastels from the period.

Many consider Honfleur the most attractive port in Normandy and one of the most popular spots in northern France. Along with other old ports like Étretat and Fécamp, Honfleur has long been a favourite with Parisians looking for properties to buy for their weekend breaks on the coast. Commuters from Caen and Rennes have also driven prices up. Consequently, a two-bedroom property starts at €186,000. ●

KEY FACTS

■ **Schools** Contact the Rectorat de l'Académie de Caen, 168 rue Caponière, BP 6184, 14061 Caen Cedex, Tel: +33 231 30 15 00, Fax: +33 231 30 15 92, for advice on education in the region
■ **Medical** Centre Hospitalier de La Plane-Equemauville, 14600 Honfleur, Tel: +33 231 89 89 89, Fax: +33 231 89 88 81
■ **Rentals** One of the most popular resorts on the Calvados coastline ■ Honfleur and surrounding area are excellent for property lets ■ Popular with Parisian daytrippers, Honfleur has huge local rental potential ■ The average price for a three-bedroom rental property is €720 ■ The annual rental yield is good, particularly from April to September
■ **Pros** Honfleur has become increasingly upmarket in recent years ■ Located close to Le Havre, the area is easily accessible ■ Although very popular with tourists, Honfleur retains its quaint and tranquil air
■ **Cons** Honfleur is an attractive coastal resort but lacks a beach ■ There is relatively little economic prosperity ■ Commuters from Paris, Caen and Rennes have flooded the market and raised prices.

HOTSPOTS

4. Rouen

ESSENTIALS ■ **Population** 102,000 ■ **Taxes** Taxe d'habitation: 6.53%, Taxe foncière: 13.16% ■ **Airport** Aéroport Rouen, Vallée de Seine, 76520 Boos, Tel: +33 235 79 41 00

KEY FACTS

■ **Schools** Contact the Rectorat de l'Académie de Rouen, 25 rue de Fontenelle, 76037 Rouen, Cedex, Tel: +33 235 14 75 00 for advice on education
■ **Medical** Rouen University Hospital, 1 rue Germont, 76000 Rouen, Tel: +33 232 88 89 90
■ **Rentals** Rouen is not a major holiday rentals centre, tending to concentrate more on industry than tourism, however there is a market for long-term lets ■ In Rouen's old town, rental property can cost from €580 a week for a two-bedroom property
■ **Pros** A diverse and cultured city, Rouen combines industry and trade with a rich historical tradition ■ It offers a number of museums and churches, the tour-de-force being beyond doubt Notre-Dame cathedral ■ The majority of Rouen's streets are modern and sophisticated ■ As Rouen is a large city, there is an abundance of services and attractions ■ Property is affordable with a two-bedroom house costing from €135,000
■ **Cons** As you leave the inner quartier, you come upon the sprawling industrial and dockyard areas ■ Rouen is an area covered only by French estate agents, who often have limited experience of dealing with foreign buyers.

Capital of the Seine-Maritime *département* and France's fifth largest port, Rouen has a vivid cultural and architectural heritage. The city is expensive and densely populated, serving as a catchment area for Parisians who commute 30 to 40 kilometres to work. The old city, on the Right Bank, has been called the 'museum town' as it numbers 700 beamed, timber-framed medieval houses along its narrow pedestrian streets, many made of brick and wood, and decorated with statues. Other attractions include the Gothic cathedral, Archbishop's Palace and the tower where Joan of Arc was kept prisoner. Arts lovers can savour the Flaubert Museum, and the Museum of Fine Arts and Ceramics which holds a collection of 17th to 18th-century French-European paintings by Caravaggio and Monet, along with porcelain and *faïence* from the 16th to 18th centuries. The city is excellent for shopping, with plenty of cafés.

Central Rouen is very expensive, but once you move into the countryside, property prices drop. The area is dominated by the French market and local estate agents are reluctant to deal with foreign buyers. Property styles include the traditional Norman beamed buildings, manor houses and the *maison de maître* built in the classical colonial style. A standard four-bedroom home can cost from €240,130. ●

5. Caen

ESSENTIALS ■ **Population** 117,000 ■ **Taxes** Taxe d'habitation: 5.37%, Taxe foncière: 11.88% ■ **Airport** Caen Airport, Aéroport de Caen Carpiquet, 14000 Caen, Tel: +33 231 71 20 10

KEY FACTS

■ **Schools** Contact the Rectorat de l'Académie de Caen, 168 rue Caponière, BP 6184, 14061 Caen Cedex, Tel: +33 231 30 15 00, for advice on education
■ **Medical** Central Hospital Caen, av Côte de Nacre, 14000 Caen, Tel: +33 231 06 31 06
■ **Rentals** Rental prices in the city are much higher than in the surrounding countryside ■ Large cities, such as Caen, tend to attract long-term rentals rather than short-term ones ■ Demand for rentals in the city comes from the local market ■ A two-bedroom property will rent for €560 a week
■ **Pros** Caen is a dynamic and pleasant city ■ Easily accessible from the UK, it has its own port and airport ■ A bustling university city with many amenities and attractions ■ Ideal for a buyer who seeks a vibrant metropolis ■ Homes are affordable here with a two-bedroom house costing from €133,000, and a one-bedroom apartment from €63,000
■ **Cons** You may have to learn French to live and work here, as this is not a predominantly international city ■ As ever, proximity to a city drives property prices up.

Caen is a history lover's dream, with its roots dating back to the relic of William the Conqueror, whose femur is held in the Abbaye aux Hommes. The city was heavily bombed during World War II, hence concrete buildings mingle with the 16th-century architecture. Learn more about the D-Day landings at the Caen Memorial, a museum dedicated to World War II, and rekindle the spirit of the Norman conquest at the ramparts of Caen castle, built by William in his early days as Duke of Normandy. One of Europe's biggest castles, it is also home to a fine art museum.

The surrounding lush landscape produces celebrated cheeses like Livarot, Pont L'Evêque and Camembert, and Caen's proximity to the coastline ensures a ready supply of top-class seafood. This is also the place to live if you prefer the quiet life. Caen's beaches may not possess the glitz of the Côte d'Azur, but they offer instead an unhurried lifestyle, with scenic charm. Within the city, on Rue Saint-Sauveur, a huge market is held on Fridays. The Rue Froide and Caen's centre offer many Parisian department stores.

Property in Caen has a quick turnover and is primarily dominated by the local French market. A large three-bedroom house just 10 minutes from Caen with swimming pool commands €470,000. ●

6. Avranches

ESSENTIALS ■ **Population** 52,471 ■ **Taxes** Taxe d'habitation: 6.98%, Taxe foncière: 11.04% ■ **Airport** Aéroport de Caen Carpiquet, 14000 Caen, Tel: +33 231 71 20 10

Avranches is a small, rural town with tourist appeal, situated on a wooded hill in the La Manche *département* of Normandy, close to Mont-Saint-Michel and near the border with Brittany. A historically important, busy town, it serves as a convenient base for visits to the D-Day beaches, and the city of Bayeux is just one hour away. There are regular traditional fêtes, a Saturday market, and daily local markets in the surrounding area, even on Sundays. The town commands fine views westward of the bay and rock of Mont-Saint-Michel, a renowned World Heritage site and France's second most popular tourist attraction after the Eiffel Tower. Avranches itself is surrounded by avenues which trace the ancient ramparts, and secreted within is a secluded botanical garden.

There is a highly active British property market in and around Avranches, and the prices are relatively cheap compared to the Calvados area and more industrial region of Upper Normandy. A four-bedroom house starts at around €195,000. If you are looking for a property to restore, a small farmhouse can be purchased for around €100,000. The market has remained constantly busy for the past decade, and most British prefer to buy than rent as prices are so affordable. A two-bedroom house can be purchased for €100,000. ●

KEY FACTS

■ **Schools** Contact the Rectorat de l'Académie de Rennes, 96 rue d'Antrain, 35044 Rennes, Cedex, Tel: +33 299 28 78 78, Fax: +33 299 28 77 72 for advice on education
■ **Medical** Centre Hospitalier Avranches-Granville, 59 rue Liberté, 50300 Avranches, Tel: +33 233 89 40 20, Fax: +33 233 89 41 25
■ **Rentals** Avranches is located in an extremely active tourist area, with a buoyant holiday rental market ■ Many holiday-makers are drawn to this area due to its proximity to Mont-Saint-Michel ■ The long-term rental market is cheap, but properties tend to be shabby and not geared towards the foreign holiday market ■ The short-term holiday rentals market is booming and runs between April and September ■ A two-bedroom house rents for €450 a week
■ **Pros** Located close to the port of Cherbourg and the coast ■ This is an excellent location for purchasing a property ■ There is a highly active foreign community ■ An excellent, sunny climate
■ **Cons** Avranches itself is very expensive, and many people buy 20 and 30 kilometres away, where prices are lower.

7. Dieppe

ESSENTIALS ■ **Population** 36,000 ■ **Taxes** Taxe d'habitation: 24.13%, Taxe foncière: 57.08% ■ **Airport** Aéroport de Caen Carpiquet, 14000 Caen, Tel: +33 231 71 20 10

Dieppe, France's first seaside resort, has undergone a transformation in recent years. The port has shaken off its reputation as a visual eyesore, the ugly terminal buildings having been replaced by a breezy promenade. The sea front is now set back from the shore, creating space for an expanse of lawns, waterside restaurants and family play areas nearly two kilometres long. Dieppe has long enjoyed its status as a destination for writers, musicians and painters. Visit the Café des Tribunaux, the favourite haunt of Renoir, Monet, Guy de Maupassant and Oscar Wilde. While in exile from England, Wilde came here to write his *Ballad of Reading Gaol*.

High on a cliff, the castle museum contains a collection of exhibits reflecting Dieppe's maritime history, including 16th-century ivory sculptures carved by local sailors, and a number of paintings by Picasso. There are plenty of fêtes throughout the year, including a kite festival and the Festival of the Flowers. Out of town, you can see the birthplace of Guy de Maupassant at the Château de Miromesnil.

There is fair British interest in Dieppe due to the ease of access from the UK. In recent years, however, interest has waned in the Dieppe area as the Normandy Riviera in Calvados and the Manche peninsula have developed, but a two-bedroom property is affordable at €112,000. ●

KEY FACTS

■ **Schools** Rectorat de l'Académie de Rouen, 25 rue de Fontenelle, 76037 Rouen, Cedex, Tel: +33 235 14 75 00, Fax: +33 235 71 56 38
■ **Medical** Hospitalier de Dieppe, av Pasteur, 76200 Dieppe, Tel:+33 232 14 76 76
■ **Rentals** This is less of a holiday centre than it used to be ■ Prices are expensive compared to the Lower Normandy area ■ Foreign holiday-makers do not desire to rent a property in Dieppe
■ **Pros** It used to be a thriving seaside resort for the French and English in the 19th century, and it retains much of its authentic charm today ■ It is still an interesting and attractive place to visit, and is highly accessible ■ Dieppe offers many attractions, both modern and historical ■ It is more welcoming than many of the neighbouring towns along the Seine-Maritime coast
■ **Cons** Property in the centre of Dieppe is expensive, and most people buy cheaper homes 20 minutes out of town ■ This town is less of a tourist resort than a thriving industrial and commercial port.

USEFUL CONTACTS

PRÉFECTURE
Préfecture de la Région
Basse-Normandie
Rue Daniel Huet
14038 Caen Cedex
Tel: +33 231 30 64 00
Fax: +33 231 30 64 90
www.basse-normandie.pref-gouv.fr

Préfecture de la Région
Haute-Normandie
7 Place de la Madeleine
76036 Rouen Cedex
Tel: +33 232 76 50 00
Fax: +33 235 98 10 50
www.haute-normandie.pref.gouv.fr

Préfecture de l'Eure
Boulevard Georges Chauvin
27022 Évreux Cedex
Tel: +33 232 78 27 27
Fax: +33 232 38 24 15
www.eure.pref.gouv.fr

Préfecture de l'Orne
39 Rue Saint Blaise
BP 529
61018 Alençon Cedex
Tel: +33 233 80 61 61
Fax: +33 233 80 61 65
Email:
admin.sitepref61@wanadoo.fr
www.orne.pref.gouv.fr

Préfecture de Manche
Place de la Préfecture
50009 Saint-Lo Cedex
Tel: +33 233 06 50 50
Fax: +33 233 57 36 66
www.manche.pref.gouv.fr

LEGAL
Chambre des Notaires
du Calvados
6 Place Louis Guillouard
14000 Caen
Tel: +33 231 85 42 62

Fax: +33 231 85 99 66
www.chambre-calvados.notaires.fr

Chambre des Notaires
de la Seine-Maritime
39 Rue du Champ des Oiseaux
BP 248
76003 Rouen
Tel: +33 235 88 63 88
Fax: +33 235 98 70 61
Email: chambre76@notaires.fr

FINANCE
Direction des Impôts du
Nord
13–15 Boulevard de la Liberté
59800 Lille
Tel: +33 320 17 64 90
Fax: +33 320 17 64 99

Direction des Impôts de
l'Ouest
6 Rue Jean Guéhenno,
CS 14208
35042 Rennes Cedex
Tel: +33 299 87 18 30
Fax: +33 299 63 28 90

BUILDING & PLANNING
Caue de la Manche
2 Place du Général de Gaulle
50000 Saint-Lo
Tel: +33 233 77 20 77
Fax: +33 233 77 20 80
Email: courrier@caue50.fr
www.caue50.fr

Caue de l'Orne
54 Rue Saint Blaise
61000 Alençon
Tel: +33 233 26 14 14
Fax: +33 233 26 13 00
Email: caue.orne@wanadoo.fr

Chambre Régionale de
Métiers de Basse-
Normandie
10 Rue Claude Bloch

14000 Caen
Tel: +33 231 95 42 00
Fax: +33 231 95 99 30
www.crm-basse-normandie.fr

Chambre Régionale de
Métiers de Haute-
Normandie
5-9 Avenue de Caen
BP 1153
76176 Rouen Cedex
Tel: +33 232 18 06 40
Fax: +33 232 18 06 49
www.crm-haute-normandie.fr

Caue du Calvados
28 Rue Jean Eudes
14000 Caen
Tel: +33 231 15 59 60
Fax: +33 231 15 59 65
http://caue14.free.fr

Caue de Seine-Maritime
5 Rue Louis Blanc
BP 1283
76178 Rouen
Tel: +33 235 72 94 50
Fax: +33 235 72 09 72
www.caue76.org

EDUCATION
Rectorat de l'Académie
de Caen
168 Rue Caponière
14061 Caen Cedex
Tel: +33 231 30 15 00
Fax: +33 231 30 15 92
www.ac-caen.fr

Rectorat de l'Académie
de Rouen
25 Rue de Fontenelle
76037 Rouen Cedex
Tel: +33 235 14 75 00
Fax: +33 235 71 56 38
www.ac-rouen.fr

HEALTH
Caisse Primaire d'Assurance

Maladie du Calvados
BP6048
Boulevard Général Weygand
14031 Caen Cedex 4
Tel: +33 231 45 79 00
Fax: +33 231 45 79 80
www.cpam14.fr

Caisse Primaire d'Assurance
Maladie de Rouen
50 avenue Bretagne
76039 Rouen
Tel: +33 235 03 63 63
Fax: +33 235 03 63 03
www.cpam76.fr

Caisse Primaire d'Assurance
Maladie de l'Eure
1bis Place Saint-Taurin
27030 Évreux Cedex
Tel: +33 232 29 20 00
Fax: +33 232 29 22 99
www.cpam27.com

Caisse Primaire d'Assurance
Maladie de l'Orne
34 Place du Général Bonet
61012 Alençon Cedex
Tel: +33 820 90 41 61
Fax: +33 233 32 35 40
www.alencon.ameli.fr

Caisse Primaire d'Assurance
Maladie de Manche
Montée du Bois André
50012 Saint-Lo Cedex
Tel: +33 820 90 41 78
Fax: +33 233 72 21 56
Email: contact-ecoute-conseil@cpam-st-lo.cnamts.fr
www.saint-lo.ameli.fr

87

€20,000–€100,000
(£13,889–£69,444)

There are some great investment properties to be had at very good prices

€23,690
CODE AMR

MANCHE/CALVADOS BORDER

A potential holiday cottage requiring complete renovation, comprising 2 buildings
£16,451

🛏 – 🌸 *Small garden* 🏘 *Situated in a small village* 🚧 *Not located on a main road*
🏠 *Room for parking*

€81,520
CODE FRA

NEAR PONT-D'OUILLY, CALVADOS

This bungalow is in an exceptional position with wonderful views and a large garden
£56,611

🛏 2 🌸 *1,500m²* 🏘 *Situated in the village centre* 🚧 *Not located on a main road*
🏠 *Room for parking, with a garage*

€90,212
CODE FRA

NEAR LESSAY, MANCHE

A country house to renovate on a large plot of land, with a new roof
£62,647

🛏 3 🌸 *980m²* 🏘 *Situated in a small village* 🚧 *Not located on a main road*
🏠 *Room for parking, with a garage*

€94,480
CODE FRA

NEAR VALOGNES, BASSE-NORMANDIE

A lovely little house in the country with an outbuilding and an attic to be converted
£65,611

🛏 3 🌸 *650m²* 🏘 *Situated in the countryside* 🚧 *Not located on a main road*
🏠 *Room for parking*

€95,355
CODE FRA

NEAR COUTANCES, MANCHE

This stone-built house has an attached wine cellar and various outbuildings
£66,219

🛏 2 🌸 *2,000m²* 🏘 *Situated in the countryside* 🚧 *Not located on a main road*
🏠 *Room for parking*

€100,000–€200,000
(£69,444–£138,889)

A selection of pretty family homes, often with potential for expansion

€104,100 CODE FRA

MANCHE
A very pretty chalet set in beautiful countryside with spectacular views
£72,292

🛏 2 ❀ 1,000m² 🏡 *Situated in beautiful countryside* 📵 *Not located on a main road*
🏠 *Room for parking, with a garage*

€125,000 CODE LAT

NEAR TRUN, CALVADOS
A charming old country house set in large grounds, with an outbuilding and a well
£86,806

🛏 2 ❀ 2,500m² 🏡 *Situated at the edge of a small village* 📵 *Not located on a main road*
🏠 *Room for parking*

€160,000 CODE LAT

NEAR NEUFCHÂTEL-EN-BRAY, SEINE-MARITIME
A delightful *colombage* house with garage and outbuildings in a large garden
£111,111

🛏 2 ❀ 1,096m² 🏡 *Situated in the village centre* 📵 *Not located on a main road*
🏠 *Room for parking, with a garage*

€180,000 CODE FRA

NEAR COUTANCES, MANCHE
A large renovated farmhouse with room for further expansion
£125,000

🛏 4 ❀ 1,300m² 🏡 *Situated in a sleepy hamlet* 📵 *Not located on a main road*
🏠 *Room for parking, with a double garage*

€197,950 CODE FRA

NEAR BERNAY, CALVADOS
A lovely Norman house in a quiet rural location with outbuildings to renovate
£137,465

🛏 2 ❀ 2,500m² 🏡 *Situated just outside the village* 📵 *Not located on a main road*
🏠 *Room for parking*

PRICE GUIDE

€200,000–€350,000
(£138,889–£243,056)

A selection of large traditional properties that won't break the bank

€220,000   CODE FRA
NEAR L'AIGLE, ORNE
An attractive Norman house nestled in rolling countryside with a conservatory
£152,778

🛏 5 ❀ 4,000m² 📷 Situated a short drive from town 🚩 Not located on a main road
🏠 Room for parking, with a garage

€244,000   CODE FRA
NEAR FROBERVILLE, SEINE-MARITIME
A superb detached rural house set in large grounds, in excellent condition throughout
£169,444

🛏 3 ❀ 2,660m² 📷 Situated in a quiet rural area 🚩 Not located on a main road
🏠 Room for parking

€244,370   CODE FRA
NEAR AVRANCHES, MANCHE
A fully restored stone cottage with the possibility of a further bedroom
£169,701

🛏 3 ❀ 1,350m² 📷 Situated in the countryside 🚩 Not located on a main road
🏠 Room for parking, with a garage

€250,000   CODE LAT
NEAR LISIEUX, CALVADOS
A beautiful 19th-century property with outbuildings, requiring some work
£173,611

🛏 6 ❀ 6,000m² 📷 Situated in a small hamlet 🚩 Not located on a main road
🏠 Room for parking, with a garage

€261,777   CODE FRA
NEAR CANISY, MANCHE
A lovely stone farmhouse with numerous outbuildings, requiring finishing touches
£181,790

🛏 4 ❀ 98,000m² 📷 Situated in a quiet rural area 🚩 Not located on a main road
🏠 Room for parking

€261,800
CODE FRA

NEAR ST-MARTIN-DES-BESACES, MANCHE
A lovely stone house in large grounds, with a picturesque well and convertible attic
£181,806

🛏 3　❄ 3,000m²　🏙 *Situated just outside the village*　🛤 *Not located on a main road*
🏠 *Room for parking, with a large garage*

€296,565
CODE FRA

NEAR DUCEY, MANCHE
A character stone-built property with 2 independent flats, currently run as a B&B
£205,948

🛏 7　❄ 24,000m²　🏙 *Situated on the outskirts of town*　🛤 *Not located on a main road*
🏠 *Room for parking, with 4 garages*

€315,000
CODE FPS

NEAR DIEPPE, SEINE-MARITIME
A multi-purpose property with a number of outbuildings, including a large apartment
£218,750

🛏 3　❄ *Covered courtyard*　🏙 *Situated near the town*　🛤 *Not located on a main road*
🏠 *Room for parking*

€332,800
CODE FPS

DEAUVILLE, CALVADOS
A beautiful property in a sought-after complex, with communal pool and tennis courts
£231,111

🛏 2　❄ *Communal gardens*　🏙 *Just 700m from the beach*　🛤 *Not located on a main road*
🏠 *Private parking*

€336,000
CODE LAT

NEAR VIMOUTIERS, ORNE
A charming house with a thatched roof, guest house and swimming pool
£233,333

🛏 8　❄ 11,800m²　🏙 *Situated 2 kms from the village*　🛤 *Not located on a main road*
🏠 *Room for parking*

€350,000
CODE FPS

NEAR ROUEN, SEINE-MARITIME
Built in 1909, this imposing property has many original features and lots of potential
£243,056

🛏 4　❄ 9,884m²　🏙 *Situated in a peaceful location*　🛤 *Not located on a main road*
🏠 *Room for parking, with 2 garages*

PRICE GUIDE

Destination France?

FranceSolutions®!

Your piece of France with peace of mind

Register now for full details of FranceSolutions*,
the new service from Barclays France if you live,
work or own a property in France, or are thinking
of doing any of these!
For more information call 0800 917 0157*
or visit Destination France at www.barclays.fr

BARCLAYS

€350,000+
(£243,056+)

Snap up a traditional *colombage* or château with great business potential

€385,000
CODE LAT

VIMOUTIERS

A newly restored 17th-century property with 2 gîtes and a swimming pool

£267,361

 6 ❀ 15,200m² 🏡 *Situated in a pretty little hamlet* 🚫 *Not located on a main road* 🏠 *Room for parking*

€460,000
CODE FRA

NEAR VILLERS-BOCAGE, CALVADOS

A substantial old property with outbuildings, including a wine cellar and a bakery

£319,444

5 ❀ 10,000m² 🏡 *Situated in a quiet location* 🚫 *Not located on a main road* 🏠 *Room for parking, with a garage*

€483,000
CODE FPS

LOUVIGNY, CALVADOS

A large 18th-century house in a picturesque village just outside Caen

£335,417

5 ❀ 2,600m² 🏡 *Situated in the village centre* 🚫 *Not located on a main road* 🏠 *Room for parking*

€504,700
CODE AMR

NEAR RÂNES

A 4-bed converted stone barn plus a gîte sleeping 6, and much more

£350,486

4 ❀ 12,000m² 🏡 *Situated in the village centre* 🚫 *Not located on a main road* 🏠 *Room for parking*

€536,842
CODE FRA

BERNAY

A charming Chambre d'Hôtes complex in large grounds, ideal for nature lovers

£372,807

7 ❀ 44,000m² 🏡 *Situated at the edge of the village* 🚫 *Not located on a main road* 🏠 *Room for parking, with a garage*

€550,000   CODE LAT

NEAR AVRANCHES

A lovely old farmhouse with a detached apartment and other outbuildings

£381,944

🛏 4 ❀ 1,800m² 🏚 Situated in a small hamlet 🛤 Not located on a main road
🏠 Room for parking

€550,000   CODE LAT

NEAR BEAUVAIS

A beautiful *colombage* house with a convertible outbuilding. Full of period features

£381,944

🛏 4 ❀ 725m² 🏚 Situated in the village centre 🛤 Not located on a main road
🏠 Room for parking

€700,000   CODE LAT

VIMOUTIERS, ORNE

A stunning 18th-century house set in large grounds with small outbuildings

£486,111

🛏 6 ❀ 46,400m² 🏚 Situated in the village centre 🛤 Not located on a main road
🏠 Room for parking

€722,105   CODE FRA

NEAR DEAUVILLE, CALVADOS

A beautifully restored *manoir* with a large barn for conversion and lovely views

£501,462

🛏 6 ❀ 22,000m² 🏚 Just a short walk from the beach 🛤 Not located on a main road
🏠 Room for parking

€740,900   CODE SIF

NEAR CAEN

An elegant late 19th-century *manoir* with an artist's studio and other outbuildings

£514,513

🛏 8 ❀ 47,440m² 🏚 Situated 5 minutes from the sea 🛤 Not located on a main road
🏠 Room for parking

€869,000   CODE FRA

NEAR LE HAVRE, SEINE-MARITIME

A 17th-century château in excellent condition with a swimming pool

£603,472

🛏 8 ❀ 140,000m² 🏚 Situated just out of town 🛤 Not located on a main road
🏠 Room for parking

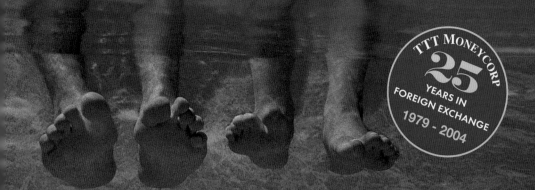

Buying in France?

Before jumping in with both feet, talk to us

Fluctuating exchange rates directly affect the Sterling price that you will pay for your property. By calling Moneycorp, you can save money and enjoy peace of mind.

Our friendly, expert staff won't baffle you with jargon, but will guide you to the most competitive exchange rates available and protect you from adverse currency fluctuations. What is more, with Moneycorp, there is no commission charge for our service and no obligation to buy your currency from us. We are confident that you will not find better rates or service anywhere else.

Contact us now on +44 (0) 20 7589 3000 to find out how Moneycorp can help you.

Don't let foreign exchange be an afterthought...

MONEYCORP
Commercial Foreign Exchange

100 Brompton Road
London SW3 1ER UK
+44 (0) 20 75 89 30 00

www.moneycorp.com

Nord Pas-de-Calais & Picardy

Gothic cathedrals, rolling countryside and cultured Lille

JUSTIN POSTLETHWAITE

FACT BOX 2005

■ **Population** 5,854,069 (+1.7% from 1990)
Nord Pas-de-Calais: 3,996,588 (+0.8% from 1990),
Picardy: 1,857,481 (+2.6% from 1990)
■ **Foreign residents** 193,341
■ **Migration** 308,079 international migrants Nord
Pas-de-Calais: 208,163 international migrants, Picardy:
99,916 international migrants
■ **Unemployment** 159,190
■ **Median house price** €133,400
■ **House price increase** Since 2002 Nord has
experienced a 2.1% increase in house prices while
Picardy has seen an increase of 8%

Price Guide

Area profile

GETTING THERE

AIR Ryan Air (0871 246 0000;
www.ryanair.com) flies into Beauvais from
Dublin and Glasgow. **Air France** (0845
359 1000; www.airfrance.co.uk) flies from
Heathrow into Lille-Lequin airport, while
Lyddair (01797 320000;
www.lyddair.co.uk) flies into Le Touquet
from Lydd.
SEA P&O (0870 520 2020;
www.posl.com) sails from Dover to Calais,
as does SeaFrance (0870 571 1711;
www.seafrance.com). **Norfolkline** (0870
870 1020; www.norfolkline.com) sails
between Dover and Dunkirk, while
Hoverspeed (0870 240 8070;
www.hoverspeed.co.uk) operates services
between Dover and Calais.
ROAD From Calais port the A26 runs
through Pas-de-Calais and Picardy. The A1
runs from Arras through to Picardy, while
the A16 runs along the coast, linking up
all the coastal resorts. The A16 and A25
also run from Calais to Lille, and if you are
flying into Paris the A16 runs through to
Amiens and on into Nord Pas-de-Calais.
Eurolines (0870 514 3219;
www.eurolines.com) operates services to
Amiens, Boulogne, Calais and Lille.
RAIL The Eurotunnel runs from Dover to
Calais, and the **Eurostar** (08705 186186;
www.eurostar.co.uk) runs from London
through to Lille or Paris. The **TGV
network** serves Lille, Calais and Dunkirk;
call **Rail Europe** (0870 584 8848;
www.raileurope.co.uk) for all details of
local services.

THE NORTHWEST REGIONS OF NORD PAS-DE-CALAIS AND PICARDY ARE
often overlooked by British homebuyers, although the hypermarkets are
certainly not! Calais may not be the best introduction to France, but travel
a little further and there is much to discover.

Lille, the capital of Nord Pas-de-Calais, is France's fourth largest city and
just two hours from Waterloo on the Eurostar. As the 'European City of
Culture' in 2004, Lille has benefited from the huge grants awarded with its
title. Distinctly Flemish in flavour, the streets are dotted with bustling cafés
and good shops. The western coast is home to a number of small towns,
the best of which is Le Touquet, with its dunes, pine woods and Art Deco
tea rooms. Nord Pas-de-Calais also has three large regional parks with a
wealth of waterways and hiking trails.

Picardy's delightful and varied landscape has witnessed some of the
worst battles ever, most notably the Battle of the Somme in World War I.
The region's largest city, Amiens, is home to France's largest Gothic
structure, the Cathédrale Notre Dame, and it is situated in an area with
many monuments. The coastal stretch is studded with small seaside resorts
and sandy bays, and the south of the region is blessed with rolling hills,
winding rivers and large forests.

Much of the cuisine in northwest France has a Flemish flavour. Popular
dishes include *carbonnade flamande* (beef in beer), *tarte aux maroilles* (cheese
tart) and *waterzooi*, a fish and vegetable stew. This is also the only area of
France where locals tend to drink more beer than wine.

The economy and housing market

Lille is France's second largest print and publishing centre, the third largest
centre for mechanical and electrical industry and the fourth largest food
processing site. Amiens, too, is a commerce-rich city and pharmaceutical
production takes place in both Calais and Lille. Calais firm Nikko exports
toys to Japan. The economy is also bolstered by British 'booze cruisers'

Lille – European City of Culture, 2004

who flock across the Channel with the hope of finding bargains in the hypermarkets of Calais.

Canny property buyers after good resale potential like Calais because of its vibrancy and popularity with French purchasers looking to live and work there. Prices are rising steadily and there is little available on the market for less than £60,000. Despite this, prices are obviously still competitive compared with Britain.

Over the past 15 years, price rises in Calais have been triggered by investment from the French Government in its once ailing industry, thus reversing the trend of locals migrating from Nord Pas-de-Calais to seek employment. New residents also flock to the region in search of employment, helping to fuel property prices. The attraction of new businesses to the area also puts added pressure on the market. Foreign purchaser interest centres around the Seven Valleys area, including the Opal coast, Montreuil, Hesdin and St Pol.

In the chic seaside resort of Le Touquet, apartment prices start from around £140,000, and house prices from £200,000. It's popular with Parisian weekend visitors and foreign purchasers looking for cheaper price tags than the UK has to offer will discover little here – Le Touquet hasn't yet experienced much foreign interest. French buyers have pushed up prices in Amiens and Lille, but there is still a good range of property available for around £100,000. Lille's ease of access from Waterloo makes it an attractive option and, as mentioned, it was European City of Culture in 2004. This award has helped enrich the city's cultural life and immeasurably improved its public parks and transport infrastructure – benefits that it is hoped will be felt for many years to come.

Throughout the region, property prices rose by around 14 per cent in the first three quarters of 2004. There have been few new builds and demand has outstripped supply. These days, there are very few renovation properties available for under £40,000 – a price level that was commonplace until recently.

Social groups

While a small number of British buyers make the daily commute to southeast England from Nord Pas-de-Calais, the region is primarily chosen for holiday homes or by businessmen desiring easy access to London. Dutch and Germans are the main foreign buyers, especially civil servants working in Brussels, who find it cost effective to commute from the region as Belgium's lack of space and lack of new builds has made for an expensive market.

Only one in 10 British buyers choose to buy on the coast, as most foreign interest is centred around inland locations, primarily within easy reach of the ports. The region's transport links to Britain have allowed buyers from southern England to purchase and enjoy weekend homes, not to mention created a more expensive property market. ●

"The western coast is home to a number of small towns, the best of which is Le Touquet, with its sand dunes, pine woods and lovely Art Deco tea rooms"

Average monthly temperature °C (Celsius)

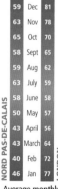

Average monthly rainfall mm (millimetres)

AVERAGE HOUSE SALE PRICES

Hotspot	2-bed	3-bed	4-bed	5/6-bed
Le Touquet	€230K (£160K)	€467K (£324K)	€575K (£399K)	€704K (£489K)
Amiens	€116K (£81K)	€148K (£103K)	€258K (£179K)	€322K (£224K)
Lille	€108K (£75K)	€177K (£123K)	€218K (£152K)	€344K (£239K)
Somme Valley	€102K (£71K)	€134K (£93K))	€244K (£169K)	€283K (£197K)
Montreuil & Hesdin	€110K (£76K)	€157K (£109K)	€162K (£113K)	€329K (£228K)

Property hotspots

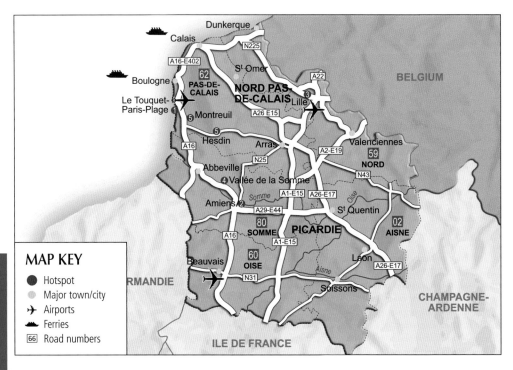

MAP KEY

● Hotspot
● Major town/city
✈ Airports
⛴ Ferries
66 Road numbers

1. Le Touquet Paris Plage

ESSENTIALS ■ **Population** 6,000 ■ **Taxes** Taxe d'habitation 7.83%, Taxe foncière 9.70% ■ **Airport** Aéroport du Touquet, Côte d'Opale, 62520 Le Touquet-Paris-Plage, Tel: +33 321 05 03 99

KEY FACTS

■ **Schools** École Active Bilingue Jeannine Manuel – École Internationale de Lille Métropole, 418 bis rue Albert Bailly, 59700, Marcq-en-Baroeul, Lille, Tel: +33 320 65 90 50
■ **Medical** Centre Hospitalier Docteur Duchenne, all. Jacques Monod, 62200 Boulogne sur Mer, Tel: +33 321 99 33 33
■ **Rentals** There are numerous tourist properties in Le Touquet Paris Plage ■ Le Touquet is unique in that there is a guaranteed summer rental season and a vibrant out-of-season rental market ■ Rental properties can cost from €730 a week for two-bedrooms up to €1,480 for four-bedrooms
■ **Pros** Le Touquet Paris Plage is an affluent area with a sophisticated atmosphere ■ Situated within two hours drive of London ■ This is a very active resort, offering wide beaches, sand dunes and unique architecture
■ **Cons** Can get very crowded in summer ■ This is a very expensive area in which to live and buy, with a two-bedroom property costing an average of €230,000 ■ Most foreign buyers buy in the Stella-Plage, on the edge of Le Touquet.

Reflecting its creation by the British a century ago, this sophisticated seaside resort was a magnet for wealthy celebrities who flocked here in the 1920s and 30s to play cricket and polo by day, then party by night. Marketed by the local tourist board as a 'four seasons' resort, throughout the year events from wine festivals to sports are held. The town is flourishing, thanks to the Channel Tunnel and Lydd Air's direct flights from Lydd in Kent, and many British commute daily to work in London.

The beach, stretching for seven miles, is ideal for sunbathers, while nature lovers can savour The Park of the Estuary, a sign-posted reserve composed of 42 hectares, situated to the north of Le Touquet. A grandiose 1930s covered market draws shoppers every Thursday and Saturday, while the rue de Metz and rue St Louis are lined with excellent speciality *charcuteries*, *traiteurs* and bakeries.

Further inland from Le Touquet are the cheaper towns of Hesdin and Montreuil, which attract many who want to live in the Le Touquet area. Le Touquet itself is popular with Parisians escaping at weekends, and consequently this is an expensive area to buy in due to high demand; a four-bedroom house can cost an average of €575,000. As a result, it's not considered good value for money for foreign investors. ●

2. Amiens

ESSENTIALS ■ **Population** 132,000 ■ **Taxes** Taxe d'habitation 9.51%, Taxe foncière 13.16% ■ **Airport** Aéroport de Beauvais, Service Chamco 60000, Beauvais, Tel: +33 344 11 46 66

Picardy's largest city, Amiens, is a university city in the Somme *département* renowned for its great Gothic architecture, notably the Cathédrale Notre Dame, the biggest Gothic building in France, which can be viewed from anywhere in the city. Construction first started in 1218, when the citizens wanted a worthy monument to house what they believed to be John the Baptist's head.

The medieval quarter of St Leu, once the city's centre for its textile industry, lies to the north of the cathedral with its network of canals, renovated into neat brick cottages, while the waterfront sparkles with restaurants and clubs. Each canal still functions as a waterway for the *hortillonnages*, a series of fertile market gardens reclaimed from the marshes created by the slow-flowing Somme river. Farmers travel about the canals in black punts, and a few still take their produce into the city by boat for the Saturday morning *marché sur l'eau*. Jules Verne, science-fiction writer and Amiens's most prominent former citizen, lived in the city from 1856 until his death in 1905. The Maison Jules Verne at 2 Rue Charles Dubois has a model of a flying machine and the Nautilus.

Amiens caters for the local French market and is not popular with the foreign buyer. A three-bedroom house in Amiens starts at €148,000, and the city is affordable compared with much of the region. ●

KEY FACTS

■ **Schools** École Active Bilingue Jeannine Manuel – École Internationale de Lille Métropole, 418 bis rue Albert Bailly, 59700, Marcq-en-Baroeul, Lille, Tel: +33 320 65 90 50
■ **Medical** Centre Hospitalier Universitaire, pl Victor Pauchet 2, 80080 Amiens, Tel: +33 322 66 80 00
■ **Rentals** Amiens caters mainly for long-term rentals ■ There are many business-connected rentals in this area, primarily from the French market ■ A weekly rental in a two-bedroom house would cost an average of €610
■ **Pros** Boasts a lively atmosphere, due to the presence of 25,000 students ■ A vibrant, cosmopolitan city, excellent for those who desire a metropolitan lifestyle ■ Amiens is affordable when compared with much of the region; a two-bedroom property costs an average of €116,050
■ **Cons** Property turnover is very rapid in Amiens and it is primarily a French market ■ British buyers don't tend to buy in Amiens unless it is for work purposes ■ Many French estate agents prefer not to deal with the foreign market, but with the local French market.

3. Lille

ESSENTIALS ■ **Population** 1,100,000 ■ **Taxes** Taxe d'habitation 7.83%, Taxe foncière 9.70% ■ **Airport** Lille Airport, BP 227, 59812 Lesquin Cedex Tel: +33 320 49 68 68

European Capital of Culture in 2004, Lille is France's fourth-largest city with plenty of stunning architecture, delectable food and drink, and sophisticated shopping. Lying in the Nord *département*, bordering Belgium, Lille combines a typically French atmosphere with a distinctive Flemish flavour.

Notable is the old quarter, Vieux Lille, which has been tastefully revived in Flemish style, in particular the Vielle Bourse. Also the immense Place du Général de Gaulle, called simply 'Grand Place' by locals. Don't miss the Musée des Beaux-Arts, a classical and modern architectural gem, with its priceless collection of paintings from Goya to Rubens. There are plenty of good cafés and brasseries serving local fare like *carbonnades* (beef braised in beer) and mussels. The city's student population ensures that the streets are buzzing into the early hours. Cinemas and bars are found in the Halles district and old quarter, while the jazz scene is also popular. Events in Lille include the September beer festival and the December Christmas markets.

Lille only attracts foreign buyers who seek to move to the area for employment purposes. Otherwise, the area is dominated by the locals. A one-bedroom apartment costs an average of €78,000, while a three-bedroom house will cost an average of €177,000. ●

KEY FACTS

■ **Schools** École Active Bilingue Jeannine Manuel – École Internationale de Lille Métropole, 418 bis rue Albert Bailly, 59700, Marcq-en-Baroeul, Lille, Tel: +33 320 65 90 50
■ **Medical** Centre Hospitalier Régional Universitaire de Lille, av Oscar Lambret, 59037 Lille Cedex, Tel: +33 320 44 59 62
■ **Rentals** This is not a tourist area and therefore long-term rentals are the norm ■ Lille is dominated by the business market and by the local French market ■ An expensive weekly rental rate; expect to pay €750 for a two-bedroom house
■ **Pros** Lille is renowned for its dynamic shopping centres and abundance of retail outlets ■ Lille has an extremely buoyant property market, albeit primarily a local French market
■ **Cons** Lille is essentially a French market dominated by the French buyer, and is a city where the French live and work ■ This is an expensive city in which to live, and property prices are high due to the demand and rapid turnover of property.

4. The Fishing Lakes of the Somme Valley

ESSENTIALS ■ **Population** Le Quesnoy 5,089, St Quentin 69,287 ■ **Taxes** Taxe d'habitation 9.51%, Taxe foncière 13.16%
■ **Airport** Aéroport du Touquet, Côte d'Opale, 62520 Le Touquet-Paris-Plage, Tel: +33 321 05 03 99

KEY FACTS

■ **Schools** École Active Bilingue Jeannine Manuel –
École Internationale de Lille Métropole, 418 bis Rue
Albert Bailly, 59700, Marcq-en-Baroeul, Lille,
Tel: +33 320 65 90 50
■ **Medical** Centre Hospitalier Universitaire, pl Victor
Pauchet 2, 80080 Amiens, Tel: +33 322 66 80 00
■ **Rentals** There is huge rental potential for
lakeside properties ■ This is a very popular area
with anglers and tourists on activities holidays ■
Rentals are affordable, with a two-bedroom property
costing from €495 per week
■ **Pros** Can be an excellent and profitable business
buying a fishing lake in Picardy ■ The Avesnois
regional park is a stunning natural park and there is
great demand for property in this area ■ This is a
must for those who love nature and outdoor or
adventure sports ■ A great area for those who
desire to be close to the south-east of England ■
The cheapest property in the region, a two-bedroom
house starts at €103,000
■ **Cons** Prices are increasing all the time due to the
rising demand from the British market ■ Costs for
lakeside properties are constantly altering and are
inconsistent ■ This is not a huge international
buying area and parts of Picardy are undiscovered.

Picardy is a haven for anglers, especially the lakes of the
Somme and the Oise, with their rich flora and fauna.
You can catch many different types of fish including
trout, carp and gudgeon in this undiscovered area of
France. For the invigorating country life, choose the
Avesnois, close to the Ardennes. Situated in the south-
east of the Nord *département*, at the very tip of Nord-Pas-de-Calais
against the Belgian border, this area is fondly referred to as 'little
Switzerland', with its extensive network of rivers, canals and lakes
making fishing, canoeing and other water sports very popular.

A designated nature park, the Avesnois valleys and pine forests are
interspersed with lush pastures and ancient walled towns. Val Joly at
Eppe Sauvage is the largest lake north of Paris, with facilities including
sailing, mini-golf and tennis. Many of the traditional arts and crafts of
Nord are still practised in this area. Le Quesnoy boasts three-and-a-half
kilometres of perfectly preserved 17th-century fortifications, bearing
witness to centuries of invasion.

Angling is an increasingly popular activity, and there is huge demand
from the foreign market for angling businesses. A house in the Somme
Valley costs from €103,000, while a four-bedroom home will set you
back €245,000. A fishing business near Calais costs from €375,000. ●

5. Montreuil and Hesdin

ESSENTIALS ■ **Population** Montreuil 2,688, Hesdin 2,763 ■ **Taxes** Taxe d'habitation 7.83%, Taxe foncière 9.70%
■ **Airport** Aéroport du Touquet, Côte d'Opale, 62520 Le Touquet-Paris-Plage, Tel: +33 321 05 03 99

KEY FACTS

■ **Schools** École Active Bilingue Jeannine Manuel –
École Internationale de Lille Métropole, 418 bis rue
Albert Bailly, 59700, Marcq-en-Baroeul, Lille,
Tel: +33 320 65 90 50
■ **Medical** Hôpital Rural, bd Richelieu 13, 62140
Hesdin, Tel: +33 321 86 86 54
■ **Rentals** A short-term lets area, there is good
demand for rentals, and many people buy with the
intention of letting ■ Easy access means people
come for short breaks, especially golfers ■ There is a
lot of demand for hotels, rather than cottages and
gîtes ■ A two-bedroom house will rent for an
average of €320 a week
■ **Pros** A major focal point in Pas-de-Calais for the
British buyer ■ Located within 45 minutes to an
hour of Calais, there is easy access to the UK ■
Exactly the attractive and affordable rural area the
British buyer loves ■ Many international buyers are
investing in the area, such as civil servants from
Brussels, plus many Dutch and Germans
■ **Cons** This area has experienced a huge increase
in prices in recent years ■ It is almost impossible to
secure a habitable property for less than €100,000.

At the heart of the historic Seven Valleys region, the
town of Hesdin, with its bridges, red brick and white
stone *maisons de maitre*, is famed as a former outpost of
the Austro–Hungarian Empire. The town is crossed by
the rivers Canche and Ternoise, the focal points are the
Town Hall, formerly the residence of Emperor Charles
V's sister, Marie of Hungary, and The Wine Society, directly across the
square. This is a good base for exploring the battle site and museum at
Agincourt. Other attractions include the flower-decked village of
Boubers-sur-Canche, and the Opal Coast, named after its white sandy
beaches. The state-owned forestland in Hesdin stretches for more than
1,020 acres and lies upon a limestone plateau, soaring above the
Ternoise, Canche and Planquette valleys. A *son et lumiére* is acted
biannually in the town in memory of Victor Hugo, who wrote the
local mayor into the plot of Les Misérables.

Houses are excellent value compared to English equivalents, while
buyers from the Netherlands, Belgium and Germany will find property
is comparably cheap. Nevertheless, compared with last year's prices,
there has been a sharp increase as demand has risen. A two-bedroom
Montreuil-sur-Mer house starts at €110,000, whereas a four-bedroom
property can sell for anything upwards of €163,000. ●

HOTSPOTS

€50,000–€100,000
(£34,722–£69,444)

Smaller apartments and houses to suit all tastes

€65,000   CODE LAT

LES VILLAS D'OPALE, BERCK-SUR-MER
New studio apartments with fantastic sea views and good rental potential
£45,139

🛏 1 　❋ – 　🏞 Situated close to the beach 　🛣 Not located on a main road
🏠 Parking spaces available to buy

€67,080   CODE LAT

AUMALE-FORMERIE, OISE
Detached brick-built house with outbuildings, set in an acre of grounds
£46,583

🛏 3 　❋ 4,054m² 　🏞 Situated close to Aumale 　🛣 Not located on a main road
🏠 Room for parking

€80,000   CODE FPS

FRUGES, PAS-DE-CALAIS
A regional farmhouse with outbuildings; in need of some internal renovation
£55,555

🛏 2 　❋ 1,000m² 　🏞 Situated in a quiet village 　🛣 Not located on a main road
🏠 Room for parking, with a garage

€87,000   CODE LAT

VALLEE DE LA PLANQUETTE, PAS-DE-CALAIS
A charming restored house with period features and a small garden
£60,417

🛏 2 　❋ – 　🏞 Situated in a quiet village 　🛣 Not located on a main road
🏠 Room for parking

€97,000   CODE LAT

LES AMARELLES, ETAPLES, PAS-DE-CALAIS
An apartment in a traditionally built new development, with stunning views
£67,361

🛏 1 　❋ – 　🏞 Situated near a nature reserve and marina 　🛣 Not located on a main road
🏠 Room for parking

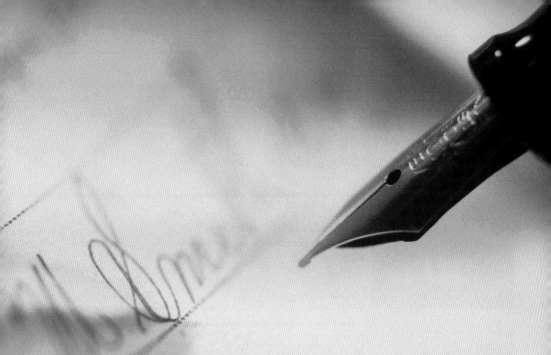

Writing out a big cheque?

When buying your place in France, Caxton FX can help you save money on your currency exchange. We offer excellent rates and free international transfers.

On top of that we understand that service matters – which is why we bend over backwards, sideways and forwards to make sure that your transaction happens quickly and smoothly.

To learn about our specialist foreign exchange service for property buyers, call James Hickman, our senior dealer, or one of his team today on 0845 658 2223. We will be pleased to hear from you.

Caxton FX Ltd. 2 Motcomb Street, London SW1X 8JU
Telephone 0845 658 2223 · www.caxtonfx.com

CAXTON*fx*

€100,000–€200,000
(£69,444–£138,889)

Beautiful properties set in attractive French countryside

€118,000   CODE LAT

CANCHE VALLEY, PAS-DE-CALAIS

A typical *fermette* with outbuildings, set in almost half an acre of garden
£81,944

🛏 3   ❋ 1,651m²   🏞 *Situated in the Canche Valley*   🛤 *Not located on a main road*
🏠 *Room for parking, with a garage*

€157,000   CODE LAT

AUMALE, SOMME

A pretty Picardy-style house set in over a quarter of an acre of wooded gardens
£109,028

🛏 3   ❋ 1,200m²   🏞 *Situated in the village centre*   🛤 *Not located on a main road*
🏠 *Room for parking*

€164,650   CODE LAT

AUMALE, SOMME

An L-shaped *colombages*-style house with outbuildings, bordered by a river
£114,340

🛏 4   ❋ 916m²   🏞 *Between Aumale and Blagny-sur-Bresles*   🛤 *Not located on a main road*
🏠 *Room for parking*

€172,200   CODE LAT

FORGES-GERBEROY, OISE

An attractive detached house set in half an acre of grounds, bordered by a river
£119,583

🛏 3   ❋ 1,500m²   🏞 *Between Forges and Gerberoy*   🛤 *Not located on a main road*
🏠 *Room for parking, with a garage*

€183,750   CODE SIF

NEAR ST OMER, PAS-DE-CALAIS

This pretty *fermette*-style house has seven main rooms and substantial grounds
£127,604

🛏 3   ❋ 950m²   🏞 *Situated in the village centre*   🛤 *Not located on a main road*
🏠 *Room for parking*

€200,000–€300,000
(£138,889–£208,333)

There's a huge selection of property available in this price range

€211,500   CODE LAT

VALLEE DE L'AUTHIE, PAS-DE-CALAIS

A charming detached house and garage set in half an acre of gardens

£146,875

🛏 4 ⚜ 2,000m² 🏞 *Situated in a peaceful location* 🚫 *Not located on a main road*
🏠 *4-car garage*

€211,680   CODE LAT

AUMALE-HORNOY-LE-BOURG, SOMME

A pretty Normandy-style house set in half an acre of grounds

£147,000

🛏 3 ⚜ 1,412m² 🏞 *Situated in a peaceful village* 🚫 *Not located on a main road*
🏠 *Room for parking, with a garage*

€212,000   CODE LAT

FORMERIE, OISE

An L-shaped house with outbuildings and a triple garage, set in an acre of gardens

£147,222

🛏 5 ⚜ 4,000m² 🏞 *Situated in a lively village with shops* 🚫 *Not located on a main road*
🏠 *Room for parking*

€214,000   CODE LAT

NEAR MONTREUIL-SUR-MER, PAS-DE-CALAIS

A charming renovated *fermette* with garage and outbuildings in large grounds

£148,611

🛏 5 ⚜ 3,000m² 🏞 *Situated in a quiet village* 🚫 *Not located on a main road*
🏠 *Room for parking, with a garage*

€240,450   CODE SIF

NEAR BERCK-SUR-MER, PAS-DE-CALAIS

A magnificent farmhouse dating from 1821, set in a green and peaceful setting

£166,979

🛏 5 ⚜ 1,000m² 🏞 *Situated in the village centre* 🚫 *Not located on a main road*
🏠 *Room for parking*

€251,540   CODE LAT

GOURNAY-EN-BRAY, OISE

Colombages and brick-built house with a quarter of an acre of gardens
£174,680

🛏 3   ❀ 1,000m²   🖼 *Situated near Gournay-en-Bray*   🏔 *Not located on a main road*
🏠 *Room for parking, with a garage*

€254,000   CODE LAT

BOULOGNE AREA, PAS-DE-CALAIS

A beautiful country house set in a quarter of an acre of well-kept grounds
£176,389

🛏 4   ❀ 1,000m²   🖼 *Situated north of Boulogne*   🏔 *Not located on a main road*
🏠 *Room for parking, with a large garage*

€270,000   CODE LAT

AUTHIE VALLEY, PAS-DE-CALAIS

A charming countryside house with outbuildings and a large garden with an orchard
£187,500

🛏 4   ❀ 4,800m²   🖼 *Situated in a peaceful location*   🏔 *Not located on a main road*
🏠 *Room for parking, with 3 garages*

€283,500   CODE SIF

NEAR ETAPLES, PAS-DE-CALAIS

A pretty *fermette* bordered by a small stream, set in half an acre of enclosed grounds
£196,875

🛏 4   ❀ 1,880m²   🖼 *Situated near to the port of Etaples*   🏔 *Not located on a main road*
🏠 *Room for parking, with a garage*

€289,600   CODE LAT

VALLEE DE L'AUTHIE, PAS-DE-CALAIS

A charming detached house set in 12.5 acres of woodland with an orchard and a lake
£201,111

🛏 3   ❀ 50,000m²   🖼 *Situated 15 minutes from the sea*   🏔 *Not located on a main road*
🏠 *Room for parking, with a garage*

€296,000   CODE SIF

PAS-DE-CALAIS

This property comprises a mill and a separate house on the banks of the river
£205,555

🛏 5   ❀ 5,840m²   🖼 *Situated on the banks of the river*   🏔 *Not located on a main road*
🏠 *Room for parking, with a garage*

€300,000–€400,000
(£208,333–£277,778)

Large houses with spacious grounds and gorgeous locations

€319,147   CODE LAT

NEAR COLEMBERT, PAS-DE-CALAIS

Southeast-facing thatched house with almost half an acre of gardens and lovely views

£221,630

🛏 4   ❀ 1,760m²   🏞 Situated near Colembert   🚶 Not located on a main road

🏠 Room for parking, with a garage

€335,000   CODE LAT

VALLEE DE L'AUTHIE, PAS-DE-CALAIS

A spacious detached house with large grounds and a substantial basement area

£232,639

🛏 5   ❀ 2,600m²   🏞 Situated in a quiet location   🚶 Not located on a main road

🏠 Parking for 6 cars

€345,000   CODE LAT

HESDIN, PAS-DE-CALAIS

An attractive property with a garage, set in large grounds with views over the valley

£239,583

🛏 4   ❀ 2,500m²   🏞 Situated near the town of Hesdin   🚶 Not located on a main road

🏠 Room for parking, with a garage

€350,000   CODE LAT

NEAR MONTREUIL, PAS-DE-CALAIS

Turn-of-the-century property with outbuildings and a courtyard in wooded grounds

£243,056

🛏 6   ❀ 5,000m²   🏞 Situated in beautiful woodland   🚶 Not located on a main road

🏠 Room for parking, with 4 large garages

€369,000   CODE LAT

NEAR HESDIN, PAS-DE-CALAIS

A delightful character house set in more than an acre of partly wooded grounds

£256,250

🛏 7   ❀ 4,768m²   🏞 Situated just 5 minutes from Hesdin   🚶 Not located on a main road

🏠 Room for parking, with 2 garages

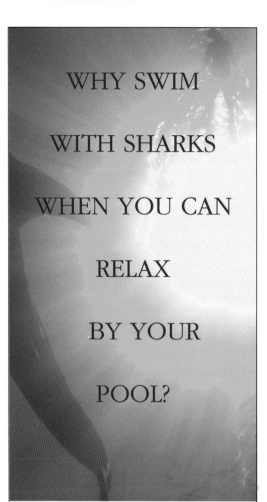
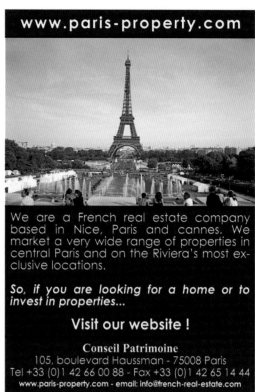

Île-de-France

The Eiffel Tower, Notre Dame, the Champs-Élysées, Versailles…

FELIX STENSSON

FACT BOX 2005

■ **Population** 10,952,037
■ **Migration** 1,965,321
■ **Unemployment** 295,346
■ **Median house price** €505,780
■ **House price increase** Since 2002, house prices in Île-de-France have increased by 14.5%

Price Guide

GETTING THERE

AIR Air France (0845 084 5111; www.airfrance.co.uk), **easyJet** (0871 750 0100; www.easyjet.com), **Flybe** (0871 700 0535; www.flybe.com), **British Airways** (0870 850 9850; www.britishairways.com), **BMI Baby** (0870 264 2229; www.flybmi.co.uk) all fly to Charles de Gaulle airport in Paris. Orly Airport is visited by domestic and intra-European flights, with Air France and Flybe services to Orly from London. **SEA SeaFrance** (0870 571 1711; www.seafrance.com) provides ferries to Calais, as does **Hoverspeed Fast Ferries** (0870 240 8070; www.hoverspeed.co.uk) and **P&O Ferries** (0870 520 2020; www.poferries.com) operates ferries to Le Havre, and from all ports access to Paris is very straightforward.

ROAD From Calais and the Channel Tunnel, take the A16 south to Amiens, and from there the A16 continues to the Parisian environs. From Le Havre the A15 runs to Rouen and then the A14 runs on into Paris, and the A4 runs into Paris from Reims.

COACH An express coach service operates from London Victoria Coach Station to Gare Routière **Eurolines** Coach Station (0870 514 3219; www.eurolines.com).

RAIL Eurostar (0870 518 6186; www.eurostar.co.uk) operates services from London, Waterloo to the Gare de Nord station, Paris. **SNCF** offers services to Versailles and Fontainebleau (www.sncf.com) or contact **Rail Europe** (0870 830 2008; www.raileurope.co.uk) for details of services.

PARIS METRO Paris has a comprehensive public transport system that is easy to navigate. The 14-line metro system is part of the RATP, which incorporates bus, metro RER trains and tramways to the city's outskirts.

Area profile

ÎLE-DE-FRANCE IS ESSENTIALLY PARIS AND ITS ENVIRONS. THE REGION'S population is almost 11 million, nearly a fifth of the nation's total, which is remarkable when you consider that, geographically, France is the third largest country in Europe.

Glamorous and cosmopolitan, Paris is quite simply one of the world's great cities, both culturally and architecturally. Historically a haven for artists and writers from all over the world, the streets and expansive boulevards are lined with great cafés, bars and restaurants. The capital's architectural riches are manifold; Notre Dame, the Louvre, Centre Pompidou, the Eiffel Tower, Musée d'Orsay… the list goes on and on.

Paris has a long and proud history dating back 2,000 years. Conquered by Julius Caesar in 53 BC, it was a Roman centre until the Middle Ages and later, the scene of the storming of the Bastille during the French Revolution in 1789. Modern Paris owes its glorious architectural style and structure to Napoléon III's civic planner, Baron Haussmann, who removed the slums and laid out the elegant avenues, boulevards and parks. The city is divided into 20 *arrondissements*; they're organised numerically and spiral out of the centre clockwise.

Although Paris is arguably the world's greatest gastronomic centre, there are few dishes that are specifically Parisian. The city has a wealth of ethnic fare and the North African and Vietnamese restaurants are often superb.

The economy and housing market

A quarter of France's manufacturing industry is situated in Paris, and chemicals, pharmaceuticals, computer software, and electrical equipment are all produced here. Paris is also an established centre of art, publishing, high-fashion clothes and jewellery; more than 8,000 foreign companies, including Esso, IBM, Kodak, Honda, and Proctor & Gamble have

Paris is one of the world's most culturally admired cities

THIERRY DANIEL

headquarters there. Galleries, bookshops, antique dealers and restaurants all dominate the 6ème arrondissement, while La Défense business centre houses ELF, Esso and IBM. East of Paris, Disneyland is a major employer.

Property prices are high in the capital but if you're prepared to explore up-and-coming areas you will get better value for money. Regaining its old status as an artists' quarter, Montmartre, in the 18ème, has some of the cheapest prices in the city. The thriving 9ème and Montparnasse, in the not-so-glitzy 14ème, also feature affordable properties. Classic Haussmann-style buildings with high price tags, left in their original state and not divided into apartments dominate the 16ème.

The Champs Élysées, Avenue Montaigne and Avenue George V in the 1ème and 2ème are popular with Middle Eastern purchasers. The smart and exclusive 16ème offers a quiet life (middle-aged couples and families are the major buyers). The 6ème's lively nightlife suits students at upmarket universities and foreign buyers seeking a central pied-à-terre, while the 8ème's recent overhaul is attracting younger residents.

With new art galleries and squares emerging towards Clichy, the Avenue de Clichy and Batignolles areas in the 17ème have seen major price hikes. Parisian Haussmann apartments in the 8ème, 16ème and 17ème are at a premium, selling at £11,000 per square metre. Non-French purchasers form about seven per cent of the 1ème and 2ème's purchasing power, making these areas the next most expensive to live in after the 7ème and 16ème. This figure is doubled in the more desirable 6ème, 7ème, 16ème and parts of the 17ème.

Neuilly, Boulogne, Saint-Cloud and Levallois to the west of Paris represent peaceful *banlieue,* popular with families and central Parisian workers, as does Versailles. Cheaper properties have helped Versailles develop from being purely the site of King Louis XIV's château, into a self-contained community with its own identity. Houses offer more space and a garden for the same price as some Parisian apartments, hence Parisians often rent homes here. Avenue de la Reine or Queen's Avenue offers a fabulous, central location, overlooked by the château.

Social groups

The capital is home to large groups of immigrants from France's former colonies in Africa and Asia including Algerian, Senegalese and Vietnamese. Like any cosmopolitan city, Paris is home to many nationalities. ●

> *"Modern Paris owes its architectural style and structure to Napoléon III's great civic planner, Baron Haussmann, who laid out the avenues, boulevards and parks"*

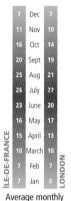

Average monthly temperature °C (Celsius)

Average monthly rainfall mm (millimetres)

PROFILE

AVERAGE HOUSE SALE PRICES

Hotspot	2-bed	3-bed	4-bed	5-bed+
Arrondissement 1	€550K (£382K)	€760K (£528K)	€1,100K (£764K)	€1,780K (£1,236K)
Arrondissement 2	€475K (£330K)	€825K (£573K)	€1,128K (£846K)	€2,430K (£1,688K)
Arrondissement 3	€434K (£301K)	€753K (£523K)	€1,033K (£717K)	€1,317K (£915K)
Arrondissement 4	€473K (£329K)	€730K (£507K)	€1,375K (£955K)	€1,773K (£1,231K)
Arrondissement 6	€525K (£365K)	€714K (£496K)	€1,075K (£747K)	€1,916K (£1,331K)
Arrondissement 7	€560K (£389K)	€860K (£597K)	€980K (£681K)	€1,423K (£988K)
Arrondissement 8	€360K (£250K)	€835K (£580K)	€1,123K (£780K)	€2,000K (£1,389K
Arrondissement 16	€595K (£413K)	€975K (£677K)	€1,426K (£990K)	€2,663K (£1,849K)
Arrondissement 17	€550K (£382K)	€785K (£545K)	€1,159K (£805K)	€3,143K (£2,183K)
Versailles	€535K (£372K)	€607K (£422K)	€803K (£558K)	€1,753K (£1,217K)

Property hotspots

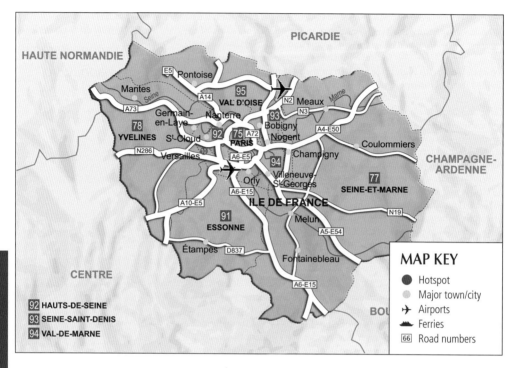

HOTSPOTS

Map labels: PICARDIE, HAUTE NORMANDIE, Pontoise, E5, Mantes, Seine, A14, 95, VAL D'OISE, N2, Meaux, Marne, A73, Germain-en-Laye, Nanterre, 93, N3, 78, 92, 75, A72, Bobigny, A4-E50, Coulommiers, YVELINES, St-Cloud, PARIS, Nogent, N286, Versailles, A6-E5, Champigny, CHAMPAGNE-ARDENNE, Orly, 94, Villeneuve-St-Georges, 77, SEINE-ET-MARNE, A6-E15, A10-E5, ÎLE DE FRANCE, N19, 91, Melun, ESSONNE, A5-E54, Étampes, D837, Fontainebleau, CENTRE, A6-E15, BOU

MAP KEY
- ● Hotspot
- ● Major town/city
- ✈ Airports
- ⛴ Ferries
- 66 Road numbers

92 HAUTS-DE-SEINE
93 SEINE-SAINT-DENIS
94 VAL-DE-MARNE

1. Arrondissement 1

ESSENTIALS ■ **Population** 1999: 16,895 ■ **Taxes** Taxe d'habitation: 5.88%, Taxe foncière: 6.65%
■ **Airport** Aéroport de Paris Orly, Orly Sud, Orly Aérogare Cedex; Tel: +33 1 49 75 15 15; www.adp.fr

KEY FACTS

■ **Schools** Nearest: 8ème and 7ème.
■ **Medical** Clinique du Louvre, 17 rue des Prêtes, Saint-Germain l'Auxerrois, 75001 Paris; +33 1 53 40 60 60; www.cliniquedulouvre.com ■ Clinique Mont-Louis, 8, 10 rue de la Foile, Régnaut, 75011 Paris; Tel: +33 1 43 56 56 56; www.clinique-mont-louis.fr
■ **Rental** Excellent. Arguably the most popular arrondissement with tourists, the rental season is year-round here ■ Weekly prices for the rent of a two-bedroom apartment range between €500 and €1,700 depending on the arrondissement
■ **Pros** A sense of community exists ■ A car is not necessary, because of the proximity to other arrondissements and the metro ■ Many roads are pedestrianised and it is a lively locale ■ It borders the nightlife and clubs of La Seinne and Le Marais
■ **Cons** It becomes packed with tourists ■ Property prices are high as the locale is exclusive

Located on the Right Bank, the 1er arrondissement is the geographical and historical heart of the capital. It's the setting for the Louvre, Les Halles, the Palais Royal. You can also find unusual, little-known residences, one being the US Consulate, located in the one-time palace of the famous Talleyrand. There are magnificent apartments for sale in blocks on the Rue de Rivoli overlooking the Tuileries and Palais Royal gardens, and renovated apartments are available near Les Halles. Place Vendôme is another elegant area.

Ile de la Cité is home to some of the greatest sights – the Gothic Notre-Dame Cathedral; Sainte-Chapelle, with its spectacular stained glass windows; and the Conciergerie, where Marie Antoinette was held prisoner. Spacious, quiet apartments with high ceilings and thick walls are hidden behind the courtyards of a few select commercial façades.

Home to the second most expensive property market in Paris, you can easily pay well into the millions for both apartments and houses here. The starting price for a two-bedroom apartment in a Directoire building is about €500,000. Be aware that the 18th- and 19th-century listed buildings here cannot be altered in any way. The majority of buyers remain between 25 and 45 and although international demand has seen prices more than treble in 10 years, the market has stabilised. ●

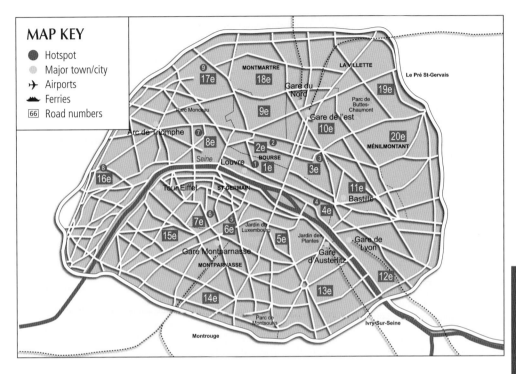

MAP KEY

- 🔴 Hotspot
- 🔘 Major town/city
- ✈ Airports
- ⛴ Ferries
- 66 Road numbers

2. Arrondissement 2 ∎

ESSENTIALS ∎ **Population**: 1999: 90,697 ∎ **Taxes** Taxe d'habitation: 5.88%, Taxe foncière: 6.65%
∎ **Airport** Aéroport de Paris Orly, Orly Sud, Orly Aérogare Cedex; Tel: +33 1 49 75 15 15; www.adp.fr

Primarily a business district and home to the Paris stock market (Bourse) and the Bibliothèque Nationale, the 2ème arrondissement is located between the Palais Royal and the grand boulevards. In the last couple of years, prices in this area have increased more than in any other. Although most Parisians tend to rent here, buyers can occasionally find a bargain apartment near the Bourse.

Once the workers have left the area for the weekend, the district acquires a much more laid back feel. You will find bargains in old-style shops among the maze of small alleys, cinema buffs can delight in exploring the cinemas, along the Boulevard des Capucines, and the Rex, an art deco building famous for its star-studded vault is located at 1 Boulevard Poissonnière. Gourmets may wish to visit Legrand, a family-run *épicerie* and wine merchant which has delighted Parisians since 1880, or you could dine at Vaudeville, which is a classic 1930s brasserie, very popular with finance workers. Property here is not as expensive as in the 1ème, 6ème and 7ème.

You could acquire a south-facing two- or three-bedroom apartment of 86 square metres in a 17th-century building with exposed beams, fireplace, living room, equipped kitchen, bedroom overlooking a courtyard and basement parking from around €550,000. ●

KEY FACTS

∎ **Schools** Nearest: 8ème, as listed.
∎ **Medical** Centre de Santé, Réaumur, 75008 Paris; Tel: +33 1 55 80 56 18
∎ **Rental** The letting potential is excellent; there is no real end of season here ∎ The months from November to January are slightly cheaper ∎ Average weekly price for a one-bedroom apartment is €680 and you can double this figure for two bedrooms ∎ Location, decor and size are the key deciding factors for cost ∎ It is a business district first, but tourist favourites are included in the mix, so it offers a good mix of potential tenants
∎ **Pros** A fabulous place to live, there is no need for a car here and it is easy to walk to the opera district in the nearby 9ème arrondissement
∎ **Cons** 18th- and 19th-century buildings that are listed in this locale cannot be changed in any way

3. Arrondissement 3 (Le Marais quarter) ▬▬▬▬▬▬▬

ESSENTIALS ■ **Population** 1999: 34,248 ■ **Taxes** Taxe d'habitation: 5.88%, Taxe foncière: 6.65%
■ **Airport** Aéroport de Paris Orly, Orly Sud, Orly Aérogare Cedex; Tel: +33 1 49 75 15 15; www.adp.fr

KEY FACTS

■ **Schools** Nearest: 15ème, 8ème
■ **Medical** Centre Médico Social OSE, 106 rue Vieille du Tenyle, 75003 Paris;
Tel: +33 1 48 87 87 85
■ **Rental** Excellent, purchasing property in this arrondissement is a surefire investment ■ Factors such as an apartment's decor can attract higher fees ■ The average weekly rental cost for a one-bedroom apartment is €850 ■ Three-bedroom apartments cost around €1,800 per week, and five-bedroom homes almost €3,000
■ **Pros** A quiet, dignified area where many 17th-century homes remain ■ The Picasso Museum and the Carnavalet Museum are located here, making it a great area for buying to let ■ The métro and proximity to central Paris make a car unnecessary ■ The 1er, 2ème, 4ème, 11ème and 10ème arrondissements surround the 3ème, so there are incredible amenities on the doorstep
■ **Cons** A lively, buzzy area, there is always a lot of activity and buyers wanting a quiet life could find it rather noisy

The Marais quarter (3ème arrondissement) is a trendy area with a lively, cultural feel. It features the oldest buildings in Paris, some of which are medieval, while many 17th-century mansions that once belonged to the noblest Parisian families and merchants are still to be seen in this quiet, impressively preserved neighbourhood. Originally, monks and knights settled in this arrondissement that was once just a patch of marshland but it was only at the beginning of the 17th century that the Marais began its reputation as a centre of regal elegance.

Generally high-priced with a few exceptions along the Right Bank, there are discreet cobbled lanes hiding courtyards, gardens, and grand timbered apartments. There are also a few renovated offices, offering tall ceilings and huge windows. Many lesser-known museums like the Jewish Art and History Museum and Musée Carnavalet, which portrays Parisian history, are within walking distance. Few green open spaces exist, except for the exclusive Place des Vosges.

Properties in the 3ème have characteristically high ceilings and are generally smaller. Prices start at around €300,000 for a two-bedroom apartment but you can pay more than double this amount if you buy a place in a classic 19th-century Parisian building. ●

4. Arrondissement 4 (The Jewish quarter) ▬▬▬▬▬▬▬

ESSENTIALS ■ **Population** 1999: 30,675 ■ **Taxes** Taxe d'habitation: 5.88%, Taxe foncière: 6.65%
■ **Airport** Aéroport de Paris Orly, Orly Sud, Orly Aérogare Cedex; Tel: +33 1 49 75 15 15; www.adp.fr

KEY FACTS

■ **Schools** Nearest 15ème and 7ème, as listed
■ **Medical** Hôpital Hôtel Dieu, 1, place Pacuis Notre Dame, 75004 Paris; Tel: +33 1 42 34 82 34
■ **Rental** Excellent, there is no shortage of tourists renting here, so purchasing a property here is a sensible investment ■ November to January is considered a little quieter, but no firm rental end of season ■ The second most expensive area in Paris, a one-bedroom apartment costs on average €980 per week ■ Four-bedroom houses cost more than €3,000 per week
■ **Pros** The historic heart of the city, its oldest landmarks, Île Saint-Louis, Île de la Cité, the Saint-Chapelle and Notre-Dame churches are here ■ Offering trendy designer boutiques, bars and restaurants and the Centre Pompidou ■ A strong alternative scene, with plenty of theatres
■ **Cons** A busy and noisy area, it is not to every buyer's taste, as this is where many Parisians come to be entertained

The centre of the Marais is a fun, lively and mainly young neighbourhood with a strong Bohemian flavour and it houses many trendy bars, shops, and restaurants. The Rue des Rosiers is a centrepiece of Jewish lifestyle in Paris, while the Ile Saint-Louis and the Ile de la Cité are the oldest parts of Paris. Nestled between the Latin Quarter and the Marais, leafy Ile Saint-Louis has a tranquil village atmosphere and is especially popular with well-heeled Parisians and international residents. Past luminaries include Voltaire, Cézanne, Baudelaire, Helena Rubenstein, and the Rothschilds. In summer, the island's quay is the city's favourite sunbathing spot. In the north of the locality you can find landmark attractions such as the Pompidou Centre at the heart of the Beaubourg neighbourhood. To savour fine 17th- and 18th-century architecture, explore the neighbourhood from Saint Gervais-Saint Paul (between the Rue Saint-Antoine and the Rue de Rivoli) stopping by at the Musée de la Curiosité et de la Magie, the Maison Européenne de la Photographie and the l'Hôtel de Sens, with its collection of decorative arts from the Middle Ages.

Considered trendy, as it has become increasingly popular and grown in stature, prices have risen accordingly. Three-bedroom apartments cost on average €920,000, and four-bedroom homes €1,100,000. ●

HOTSPOTS

5. Arrondissement 6 (Saint-Germain-des-Prés)

ESSENTIALS ■ **Population** 1999: 44,903 ■ **Taxes** Taxe d'habitation: 5.88%, Taxe foncière: 6.65%
■ **Airport** Aéroport de Paris Orly, Orly Sud, Orly Aérogare Cedex; Tel: +33 1 49 75 15 15; www.adp.fr

 Once the favourite haunt of Bohemians and intellectuals, this Left Bank neighbourhood, known as Saint-Germain-des-Prés, has undergone regeneration and is now fashionably chic. Designer boutiques, art galleries and bistros like Polidor, which has been serving basic hearty food since 1845, can be found throughout this district. Stop for coffee at Les Deux Magots, the place where Jean-Paul Sartre and Simone de Beauvoir spent their days absorbed in their writing, or relax in the Palais de Luxembourg gardens. Saint-Germain's legendary nightlife remains a major draw.

Buyers who appreciate period architecture will find some superb 19th-century properties in this district. Two-bedroom homes average at around €525,000, and if you want five bedrooms expect to pay upwards of €2,000,000.

Alternatively there is the classic six or seven-storey classic Haussmann mansion apartment, complete with wrought-iron balconies, railings and ornamental stonework. Close to the Jardin de Luxembourg, you can find apartments with wood panelling and high ceilings, but they sell at a premium. Popular with foreign businessmen and well heeled students at universities, two-bedroom apartments often cost more than €600,000, and you can spend much more than this. ●

KEY FACTS

■ **Schools** Nearest: 15ème, as listed
■ **Medical** Institut Arther Vernes, 36 rue d'Assas, 75006 Paris; +33 144 39 5300; www.institut-vernes.fr
■ **Rental** Excellent potential as one of the top four tourist arrondissements, guaranteeing year-round rental income ■ One-bedroom apartments can be let for around €800 per week ■ Three-bedroom homes fetch around €2,000 per week
■ **Pros** On the Left Bank, it is part of the famous Latin Quarter and home to the Luxembourg Palace, art, antiques, bookshops and stylish boutiques ▥ An up-and-coming, chic part of Paris following a makeover from its Bohemian roots, it is currently 'the' arrondissement ■ Posh boutiques, art galleries, theatres, nightclubs and restaurants are in plentiful supply ▥ Near to the Eiffel Tower, in the 7ème
■ **Cons** Properties here can cost from €6,500 per square metre. ▥ One of the most sought-after areas

6. Arrondissement 7

ESSENTIALS ▥ **Population** 1999: 56,988 ■ **Taxes** Taxe d'habitation: 5.88%, Taxe foncière: 6.65%
■ **Airport** Aéroport de Paris Orly, Orly Sud, Orly Aérogare Cedex; Tel: +33 1 49 75 15 15; www.adp.fr

 The 7ème is one of the city's chic postcodes, with traditional, bourgeois character. Bordered to the north by the Seine, with the 6ème to the east and the 15ème lying southwest, it is a draw for tourists. Here you will find the Musée d'Orsay with its Impressionist art collections, Les Invalides, where you can stroll along the impressive esplanade, and the Eiffel Tower. It's also home to the Assemblée Nationale, where you can drop in to listen to a debate. This expensive, well kept area with chic apartments has a reputation for being quiet and safe; indeed, the French prime minister and several of the ministries are housed around Faubourg and Saint Germain.

The grand and private Boulevard des Invalides affords some beautiful architecture. Most of the period buildings are handsome, solid and discreet, but there are modern exceptions. A penthouse with magical views overlooking the main monuments and Montmartre sell for between €1,500 000 and €2,500 000.

The 7ème is an expensive part of town and prices are higher than in the Marais. Apartments in mansion blocks have underground parking and security. The west side, from Esplanade des Invalides up to the 15ème, is much cheaper. Two-bedroom apartments here average at around €760 000; four-bedroom homes cost around €1,000,000. ●

KEY FACTS

■ **Schools** Nearest: 7ème, 15ème, as listed
■ **Medical** Hôpital de Jour 39, rue Varennes, 75007 Paris; Tel: +33 1 45 48 96 31
■ **Rental** Excellent. One of the top four tourist arrondissements so any property purchase here is a watertight investment ▥ Pretty much a year-round rental season, though slightly more quiet in the winter months ■ The average weekly letting price for a two-bedroom apartment is €1,170 ■ Four-bedroom homes can raise €2,200 per week
■ **Pros** A sought-after, select residential arrondissement. The main highlights are the Eiffel Tower, the Musée d'Orsay and the Hôtel des Invalides, where Napoleon's tomb is located ▥ A wealthy, Left Bank district ■ Filled with dwellings and offices, this central location affords good employment opportunities ▥ A central location where a car is not necessary ▥ Other attractions are Parc Georges Brassens, the swimming pool theme park Aquaboulevard and the Musée Rodin
■ **Cons** Very busy at weekends in the west side of the arrondissement, it attracts lots of tourists ▥ Fewer shops, restaurants and cinemas

HOTSPOTS

7. Arrondissement 8

ESSENTIALS ■ **Population** 1999: 39,303 ■ **Taxes** Taxe d'habitation: 5.88%, Taxe foncière: 6.65%
■ **Airport** Aéroport de Paris Orly, Orly Sud, Orly Aérogare Cedex; Tel: +33 1 49 75 15 15; www.adp.fr

KEY FACTS

■ **Schools** Nearest: 8ème, as listed
■ **Medical** Hôpital Européen Georges Pompidou, 20 rue Leblanc, 75908 Paris Cedex 15; www.hbroussais.fr/HEGP/
■ **Rental** Good. The best sized property is a two-bedroom property and for higher rates it is best to offer rental on a short-term basis ■ Two-bedroom apartments can fetch €1,700 per week ■ There is less of a rental scene, but it is still a prime area ■ Management costs for rental properties can be high
■ **Pros** Encompasses the Champs-Elysées, the Arc de Triomphe, the Elysées Palace, the Madeleine Church and the Avenue Montaigne and Faubourg Saint-Honoré fashion houses ■ The traditional Paris, it features the more residential, Haussmann-style buildings ■ Property prices are slightly lower than in 1ème to 6ème ■ A car is unnecessary, as there is excellent public transport
■ **Cons** Tourists from all over the world flock here ■ Surrounding cafés, bars and restaurants are fearsomely expensive

This Right Bank arrondissement of 8ème is the city's most expensive neighbourhood. You can discover elegant hotels and first-class restaurants, such as the Buddha Bar, in this vibrant and elite arrondissement, along with the presidential Elysée Palace, the Champs-Elysées, the *haute couture* boutiques of the Rue Saint-Honoré and palatial hotels like the George V and the Crillon.

In the area to the east, between the Champs-Elysées and Place de la Madeleine, there is a mixture of 19th-century buildings interspersed with businesses. History buffs can visit Place de la Concorde, the Luxor obelisk, and Eglise de la Madeleine for sculpture and architecture.

One of the most sought-after locales, this is a family-orientated, beautiful part of Paris. It is also close to the lively 4ème, and yet it offers a tranquil retreat. Hugely sought after by international buyers, the 8ème arrondissement is a quiet residential area and an excellent investment for those who can afford it.

If you appreciate scenic views, you can buy a top-floor, four-room apartment from around €1,600,000. At the top end of the market, a third-floor apartment inside a Haussmann-period mansion block costs around €2,300,000. However, it is still possible to pick up a one-bedroom apartment for under €350,000. ●

8. Arrondissement 16

ESSENTIALS ■ **Population** 1999: 161,817 ■ **Taxes** Taxe d'habitation: 5.88%, Taxe foncière: 6.65%
■ **Airport** Aéroport de Paris Orly, Orly Sud, Orly Aérogare Cedex; Tel: +33 1 49 75 15 15; www.adp.fr

KEY FACTS

■ **Schools** Nearest: 16ème, 8ème (as listed)
■ **Medical** Hôpital Européen Georges Pompidou, 20 rue Leblanc, 75908 Paris Cedex 15; www.hbboussais.fr/HEGP/ ■ Centre Médical Edouaurd Rist, 14, rue Boileau, 75016 Paris; Tel: +33 1 40 50 52 00
■ **Rental** Good, but priced slightly lower than other areas ■ Short-term rentals are better value and two-bedroom properties are most popular ■ One-bedroom flats average at just over €700 per week ■ Expect to receive around €940 for a two-bedroom apartment ■ Steep management costs for short-term lets ■ Older residents means it is not as lively as the 1er to 8ème
■ **Pros** The locale of wealthy Parisians ■ The Bois de Boulogne and Trocadéro are here (home to government institutions) ■ A growing number of international buyers ■ Near the Trocadéro, the Musée de la Marine and the well known Musée de l'Homme, specialising in anthropology
■ **Cons** This quiet locale would not suit every purchaser or tenant ■ Not much nightlife

This residential area – formerly the village of Passy and one of the biggest arrondissements – runs west from the Arc de Triomphe out to Bois de Boulogne, the city's huge, rambling park where many locals run or ride horses. It is another area of expensive property, with large apartments both old and modern. In the west of the arrondissement, there is little street life and it is a quiet area at night. Further west, the district of Neuilly, is similar and ideal for buyers seeking tranquility.

Literary lovers can visit the apartment of Balzac, who wrote the Comédie Humaine. Close by, the Musée Marmottan boasts the largest number of Monet paintings in the world.

Geographically the largest arrondissement, the 16ème is very smart. Property is frequently owned and let by insurance companies and a growing number of Middle-Eastern purchasers are buying here. With more residential emphasis than in other arrondissements, classic Haussmann buildings can sell for many millions of euros.

The older areas with very quiet avenues, are located in the south and east near the Trocadéro, and apartments here cost slightly more than the area's average. On the whole, two-bedroom apartments average at €518,000, and four-bedroom homes cost around €1,500,000. ●

9. Arrondissement 17

ESSENTIALS ■ **Population** 1999: 161,138 ■ **Taxes** Taxe d'habitation: 5.88%, Taxe foncière: 6.65%
■ **Airport** Aéroport de Paris Orly, Orly Sud, Orly Aérogare Cedex; Tel: +33 1 49 75 15 15; www.adp.fr

This diverse district contains several residential areas, including the upmarket western part near the Arc de Triomphe. It is generally a chic area, but smaller and more accessible than the 16ème; it shares the pleasant Monceau park with the 8ème. Many embassies are based here, and there are more artists' studios than any other arrondissement. Areas like the Place des Ternes have a lively feel to them, while the Marché des Moines is one of the cheapest markets in the capital, with a warm and lively atmosphere. Luxury boutiques such as Kenzo, Armani and Louis Vuitton can be found here too.

It's a quiet, deserted area after office hours, although you can visit the Palais des Congrès which hosts various exhibitions. Most buildings are 19th-century and have bigger rooms than most other arrondissements.

One to three-bedroom apartments, with security and underground parking can be found for between €300,000 and €1,000,000. Alternatively, the quiet residential area between Portes de Champerret and Maillot, close to the Arc de Triomphe is ideal for a brand new, two-bedroom apartment. The classic Haussmann-style apartments start from around €490,000. Prices in the Arc de Triomphe and Parc Monceau area to the west are more expensive. Prices increase in neighbourhoods near to Neuilly in the north. ●

KEY FACTS

■ **Schools** Nearest: 16ème, 8ème and 17ème
■ **Medical** Centre Médico-Physique, 174, rue Courcelles, 75017 Paris; Tel: +33 1 45 74 75 15
■ **Rental** Lower rental available, but still a good location. Traditional Haussmann buildings are found in this residential part of the city. Short-term lets are better value ■ Two-bedroom properties are the best investment for buyers to let; they fetch on average about €1,400 per week ■ There is no real end of season here; perhaps November to January tend to be slightly cheaper ■ High management costs for short-term lets ■ Parts of the area are quiet, which could deter tourist tenants
■ **Pros** One of the more wealthy areas ■ A growing number of international foreign buyers ■ Smaller than the 16ème, it has a sense of community ■ A lively outlook, it has great restaurants, bars and nightclubs
■ **Cons** High management costs for short-term lets ■ Parts of the area are considered as lacking in life and activity, which could deter tourist tenants

10. Versailles

ESSENTIALS ■ **Population** 1999: 85,726 ■ **Taxes** Taxe d'habitation: 4.80%, Taxe foncière: 4.60%
■ **Airport** Aéroport de Paris Orly, Orly Sud, Orly Aérogare Cedex; Tel: +33 1 49 75 15 1;, www.adp.fr

Situated in département 78, Versailles is undoubtedly best known for the sumptuous palace of the same name that was created by Louis XIV to glorify his reign as the Sun King. Yet Versailles is also a stylish suburb of Paris, where elegant homes are to be found and there is easy access to the city centre by means of the train. It's well served by the Paris D10 and A13 autoroutes, but far enough out to feel a whole world away from the life of the city.

Versailles will be especially attractive to those property buyers who are happy to commute in return for plenty of spacious parkland. King Louis XIV was a great patron of the arts, hence theatre, festivals and fêtes dominate the cultural scene.

Characterised by its 17th- and 18th-century buildings, a market, shops and the Rive Gauche railway station with routes into central Paris, the Left Bank Saint-Louis area of Versailles is the oldest quarter, and has been regenerated over the past decade. Filled with exclusive boutiques, it's a desirable locale. The average four-bedroom home costs €800,000, but you can pay a lot more for period homes. A good choice for families is the peaceful, leafy area of Gatigny. Here, a two-bedroom apartment costs around €450,000. However, those will smaller budgets will be able to find apartments for between €200,000 and €300,000. ●

KEY FACTS

■ **Schools** British School of Paris, 38 quai de l'Ecluse, 78290 Croissy-sur-Seine; Tel: 33 1 34 80 45 90 ■ Lycée International of Saint-Germain-en-Laye (American School) Rue du Fer à Cheval, BP 230, 78104 Saint-Germain-en-Laye; Tel: +33 1 34 51 74 85
■ **Medical** Clinique Internationale du Parc Monceau, 21 rue de Chazelles, 75017 Paris; Tel: +33 1 48 88 25 25; www.cinique-monceau.com
■ **Rental** Average; mostly long-term lets for people who work in the city ■ A small apartment on a long-term basis is cheaper than in central Paris, attracting young marrieds ■ Two-bedroom apartments average at around €1,300 per week
■ **Pros** An oasis of history, a select and glamorous area ■ More peaceful than the centre ■ The Avenue de la Reine, or Queen's Avenue, is a beautiful place to live ■ Good local amenities and new shopping centres ■ A community in itself
■ **Cons** Taxis from the centre are expensive ■ Traffic jams between Paris and Versailles are common ■ The RER (suburban train system) can take up to an hour to reach central Paris

DANIEL THIERRY

USEFUL CONTACTS

PREFECTURE
Préfecture de la Région d'Ile-de-France
29 rue Barbet de Jouy
75007 Paris
Tel: +33 1 44 42 63 75
www.idf.pref.gouv.fr

LEGAL
Chambre des notaires de Paris
12 avenue Victoria
75001 Paris
Tel: +33 1 44 82 24 82
www.paris.notaires.fr

Chambre Interdépartementale des Notaires de Versailles
40 avenue de Paris
78000 Versailles
Tel: +33 1 39 50 01 75
www.chambre-versailles.notaires.fr

FINANCE
Direction des Impôts d'Ile-de-France
33 avenue de l'Opéra
75002 Paris
Tel: +33 1 44 77 99 59

Centre des Impôts des Non-Résidents
9 rue d'Uzès
75094 Paris Cedex 02
Tel: +33 1 44 76 18 00

BUILDING AND PLANNING
Chambre Régionale de Métiers d'Ile-de-France
72/74 rue de Reuilly
75592 Paris Cedex 12
Tel: +33 1 53 33 53 60
www.cm-idf.fr

Union Régionale des CAUEs d'Ile-de-France
9 Rue du Docteur Berger
92330 Sceaux
Tel: +33 1 48 52 05 24

EDUCATION
Rectorat de l'Académie de Creteil (Seine-et-Marne, Seine-saint-Denis, Val-de-
Marne)
4, Rue Georges Enesco
94000 Creteil
Tel: +33 1 49 81 60 60
www.ac-creteil.fr

Rectorat de l'Académie de Paris
94 Avenue Ganbetta
75984 Paris Cedex 20
Tel: +33 1 44 62 40 40
www.ac-paris.fr

Rectorat de l'Académie de Versailles
(Essonne, Hauts-de-Seine, Val-d'Oise, Yvelines)
3 boulevard de Lesseps
78017 Versailles Cedex
Tel: +33 1 30 83 44 44
www.ac-versailles.fr

HEALTH
Caisse Primaire d'Assurance Maladie de Paris
21 rue Georges Auric
75948 Paris Cedex 19
Tel: +33 1 53 38 70 00

www.cpam-paris.fr

Caisse Primaire d'Assurance Maladie des Yvelines
92 avenue de Paris
78014 Versailles
Tel: +33 1 39 20 30 00
www.cpam-yvelines.fr

INTERNATIONAL SCHOOLS
Ecole Active Bilangue
117 Boulevard Malesherbes
75008 Paris
Tel: +33 1 45 63 47 00
www.eab.fr

Ecole Active Bilingue
Jeannine Manuel
70 rue du Théâtre
75015 Paris
Tel: +33 1 44 37 00 80
www.eabjm.com

International School of Paris
6 rue Beethoven
75016 Paris
Tel: +33 1 42 24 09 54

€200,000–€1,000,000
(£138,889–£694,444)

A selection of properties just outside and within the capital

€236,250	CODE FPS

NEAR FONTAINEBLEAU, SEINE-ET-MARNE

A very large old house in a lovely village with a convertible loft and barn

£164,062

🛏 4   ✽ *With garden*   🖼 *Situated in a quiet village*   🏠 *Located on a main road*

🏠 *Room for parking*

€310,000	CODE SIF

NEAR COULOMMIERS, SEINE-ET-MARNE

This former presbytery, dating from the 19th century, is in very good general order

£215,278

🛏 4   ✽ *4,500m²*   🖼 *Situated in a peaceful hamlet*   🏠 *Not located on a main road*

🏠 *Room for parking*

€375,000	CODE DEM

NEAR FONTAINEBLEAU, SEINE-ET-MARNE

This villa was built in 1985 and is in good condition inside and out

£260,416

🛏 4   ✽ *800m²*   🖼 *Situated at the edge of a forest*   🏠 *Not located on a main road*

🏠 *Room for parking, with a garage for 2 cars*

€575,000	CODE VEF

16ÈME

These newly built unfurnished apartments are in one of the largest *arrondissements*

£399,305

🛏 1   ✽ *No garden*   🖼 *Situated in the city*   🏠 *Located on a main road*

🏠 *No private parking*

€576,800	CODE AMR

8ÈME

This 3rd floor apartment is just 100 metres from the famous Champs-Elysées

£400,556

🛏 2   ✽ *Balcony*   🖼 *Situated in central Paris*   🏠 *Located on a main road*

🏠 *No private parking*

€634,400

TAVERNY, VAL D'OISE

This lovely detached house is set over 3 floors and has many original features
£440,556

🛏 5 ❋ 1,387m² 🖼 *Situated just outside Paris* 🚧 *Located on a main road*
🏠 *Room for parking, with 3-car garage*

€636,000

NEAR FONTAINEBLEAU, SEINE-ET-MARNE

A charming 17th-century *manoir* in good order but requiring some redecoration
£441,667

🛏 6 ❋ 10,000m² 🖼 *Situated in the countryside* 🚧 *Not located on a main road*
🏠 *Room for parking*

€814,500

VAL D'OISE

This classic 16th-century *manoir* comes with a caretaker's house to renovate
£565,625

🛏 4 ❋ 2,300m² 🖼 *Situated 2 kms from amenities* 🚧 *Not located on a main road*
🏠 *Room for parking, with a garage*

€824,749

16ÈME

A luxury apartment in the heart of Paris with a fully fitted kitchen and shower room
£572,742

🛏 3 ❋ *Balcony* 🖼 *Situated in the centre of Paris* 🚧 *Located on a main road*
🏠 *Underground parking*

€945,000

PORTE D'ORLÉANS, NEAR PARIS

This property was renovated in 2003, as was the old circus caravan in the grounds
£656,250

🛏 3 ❋ 10,000m² 🖼 *Situated 20 minutes from Paris* 🚧 *Not located on a main road*
🏠 *Room for parking*

€945,183

ESSONNE, NEAR PARIS

A beautiful 18th-century *manoir* on the banks of the Seine, with stunning views
£656,377

🛏 8 ❋ 9,400m² 🖼 *Situated in a quiet village* 🚧 *Not located on a main road*
🏠 *Room for parking*

€1,000,000–€2,000,000
(£694,444–£1,388,889)

Expect a decent apartment in the city or a substantial property a short drive away

€1,013,000	CODE AMR

16ÈME

A unique property that resembles a miniature medieval castle

£703,472

🛏 3 ✽ No garden 🖼 Situated in the centre of Paris 🚩 Located on a main road
🏠 Room for parking

€1,020,000	CODE DAK

16ÈME

A quality flat in a modern building with lovely views of the Eiffel Tower

£708,333

🛏 3 ✽ Balcony 🖼 Situated in the centre of Paris 🚩 Located on a main road
🏠 No private parking

€1,050,000	CODE CHA

NEAR CHARTRES

A classic manor house set in large grounds with outbuildings. 70km from Paris

£729,166

🛏 8 ✽ 28,000m² 🖼 Situated in beautiful parkland 🚩 Not located on a main road
🏠 Room for parking, with a garage

€1,162,000	CODE DEM

RIVER SEINE, PARIS

A luxury river boat with state-of-the-art equipment and a jacuzzi

£806,944

🛏 6 ✽ – 🖼 Moored in the centre of Paris 🚩 Located on the river
🏠 With a private docking space in Paris

€1,166,000	CODE SIF

FONTAINEBLEAU, SEINE-ET-MARNE

This superb 18th-century *manoir* is set in almost a hectare of forest land

£809,722

🛏 11 ✽ 9,880m² 🖼 Situated 75 kms from Paris 🚩 Not located on a main road
🏠 Room for parking

PRICE GUIDE

€1,300,000
CODE SIF

ESSONNE, NEAR PARIS
This historic building was once restored by the famous fascist Sir Oswald Mosley
£902,778

6 | 14,400m² | Situated in a charming park | Not located on a main road
Room for parking

€1,364,000
CODE CHA

NEAR CHEVREUSE
A charming manor house set in wooded grounds with a pool and a secondary house
£947,222

6 | 13,000m² | Situated in a quiet rural area | Not located on a main road
Room for parking, with a garage

€1,411,000
CODE AMR

NEAR PARIS
An exceptional modern residence set in large secure wooded grounds
£979,861

4 | 4,800m² | Situated 5 minutes from Paris | Not located on a main road
Room for parking

€1,440,000
CODE SIF

8ÈME
A luxuriously renovated contemporary apartment in the heart of the city
£1,000,000

2 | – | Situated in the centre of Paris | Located on a main road
With private parking

€1,500,000
CODE DEM

ESSONNE, NEAR PARIS
A large 15th-century residence split into two distinct wings with separate entrances
£1,041,667

6 | 750m² | Situated 15 kms from Paris | Not located on a main road
Room for parking, with a garage for 2 cars

€1,830,000
CODE SIF

YVELINES
A beautiful listed 18th-century château requiring extensive work throughout
£1,270,833

19 | 50,000m² | Situated in the Seine valley | Not located on a main road
Room for parking

€2,000,000+
(£1,388,889+)

Take your pick from prestigious townhouses, châteaux and even a palace

€2,100,000   CODE DEM

NEAR NEMOURS, SEINE-ET-MARNE
A luxurious estate consisting of 8 major buildings with an indoor swimming pool
£1,458,333

🛏 12 ⬡ 62,000m² 🏞 Situated in quiet location 🚫 Not located on a main road
🏠 Room for parking, with garages

€2,160,000   CODE DEM

16ÈME
This charming mansion is located on a private street in a chic part of the city
£1,500,000

🛏 4 ⬡ Large terrace 🏞 Situated in the centre of Paris 🚫 Located on a private
street 🏠 Room for parking

€2,250,000   CODE CHA

NEAR ORSAY
A prestigious manor house and estate with plenty of potential for expansion
£1,562,500

🛏 10 ⬡ 110,000m² 🏞 Situated 20km from Paris 🚫 Not located on a main road
🏠 Room for parking

€2,420,000   CODE CHA

ESSONNE, NEAR PARIS
A large contemporary property in excellent condition throughout with pool
£1,680,556

🛏 8 ⬡ 5,600m² 🏞 Situated 24km from Paris 🚫 Not located on a main road
🏠 Room for parking

€2,800,000   CODE CHA

16ÈME
A beautiful apartment in excellent condition with a studio flat in need of work
£1,944,444

🛏 4 ⬡ No garden 🏞 Situated in the centre of Paris 🚫 Located on a main road
🏠 Private parking nearby

€3,000,000   CODE SIF

NEAR PARIS
Built in 1860, this elegant property is situated in 200-year-old parkland
£2,083,333

🛏 6   🌸 3,800m²   🏞 Situated 7 minutes from La Défense   🛣 Not located on a main road   🅿 Room for parking

€3,500,000   CODE CHA

RAMBOUILLET, NEAR PARIS
This huge country estate and hunting lodge has it all, including stables and kennels
£2,430,556

🛏 12   🌸 1,000,000m²   🏞 Situated in the forest   🛣 Not located on a main road   🅿 Room for parking

€3,700,000   CODE CHA

3ÈME
This beautiful townhouse is right in the centre of Paris, next to the Pompidou Centre
£2,569,444

🛏 5   🌸 No garden   🏞 Situated in the centre of Paris   🛣 Located on a main road   🅿 Room for parking

€5,500,000   CODE CHA

SEINE-ET-MARNE
A prestigious mansion in a residential district along the Marne river
£3,819,444

🛏 5   🌸 1,600m²   🏞 Situated 10km from Paris   🛣 Not located on a main road   🅿 Underground parking for 8 cars

€6,000,000   CODE CHA

16ÈME
An impressive apartment in the largest *arrondissement* with splendid views
£4,166,667

🛏 3   🌸 No garden   🏞 Situated in the centre of Paris   🛣 Located on a main road   🅿 Room for parking, with a garage for 2 cars

€8,000,000   CODE CHA

NEAR PARIS
This exceptional Louis XIV-styled palace is set in large grounds with outbuildings
£5,555,556

🛏 6   🌸 7,131m²   🏞 Situated 10km from Paris   🛣 Not located on a main road   🅿 Room for parking

The fastest way to Brittany

Your **life in the sun** starts here

Champagne-Ardenne

Great forests, picturesque 16th-century Troyes, and Champagne

SOREN RASMUSSEN

FACT BOX 2005

■ **Population** 1,342,363
■ **Migration** 81,861
■ **Unemployment** 31,132
■ **Median home price** €128,400
■ **House price increase** Since 2002, house prices
have increased by 15.1%

Price Guide

PROFILE

AIR Ryanair (0871 246 0000; www.ryanair.com) flies to Reims from London Stansted. **Air France** (0845 359 1000; www.airfrance.co.uk), **British Airways** (0870 850 9850; www.britishairways.com), **BMI Baby** (0870 264 2229; www.bmibaby.com), **British European** (0870 567 6676; www.flybe.com) and **British Midland** all operate flights from various UK airports to Paris, where connections are available via air, rail and road to Champagne-Ardenne. For northern Champagne-Ardenne, Brussels-South Charleroi may be more convenient than Paris, and **Ryanair** flies to Charleroi from Glasgow, Liverpool and London Stansted.

ROAD The A26 runs from the ferry port at Calais straight through to Reims. Change on to the N43 at Arras for Charleville-Mézières. From Paris the A4 runs straight to Reims, and the N51 runs from Reims to Épernay.

COACH Eurolines coaches (0870 514 3219; www.eurolines.com) travel from the UK to Reims, Troyes and Chaumont.

RAIL TGV trains serve Reims, while SNCF services operate from Paris Gare de l'Est and Reims, Châlons-en-Champagne, Troyes and Charleville-Mézières. You could take the **Eurostar** (0870 518 6186; www.eurostar.co.uk) to Lille-Europe and from there SNCF services to Champagne-Ardenne. For all rail enquiries and more details about local services, contact **Rail Europe** (0870 584 8848; www.raileurope.co.uk).

Area profile

THE CHAMPAGNE-ARDENNE REGION IN THE NORTHEAST OF FRANCE IS the home of the famous sparkling wine, which has been produced here since the 17th century. The landscape encompasses the Ardenne Massif hills, consisting of hundreds of thousands of acres of forest, great lakes, and miles of waterways.

The biggest city in the region is Reims, home to one of France's finest buildings, the magnificent Gothic Cathédrale Notre-Dame which dates back to 1211. It's a handsome city with wide avenues and a wealth of parks and just two hours from Paris. South of Reims is Épernay, the Champagne-producing capital and the home of Moët et Chandon, which has 30 km of cellars. Picturesque Troyes in the south of Champagne-Ardenne is home to 16th-century half-timbered houses that sit on narrow streets.

Champagne-Ardenne's countryside has much to offer, too. The *route touristique du Champagne* is a pleasant drive through many acres of vineyards, and southwest of Reims, the *Parc Naturel Régional de la Montagne de Reims* offers lots of interesting trails, and some unusual botany to boot

Ardennes in the north provides lots of water-based activities including sailing, canoeing and fishing, while its dense forests encourage exploration on foot. The most southerly *département* is Haute-Marne, home to the feudal town of Chaumont, which has some impressive Renaissance architecture.

The cuisine in Champagne-Ardenne is characterised by the region's abundant wild game. Troyes is best-known for its speciality sausages known as *andouillettes*, which are filled with thin slices of pig's stomach and onion – you can even eat them raw – and Ardennes is renowned for its quality hams. Naturally, champagne is the region's biggest draw, although many other wines are produced, including rosés and still reds.

Like many regions in Northern France, the weather is extremely variable.

Champagne-Ardenne is covered with many acres of vineyards

THE CHAMPAGNE INFORMATION BUREAU – JOHN HODDER

Champagne-Ardenne is certainly slightly colder than the South, but the summers are mostly warm and dry.

The economy and housing market

Wine and champagne (including Moët et Chandon, Mercier and Krug) production have driven the economy of this region, specifically in Épernay and Reims, since the 16th century. Hi-tech industries are now developing in Reims and Charleville-Mézières on the industrial park, the *Centre régional d'innovation et de transfert de technologie*. Tourism is increasing in Reims and the Champagne-producing areas, and the region's countryside is popular.

Growing tourism and an established wine industry have made Reims one of the priciest locations, yet demand for relocation still makes the area a sound investment. Demand far outstrips supply, and a lack of rental properties has created a landlords' market.

Increasing numbers of foreign visitors and city centre regeneration plans for a shopping centre and recreation facilities give Châlons-en-Champagne similar long-term buy-to-let value, and a planned TGV link will increase its desirability. Civil servants from Brussels have pushed prices up in Charleville-Mézières, where prices for four and six-bedroom houses cost between £200,000 and £400,000. Cheaper renovation properties can be hunted out, though. Brussels commuters have also bolstered prices in Châlons-en-Champagne, where prices range between £95,000 and £220,000.

Épernay is a key buy-to-let area, with about 300,000 visitors a year, many of them British and American. Property prices here start at around £150,000. If a bargain area exists, the Vallée de la Marne would be it, with four-bedroom houses from £125,000. Bear in mind, however, that Champagne's association with luxury can make buyers willing to pay more.

Thriving employment markets in Charleville-Mézières and Reims make them ideal for relocators planning to live and work the French way. For long-term letting, Reims, Charleville-Mézières and Épernay are the best locations, but short-term seasonal letting is growing in Reims, with French, British, Belgian and German visitors. Charleville and Bogny-sur-Meuse offer tourist letting markets with high rents and a long season.

Prices are increasing throughout the region. A family house in Épernay costs around £220,000 and the same amount in Reims would buy a property with no garden. One hour from Paris by TGV, the market has soared in Reims and Épernay in the past two years.

In and around the heart of Champagne, prices are higher, and a four-bedroom house in the countryside around Verzy is about £300,000. Parisian buying power has pushed up prices in this area.

Social groups

The northern parts of Champagne-Ardenne – Charleville-Mézières in particular – attract a lot of Belgian buyers because of the commutable distance to Brussels. Much of the region is also just an hour by rail from Paris and this attracts many Parisian commuters. British buyers looking for a bargain tend to stay away from the 'Champagne triangle' which encompasses Reims, Épernay and Châlons-en-Champagne. ●

> *"Épernay is the Champagne capital of the world and the home of Krug, Mercier, and Moët et Chandon, which has 30 km of cellars"*

CHAMPAGNE-ARDENNE		LONDON	
6.2	Dec	7	
9.6	Nov	10	
15	Oct	14	
19	Sept	19	
35	Aug	21	
24	July	22	
23	June	20	
15	May	17	
14	April	13	
8.9	March	10	
5.6	Feb	7	
6.2	Jan	6	

Average monthly temperature °C (Celsius)

CHAMPAGNE-ARDENNE		LONDON	
58	Dec	81	
58	Nov	78	
66	Oct	70	
43	Sept	65	
58	Aug	62	
66	July	59	
53	June	58	
53	May	57	
48	April	56	
48	March	64	
38	Feb	72	
46	Jan	77	

Average monthly rainfall mm (millimetres)

AVERAGE HOUSE SALE PRICES

Hotspot	2-bed	3-bed	4-bed	5-bed+
Charleville-Mézières	€94K (£65K)	€122K (£85K)	€184K (£127K)	€563K (£391K)
Reims & Épernay	€153K (£106K)	€181K (£126K)	€192K (£133K)	€273K (£189K)
Châlons-en-Champagne	€139K (£96K)	€185K (£129K)	€205K (£143K)	€313K (£217K)

Property hotspots

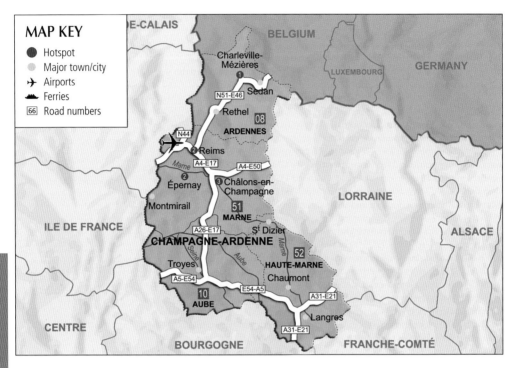

MAP KEY
- ● Hotspot
- ○ Major town/city
- ✈ Airports
- ⚓ Ferries
- [66] Road numbers

1. Charleville-Mézières and surrounds

ESSENTIALS ■ **Population** 58,092 ■ **Taxes** Taxe d'habitation: 7.68%, Taxe foncière: 12.02% ■ **Airport** Reims-Champagne Aeroport, 51450 Bétheny, Tel: +33 326 07 15 15

KEY FACTS

■ **Schools** Association des Amis de l'Enseignement International de Reims siège social, Chaussée Bocquaine, 51100 Reims, Tel: +33 326 05 15 83
■ **Medical** Centre Hospitalier, Général de Manchester, 45 avenue de Manchester, Charleville-Mézières, Tel: +33 324 58 70 70
■ **Rentals** Tourism is the main growth industry in the Ardenne area, and rental property is expensive
■ Tourists are mainly French, Dutch and Belgian, with increasing numbers of Britons ■ The average rental for a two-bedroom house stands at €270 per week
■ **Pros** Foreign buyers are mainly from Luxembourg, Denmark and Brussels ■ More English buyers are being drawn here by the many fermettes to renovate, complete with parcels of land
■ Property here is very affordable with an average two-bedroom property costing roughly €93,600
■ The perfect destination for families pursuing outdoor activity holidays
■ **Cons** Overlooked by the British market and better known to the French and Germans ■ Proximity to Brussels makes this area more expensive, with many civil servants buying property.

The region of Champagne-Ardenne is formed by deep, thickly wooded valleys, which are magnificent in any season, and it is traversed by the winding Meuse and Semoy rivers. The capital is Charleville-Mézières, formed nearly 40 years ago from two competing communities. Charleville is the birthplace of the poet Rimbaud; Mézières, the original town, was founded in AD899.

The town is now the world capital of puppetry, hosting a week-long puppet festival every three years in September. In the 17th-century Vieux Quartier, christened the 'new town', visit the Ardennes Museum; the Notre-Dame of Hope Basilica; and the Musée Rimbaud, housed in a windmill near Place Ducale, with an entire room dedicated to the young poet. A few miles away lies Sedan, site of the largest fortified château in Europe.

With more than 150,000 hectares of oak, beech and ash, the surrounding forests of the Ardenne provide plenty of hunting for wild boar and game. Local specialities reflect forest treasures, such as game cooked in wild juniper, and red turkey terrine with bacon salad. Charleville-Mézières and its surround is a popular area with foreign buyers as it is inexpensive; prices range from €93,600 for a two-bedroom house, to €183,500 for four bedrooms. ●

2. Reims and Épernay

ESSENTIALS ■ **Population** 218,358 ■ **Taxes** Taxe d'habitation: 7.68%, Taxe foncière: 12.02% ■ **Airport** Reims-Champagne Aeroport, 51450 Bétheny, Tel: +33 326 07 15 15

In the heart of Champagne, home to the vineyards of the Pinot Noir and Pinot Meunier grape varieties, historic Reims owes its fame not only to champagne, but to its numerous UNESCO treasures. The Cathedral of Our Lady is a masterpiece of Gothic architecture, housing a collection of renowned statues, and was on several occasions a coronation site for the kings of France. Even older is the Church of Saint-Rémi, half-Romanesque, half-Gothic in style, and comparable in size to the Notre-Dame-de-Paris.

Beneath the town and its suburbs are 150 miles of cellars cut into the chalk. During World War II bombing, the citizens of Reims sheltered there, but now they house more than a billion bottles of champagne! Property buyers have the pick of the champagne trail from Reims to Épernay, which covers 45 miles of Champagne's villages and the vineyards between. On the left bank of the Marne Valley, Épernay rivals Reims as a champagne producer, boasting 200 miles of cellars. If you prefer outdoor pursuits, boating on the Marne takes you past vineyards.

Buyers are prepared to pay high prices to live in the area, and interest from Paris has further increased prices. The average cost of a five-bedroom property in the area is €272,700, while two-bedroom houses start at €152,800. ●

KEY FACTS

■ **Schools** Association des Amis de l'Enseignement International de Reims siège social, Chaussée Bocquaine, 51100 Reims, Tel: +33 326 05 15 83 ■ **Medical** Centre Hospitalier Universitaire de Reims, rue Général Koenig, 51100 Reims, Tel: +33 326 78 78 78 ■ **Rentals** This area is very popular with tourists as the champagne route is centred on Reims and Épernay ■ Half the tourists are French, but there are also British, Belgians and Germans ■ The average two-bedroom property will cost €305 to rent for a week, and a four-bedroom €515 ■ **Pros** Just an hour from Paris, Reims is a popular destination and easily accessible ■ It is rich in culture and history ■ Épernay is less inspiring but is home to the champagne industry, with many cellars located in the Avenue de Champagne ■ Reims offers many smart townhouses and apartments ■ Most buyers are French, many moving here for work, not just to relocate or retire ■ The prevailing market is for permanent relocation properties ■ **Cons** Huge demand in the Reims market pushes up prices ■ Easy access from Paris to Reims also makes property very expensive ■ The demand for property is much greater than the supply.

3. Châlons-en-Champagne

ESSENTIALS ■ **Population** 48,000 ■ **Taxes** Taxe d'habitation: 6.10%, Taxe foncière: 6.48% ■ **Airport** Reims-Champagne Aeroport, 51450 Bétheny, Tel: +33 326 07 15 15

Formerly known as Châlons-sur-Marne, the creation of the capital of the Marne *département* is historically linked to Attila the Hun. Not just a champagne centre, it also produces beer, textiles and electrical equipment, and fortunately has retained its medieval architecture.

Running parallel to the Marne, the Châlons canals are spread through an area known as the Left Bank, with many stone bridges and old cafés. Close to Place Monseigneur Tissier is the town hall, which is one of the grandest buildings in the city. Also here is the famous church of Notre-Dame-en-Vaux, which is a UNESCO World Heritage site. Place Notre-Dame is surrounded by charming little ßstone houses and the Gothic cathedral of Saint-Étienne. Le Petit Jard, situated between two of the canals on the south side of town, is a peaceful riverside garden, a favourite place to stroll since the Middle Ages. Nearby, the little town of Saint-Ménéhould has contributed to the gastronomic world with its recipes for pigs' feet and carp. Just five miles from Châlons, champagne tastings take place at the Joseph Perrier estate.

In the countryside around Châlons, a renovated two-storey *maison en pierre* costs from €167,000, while within the town itself you are looking at €138,800 for a two-bedroom property. ●

KEY FACTS

■ **Schools** Association des Amis de l'Enseignement International de Reims siège social, Chaussée Bocquaine, 51100 Reims, Tel: +33 326 05 15 83 ■ **Medical** Centre Hospitalier de Châlons-en-Champagne, 51 rue du Commandant Derrien, 51000, Tel: +33 326 69 60 60 ■ **Rentals** Châlons-en-Champagne receives mainly French visitors, but many foreign tourists come between spring and autumn ■ Holiday rentals are very expensive, and rentals are mostly long term ■ Little demand for seasonal rentals, but more people are buying to let ■ A weekly rental in a two-bedroom property will cost an average of €330 ■ **Pros** Foreign tourism is on the increase, and particularly from Britain ■ The area within a three-mile radius of Châlons is very popular for buying property ■ There are excellent access routes ■ **Cons** Houses in the area are very expensive, with the lowest prices around €140,000 ■ A shortage of renovation properties here makes some people prefer to buy in the Ardenne and Argonne ■ Increasing demand for property is pushing up already high prices even further.

USEFUL CONTACTS

PRÉFECTURE

Préfecture des Ardennes

1 Place de la Préfecture
08011 Charleville-Mézières
Tel: +33 324 59 66 00
Fax: +33 324 58 35 21
Email: roger.dusart@
ardennes.pref.gouv.fr
www.ardennes.pref.gouv.fr

Préfecture de l'Aube

Rue Pierre Labonde
BP 372
10025 Troyes Cedex
Tel: +33 325 42 35 00
Fax: +33 325 73 72 26
Email:
prefecture@aube.pref.gouv.fr
www.aube.pref.gouv.fr

Préfecture de Haute-Marne

89 Rue Victoire de la Marne
52011 Chaumont Cedex
Tel: +33 325 3052 52
Fax: +33 325 32 01 26
Email: sylvain.rohrhurst@
haute-marne.pref.gouv.fr

www.haute-marne.pref.gouv.fr

Préfecture de la Région Champagne-Ardenne

1 Rue de Jessaint
51036 Châlons-en-Champagne
Cedex
Tel: +33 326 26 10 10
Fax: +33 326 26 12 63
www.champagne-
ardenne.pref.gouv.fr

LEGAL

Chambre des Notaires

Cours Jean-Baptiste Langlet 44
BP 1181
51157 Reims Cedex
Tel: +33 326 86 72 10
Fax: +33 326 86 72 21
www.chambre-
ardennes.notaires.fr

FINANCE

Direction des Impôts de l'Est

Rue du Cardinal Tisserant 2
BP 70307

54006 Nancy Cedex
Tel: +33 383 36 32 80
Fax: +33 383 36 32 89

BUILDING & PLANNING

Chambre Régionale de Métiers de Champagne-Ardenne

Rue Titon 42
51000 Châlons-en-Champagne
Tel: +33 326 68 10 55
Fax: +33 326 66 88 06
Email: crm.ca@wanadoo.fr

Caue de Haute-Marne

Maison de l'Habitat
BP 178
Rue des Abbés Durand 16
52006 Chaumont Cedex
Tel: +33 325 32 52 62
Fax: +33 325 02 37 16
Email: caue.52@wanadoo.fr

EDUCATION

Rectorat de l'Académie de Reims

Rue Navier 1

51082 Reims Cedex
Tel: +33 326 05 69 69
Fax: +33 326 05 69 42
www.ac-reims.fr

HEALTH

Caisse Primaire d'Assurance Maladie de la Marne

Rue Ruisselet 14
51086 Reims Cedex
Tel: +33 820 90 41 47
Fax: +33 326 84 41 10
www.ameli.fr

Caisse Primaire d'Assurance Maladie de Haute-Marne

18 Boulevard du Maréchal de
Lattre de Tassigny
BP 2028
52915 Chaumont Cedex 9
Tel: +33 325 02 85 85
Fax: +33 325 32 63 32
Email: general@cpam-
chaumont.cnamts.fr
www.cpam-chaumont.fr

The wine and champagne industry dominates the region's economy

THE CHAMPAGNE INFORMATION BUREAU + JOHN HODDER

HOTSPOTS

€100,000–€150,000
(£69,444–£104,166)

Despite high property prices throughout the region, bargains can still be found

€103,000　　　　　　　　　　　　　　CODE AMR

NEAR ÉPERNAY, MARNE

A lovely old townhouse with outbuildings and large attic space for conversion

£71,527

🛏 4 　✳ Courtyard 　🖼 Situated 25kms from Épernay 　🚏 Located on a main road

🏠 Room for parking

€105,961　　　　　　　　　　　　　　CODE ROU

CHARLEVILLE, MARNE

A medium-sized terraced house in a residential area, with a cellar and garage

£73,584

🛏 3 　✳ 100m² 　🖼 Situated on the outskirts of town 　🚏 Located on a main road

🏠 Room for parking, with a garage

€117,386　　　　　　　　　　　　　　CODE ROU

CHARLEVILLE, MARNE

A typical terraced house in Charleville with space for parking on the street

£81,518

🛏 4 　✳ 120m² 　🖼 Situated in the town centre 　🚏 Located on a main road

🏠 Room for parking

€143,302　　　　　　　　　　　　　　CODE ROU

CHARLEVILLE, MARNE

A charming, detached house with a stylish kitchen, patio and a terrace

£99,515

🛏 3 　✳ 870m² 　🖼 Situated in a quiet area 　🚏 Not located on a main road

🏠 Room for parking

€145,600　　　　　　　　　　　　　　CODE ROU

NEAR FLIZE, ARDENNES

A semi-detached stone house in a pretty hamlet, with a cellar and a garage

£101,111

🛏 3 　✳ 350m² 　🖼 Situated in a small hamlet 　🚏 Located on a main road

🏠 Room for parking, with a garage

€150,000–€175,000
(£104,166–£121,527)

Small habitable properties and larger investment opportunites

€151,686   CODE ROU

CHARLEVILLE, MARNE

A superb apartment in the centre of town, with four bedrooms and a parking space
£105,337

🛏 4 ❀ – 🖼 Situated in the town centre 🖼 Located on a main road
🏠 Room for parking

€152,000   CODE ROU

CHARLEVILLE, MARNE

A large commercial property in need of major renovation. A great investment
£105,555

🛏 – ❀ No garden 🖼 Situated in the town centre 🖼 Located on a main road
🏠 Room for parking

€152,450   CODE ROU

MAUBERT-FONTAINE, ARDENNES

A lovely old property in need of renovation, with outbuildings and a large garden
£105,868

🛏 7 ❀ 2,200m² 🖼 Situated in the village centre 🖼 Located on a main road
🏠 Room for parking

€167,560   CODE VEF

LAON, AISNE

A newly built cottage on the river bank, set in beautiful countryside
£116,361

🛏 3 ❀ With garden 🖼 Situated on the river bank 🖼 Not located on a main road
🏠 Room for parking

€174,554   CODE ROU

NEAR CHARLEVILLE, MARNE

A modern four-bedroom family home with a games room and a garage
£121,218

🛏 4 ❀ 1,250m² 🖼 Situated 15km from Charleville 🖼 Not located on a main road
🏠 Room for parking, with a garage

€175,000–€240,000
(£121,527–£166,666)

Take your pick from smart urban apartments and large rural retreats

€183,000   CODE FPS
AUBE
A charming fermette with a separate small house and two barns to convert
£127,083

🛏 3   ❋ 2,600m²   🏡 Situated in the village centre   🛣 Not located on a main road

🏠 Room for parking

€183,750   CODE ROU
NEAR CHARLEVILLE
A lovely modern villa with a fitted kitchen, set in well kept large grounds
£127,604

🛏 4   ❋ 662m²   🏡 Situated in the village centre   🛣 Not located on a main road

🏠 Room for parking, with a garage for two cars

€190,000   CODE ROU
CHARLEVILLE, MARNE
This modest detached house is in a lovely location, with a cellar, garage and terrace
£131,944

🛏 3   ❋ 1,620m²   🏡 Situated just outside Charleville   🛣 Not located on a main road

🏠 Room for parking, with a garage

€222,575   CODE ROU
CHARLEVILLE, MARNE
A large apartment in a pleasant area, with a small, private garden and a terrace
£154,565

🛏 4   ❋ 200m²   🏡 Situated in the town centre   🛣 Located on a main road

🏠 Room for parking

€228,700   CODE ROU
VIREUX, NEAR CHARLEVILLE, MARNE
A pretty, detached cottage in a quiet rural area, 50km north of Charleville
£158,819

🛏 5   ❋ 876m²   🏡 Situated in an idyllic rural location   🛣 Not located on a main road

🏠 Room for parking, with two garages

€240,000–€550,000
(£166,666–£381,944)

From lovely big houses in excellent condition to a barge on the Seine

€243,900 CODE ROU

SEDAN, ARDENNES

A beautiful old house in excellent condition, with a terrace and large grounds
£169,375

🛏 4 ✿ 6,200m² 🏙 Situated in the town centre 🛣 Not located on a main road
🏠 Room for parking, with a garage

€350,600 CODE ROU

SEDAN, ARDENNES

A splendid modern villa with under-floor heating and a swimming pool
£243,472

🛏 5 ✿ 6,600m² 🏙 Situated on the outskirts of town 🛣 Not located on a main road
🏠 Room for parking, with a garage for two cars

€380,000 CODE DEM

RIVER SEINE, CHAMPAGNE-ARDENNE

This lovely old barge was built in 1931 and is moored on the Seine, 100km from Paris
£263,889

🛏 6 ✿ – 🏙 Moored in a charming old city 🛣 –
🏠 –

€380,000 CODE ROU

CHARLEVILLE, MARNE

A beautiful villa set in generous grounds with wonderful views over the countryside
£263,889

🛏 6 ✿ 2,500m² 🏙 Situated on the outskirts of town 🛣 Not located on a main road
🏠 Room for parking, with a garage for three cars

€520,000 CODE SIF

MARNE

This large 19th-century property is built above cellars and comprises 15 main rooms
£361,111

🛏 11 ✿ 7,000m² 🏙 Situated on the edge of a village 🛣 Not located on a main road
🏠 Room for parking, with a garage for three cars

€550,000+
(£381,944+)

An abundance of beautiful châteaux and prestigious rural properties

€816,046   CODE SIF

HAUTE-MARNE

Built in 1745, this charming baroque-style property is set in formal gardens

£566,698

🛏 4 ✸ 2,500m² 🖼 Situated 10 minutes from amenities 🚗 Not located on a main road
🏠 Room for parking, with a large garage

€990,000   CODE SIF

NEAR SEDAN, ARDENNES

This 16th-century château is in habitable condition and includes two apartments

£687,500

🛏 6 ✸ 30,000m² 🖼 Close to town and amenities 🚗 Not located on a main road
🏠 Room for parking

€1,000,000   CODE DEM

NEAR CHARLEVILLE, MARNE

This beautiful listed château was once owned by Louis XIV's cardinal

£694,444

🛏 6 ✸ 30,000m² 🖼 Situated near the river Meuse 🚗 Not located on a main road
🏠 Room for parking

€1,295,000   CODE SIF

ARDENNES

A superb restored château with some five hectares of enclosed woods and parkland

£899,305

🛏 6 ✸ 50,000m² 🖼 Situated at the edge of the village 🚗 Not located on a main road
🏠 Room for parking, with a double garage

€1,590,000   CODE SIF

AUBE

This immense château has several outbuildings, a tennis court and a lovely chapel

£1,104,166

🛏 10 ✸ 160,000m² 🖼 Situated in a quiet area 🚗 Not located on a main road
🏠 Room for parking, with garages

Alsace, Lorraine & Franche-Comté

Strasbourg, the Vosges mountains and strong Germanic influences

CIVA

FACT BOX 2005

■ **Population** 5,161,580
■ **Migration** 474,443
■ **Unemployment** 89,304
■ **Median home price** €145,630
■ **House price increase** Since 2002, house prices in Alsace have increased by 14%, prices in Lorraine have increased by 7.3% and prices in Franche-Comté have increased by 3.1%

Price Guide

Area profile

AIR Air France (0845 084 5111;
www.airfrance.co.uk) flies directly from
Gatwick to Strasbourg. For the northern
Lorraine area, it is easier to fly with
Ryanair (0871 246 0000;
www.ryanair.com) to Brussels-South
Charleroi; **Ryanair** flies from Glasgow,
Liverpool and Stansted to Charleroi.
ROAD The A26 runs from the Calais
ferryport to Reims, and from there the A4
continues to Metz and Strasbourg. From
Metz take the A31 south to Nancy and,
for Besançon, follow the A26 from the
Channel ports, or the A5 from Paris to
Troyes, continuing on the A5 and the A31
for Dijon, changing to the A39 and then
the A36. From Paris, the A4 runs through
Reims to Metz and Strasbourg.
COACH Eurolines (0870 514 3219;
www.eurolines.com) runs services from
the UK to Belfort, Besançon, Colmar,
Metz, Mulhouse, Nancy and Strasbourg.
RAIL TGV services operate between Paris
Gare de l'Est, and Nancy, Metz and
Strasbourg. Paris Gare de Lyon operates
services to Besançon, while the **Eurostar**
(0870 518 6186; www.eurostar.co.uk)
runs from the UK to Lille, where TGV
services run on to Besançon. From Lille-
Flandres there are direct train services to
Metz. For all enquiries and more details
on local services, contact **Rail Europe**
(0870 830 2008; www.raileurope.co.uk).

FRANCE'S NORTHEASTERN REGIONS PROVIDE AN INTERESTING AND
distinctly Germanic cultural contrast from many other parts of the country.
While Franche-Comté in the south shares its boundary with Switzerland,
Lorraine and Alsace share much of their eastern borders with Germany,
and at various times in their history have been under German rule.

Lorraine, the largest of the three regions, is home to two handsome,
appealing cities, Nancy and Metz. Nancy is characterised by some fabulous
Art Nouveau architecture, while Metz, 50 kilometres further north, has an
impressive Gothic cathedral. Sixty kilometres east of Metz is the small
town of Verdun, the scene of World War I's worst battle in which
hundreds of thousands of men died. The triangle of land between the three
towns encompasses the Lorraine Regional Park: 2,000 square kilometres of
forests, streams and lakes.

The Alsace region is separated from Lorraine by the Vosges mountains
and by the Rhine from Germany. At various times in its history, Alsace has
been ruled by Germany, and this is reflected in the architecture, language
and traditions. Regional capital Strasbourg has for centuries been a
crossroads, linking northern Europe with Mediterranean Europe. It's a
cosmopolitan city, home of the European Parliament and the European
Court of Human Rights, while the ancient Grand Île area is a World
Heritage site. The capital of Franche-Comté is Besançon, a lively city with
a large student population and lots of decent bars and restaurants.

The regional cuisine includes dishes influenced by other parts of
Europe, particularly Germany. *Choucroute* is white cabbage marinaded in
beer and often includes sausage, bacon and pork – it's usually served with a
large glass of beer, too. Fresh fish stews and creamy onion tarts are also
local specialities. A lot of French beer is brewed in the region – the famous

There's plenty of short-term rental potential in the area

Kronenberg brewery is in Strasbourg. The wine is also German-influenced, and there are some excellent Rieslings.

The economy and housing market

Service and tertiary industries provide a lot of employment in these regions – 58 per cent of workers are employed in the service industry. Agriculture, chemicals and plastics are also major industries. More than half of France's toys and 80 per cent of the country's eyewear is produced in Franche-Comté's Jura *département*. The telecommunications industry is big in Metz – the Technopole Metz 2000 base is a big employer. Nancy and Strasbourg, too, are centres of commerce and industry.

Strasbourg has great buy-to-let investment potential, despite the high price tag of £350,000 for a four to six-bedroom home in the centre. The constant influx of well-to-do workers ensures that profits are made on sales. Traditional buildings in the Orangerie district are the most expensive in Strasbourg because of their historic links and a lack of available land. Four-bedroom homes on the city's outskirts sell for around £200,000.

Prices are higher in Metz, which is popular with Luxemburgers looking for bargains across the border. Four-bedroom houses start from £300,000, but renovation properties in surrounding villages can be purchased from as little as £40,000. Metz and Nancy's prices have increased dramatically in the past five years, driven by a demand that supply is not meeting. A stable rental market exists in Metz and a central apartment is hard to find. Nancy and Clairvaux have four to six-bedroom homes starting at £150,000, but the Jura is a rising star for purchasers wishing to buy-to-let. A renovation property can be found in Lons-le-Saunier from £55,000 and, with regular Swiss and German visitors, there is very good investment potential in the area as a whole.

If holiday gîtes/homes and short-term rentals are your aim, Metz and Strasbourg's Christmas markets attract winter rental. The Jura offers established gîte country, with 48 per cent of Franche-Comté's gîtes found here. It's placed consistently high in France's best quality of life list and its vast swathes of forest make it a relaxing location. For winter gîtes, Metabief and Les Rousses are developing ski resorts, where the populations double in winter. Haut-Doubs is a big draw because of its winter sports potential.

Besançon's prices are increasing, but still offer good value, with a four to six-bedroom home priced from £200,000. Although prices are higher than the French average, demand is still high. The Velotte district is very exclusive and buyers are paying premium prices for new executive homes in Besançon.

Social groups

The region as a whole has lots of German and Swiss residents; much of Alsace is German-speaking. Strasbourg has a multinational population because of its European institutions. ●

> "At various times in its history, Alsace has been ruled by Germany and this is reflected in the language, traditions and architecture"

Average monthly temperature °C (Celsius)

Average monthly rainfall mm (millimetres)

AVERAGE HOUSE SALE PRICES

Hotspot	2-bed	3-bed	4-bed	5-bed+
Strasbourg	€176K (£122K)	€278K (£193K)	€360K (£250K)	€556K (£386K)
Metz & Nancy	€161K (£112K)	€201K (£139K)	€229K (£159K)	€322K (£223K)
The Vosges	€150K (£104K)	€181K (£126K)	€257K (£178K)	€348K (£242K)
Besançon	€161K (£112K)	€236K (£164K)	€337K (£234K)	€395K (£274K)
Lons-le-Saunier, Haut-Jura & Vallée des Lacs	€80K (£55K)	€120K (£83K)	€183K (£127K)	€294K (£204K)

Property hotspots

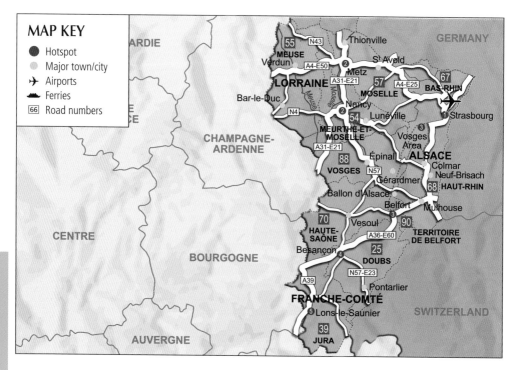

MAP KEY
- ● Hotspot
- ● Major town/city
- ✈ Airports
- ⛴ Ferries
- 66 Road numbers

1. Strasbourg

ESSENTIALS ■ **Population** 267,051 ■ **Taxes** Taxe d'habitation: 6.97%, Taxe foncière: 6.35% ■ **Airport** Strasbourg International Airport,67960 Entzheim, Tel: +33 388 64 67 67

KEY FACTS

■ **Schools** Lycée International des Pontonniers, 1 Rue des Pontonniers, 67081, Tel: + 33 (0) 388 37 15 25, www.scolagora.com/ponto/Site_Web
■ **Medical** Centre Hospitalier Universitaire, 1 Place de l'Hôpital, 67000, Tel: +33 388 11 67 68
■ **Rentals** International students create a long-term lets market, but there is a good demand for holidays ■ Many tourists visit for the Christmas market ■ Prices vary from €490 for a weekly rent in a two-bedroom property ■ Strasbourg is a tourism magnet, especially for families
■ **Pros** Mainly demand from the French and German market, but some international appeal ■ Strasbourg is a prominent and wealthy industrial city ■ Accessible and well positioned for Europe ■ Property is expensive when compared with the rest of the French market; a four-bedroom house costs from €360,200
■ **Cons** Demand makes property and land very expensive ■ Proximity to the border increases demand and prices ■ Huge demand for renovation property, which is scarce due to a lack of migration.

Flanking the Franco–German border, Strasbourg is the base of the European Union, with a truly cosmopolitan air. Also a UNESCO World Heritage site, Strasbourg has a medieval centre with a maze of cobbled squares, half-timbered houses and meandering canals. The pink sandstone Gothic Cathedral of Notre-Dame displays a rich tapestry of carved doorways, gargoyles and a rose window.

The historic Grande Île is encircled by waterways. A guided walk from its western corner through Petite France shows the French and German influences that shaped the Old Town, where millers, tanners and fishermen lived. Narrow streets with half-timbered houses are criss-crossed by canals, with the watchtowers of the Ponts Couverts, part of the 14th-century fortifications, and the Vauban Dam, built to protect Strasbourg from river-bound attack, standing by. For an insight into Alsace life, do not miss the Musée Alsacien and the famous Christmas market in December.

Many foreigners have chosen to make Strasbourg their home and this is partly due to its strategic position on the border. There are many German buyers in particular purchasing in the area, as well as foreign language students who fuel the rentals market. This high demand has pushed prices up; a two-bedroom house will sell for €176,000. ●

HOTSPOTS

2. Metz and Nancy

ESSENTIALS ■ **Population** 233,328 ■ **Taxes** Taxe d'habitation: 5.81%, Taxe foncière: 6.47% ■ **Airport** Strasbourg International Airport, 67960 Entzheim, Tel: +33 388 64 67 67

Metz, just 40 miles from the German border, became part of France in 1552, but fell under German occupation from 1870 to 1918 and again during World War II. Not awash with tourists like Strasbourg, its ochre stone lends warmth to its Renaissance buildings. Leafy paths trace the Roman and medieval ramparts, and follow the Seille and Moselle rivers. Late Gothic stained glass and additions by Marc Chagall adorn the Cathedral of Saint-Etienne, the third highest in France, with statues of the 'Graouly', the legendary dragon who haunted the ruins of the city's Roman amphitheatre. In Place de la Comédie is the oldest working theatre in France, built between 1738 and 1753. Another gem, the Arsenal, built under Napoleon III, is now a concert hall.

Upstream lies the university town of Nancy, the historical capital of Lorraine founded at a European crossroad. Its famed Place Stanislas, created by the Polish exiled King Stanislas Leczinski, is one of Europe's finest with many beautiful churches, including the 15th-century Franciscan and 18th-century Saint-Sebastien churches and Notre-Dame-de-Bon-Secours.

A two-bedroom house costs from €161,300, while at the top end of the market a five-bedroom home can set you back from €322,000. ●

KEY FACTS

■ **Schools** Rectorat de l'Académie de Nancy-Metz, rue Philippe-de-Gueldres 2, BP13, 54035 Nancy, Tel: +33 383 86 20 20
■ **Medical** Hôpital Clinique Claude Bernard, 97 rue Claude Bernard, BP45050, 57072 Metz, Tel: +33 387 39 66 66 ■ Centre Hospitalier Universitaire, 29 avenue Maréchal de Lattre de Tassigny, 54000 Nancy, Tel: +33 383 85 85 85
■ **Rentals** Peak season is from July until August and there is rental activity until the end of September ■ Metz attracts many tourists, and both cities are popular rental areas ■ The popular nature of the rentals market makes this a good area for investment ■ A two-bedroom property would rent for €330 a week
■ **Pros** The rental market is very stable in Metz, if expensive ■ Prices in both areas have increased dramatically during the last five years; a two-bedroom property costs €161,300 ■ Both cities are culturally and architecturally rich ■ There is high demand from Luxembourgers for cheap property ■ Apartments in both city centres are very popular
■ **Cons** City centres are very expensive ■ Huge demand for renovation properties on the outskirts of the cities, but with limited property available.

3. The Vosges

ESSENTIALS ■ **Population** 100,065 ■ **Taxes** Taxe d'habitation: 6.97%, Taxe foncière: 6.35% ■ **Airport** Strasbourg International Airport, 67960 Entzheim, Tel: +33 388 64 67 67

The mountainous Vosges in western Alsace present an inviting panorama to buyers, with high forests, lakes, gorges and waterfalls. Two regional parks, one in the south, covering the Vosges massif from the valley of Sainte-Marie-aux-Mines to the edge of Belfort and Luxeuil-les-Bains, and a northern one featuring a forest at its centre, are both excellent for outdoor pursuits.

In Haut Alsace, the Ballons des Vosges is dominated by a series of rounded peaks or ballons. This land of the *marcaires* (or mountain farmers), tending their herds on moorland pastures, boasts geological splendours, with large quartz and feldspar crystals in its granite. Notable are the eroded volcanic hills of Petit Ballon and Grand Ballon.

Gérardmer is a popular southern Vosges resort, offering the surrounding winter skiing slopes of the Vosges cristallines or its lake for activities in summer. Between the southern Vosges and the northern reaches of the Jura mountains, attractive Belfort has a restored old town with buildings displaying a harmonious range of colours. Dominated by a fortified castle and Bartholdi's red sandstone lion marking the city's resistance to siege during the Prussian War, Belfort is known for its antiques market. Expect to pay €150,000 for a habitable two-bedroom property. ●

KEY FACTS

■ **Schools** Rectorat de l'Académie de Besançon, rue de la Convention 10, 25030 Besançon Cedex, Tel: +33 381 65 47 00, www.ac-besancon.fr
■ **Medical** Centre Hospitalier de Belfort-Montbéliard, 14 rue Mulhouse, 90000 Belfort, Tel: +33 384 57 40 00
■ **Rentals** A year-round rental season, mainly for outdoor holiday-makers ■ Growing tourist interest in the area, mostly from the French ■ Winter is the most popular season, especially for skiing ■ An excellent rental/investment area ■ Short-term rental is the main trend ■ Gérardmer is the area's main draw ■ A two-bedroom property costs €510 a week
■ **Pros** The area boasts many outdoor activities, such as climbing and mountain biking ■ Forested mountains, lakes and wine routes stretch along the Rhine from Strasbourg ■ Belfort is popular with international buyers, particularly the Germans and Dutch, but the French remain the main buyers ■ Property prices are affordable with a three-bedroom house costing from €181,200
■ **Cons** Prices are increasing as demand rises ■ There is a limited supply of sought-after renovation properties.

4. Besançon and area

ESSENTIALS ■ **Population** 125,000 ■ **Taxes** Taxe d'habitation: 7.00%, Taxe foncière: 9.70% ■ **Airport** Strasbourg International Airport,67960 Entzheim, Tel: +33 388 64 67 67

KEY FACTS

■ **Schools** Rectorat de l'Académie de Besançon, rue de la Convention 10, 25030 Besançon Cedex, Tel: +33 381 65 47 00, www.ac-besancon.fr
■ **Medical** Hôpital Universitaire St Jacques, 2 Place Saint Jacques, 25030 Besançon Cedex, Tel: +33 381 66 81 66
■ **Rentals** This area is largely ignored by foreign tourists, making for a slow rentals market ■ It is difficult to rent property out seasonally, but it can be done ■ The winter rentals market is particularly poor ■ The peak season here is between May and September, when foreign tourists visit, primarily from Germany and America ■ A four-bedroom property rents from €865 a week
■ **Pros** There are good bargains to be found in this area, especially for those seeking winter rather than summer holiday homes ■ Prices are on the increase, but property is still currently good value for money ■ Investment is good as property is affordable; a two-bedroom home costs from €161,250
■ **Cons** Property prices are higher than average for the region ■ Growing demand is causing prices to rise and a shortage of available property has also caused increases ■ There is a lack of both renovated properties and of properties to renovate.

The ancient, attractive grey-stone capital of Franche-Comté lies between Alsace and Burgundy on the northern edge of the Jura mountains, encircled by a bend in the River Doubs. Having first begun as a Gallo-Roman city, Besançon absorbed different identities as a Spanish settlement, then provincial town. Its astronomical clock – with 30,000 parts – at Saint-Jean Cathedral identifies this as a famous clock-making town. Also the birthplace of artificial silk, or rayon, in 1890, the city counts among its native sons the pioneering Lumière brothers and epic novelist Victor Hugo.

Located on the banks of the Moulin Saint-Paul canal, in the heart of the town, Besançon Port enjoys a scenic setting, with facilities to accommodate pleasure boats, house boats and floating hotels. Sampling its waterside charms by barge is a must, passing through tunnels dug under the 19th-century citadel via the lock of the Saint-Paul windmill. There are plenty of lively and inexpensive restaurants, cafés and bars by the river near place Battant, particularly along the riverside streets.

Property in Besançon is currently affordable, although this is likely to change as demand continues to increase. Prices are further fuelled by the limited number of renovation properties available. Currently a two-bedroom property would set you back an average of €161,250. ●

5. Lons-le-Saunier, Haut-Jura and Vallée des Lacs

ESSENTIALS ■ **Population** 43,601 ■ **Taxes** Taxe d'habitation: 8.46%, Taxe foncière:15.58% ■ **Airport** Geneva International Airport, PO Box 100, CH1215, Geneva 15, Tel: +41 227 17 71 11

KEY FACTS

■ **Schools** Rectorat de l'Académie de Besançon, rue de la Convention 10, 25030 Besançon Cedex, Tel: +33 381 65 47 00, www.ac-besancon.fr
■ **Medical** Hospitalier Général de Lons-le-Saunier, 55 rue du Docteur Jean-Michel, 39000 Lons-le-Saunier, Tel: +33 384 35 60 00
■ **Rentals** Highly popular range of outdoor activities ■ Lons-le-Saunier attracts short-term rentals ■ Rental potential comes from the popular Jura ski resort, Les Rousses ■ Main rental season from May to September ■ Prices vary from €325 for a two-bedroom property to €565 for four beds
■ **Pros** The mountains attract winter sports and nature lovers ■ The Jura region is increasingly popular ■ Prices are relatively low with a two-bedroom house costing an average of €79,800 ■ Most demand is French, but increasingly Dutch, German and British ■ Most buyers seek relocation properties priced below €150,000
■ **Cons** Renovation properties are in high demand, but are rare ■ Increasing local demand makes international buys difficult ■ Proximity to Geneva and Brussels is making this area more popular, which could result in increased prices.

Close to Switzerland, the Haut Jura and Doubs *départements* share an exceptional setting in a regional park full of opportunities for winter sports enthusiasts and nature lovers in summer. At altitudes ranging from 800 to 1,600m and just an hour from Geneva, Haut Jura is the most authentic of French mountain ranges. With villages nestling at the foot of its valleys, Haut Jura sets the scene for the Transjurassienne, the cross-country ski race attracting thousands of participants from all over the world. Saint-Claude, the largest city, lies close to the ski resort of Les Rousses and has a history of pipe making and diamond cutting, while Morbier is renowned for its creamy cheese.

At high altitude, Haut Doubs often experiences harsh winters, though summers are pleasant for swimming, fishing and sailing in the lakes and rivers. From the bitter roots of the gentian, distilleries throughout this region produce excellent apéritifs and liqueurs, and Pontarlier, the dynamic capital and second-highest town in France, produced absinthe until 1915.

This is a popular area with foreign buyers and it is typified by the colourful houses and swathes of rustic villages and hills. A three-bedroom property in this region will set you back €120,000, while a habitable two-bedroom property is an affordable €79,800. ●

HOTSPOTS

USEFUL CONTACTS

PRÉFECTURES

Préfecture de la Région Alsace
5 Place de la République
67073 Strasbourg Cedex
Tel: +33 388 21 67 68
Fax: +33 388 21 61 55
www.alsace.pref.gouv.fr

Préfecture de la Région Lorraine
Place de la Préfecture
57034 Metz Cedex 1
Tel: +33 387 34 87 34
Fax: +33 387 32 57 39
www.lorraine.pref.gouv.fr

Préfecture de la Région Franche-Comté
8 Bis Rue Charles-Nodier
25035 Besançon Cedex
Tel: +33 381 25 10 00
Fax: +33 381 83 21 82
www.franche-comte.pref.gouv.fr

Préfecture-Territore-de-Belfort
Place de la République
90020 BELFORT
Tel: +33 384 57 15 41
Fax: +33 384 21 32 62
Email: communication@pref90.net
www.territoire-de-belfort.pref.gouv.fr

Préfecture-Haut-Rhin
7 Rue Bruat
68020 Colmar Cedex
Tel: +33 389 24 70 00
Fax: +33 389 23 36 61
www.haut-rhin.pref.gouv.fr

Préfecture-Jura
55 Rue Saint-Désiré
39030 Lons-le-Saunier Cedex
Tel: +33 384 85 86 00
Fax: +33 384 24 71 29
www.jura.pref.gouv.fr

Email: info@jura.pref.gouv.fr

Préfecture-Haute-Saône
1 Rue de la Préfecture
BP 429
70013 Vesoul Cedex
Tel : +33 384 77 70 00
Email: préfecture@haute-saone.pref.gouv.fr
www.haute-saone.pref.gouv.fr

LEGAL

Chambre des Notaires du Doubs
22a Rue de Trey
25000 Besançon
Tel: +33 381 50 40 52
+33 381 50 77 79
Email: conseil-regional.besancon @notaires.fr

Chambre des Notaires du Bas-Rhin
2 Rue des Juifs
67000 Strasbourg
Tel: +33 388 32 10 55
Fax: +33 388 23 40 39
Email: chambre-bas-rhin @notaires.fr

Chambre des Notaires de la Moselle
1 Rue de la Pierre Hardie
57000 Metz
Tel: +33 387 75 27 93
Fax: +33 387 74 08 20
Email: chambre.57 @notaires.fr

FINANCE

Direction des Impôts de l'Est
2 Rue du Cardinal Tisserant
BP 70307
54006 Nancy Cedex
Tel: +33 383 36 32 80
Fax: +33 383 36 32 89

BUILDING & PLANNING

Chambre Régionale de Métiers d'Alsace
Espace Européen de l'Entreprise
30 Avenue de l'Europe
67300 Schiltigheim
Tel: +33 388 19 79 79
Fax: +33 388 19 60 65

Chambre Régionale de Métiers de Franche-Comté Valparc
Espace Valentin Est
25048 Besançon Cedex
Tel: +33 381 47 45 50
Email: crmfc@wanadoo.fr

Chambre Régionale de Métiers de Lorraine
2 Rue Augustin Fresnel
57082 Metz Cedex 3
Tel: +33 387 20 36 80
Fax: +33 387 75 41 79
Email: crmlorraine@wanadoo.fr

Caue du Bas-Rhin
5 Rue Hannong
67000 Strasbourg
Tel: +33 388 15 02 30
Fax: +33 388 21 02 75
Email: caue67@wanadoo.fr

Caue du Doubs
14 Passage Charles de Bernard
25000 Besançon
Tel: +33 381 82 19 22
Fax: +33 381 82 34 24
Email: caue25@wanadoo.fr

Caue du Jura
9 Avenue Jean Moulin, BP 48
39002 Lons-le-Saunier Cedex
Tel: +33 384 24 30 36
Fax: +33 384 24 63 89
Email: caue39@wanadoo.fr

EDUCATION

Rectorat de l'Académie de Nancy-Metz

2 Rue Philippe-de-Gueldres
BP 13
54035 Nancy Cedex
Tel: +33 383 86 20 20
Fax: +33 383 86 23 01
www.ac-nancy-metz.fr

Rectorat de l'Académie de Strasbourg
6 Rue de la Toussaint
67081 Strasbourg Cedex 9
Tel: +33 388 23 37 23
Fax: +33 388 23 39 99
www.ac-strasbourg.fr

Rectorat de l'Académie de Besançon
10 Rue de la Convention
25030 Besançon Cedex
Tel: +33 381 65 47 00
Fax: +33 381 65 47 60
www.ac-besancon.fr

HEALTH

Caisse Primaire d'Assurance Maladie du Doubs
2 Rue Denis Papin
25000 Besançon
Tel: +33 381 47 53 00
Fax: +33 381 47 53 40
Email: passerelle@cpam-besancon.cnamts.fr

Caisse Primaire d'Assurance Maladie de la Moselle
18 Rue Haute Seille
57751 Metz
Tel: +33 387 39 36 36
Fax: +33 387 76 15 71
www.cpam-metz.com

Caisse Primaire d'Assurance Maladie du Bas-Rhin
16 Rue Lausanne
67000 Strasbourg
Tel: +33 820 90 41 50
Fax: +33 388 76 88 99
www.cpamstrasbourg.fr

HOTSPOTS

€30,000–€150,000
(£20,833–£104,166)

A decent selection of habitable properties requiring some work

€33,500   CODE AMR

MOSELLE, LORRAINE
A small first-floor flat in a late 19th-century building
£23,263

1 | No garden | Situated in the town centre | Located on a main road
No private parking

€83,760   CODE DEV

LORRAINE
This tidy 3-bedroom village house has central heating and a large garage
£58,166

3 | With a garden | Situated in the village centre | Not located on a main road
Room for parking, with a garage

€110,000   CODE DEV

LORRAINE
A totally restored village house with central heating, a large garage and a storeroom
£76,388

3 | Garden at rear | Situated in the village centre | Not located on a main road
Room for parking, with a garage

€111,500   CODE DEV

LORRAINE
A modern villa set in large grounds, with central heating and an attic to convert
£77,430

3 | With a garden | Situated in the village centre | Not located on a main road
Room for parking

€131,700   CODE FPS

LONS-LE-SAUNIER, JURA
A typical farmhouse in large grounds with a cellar and dove house to restore
£91,458

2 | 2,440m² | Situated in the village centre | Not located on a main road
Room for parking, with a garage

€150,000–€200,000
(£104,166–£138,889)

Some lovely farmhouses and village dwellings set in beautiful countryside

€152,000	CODE DEV

LORRAINE

An attractive old farmhouse with stables, barns and other outbuildings to convert

£105,555

🛏 3   ⊛ 30,000m²   Situated in a rural area   Not located on a main road

Room for parking, with garages

€155,868	CODE DEV

LORRAINE

A farmhouse with central heating, barns and stables in large grounds

£108,241

🛏 2   ⊛ Large grounds   Situated in a peaceful hamlet   Not located on a main road

Room for parking

€185,000	CODE DEV

LORRAINE

This grand village house has a courtyard, 2 secondary houses and plenty of land

£128,472

🛏 8   ⊛ 15,000m²   Situated in the village centre   Located on a main road

Room for parking, with garages

€191,940	CODE FPS

JURA, FRANCHE-COMTÉ

A superb detached property in great condition throughout, with a swimming pool

£133,291

🛏 4   ⊛ 3,000m²   Situated in the village centre   Not located on a main road

Room for parking

€196,000	CODE FPS

JURA, FRANCHE-COMTÉ

A detached farmhouse with an outbuilding to convert, stables and a barn

£136,111

🛏 4   ⊛ 12,300m²   Situated in a small hamlet   Not located on a main road

Room for parking

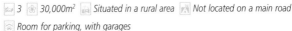

PRICE GUIDE

149

€200,000–€300,000
(£138,889–£208,333)

Large rural properties, often with potential for further expansion

€225,000   CODE FRO

MULHOUSE, ALSACE

This traditional villa set over 3 levels offers spacious living at a bargain price
£156,250

5   450m²   *Situated in the village centre*   *Not located on a main road*
Room for parking, with a garage for 3 cars

€244,600   CODE FPS

JURA, FRANCHE-COMTÉ

This large detached stone property has recently been fitted with a new roof
£169,861

6   2,400m²   *Situated on the outskirts of town*   *Not located on a main road*
Room for parking, with a garage

€260,000   CODE FPS

LONS-LE-SAUNIER, JURA

A stone end-terrace house with a fitted kitchen and a lovely fireplace in the lounge
£180,555

5   1,680m²   *Situated in the village centre*   *Not located on a main road*
Room for parking, with a garage

€271,200   CODE FPS

JURA, FRANCHE-COMTÉ

This large detached property has lots of character and is set in pretty surroundings
£188,333

4   1,560m²   *Situated on the outskirts of town*   *Not located on a main road*
Room for parking, with a garage

€292,000   CODE FRO

BOLLWILLER, ALSACE

A good-sized villa in a lovely old village, with easy access to all amenities
£202,778

7   538m²   *Situated in the village centre*   *Not located on a main road*
Room for parking, with a double garage

€300,000–€500,000
(£208,333–£347,222)

Beautiful houses set in spectacular locations near forest, rivers and mountains

€310,000   CODE FRO

WITTELSHEIM, ALSACE
This traditional villa is set in large grounds with a terrace and ample secure parking
£215,277

🛏 5   ⊕ 2,000m²   🖼 *Situated in the village centre*   🏠 *Not located on a main road*
🏠 *Room for parking, with a garage for 3 cars*

€323,000   CODE DEM

NEAR VITTEL, VOSGES
An 18th-century master's house, with a large farmhouse and another outbuilding
£224,305

🛏 8   ⊕ 12,000m²   🖼 *Situated in a small village*   🏠 *Not located on a main road*
🏠 *Room for parking, with a garage*

€335,000   CODE FRO

GOMMERSDORF, ALSACE
A large modern villa offering spacious living, with a swimming pool
£232,638

🛏 8   ⊕ 740m²   🖼 *Situated in the village centre*   🏠 *Not located on a main road*
🏠 *Room for parking, with a double garage*

€365,000   CODE FRO

LUTTERBACH, ALSACE
This large villa has a lovely swimming pool and is set in a beautiful part of Alsace
£253,472

🛏 6   ⊕ 672m²   🖼 *Situated in a peaceful area*   🏠 *Not located on a main road*
🏠 *Room for parking, with a double garage*

€373,000   CODE DEM

MEUSE, LORRAINE
A modern house set in large grounds amidst a beautiful forest
£259,027

🛏 3   ⊕ 23,000m²   🖼 *Situated 5 km from amenities*   🏠 *Not located on a main road*
🏠 *Room for parking, with a garage*

€385,000 CODE FRO

MASEVAUX, ALSACE

A massive villa set in a peaceful rural area, with a separate guest house

£267,361

🛏 7   4,000m²   Situated in a quiet area   Not located on a main road
Room for parking, with a double garage

€390,269 CODE DEM

NEAR ÉPINAL, VOSGES

This former hunting inn is currently operating as a restaurant and conference centre

£271,020

🛏 8   6,000m²   Situated in peaceful countryside   Not located on a main road
Room for parking

€399,000 CODE FPS

JURA, FRANCHE-COMTÉ

This magnificent *maison de maître* has large vaulted cellars and a stable

£277,083

🛏 5   8,000m²   Situated in a small hamlet   Not located on a main road
Room for parking

€448,000 CODE FPS

JURA, FRANCHE-COMTÉ

This fully restored character property is set in mature, landscaped grounds with a pool

£311,111

🛏 7   800m²   Situated in a small hamlet   Not located on a main road
Room for parking, with a garage

€480,000 CODE FRO

NIFFER, ALSACE

A traditional-style modern villa in the centre of a pretty village

£333,333

🛏 7   600m²   Situated in the village centre   Not located on a main road
Room for parking, with a double garage

€485,000 CODE FRO

HEIMSBRUNN, ALSACE

A lovely villa with a large cellar and store room, plus a swimming pool

£336,805

🛏 6   970m²   Situated in the village centre   Not located on a main road
Room for parking, with a garage for 3 cars

PRICE GUIDE

€500,000+
(£347,222+)

A mix of old and new properties at the top end of the scale

€567,000   CODE FPS

JURA, FRANCHE-COMTÉ

A luxuriously appointed, detached property within easy reach of Lyon and Geneva

£393,750

🛏 4   ⬡ 10,000m²   Situated on the outskirts of town   Not located on a main road   Room for parking, with a garage

€602,173   CODE DEM

NEAR STRASBOURG, ALSACE

A modern residence just 25km west of Strasbourg, with a separate studio apartment

£418,175

🛏 4   ⬡ 2,500m²   Situated in a quiet rural area   Not located on a main road   Room for parking, with a double garage

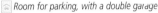

€770,000   CODE SIF

DOUBS

A former convent with artist's studio, with original features and buildings to convert

£534,722

🛏 5   ⬡ 48,600m²   Situated near the Swiss border   Not located on a main road   Room for parking, with a garage

€980,000   CODE SIF

DOUBS

A beautiful 14th-century château built on medieval foundations. Requires renovation

£680,555

🛏 12   ⬡ 14,000m²   Situated in beautiful countryside   Not located on a main road   Room for parking

€1,800,000   CODE SIF

HAUTE-SAÔNE

A part-renovated 19th-century château with numerous outbuildings

£1,250,000

🛏 18   ⬡ 100,000m²   Situated in a peaceful rural area   Not located on a main road   Room for parking, with garages

PRICE GUIDE

154

The Loire

Magnificent rivers and valleys and stunning medieval châteaux

COMITÉ RÉGIONAL DU TOURISME ET DES LOISIRS

FACT BOX 2005

◢ **Population** 5,662,390
◢ **Migration** 257,108
◢ **Unemployment** 112,255
◢ **Median house price** €55,130
◢ **House price increase** Since 2002, house prices in the Loire have increased by 10.8%, on average

Price Guide

GETTING THERE

AIR Air France (0845 084 5111;
www.airfrance.co.uk), **Flybe** (0871 700
0535; www.flybe.com) and **GB Airways**
(0870 551 1155; www.gbairways.com)
operate flights from Gatwick to Nantes;
Ryanair (0871 246 0000;
www.ryanair.com) serves Tours,
La Rochelle and Poitiers from Stansted,
and **British Airways** (0870 850 9850;
www.britishairways.co.uk) flies from
Heathrow to Nantes.
ROAD Take the A26 from Calais and
continue on to the A16-E40 and then the
A16 and A26. From there follow the A16-
E402 to Rouen, taking the A28 on to the
A28-E402 at junction 23. From Le Havre
the A13-E46 runs down to Rennes, and
the N137 or the A81-E50 continues on
into the Pays de la Loire. From Paris the
A10-E6 runs into the centre and
continues on to the south of the region,
and the A11-E50 then runs on into Pays
de la Loire.
RAIL Rail Europe (0870 830 2008;
www.raileurope.co.uk) operates TGV
trains to Le Mans, Angers, Nantes,
Poitiers, La Rochelle and Angoulême
from Paris Gare Montparnasse.
COACH Eurolines (0870 514 3219;
www.eurolines.com) offer services to La
Roche sur Yonne, Le Mans, Les Sables
d'Olonne, Nantes, Orléans and Tours.

Area profile

THE LOIRE IS FRANCE'S LONGEST RIVER AND IT CUTS THROUGH TWO
of the country's most beautiful regions, Centre and Pays de la Loire.
Encompassing fertile farmland, stunning Renaissance châteaux and the
magnificent Loire Valley, Centre is rich in history, and tourists flock to
the region's medieval fortresses and plentiful vineyards. UNESCO has
designated the long stretch between Sully-sur-Loire and Chalonnes as
a protected World Heritage Site.

The capital is Orléans, famous for its association with Joan of Arc
who liberated the city in 1429. Much of the centre's historic Roman
architecture remains intact and there are some excellent museums and a
Gothic cathedral. Further southwest is Tours, a large and cosmopolitan
university city with wide, attractive avenues and boulevards, which are
lined with busy cafés.

Pays de la Loire is home to the National Equestrian School at Saumur,
and the beautiful surroundings provide great horseriding country. Saumur
is also famous for its huge caves where wine is stored and mushrooms are
grown – almost 70 per cent of France's button mushrooms are produced
here. Northeast of Saumur is Angers, a Roman city that sits above the
Maine river. Its majestic 13th-century Château d'Angers houses the
historic L'Apocalypse, a tapestry that illustrates the last book in the Bible.

The region's coastline plays host to picturesque fishing ports, small
seaside resorts and sloping sandy beaches. Les Sables d'Olonne is a cheerful
port with a large fish market which supplies the town's wealth of seafood
restaurants. Pays de la Loire's capital is Nantes, a large and lively university
city, which has splendid botanical gardens and a grand Gothic cathedral.

The Loire's lush landscape and the Atlantic coast provide a rich choice
of gastronomic delights. Game stews and baked fruit dishes are a speciality;
clafoutis is a sweet dish of cherries coated in batter. Freshwater fish cooked
in white wine, onions and garlic is also popular.

The Loire is famous for its vineyards and châteaux

The economy and housing market

A landscape of forests, small towns and villages dotted along the Loire's river lends itself particularly to *gîte* tourism. However, the celebrated wine industry, with wines ranging from *Sancerre* and *Pouilly Fumé* in the east of the region to *Muscadet* in the area around Nantes, together with agricultural production still offers a stable support to the region's economy. Industry and commerce in the major towns of Le Mans and Nantes are strong supporters of the economy.

House prices have increased on average by 25 per cent in the Loire in recent years. The volume of tourists maintains and boosts the rental market and guarantees a return upon the investment made by those who buy in the area. Generally speaking, the market is extremely healthy, but prices remain competitive, making it an excellent time to invest. With the neighbouring region of Brittany becoming saturated and the increase of budget flights into the Loire region, prices will continue to rise.

The pretty tourist areas of Touraine and Anjou offer safe investments, with prices from £30,000 for a renovation project, to £700,000 for a prestigious property. Baugé, Chandelais, Saumur and Angers are very popular destinations. Tourists flock to these areas and despite rising prices, they mostly represent sound investments. The property market in Le Mans has stagnated recently; prices have been pushed up by Parisian second-home buyers and properties have become increasingly expensive in the commuter belt. Prices in Tours have risen sharply due to French relocators moving into the region.

The coastal towns of the Vendée are top holiday-home destinations for Parisians. Les Sables d'Olonne has long, clean beaches, a thriving market, and is just a two-hour train journey from the capital. Many French purchasers buy their holiday homes here, with a view to retiring. This makes the region an excellent area for purchasing because of the resale value and holiday market potential.

The wealth of employment opportunities in Nantes make the city perfect for those who are looking to work in the Loire. *Gîtes* are ideal for relocators looking to run their own businesses. Tours, Ambilou and Saumur and the surrounding towns and villages are key *gîte* areas with year-round rental yields, and old properties are available from around £75,000. Some *gîte* owners have introduced specialist holidays, including painting, to counter disruption to the market caused by world events.

Buyers who are looking to renovate properties and let them out should consider adding a swimming pool to a renovation property because it vastly increases the potential for rental income.

Social groups

Parcay les Pins stands out because of its almost 40 per cent British home ownership. However, the rest of the region is generally made up of the indigenous French population. ●

> *"UNESCO has designated the stretch between Sully-sur-Loire and Chalonnes as a protected World Heritage Site"*

THE LOIRE		LONDON		THE LOIRE		LONDON
8	Dec	7		64	Dec	81
12	Nov	10		62	Nov	78
17	Oct	14		60	Oct	70
22	Sept	19		58	Sept	65
24	Aug	21		60	Aug	62
25	July	22		52	July	59
23	June	20		52	June	58
16	May	17		60	May	57
17	April	13		42	April	56
11	March	10		44	March	64
8	Feb	7		56	Feb	72
9	Jan	6		60	Jan	77

Average monthly temperature °C (Celsius)   Average monthly rainfall mm (millimetres)

AVERAGE HOUSE SALE PRICES

Hotspot	2-bed	3-bed	4-bed	5-bed+
Vendée coast	€176K (£122K)	€218K (£151K)	€270K (£188K)	€293K (£204K)
Saumur & Angers	€154K (£107K)	€171K (£119K)	€233K (£161K)	€313K (£217K)
Nantes	€167K (£116K)	€241K (£167K)	€290K (£201K)	€362K (£251K)
Le Mans	€131K (£91K)	€153K (£166K)	€208K (£144K)	€342K (£238K)

Property hotspots

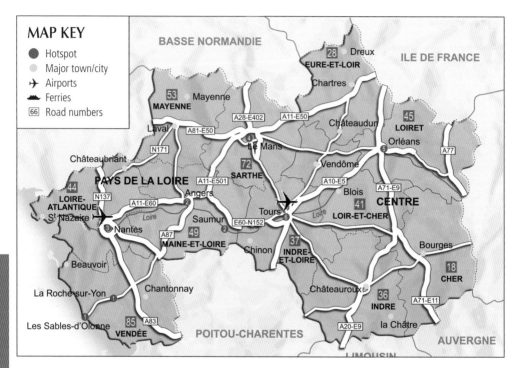

MAP KEY
- ● Hotspot
- ○ Major town/city
- ✈ Airports
- ⛴ Ferries
- 66 Road numbers

BASSE NORMANDIE

ILE DE FRANCE

28 Dreux
EURE-ET-LOIR
Chartres

53 Mayenne
MAYENNE
Laval
A28-E402   A11-E50
Châteaudun
45 LOIRET
Orléans
A77

N171
Le Mans
A81-E50

Châteaubriant
72 SARTHE
Vendôme
A10-E5
Blois
A71-E9

44 PAYS DE LA LOIRE
A11-E501
N137
Angers
41 CENTRE
LOIR-ET-CHER

LOIRE-ATLANTIQUE
St Nazaire
A11-E60
Tours
Loire
3 Nantes
Saumur
E60-N152
A87   49
MAINE-ET-LOIRE
Chinon
37 INDRE-ET-LOIRE

Beauvoir
Bourges
18 CHER

La Roche-sur-Yon
Chantonnay
Châteauroux
36 INDRE
A71-E11

85 A83
VENDÉE
Les Sables-d'Olonne
POITOU-CHARENTES
A20-E9   la Châtre
AUVERGNE

LIMOUSIN

1. Vendée Coast

ESSENTIALS ■ **Population** 68,992 ■ **Taxes** Taxe d'habitation: 8.19% , Taxe foncière: 16.76% ■ **Airport** Nantes-Atlantique Airport, 44346 Bouguenais Cedex, Tel: +33 240 84 95 33

KEY FACTS

■ **Schools** Cité Scolaire Internationale Grand Air, Lycée et Collège de Grand Air, 77 Avenue du Bois d'Amour, 44500 La Baule Escoublac, Nantes, Tel: +33 240 11 58 00
■ **Medical** Centre Hospitalier Côte-de-Lumière, 75 Avenue d'Aquitaine, 85119 Les Sables-d'Olonne, Tel: +33 251 21 85 85
■ **Rentals** Les Sables d'Olonne is a popular Atlantic coast resort with plenty of summer tourists to generate rental income ■ Good long-term rentals in La Roche-sur-Yon ■ Average rental prices are €710 per week,for a two-bedroom property in peak season
■ **Pros** Easily accessible, the Vendée is well served by transport links via the N160 and nearby TGV links ■ Popular with permanent relocators ■ There is no shortage of activities that can be pursued and enjoyed in this area ■ The Vendée offers good weather ■ Property here is affordable with a two-bedroom property costing €176,000
■ **Cons** There is little rental activity in winter ■ This is predominantly a French speaking area ■ It can get very crowded in the summer months

The Vendée, named after a river that runs through the southeast of the *département*, features a variety of different landscapes, from coastal areas to the flat grasslands and lush *bocage* countryside. With near–white sand stretching for 250 kilometres and rocky escarpments tucked behind the Atlantic ocean's shores, safe bathing and gently sloping beaches offer a desirable location for families. Les Sables d'Olonne is a fishing port where cheerfully painted villas with sculpted décor lead onto a long promenade with sea-facing bistros. Famous for its fish market on the quayside, Les Sables d'Olonne also has a large indoor food market and an extensive shopping area, including designer clothes boutiques and a variety of exclusive eateries. The town of La Roche-sur-Yon was founded by Napoleon in 1804 and was once an isolated village. It has since become the principal town in the Vendée, and locals are proud of their theatre – a temple-based design in a classic Italian style – and the National Stud. The town is flanked by countryside and provides a natural North/South divide between La Roche-sur-Yon and Pays Yonnais. It's a popular, easily accessible area with a healthy rentals and property market. A modern four-bedroom villa in Les Sables d'Olonne starts at €270,000, while a two-bedroom house in La Roche costs from €176,000. ●

2. Saumur and Angers

ESSENTIALS ■ **Population** Saumur 31,443, Angers 151,279 ■ **Taxes** Taxe d'habitation: 6.08%, Taxe foncière: 9.35%
■ **Airport** Nantes-Atlantique Airport, 44346 Bouguenais Cedex, Tel: +33 240 84 95 33

Saumur is an historic, wine-making city, built into chalky white tufa stone that is characteristic of the Loire Valley. Its speciality is sparkling wine and its stunning clifftop château houses two magnificent museums: the decorative arts museum and the horse museum. Saumur is home to France's premier equestrian centre and horse lovers should visit the Cadre Noir, headquarters of the world-famous National Horse and Riding School. At the western end of the Loire Valley, Angers occupies a site above the Maine river. During Roman times it served as a crossroads for routes from Rennes, Nantes and Tours. Today it is known for its flowers, wines, liqueurs and umbrella production. Impressive features include its castle and some fine examples of Plantagenet Gothic architecture.

The area makes for a sound investment and there is a huge demand for rentals. The cheapest properties start at €70,000 for a farmhouse in need of renovation. These cities are cheaper than the neighbouring Dordogne and, therefore, hugely attractive to buyers and investors who now spill over into the Loire region. Angers offers a buoyant property market and its excellent transport links ensure many people are drawn to the area. Prices start at €154,000 for a two–bedroom property while a five–bedroom property will set you back by around €313,000. ●

KEY FACTS

■ **Schools** Cité Scolaire Internationale Grand Air, Lycée et Collège de Grand Air, 77 Avenue du Bois d'Amour, 44500 La Baule Escoublac, Nantes, Tel: +33 240 11 58 00
■ **Medical** Centre Hospitalier de Saumur, Route de Fontevraud, 49400 Saumur, Tel: +33 241 53 30 30, www.ch-saumur.fr
■ **Rentals** Both Saumur and Angers are major tourism centres and there is great potential for those buying property to let ■ Good annual rentals with more long-term than short-term demand in Angers ■ Average prices for a two-bedroom property are €415 euros per week
■ **Pros** The area boasts excellent weather and attractive surroundings ■ Angers has been voted best French city for three years running ■ The area houses a strong British community ■ Angers is extremely cosmopolitan, with a large developing population ■ There is an excellent transport network ■ Property is affordable with a two-bedroom dwelling costing an average of €171,350
■ **Cons** The market is extremely unreliable and prone to oscillating prices ■ With little commercial industry, Angers relies on agriculture ■ The rental market experiences huge competition.

3. Nantes

ESSENTIALS ■ **Population** 150,605 ■ **Taxes** Taxe d'habitation: 6.50% ■ Taxe foncière: 6.24% ■ **Airport** Nantes-Atlantique Airport, 44346 Bouguenais Cedex, Tel: +33 240 84 95 33

Nantes is officially part of the Loire region yet many of its residents regard themselves as Brétons. It's situated in northwest France at the intersection of the Loire, Erdre, and Sèvre rivers. The Château des Ducs de Bretagne, where the edict was signed, still occupies a central place in the city and houses a striking 14th-century tapestry that stretches over 100 metres.

Although France's seventh biggest city is geared towards innovation, encapsulated by Nantes resident Jules Verne in his novels, the old town features many historical gems. Its fine cathedral, half-timbered mansions and art galleries, such as the Musée des Beaux Arts with collections by Kandinsky, are worth a look. Nantes's 850 acres of parks, including the Japanese-style garden on the Île de Versailles on the Erdre, are ideal starting points for touring the rivers, and pleasure steamers regularly leave from the quays to explore the Muscadet vineyards.

A relatively new property hotspot, Nantes is a technological and research centre dominated by the presence of local buyers. This is not an area dominated by second home buyers and investors, although the region has experienced a 12 per cent appreciation – most tend to settle in the surrounding countryside. Despite Nantes's status as a city, property is affordable and a two-bedroom house will set you back €167,000. ●

KEY FACTS

■ **Schools** Contact Rectorat de l'Académie de Nantes, 4 rue de la Houssinière, BP 72616, 44326 Nantes, Tel: +33 240 37 37 37 for advice
■ **Medical** Hôpitaux dy CHU de Nantes, 1 Pl Alexis Ricordeau, 44000 Nantes, Tel: +33 240 08 33 33
■ **Rentals** There is a good long-term rentals market, mainly for locals and long-term visitors ■ Average rentals for Nantes throughout the year are €660 for a two-bedroom property and €855 per week for a three-bedroom property
■ **Pros** The area has excellent business and employment prospects ■ Nantes is a cosmopolitan city ■ There are excellent transport routes, with cheap flights from the UK ■ The old town centre is very attractive, as is the Château des Ducs de Bretagne ■ A big city, popular with relocators ■ Property in Nantes is affordable with a two-bedroom house costing just €167,000
■ **Cons** The architecture can be ugly and modern ■ Not a typical tourist destination so the buy-to-let market is limited ■ The popular commuter belt including Sautron, Clisson, Haute Goulaine and Baine Goulaine offers very expensive properties.

HOTSPOTS

4. Le Mans

ESSENTIALS ■ **Population** 150, 605 ■ **Taxes** Taxe d'habitation: 7.64%, Taxe foncière: 10.74% ■ **Airport** Aéroport Tours Val de Loire, 40 rue de l'Aéroport, 37100 Tours, Tel: +33 247 49 37 00

KEY FACTS

■ **Schools** Contact the Rectorat de l'Académie d'Orléans-Tours, 21 rue Saint Étienne, 45043 Orléans Cedex 1, Tel: +33 238 79 38 79
■ **Medical** Centre Hospitalier Régional du Mans, 194 Avenue Rublillard, 72000 Le Mans, Tel: +33 243 43 43 43
■ **Rentals** Primarily a local, long-term rental market, Le Mans has a busy short-term, tourist rental market from May to July ■ The average price per week for a two-bedroom property is €560, and €1,000 per week for three bedrooms
■ **Pros** Popular with Parisians for second homes; property prices continue to rise ■ Perfect for commuting to Paris ■ The development of a popular commuter belt means property is guaranteed a price rise ■ This is one of the cheapest areas in the Loire for property with a two-bedroom home setting you back only €130,500
■ **Cons** Le Mans is very industrial and not traditionally popular with relocators to the Loire or for holiday rentals ■ The city has a limited tourist appeal ■ People tend to buy on the outskirts or in the surrounding countryside.

Le Mans – located in the Sarthe *département;* a pageant of blossom in May – is synonymous with motor racing but has a satisfying cultural scene. Visit the lovely old quarter enclosed within Gallo-Roman walls to view its medieval cobbled streets and half-timbered houses. The film *Cyrano de Bergerac* with Gérard Depardieu was filmed in the shadow of the glorious Cathedral Saint-Julien, a Gothic monument to the Plantagenet kings, while the car museum – part of the 24-hour race circuit complex – is a must for motor enthusiasts. Visit the Musée de la Reine Bérengère to view various arts and crafts, while the Lude castle is also a must see. Additionally, pay a trip to the Manoir de la Possonnière, beloved by the poet Pierre de Ronsard, or the war museum at Lavardin and the Benedictine abbey of Solesme.

The property market here is increasingly buoyant due to the influx of Parisian buyers and those who work in the capital. The city is very industrialised and consequently, not a popular location for foreign buyers. Buy to lets also offer a limited market because, despite the cosmopolitan atmosphere induced by the Le Mans race, most of the year the rental and property market is dominated by the locals. A four-bedroom property will set you back an average of €208,000. ●

5. Orléans

ESSENTIALS ■ **Population** 150,605 ■ **Taxes** Taxe d'habitation: 5.26%, Taxe foncière:8.28% ■ **Airport** Aéroport Tours Val de Loire, 40 rue de l'Aéroport, 37100 Tours, Tel: +33 247 49 37 00

KEY FACTS

■ **Schools** Contact the Rectorat de l'Académie d'Orléans-Tours, 21 rue Saint Étienne, 45043 Orléans Cedex 1, Tel: +33 238 79 38 79
■ **Medical** Centre Hospitalier Régional d'Orléans, 1 rue Porte Madeleine, BP 2439, 45032 Orléans Cedex 1, Tel: +33 285 14 444
■ **Rentals** With a good annual rental market, Orléans is more of a tourist area ■ Average prices throughout the year in Orléans start at €300 a week for a one-bedroom apartment and extend to €1,020 a week for a five-bedroom house
■ **Pros** Offers easy access to the capital, so commuting is easy and prices are lower ■ Subject to the pleasant, Loire micro-climate, the weather is attractive ■ Plenty of historic tourist attractions, this is the city of Joan of Arc, with two impressive cathedrals ■ There are many employment and educational opportunities.
■ **Cons** There are some concerns over the inconsistent nature of the rental market ■ Property is fairly steep with a two-bedroom house costing from €167,000

Orléans is the capital of the Loire Valley and famous for Joan of Arc, and its regional châteaux. Liberated by Joan of Arc in 1429, Orléans expresses its annual gratitude to the Maid of Orléans via a Medieval Pageantry Festival on May 8th. As France's intellectual capital in the 13th century, it was the royal court of Emperor Charlemagne who attracted artists, poets and troubadours to seek his patronage. Although many of the old buildings were destroyed during the Second World War, huge reconstruction efforts have been made since then in order to recover the city's former splendour. Of particular note are the Cathédral Saint Croix, the Musée des Beaux Arts, the Natural Science Museum and the Maison de Jeanne d'Arc.

Orléans draws many tourists, providing a healthy rentals market and making it a safe investment for those who decide on buying to rent. Being close to Paris, many Orléanais go to the capital for evenings out as well as commuting there to work. Property is reasonably priced but prices rise considerably once you reach the environs.

As with many areas, the best property prices are often found in the city's surrounding countryside. Currently the average two-bedroom property will set you back around €166,800, and a four-bedroom property, around €259,000. ●

6. Tours and the Touraine

ESSENTIALS ▰ **Population** Tours 132,820 ▰ **Taxes** Taxe d'habitation: 6.32%, Taxe foncière: 7.92β% ▰ **Airport** Aéroport Tours Val de Loire, 40 rue de l'Aéroport, 37100 Tours, Tel: +33 247 49 37 00

Tours was the capital of France and a centre for silk production under the reign of Louis XI. Today it attracts many tourists keen to maximise its location as a gateway to the Touraine *département*, with its remarkable châteaux and the Loire vineyards. Elegant Tours old town abounds with Renaissance and neo-classic architecture. Nearby is the fairy-tale Château de Chenonceau, also known as the 'ladies' castle', because its history was shaped by a series of aristocratic women, including Catherine de Medici. Touraine is known as the 'garden of France' for its abundance of fruit, flowers and red wines – which contrast with its many troglodyte dwellings carved from the local tuffeau rock.

The property market is very healthy in this popular area of the Loire. There are many unique and luxurious châteaux for sale. Due to the demand in the market, property is more expensive than in other parts of the Loire, and much of this demand has come from the local French market. However, with the increase in budget flights to this delightful area, international interest is also increasing. Typically a two-bedroom property will cost you around €136,600, and a four-bedroom property upwards of €272,000. ◗

KEY FACTS

▰ **Schools** Contact the Rectorat de l'Académie d'Orléans-Tours, 21 rue Saint Étienne, 45043 Orléans Cedex 1, Tel: +33 238 79 38 79
▰ **Medical** Hôpital Bretonneau, 2 boulevard Tonnellé, 37044 Tours, Cedex 9, Tel: +33 247 47 47 47 www.chu-tours.fr
▰ **Rentals** Tours has a good annual long-term rentals market ▰ Average rentals start at €520 a week for a two-bedroom property, and €700 for a three-bedroom property ▰ The rental season lasts from March to October in the Touraine towns of Chinon and Loches
▰ **Pros** Often considered the most popular tourist area in the Loire, with UNESCO World Heritage status ▰ A large university population and thriving boutique/café culture ▰ Enjoys excellent transport links ▰ Property is reasonably priced, averaging €136,600 for a two-bedroom property ▰ There is a growing foreign (particularly British) community in Chinon and Loches
▰ **Cons** An expensive place to buy property ▰ Azay-le-Rideau and Langeais in the Touraine have few foreign buyers ▰ Some French is essential ▰ The Touraine is fairly quiet.

St-Jean beach stretches as far as the eye can see

€50,000–€200,000
(£34,722–£138,889)

These affordable restoration projects will get your foot on the ladder

€68,600

PAYS-DE-LA-LOIRE
A lovely, old cottage to restore in a beautiful rural setting
£47,639

🛏 1　❀ 1,500m²　🏞 Situated close to a village　🚗 Not located on a main road
🏠 Room for parking

€88,050

FONTENAY-LE-COMTE
A tiny house set in large grounds with numerous outbuildings and a well
£61,146

🛏 1　❀ 1,960m²　🏞 Situated in a quiet rural area　🚗 Not located on a main road
🏠 Room for parking

€99,000

PAYS-DE-LA-LOIRE
A part-restored house in a small hamlet with an enclosed courtyard and garden
£68,750

🛏 2　❀ Small garden　🏞 Situated in a peaceful area　🚗 Not located on a main road
🏠 Room for parking

€108,000

RICHELIEU/CHÂTELLERAULT
An old character house in large grounds with outbuildings, requiring some restoration
£75,000

🛏 2　❀ 12,000m²　🏞 Situated in a quiet rural area　🚗 Not located on a main road
🏠 Room for parking

€179,850

FONTENAY-LE-COMTE
A small, detached town house with a well-kept garden including summer kitchen
£124,895

🛏 3　❀ 480m²　🏞 Situated in a small town　🚗 Not located on a main road
🏠 Room for parking, with a garage

€200,000–€300,000
(£138,889–£208,333)

Beautiful old family homes in idyllic rural settings

€200,015   CODE VDR

PAYS-DE-LA-LOIRE

A beautifully restored 3-bedroom house with a lovely living room

£138,899

🛏 3 🌰 2,000m² 🏠 Situated in the village centre 🛣 Not located on a main road

🏠 Room for parking

€201,280   CODE LAT

NEAR CHENONCEAUX, INDRE-ET-LOIRE

A charming single-storey property set in large wooded grounds with fruit trees

£139,778

🛏 4 🌰 4,770m² 🏠 Situated 5km from Chenonceaux 🛣 Not located on a main road

🏠 Room for parking

€210,000   CODE VDR

PAYS-DE-LA-LOIRE

There are lovely views over the surrounding farmland from this restored cottage

£145,833

🛏 3 🌰 3,000m² 🏠 Situated in a quiet rural area 🛣 Not located on a main road

🏠 Room for parking

€212,000   CODE LAT

NEAR CHINON, INDRE-ET-LOIRE

A restored 18th-century detached house with guest cottage and original features

£147,222

🛏 2 🌰 400m² 🏠 Situated in a small hamlet 🛣 Not located on a main road

🏠 Room for parking

€291,858   CODE FPS

POUZAUGES

A fantastic detached house with marble entrance halls and landscaped gardens

£202,679

🛏 4 🌰 3,440m² 🏠 Situated in a quiet rural area 🛣 Not located on a main road

🏠 Room for parking, with a garage

€300,000–€400,000
(£208,333–£277,778)

Substantial properties with plenty of land and expansion potential

€323,192   CODE LAT

CHÂTILLON-SUR-INDRE, INDRE

Bourgeoise-style house with outbuildings, including 2 houses and a third to renovate
£224,439

🛏 7   ⚜ 1,500m²   🏙 Situated in a market town   🛣 Not located on a main road
🏠 Room for parking, with a garage

€323,300   CODE LAT

BOURGUEIL, INDRE-ET-LOIRE

A charming 19th-century house with a large attic and outbuildings
£224,514

🛏 4   ⚜ 3,800m²   🏙 Situated in the town centre   🛣 Not located on a main road
🏠 Room for parking, with a garage

€340,000   CODE LAT

NEAR DESCARTES, INDRE-ET-LOIRE

A lovely old farmhouse with gîtes set in large grounds. Includes a gym with sauna
£236,111

🛏 5   ⚜ 25,000m²   🏙 Situated in the countryside   🛣 Not located on a main road
🏠 Room for parking

€369,150   CODE SIF

INDRE-ET-LOIRE

A substantial property with numerous outbuildings and scope for development
£256,354

🛏 5   ⚜ 9,700m²   🏙 Situated 2km from a little village   🛣 Not located on a main road
🏠 Room for parking

€381,830   CODE LAT

NEAR RICHELIEU, INDRE-ET-LOIRE

A well-renovated property with marble fireplaces, wooden beams and a vaulted cellar
£265,160

🛏 6   ⚜ 2,500m²   🏙 Situated in an idyllic rural location   🛣 Not located on a main road
🏠 Room for parking

PRICE GUIDE

€400,000–€700,000
(£277,778–£486,111)

These large properties offer luxurious living and great business opportunities

€403,990   CODE LAT

AZAY-LE-RIDEAU, INDRE-ET-LOIRE

A beautifully renovated 16th-century manoir with room for plenty of expansion

£280,549

🛏 4   ❀ 250m²   🏞 Situated in a village with amenities   🛣 Not located on a main road

🏠 Room for parking

€439,900   CODE LAT

NEAR CHINON, INDRE-ET-LOIRE

A charming detached house with pool, separate guest cottage and outbuildings

£305,486

🛏 5   ❀ 5,200m²   🏞 Situated in a village with amenities   🛣 Not located on a main road

🏠 Room for parking

€470,000   CODE VDR

NEAR MAYENNE

A stunning example of 15th-century architecture in a quiet village location

£326,389

🛏 5   ❀ 4,000m²   🏞 Situated in a medieval village   🛣 Not located on a main road

🏠 Room for parking

€550,000   CODE VDR

PAYS-DE-LA-LOIRE

A superb family home in large grounds with a pool and a guest house to restore

£381,944

🛏 5   ❀ 12,000m²   🏞 Situated near the river Loire   🛣 Not located on a main road

🏠 Room for parking

€580,000   CODE VDR

NEAR ANGERS

An established B&B business with a 3-bedroom owners house and 5 letting rooms

£402,778

🛏 8   ❀ Large garden   🏞 Situated in a peaceful area   🛣 Not located on a main road

🏠 Room for parking

€700,000–€1,000,000
(£486,111–£694,444)

Live like royalty in a classic French château for less than you would think

€784,350   CODE LA

CHINON, INDRE-ET-LOIRE
A grand château with a pool, stables and a lodge, plus several other outbuildings
£544,687

🛏 8 ✴ 40,000m² 🖼 Situated near the city centre 🛤 Not located on a main road
🏠 Room for parking

€805,845   CODE VDI

PAYS-DE-LA-LOIRE
With unrivalled views over the river, this classic château dates from the 16th century
£559,615

🛏 8 ✴ 48,000m² 🖼 Situated near the river Loire 🛤 Not located on a main road
🏠 Room for parking

€807,980   CODE LA

NEAR CHINON, INDRE-ET-LOIRE
A carefully restored 15th-century property with outbuildings that require conversion
£561,097

🛏 6 ✴ 15,000m² 🖼 Situated in quiet countryside 🛤 Not located on a main road
🏠 Room for parking

€840,000   CODE SI

INDRE
A superb 16th-century château and sprawling estate requiring some modernisation
£583,333

🛏 – ✴ 247,000m² 🖼 Situated in a large estate 🛤 Not located on a main road
🏠 Room for parking

€998,000   CODE LA

AMBOISE
This beautiful Renaissance-style manor house is set in parkland with lovely views
£693,056

🛏 11 ✴ 230,000m² 🖼 Situated on the edge of a village 🛤 Not located on a main road
🏠 Room for parking

PRICE GUIDE

€1,000,000+
(£694,444+)

Immense estates in need of work and smaller mansions in a habitable condition

€1,378,000 CODE LAT

NEAR TOURS, INDRE-ET-LOIRE

A stunning 19th-century château set in large grounds with woods and a small river

£956,944

🛏 13 ❀ 1,200,000m² 🖼 Situated in a peaceful location 🚫 Not located on a main road 🏠 Room for parking

---

€1,391,000 CODE SIF

INDRE-ET-LOIRE

A delightful property with considerable potential. Requires extensive modernisation

£965,972

🛏 12 ❀ 1,020,000m² 🖼 Set in large cultivated grounds 🚫 Not located on a main road 🏠 Room for parking

---

€1,524,500 CODE SIF

LOIRET, NEAR ORLÉANS

A superb 17th-century château and outbuildings requiring substantial renovation

£1,058,681

🛏 24 ❀ 360,000m² 🖼 Situated in wooded parkland 🚫 Not located on a main road 🏠 Room for parking

---

€1,608,000 CODE SIF

LOIRE-ATLANTIQUE

This classic Breton manoir dates from the 15th century and is in excellent condition

£1,116,667

🛏 7 ❀ 100,000m² 🖼 Situated 10 minutes from the sea 🚫 Not located on a main road 🏠 Room for parking

---

€1,715,000 CODE SIF

MAINE-ET-LOIRE

A charming 19th-century château that currently operates as a health spa

£1,190,972

🛏 9 ❀ 10,000m² 🖼 Situated in large wooded grounds 🚫 Not located on a main road 🏠 Room for parking

Cinema

Documentaries

News

Learn & teach French
with **TV5**

Music

Entertainment

Sport

Drama

Le centre du monde est partout

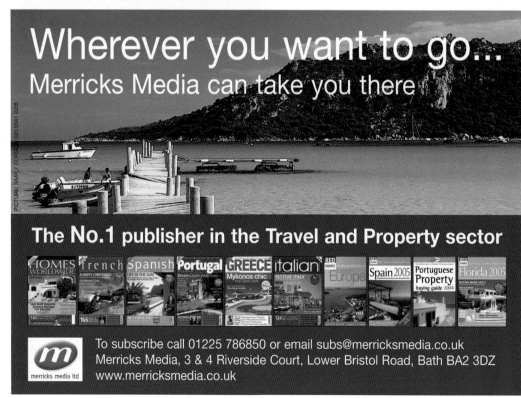

Burgundy

Vineyards, world-renowned wine and culture

JUSTIN POSTLETHWAITE

FACT BOX 2005

▥ Population 1,610,067
▥ Migration 107,803 international migrants
▥ Unemployment 31,217
▥ Median house price €119,150
▥ House price increase Since 2002 house prices in Burgundy have increased by 16.7% but the region remains the third cheapest in France

Price Guide

Area profile

AIR Air France (0845 0845 111; www.airfrance.co.uk) flies to Clermont-Ferrand and Lyon, while **British Airways** (0870 240 0747; www.britishairways.co.uk) and **Flybe** (01392 366 669; www.flybe.com) operate flights from Heathrow to Lyon. Lyon receives **easyJet** (0870 600 0000; www.easyjet.com) flights from London Stansted.

SEA The best ferry port destinations for access to Burgundy are Calais, Dieppe and Dunkirk. **P&O Ferries** (0870 520 2020; www.poportsmouth.com) operates from Dover to Calais, and Portsmouth to Le Havre, Hoverspeed (0870 240 8070; www.hoverspeed.co.uk) operates from Dover to Calais, as does **SeaFrance** (0870 571 1711; www.seafrance.com), and also between Newhaven and Dieppe. **Transmanche Ferries** (0800 917 1201; www.transmancheferries.com) sails between Newhaven and Dieppe, while **Norfolkline** (0130 421 8400; www.norfolkline.com) operates between Dover and Dunkirk.

ROAD The best route to take is from one of the northern ferry ports such as Calais. From there the A26 leads you down to Reims and then on to Troyes, from where the A5 takes you into Burgundy. The A6 from Paris will take you straight to the heart of Burgundy, passing through Sens, Chablis, Beaune, Mâcon and finally in Dijon. The A43 also runs south from Lyon through Burgundy and on into the Rhône Alps.

COACH Eurolines coaches (0870 514 3219; www.eurolines.com) operate services from destinations throughout the UK to Chalon-sur-Saône, Dijon and Mâcon.

RAIL A TGV service from London Waterloo reaches Dijon in six hours. From Paris there are numerous services to Dijon. The **Eurostar** (0870 518 6186; www.eurostar.com) runs through to Lille Europe, and from there a TGV operates between Lille and Dijon. Contact **Rail Europe** (0870 584 8848; www.raileurope.co.uk) for all details of train services in the region.

LYING AT THE HEART OF FRANCE, BURGUNDY IS A VERY PEACEFUL REGION which is renowned for its historic architecture, abundance of Michelin-starred restaurants and the production of fine wines, which are produced primarily in the Côte d'Or ('Hills of Gold') vineyard area. This is a beautiful part of the region to visit and is easy to reach, with the majority of the vineyards lining the western side of the N74 road between Dijon and Chalon-sur-Saône.

Burgundy is situated quite a distance from the coast and its climate tends to attract those who desire a cooler, less Mediterranean feel, although summers can be hot and showery. Autumn, when the grapes are harvested, is the most pleasant time of the year, when the warm, sunny days show off the beautiful landscape to the full. This is especially true in the rural La Puisaye area where there are gentle, rolling hills and long, tree-lined waterways that are perfect for cyclists or walkers.

The economy and housing market

Burgundy lacks a dominant sector in its economy besides wine, but it produces a range of agricultural and industrial products. The region's vineyards, cultural heritage and gastronomic delights also generate a healthy income from the tourist industry.

The area most in demand for property, the Côte d'Or isn't the best value for money because properties are expensive and there's relatively little land to accompany them. Since this is a wine area, there's little room for property development and this, combined with such a high demand, continues to cause an upward trend in property prices. The market here is very fast-moving and renovation properties are rare to find.

The northern areas are expensive due to the presence of Parisian holiday homes and the fact that the weather is slightly cooler than in southern Burgundy. The best value for money exists to the west of the Côte d'Or,

Burgundy's canal system attracts many holidaymakers seeking a different way to explore the region

towards the border with Central France. Morvan is also very affordable, located away from the expensive wine areas. It's extremely busy during high season but can be quite isolated during winter. Dijon is an expensive, bustling French city where buyers are primarily French.

Foreign buyers often purchase property outside the wine region, in cheaper areas such as Autun and Auxois. Auxerre in the North is also expensive, again due to the number of Parisian holiday homes.

Social groups

Relatively isolated, Burgundy has never featured highly as a favoured area for the foreign property market, which is surprising given the high standard of living that this area offers. The property market increased by approximately seven to 10 per cent in 2003, not solely because of British interest, but also due to Dutch and Belgian buyers. There aren't a great deal of British inhabitants here, given that most British buyers seek a Mediterranean climate and prefer to be nearer the coast. If you believe Burgundy is the best place for you, you should be motivated as much by its culture, history, cuisine and wine as for its affordable property. Because it's not really a family region, Burgundy is an area frequented more by couples seeking a sophisticated and peaceful retirement.

Food and drink

Perhaps most famous for its wines, made from Pinot Noir (red) and Chardonnay (white) grapes, Burgundy is in fact a gastronomic paradise, and the archaeological museum in Dijon contains detailed descriptions of food and banquets dating back to medieval times. The love of food is almost religious in the region, and the actual produce is generally very healthy, organic and fresh. Dijon is home to both the mustard and *pain d'épice* (spiced bread), while Chaource and Epoisses cheese are made in the area, with Epoisses in particular being famed for its delicate flavour and pungent smell.

The food is generally very rustic, and includes snails, boar, mushrooms, crayfish and quail, while Morvan is known more for its ham, pork and kidney dishes, as well as its stews, which are made with a considerable amount of red wine. Beef bourguignon is the most famous of these classic stews, while other specialities include *oeufs en meurette* (eggs poached in red wine with bacon, onions and mushrooms) and *jambon persillé* (strips or cubes of ham and parsley joined with a meat-wine gelatin that's served cold).

On the third Sunday in November every year, there's a charitable wine auction at the Hospices de Beaune in the centre of Beaune. The hospital was founded back in 1443 and since 1885, each of the region's 45 vineyards auctions its new wines before a very select audience to raise money to support the hospital. The ceremony is very lavish and shows off the finest Burgundy food and wine, while the amount paid for each wine is used as an indication of the vintage's quality and cost.

> "The best value for money exists to the west of the Côte d'Or, towards the border with Central France. Morvan is also very affordable, located away from the expensive wine areas"

Average monthly temperature °C (Celsius)

Average monthly rainfall mm (millimetres)

AVERAGE HOUSE SALE PRICES

Hotspot	2-bed	3-bed	4-bed	5-bed+
Côte d'Or	€132K (£83K)	€176K (£123K)	€318K (£221K)	€578K (£402K)
Saône-et-Loire	€120K (£98K)	€185K (£129K)	€229K (£159K)	€302K (£210K)
Morvan Regional Park	€109K (£76K)	€163K (£113K)	€196K (£136K)	€297K (£206K)
Auxerre	€97K (£68K)	€158K (£110K)	€210K (£146K)	€274K (£190K)
Châtillon-sur-Saône	€126K (£87K)	€216K (£150K)	€250 (£174K)	€431 (£299)

Property hotspots

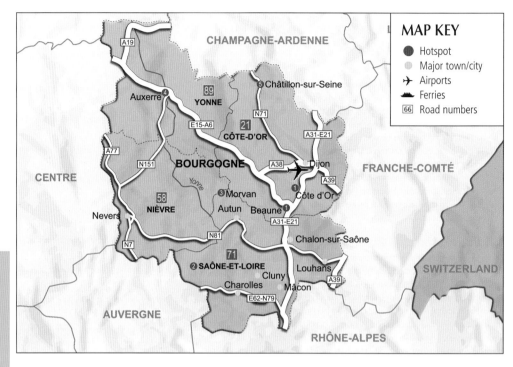

1. Cote d'Or Vineyards

ESSENTIALS ▦ **Pop** 506,755 (Beaune 21,923) ▦ **Taxes** Taxe d'habitation: 6.60%, Taxe foncière: 10.81% ▦ **Airport** Dijon-Bourgogne Aéroport, 21601 Longvic Cedex, Tel: +33 380 67 67 67

KEY FACTS

▦ **Schools** Contact the Rectorat de Dijon, 51 Rue Monge, 21033 Dijon, Tel: +33 (0) 380 44 80 00
▦ **Medical** Medical Centre Hospitalier Philippe le Bon, Avenue Guigone de Salins 21200 Beaune, Tel: +33 (0) 380 24 44 44
▦ **Rentals** Côte d'Or is guaranteed at least a seven month rental season, as September and November are months for various wine festivals and auctions
▦ This area is popular with the foreign market, and guarantees rental interest.
▦ **Pros** It is the best permanent home location because of the sense of community it offers
▦ A wealthy area due to its association with the Dukes of Burgundy and its thriving wine trade
▦ This is an ideal region for those seeking an authentic French environment ▦ Côte d'Or is the commercial and cultural epicentre of Burgundy
▦ **Cons** There is no proximity to the coast and this is not an family area ▦ The majority of British buyers purchase just outside of the Côte d'Or area to secure a cheaper property ▦ Property is limited and difficult to get hold of which pushes prices up – a two-bedroom house will set you back an average of €132,000 ▦ The market is controlled by the wealthy Parisian second-home buyer, making it expensive.

Côte d'Or is Burgundy's most famous winemaking region, and consequently experiences a huge tourist interest. Its capital, Beaune, is well-located for exploring the vineyards. A tourist draw in its own right, the old quarter is graced with a picturesque central square and the Hospice de Beaune, first created after the Hundred Years' War. In a region associated with the traditional *boeuf bourguignon*, which has long been famous outside of Burgundy, Charolais beef and top-quality goat's cheese, there are many dishes prepared *en meurette*, in a red wine and bacon sauce. Beaune also has the finest French restaurants like *Ma Cuisine*, a bistro with a 12-page wine list.

The best-known villages in the area include Meursault, Puligny-Montrachet and hillside hamlet Chassagne-Montrachet. The sleepy village of Meursault with its medieval church and Romanesque houses is home to *Château Meursault*, one of Burgundy's top wines.

The Côte d'Or is the most expensive and popular location in which to buy in the region and consequently prices in and around Beaune are above the national average. Most buyers are French locals with the occasional foreign buyer. However, the region is beginning to experience greater foreign interest and prices have appreciated by between 20 to 25 per cent in the regions towns. ●

2. Saône-et-Loire (Cluny and Macon)

ESSENTIALS ▓ **Population** 543,700 ▓ **Taxes** Taxe d'habitation: 6.60%, Taxe foncière: 10.60% ▓ **Airport** Dijon-Bourgogne Aéroport, 21601 Longvic Cedex, Tel: +33 380 67 67 67

 Not hugely popular with foreign buyers, and boasting more cattle than people, the departement of Saône-et-Loire is extremely rural. Nonetheless this historic region enjoys a number of traditional villages nestled amidst verdant hills, and sustained by the prosperous wine and tourist trade.

Macon is a vibrant tourist town situated on the banks of the river Saone. Well-connected, this industry fuelled town is central to Burgundy's wine trade. Only one hour from Geneva there is a healthy influx of Austrian and German buyers keen to take advantage of the cheap property and picturesque, cultured surroundings of the town. Ideal for sporting and leisure holidays, this is also a perfect spot for those seeking to start a bed and breakfast business.

Cluny is another draw for the foreign buyer. Birthplace of the Cistercian monks, Cluny Abbey is the region's primary tourist destination. This highly attractive and traditional village is home to the elite higher education institution, the *Grand Ecole des Ingénieurs*. This region is ideal for an investment property and tourist-based business. Predictions are that this is an area destined to blossom, and although prices vary and are on the increase you are looking at roughly €120,000 for a two-bedroom property in the region. ●

KEY FACTS

▓ **Schools** Contact the Rectorat de Dijon, 51 rue Monge, 21033 Dijon, Tel: +33 (0) 380 44 84 00 ▓ **Medical** Centre Hospitalier les Chanaux, Boulevard de l'hopital, 71018 Macon Cedex, Tel: +33 385 20 30 40/77/69 ▓ **Rentals** Burgundy is not a strong rentals market and the season is short ▓ In summer, demand is high, but in winter, tenants can be more difficult to find ▓ Lets here are mostly short term, as this is more lucrative ▓ A two-bedroom waterfront villa rents for €431 to €579 a week ▓ This is not a healthy or vibrant rentals market ▓ **Pros** There is a wealth of sporting and leisure activities you can enjoy in this region ▓ Famous for its wines there are a number of vineyards offering tastings ▓ This is an attractive region for those seeking a real flavour for the culture and history of Burgundy ▓ Property here is cheap when compared with average prices for France – a three-bedroom property retails for an average €185,000 ▓ **Cons** There is not a huge amount for children to do, so it is not an ideal place for a family relocation ▓ This is primarily a rural area and not ideal for those seeking an active city lifestyle.

3. Morvan Regional Park

ESSENTIALS ▓ **Population** 34,405 (Saulieu 2,835, Vézelay 507) ▓ **Taxes** Taxe d'habitation: 6.60%, Taxe foncière: 10.60% ▓ **Airport** Dijon-Bourgogne Aéroport, 21601 Longvic Cedex, Tel: +33 (0) 380 67 6767

 True to its Celtic name 'Morvan', meaning black mountain, this regional park is bursting with spectacular scenery. Created in 1970 to protect its cultural and natural heritage, Morvan is one of France's least densely populated areas, but is within easy reach of many tourist destinations, such as the tiny walled town of Vézelay. For centuries the park served as a backdrop for ghostly folk-tales and now many activities are focused around the forests, hills and lakes, including canoeing, mountain biking and potholing.

To the northeast of the park lies Saulieu, an ancient market town which is well worth visiting for its 17th-century basilica with animal motifs, and the bible that once belonged to Emperor Charlemagne. Saulieu also has a reputation for fine dining, championed by late, world-renowned chef, Bernard Loiseau, whose refined cuisine made The Côte d'Or into one of France's most prestigious restaurants. His signature dish, sautéed frogs' legs in puréed garlic and parsley, is still on the menu, and the restaurant is now run by Loiseau's protégé, Patrick Bertron.

Properties here are less expensive than other Burgundy areas, owing to the park's distance from major wine areas and its seasonal nature. Renovation possibilities include a barn priced at €20,000. On average expect to pay €109,000 for a two-bedroom property. ●

KEY FACTS

▓ **Schools** Contact the Rectorat de Dijon, 51 Rue Monge, 21033 Dijon, Tel: +33 380 44 84 00 ▓ **Medical** Centre hospitalier de Saulieu, 2 Rue Courtépée, 21210 Saulieu, Tel: +33 380 90 55 05 ▓ **Rentals** This is a very busy holiday area and is exceptionally busy during the rental season from April to September ▓ There are many diversions and activities, and nice surroundings to attract the rental market ▓ Generally Burgundy is not a particularly healthy rental market, however Morvan can generate enough income to cover any outgoings ▓ **Pros** This is an affordable area in which to live ▓ Morvan is an excellent area for a second home ▓ Current figures estimate that Morvan property has appreciated by 10% over the last year, making the area a healthy investment ▓ **Cons** During the winter season the area becomes rather isolated and there is less of a community feel ▓ This is not a recommended family area due to the lack of suitable activities and its isolation ▓ This area is currently experiencing price hikes and it is estimated that there are more foreign buyers here than French.

4. Auxerre

ESSENTIALS ■ **Population** 37,600 ■ **Taxes** Taxe d'habitation: 7.10%, Taxe foncière: 11.51% ■ **Airport** Dijon-Bourgogne Aéroport, 21601 Longvic Cedex, Tel: +33 380 67 67 67

KEY FACTS

■ **Schools** Contact the Rectorat de l'Académie de Dijon, 51 Rue Monge, BP 1516, 21033 Dijon Cedex, Tel: +33 380 44 84 00, Fax: +33 380 44 84 88
■ **Medical** Centre Hospitalier d'Auxerre, 2 Boulevard de Verdunn, 89011 Auxerre, Tel: +33 (0) 386 48 48 48, www.ch-auxerre.fr
■ **Rentals** A large number of Parisians own holiday homes in this area of Burgundy ■ Burgundy is not famed for it's rentals market and it can be difficult to secure seasonal rentals in Auxerre ■ The market is primarily geared at long term rentals
■ **Pros** The Yonne département is easily accessible from Paris and is considered to promote a much better lifestyle ■ Property is significantly cheaper here than it is in the départements situated closer to the capital
■ **Cons** This is a cooler area than South Burgundy, with a much milder climate ■ The presence of many Parisian holiday homes here renders prices more expensive than further south.

Situated in the Yonne departement, to the southeast of Paris, Auxerre overlooks the Yonne river and was once the capital of Burgundy. The land of the Auxerrois wine routes, where Chablis, the first of the great Burgundy whites is produced, the whole community devotes its time to the production of wine.

Rising majestically above the river, Auxerre is celebrated for its Gallo-Roman remains, while its red-brown roofs covered with distinctive flat tiles – so characteristic of northern Burgundy – frame the Gothic spires of the Cathedral of Saint-Etienne. The Romanesque bell tower of the former abbey of Saint-Germain is another popular draw, its architecture decorated by the oldest recorded frescoes in France. At dusk when the city becomes illuminated, it is wonderful to sample Burgundy truffles and cointreau–strawberry liqueur cocktails at the grand Restaurant Barnabet, a 17th-century centrally located post house.

Property is significantly cheaper in the area around Auxerre than it is in the expensive Côte d'Or wine region and the capital, Dijon. However, many Parisians own holiday homes here and in recent years this has encouraged price hikes. Just 30 minutes from Auxerre, you can buy a fully restored 200-year-old house with a detached cottage for roughly €330,000. A two-bedroom houses cost from around €97,200.●

5. Châtillon-sur-Saône

ESSENTIALS ■ **Population** 6,900 ■ **Taxes** Taxe d'habitation: 6.60%, Taxe foncière: 10.81% ■ **Airport** Dijon-Bourgogne Aéroport, 21601 Longvic Cedex, Tel: +33 380 67 67 67

KEY FACTS

■ **Schools** Contact the Rectorat de Dijon, 51 Rue Monge, 21033 Dijon, Tel: +33 380 44 84 00
■ **Medical** Hôpital Général, 3 Rue du Faubourg Raines, 21000 Dijon, Tel: +33 380 29 30 31
■ **Rentals** It is possible to rent a three-bedroom cottage from €215 ■ As the town is not a hugely popular tourist attraction, it may be difficult to generate a large amount of rental income
■ **Pros** This is a relatively new hotspot and consequently an excellent time to invest ■ A quiet area, ideal for those seeking a peaceful rural retreat ■ This is one of Burgundy's cheapest areas, a full 10 to 20% cheaper than Morvan ■ This is an undiscovered area which offers excellent appreciation potential for investors
■ **Cons** There is little of interest in the area with the main attraction being that property here is cheap ■ Rental potential is limited and this is not a huge tourist area ■ The town and surrounding landscape has been described as austere.

Located to the east of Auxerre, and situated between Champagne and Burgundy, this picturesque town is positioned in a rocky outcrop overlooking the river Seine. As a newly discovered market, there is excellent scope for foreign investors seeking an untapped market. Châtillon-sur-Saône is a quiet town, boasting an extremely attractive old quarter and a wealth of interesting architecture. It lacks the lush vegetation and rolling hills of southern Burgundy but has a number of interesting features. Among them is the 'Treasure of Rix', an exquisite hoard of pre-Roman archaeology, including 6th-century golden tiaras and a four-wheeled roman chariot. The area also offers many fishing and outdoor activity opportunities.

In terms of property prices, Burgundy remains one of France's cheapest region, despite experiencing one of the highest percentage increases in recent years. Châtillon-sur-Saône is hugely affordable with prices currently standing between 10 and 20 per cent cheaper than in the rest of Burgundy. A two-bedroom property currently costs an average of €126,000 but predictions state that within five years these properties will have appreciated dramatically as the area is discovered. Currently, investment opportunities are ideal with it being possible to purchase a habitable three-bedroom home for between €100,000 and €150,000.●

HOTSPOTS

Sending regular payments abroad?

Whether you need to transfer money to service a foreign currency mortgage each month or you live overseas and receive a pension from the UK, HIFX can save you time, stress and money. For example, fluctuating exchange rates will affect the Sterling cost of your regular mortgage transfer. We can fix the exchange rate and establish a direct debit with your UK bank.

Furthermore we transfer the funds each month free of charge.
**This could save you up to £300 per year
(or £4,500 over a 15 year mortgage).**

For further information visit our website www.hifx.co.uk/mpa
or speak to a consultant

UK office: +44(0)1753 859 159
Spanish office: (+34) 952 587 507

 HIFX PLC

mpa@hifx.co.uk

59-60 Thames Street Windsor SL4 1TX

€50,000–€100,000
(£34,722–£69,444)

There are plenty of cheap renovation projects in this lovely countryside

€66,500   CODE BUR

NEAR CLUNY, SAÔNE-ET-LOIRE

Two houses and an outbuilding in need of renovation, plus barn and stable
£46,180

2 | With garden | *Situated near the village* | *Not located on a main road*
Room for parking

€81,000   CODE BUR

NEAR AUTUN, SAÔNE-ET-LOIRE

A lovely little farmhouse in good structural condition, requiring internal renovation
£56,250

2 | 3,000m² | *Situated in a small hamlet* | *Not located on a main road*
Room for parking, with a garage

€83,800   CODE BUR

NEAR MORVAN

A stone-built village house in habitable condition with splendid views
£58,194

3 | With garden | *Situated in the village centre* | *Not located on a main road*
Room for parking

€87,000   CODE BUR

NOURUE, NEAR SAINT-GENGOUX-LE-NATIONAL

A tiny, stone-built house with plenty of character, in need of major renovation
£60,416

1 | Tiny garden | *Situated in a small hamlet* | *Not located on a main road*
Room for parking

€97,000   CODE BUR

NEAR SAINT-HONORÉ-LES-BAINS

A renovated stone farmhouse with an independent guest house and large barn
£67,361

3 | Large garden | *Situated just outside the village* | *Not located on a main road*
Room for parking

PRICE GUIDE

€100,000–€200,000
(£69,444–£138,889)

Small village houses and rural retreats requiring some attention

€110,000   CODE FRA

NEAR LONS, SAÔNE-ET-LOIRE
An old farmhouse to renovate in a peaceful village with a private garden
£76,389

3   200m²   *Situated in a small village*   *Not located on a main road*   *Room for parking*

€144,000   CODE FRA

NEAR ROANNE, LOIRE
A three-storey house in an elegantly restored château complex, with communal pool
£100,000

4   1,600m²   *Situated 6kms from Roanne*   *Not located on a main road*   *Room for parking, with a garage*

€150,000   CODE FRA

NEAR LOUHANS, SAÔNE-ET-LOIRE
A semi-detached farmhouse with numerous outbuildings and great views
£104,166

2   1,200m²   *Situated in a quiet, rural area*   *Not located on a main road*   *Room for parking*

€192,000   CODE BUR

NEAR CLUNY, SAÔNE-ET-LOIRE
This former school is currently undergoing renovation and offers three bedrooms
£133,333

3   *With garden*   *Situated just outside the village*   *Not located on a main road*   *Room for parking*

€195,600   CODE BUR

NEAR CLUNY, SAÔNE-ET-LOIRE
A restored farmhouse set in large grounds with two small wooden chalets for guests
£135,833

4   2,000m²   *Situated high in the hills*   *Not located on a main road*   *Room for parking*

PRICE GUIDE

€200,000–€300,000
(£138,889–£208,333)

A selection of character properties with gardens and superb views

€210,000   CODE BUR

CHALONAIS, SAÔNE-ET-LOIRE
A three-bedroom house in a quiet wine-growing village, with lovely views
£145,833

🛏 3   80m²   Situated in the village centre   Not located on a main road
Room for parking

€220,000   CODE FRA

CHALON-SUR-SAÔNE
A traditionally built modern house with a pool, garage and wine cellar
£152,778

🛏 4   With garden   Situated just outside the town   Not located on a main road
Room for parking, with a garage

€225,000   CODE BUR

NEAR AUTUN, SAÔNE-ET-LOIRE
A beautiful house in large grounds with a lake, set in the Morvan regional park
£156,250

🛏 3   12,500m²   Situated in a quiet hamlet   Not located on a main road
Room for parking

€235,000   CODE FRA

TOURNUS, SAÔNE-ET-LOIRE
A renovated farmhouse set in lovely grounds with outbuildings
£163,194

🛏 5   800m²   Situated in the village centre   Not located on a main road
Room for parking

€246,100   CODE BUR

NEAR LOUHANS, SAÔNE-ET-LOIRE
A traditional farmhouse renovated to a high standard, retaining original features
£170,902

🛏 3   3,300m²   Situated near the market town   Not located on a main road
Room for parking, with a garage

PRICE GUIDE

€300,000–€400,000
(£208,333–£277,778)

Many of these large houses have been renovated to a high standard

€302,500   CODE FRA

SAÔNE-ET-LOIRE

A lovely property with character in southern Burgundy, built in 1870
£210,069

🛏 3   🌳 3,695m²   🖼 Situated in the village centre   🚧 Not located on a main road

🏠 Room for parking, with a garage

€372,750   CODE FRA

NEAR DIJON, CÔTE-D'OR

A delightfully restored stone farmhouse currently run as a bed and breakfast
£258,854

🛏 8   🌳 1,300m²   🖼 Situated in a small village   🚧 Not located on a main road

🏠 Room for parking

€380,000   CODE BUR

NEAR AUTUN, SAÔNE-ET-LOIRE

A spacious house in excellent condition with a barn and chalet for conversion
£263,889

🛏 5   🌳 10,000m²   🖼 Situated on a wooded hillside   🚧 Not located on a main road

🏠 Room for parking

€385,000   CODE FRA

NEAR BEAUNE, SAÔNE-ET-LOIRE

A beautiful house with swimming pool set in a village with all amenities
£267,361

🛏 7   🌳 1,600m²   🖼 Situated in the village centre   🚧 Not located on a main road

🏠 Room for parking, with a garage

€390,000   CODE FRA

PIERRE-DE-BRESSE, SAÔNE-ET-LOIRE

A traditional country house with many local features, with numerous outbuildings
£270,833

🛏 5   🌳 4,000m²   🖼 Situated at the edge of the village   🚧 Not located on a main road

🏠 Room for parking

€400,000+
(£277,778+)

Substantial properties set in large grounds with excellent business potential

€453,000 CODE FRA

CLUNY, SAÔNE-ET-LOIRE
A lovely 18th-century property with three bathrooms and a large wine cellar
£314,583

🛏 4   ⬙ 1,830m²   Situated in the village centre   Not located on a main road
Room for parking

€458,350 CODE AMR

NEAR TOUCY, YONNE
An attractive former farmhouse comprising main house, apartment and studio
£318,298

🛏 5   ⬙ 26,000m²   Situated in a small hamlet   Not located on a main road
Room for parking

€470,000 CODE FRA

CHAGNY, SAÔNE-ET-LOIRE
A lovely property set in a quiet residential area, with lovely views
£326,388

🛏 4   ⬙ 3,000m²   Situated in a residential area   Not located on a main road
Room for parking, with a three-car garage

€480,000 CODE FRA

NEAR CHAROLLES, SAÔNE-ET-LOIRE
A recently restored period farmhouse set in large grounds with a swimming pool
£333,333

🛏 5   ⬙ 7,000m²   Situated in the village centre   Not located on a main road
Room for parking

€1,720,000 CODE AMR

NEAR FRONTENAUD, BRESSE
A luxury residence, currently a cultural centre, with numerous en-suite bedrooms
£1,194,444

🛏 –   ⬙ 88,000m²   Situated just outside the village   Not located on a main road
Room for parking

Poitou-Charentes

Beautiful wetlands, great beaches and hours of sunshine

LA ROCHELLE AQUARIUM

FACT BOX 2005

- ■ **Population** 1,640,068
- ■ **Migration** 63,750 international migrants
- ■ **Unemployment** 36,407
- ■ **Median house price** €109,100
- ■ **House price increase** Since 2002, house prices in Poitou-Charentes have increased by 7.3%

Area profile

GETTING THERE

AIR Air France (0845 084 5111;
www.airfrance.co.uk) and **GB Airways**
(0870 551 1155; www.gbairways.com)
fly from Gatwick to Nantes; **Ryanair**
(0871 246 0000; www.ryanair.com)
operates flights to Tours, La Rochelle
and Poitiers from Stansted; and Nantes
receives **British Airways** (0870 850
9850; www.britishairways.com) flights
from Heathrow.

ROAD From Paris, the A1 links with the
A10 via the N10 to Pont de Sèvres and
the A10-E5 junction with the A10. From
the A10 take the Lyon junction with the
N104 on to the A10-E5. This leads to the
N147-E62 at Junction 29 for Poitiers and
Limoges, after a right turn at the Saumur,
Angers, Nantes signpost. Take the N147
at the junction for Migné-Auxances,
which joins the N10 into Poitiers. The
A10 links Poitiers and Saintes with Paris.
To reach La Rochelle, take the N11 west
from the A10 to La Rochelle, or the N10
south to Angoulême.

COACH Eurolines (0870 518 6186,
www.eurolines.com) operates coaches to
Angoulême, La Rochelle and Poitiers.

RAIL An excellent TGV route links
Le Mans, Angers, Nantes, Poitiers,
La Rochelle and Angoulême to Paris Gare
Montparnasse. For more information
contact **Rail Europe** (0870 830 2008;
www.raileurope.co.uk).

THE POITOU-CHARENTES REGION IS SANDWICHED BETWEEN PAYS DE LA
Loire and Aquitaine on the Atlantic coast, and it encompasses the port city
La Rochelle, the region's capital Poitiers, and the world famous small town
of Cognac – the spiritual home of brandy.

Boasting 300 miles of beautiful coastline and more than 2,000 hours of
sunshine every year, Poitou-Charentes attracts tourists from spring to
autumn. Inland, the beautiful wooded valleys are dotted with vineyards that
provide the grapes for the famous Cognac, much of which is exported to
the UK and Japan. Miles of canals, wetlands and walking trails attract
canoeists, hikers and cyclists alike.

The coastline is protected by four islands, the most popular of which, Île
de Ré, attracts thousands of tourists to its beaches in the summer months.
Île de Ré actually gets more hours of sunshine than any other part of
France bar the Mediterranean. Both Île de Ré and Île d'Oléron are
attached to the mainland by long toll bridges and it costs around £10 to
cross in high season.

La Rochelle is a charming port with a wealth of seafront restaurants and
an expanding university. For centuries, it was one of France's most
prominent Atlantic ports with strong trade links to America and Canada.
Today, the city sees an influx of mainly well-to-do French holidaymakers
in July and August, and although there aren't any beaches, most travel over
the bridge to the aforementioned Île de Ré.

Sixty per cent of France's oysters are farmed in the Marenne-Oléron
basin and seafood is naturally one the region's culinary specialities. Mussels
marinated in white wine or cooked in heavy cream feature prominently
on menus, as does fish soup with white wine and *escargots* (snails) prepared
in wine. For the more adventurous, some local butchers offer beaver
sausages. Cognac, the world renowned brandy, is the region's other major
claim to fame but there are other famous wines such as Pineau des
Charentes, which blends Cognac with new grape juice.

**La Rochelle is a charming port with a wealth of seafront
restaurants and an expanding university**

The economy and housing market

Agriculture is the region's major economic driving force. Chauvigny has a number of small paper mills and its porcelain factories provide employment. Cognac's heart and soul revolve around the production of its namesake brandy. Angoulême in Charente continues its tradition of paper mills, although on a smaller scale than previously, while tourism is a developing strand of the economy. There are now 75 restaurants in the city. Tourism and mussel and oyster fishing form the mainstay of île de Ré, while fishing, tourism and commerce support La Rochelle.

Renovation properties dominate the market throughout Charente and there tend to be fewer fully modernised, habitable properties available. The area has seen some dramatic price increases and the willingness of some British buyers to pay more for properties has encouraged some agents to charge twice their market value. Property values at the lower end of the market have at least doubled in the last couple of years. The price of a detached house and barn for renovation, for example, with a large garden in a hamlet setting, could even have increased threefold. Urban properties generally stay at the cheaper end, but are less popular with many international buyers who also seek gardens.

La Rochelle is popular with Parisians looking for second homes, and though it is more expensive than other parts of the region it represents a solid investment. The average price of a three-bedroom house in La Rochelle is £160,000. Generally speaking, properties in the southeast of Charente (Châtellerault) represent excellent value, as they are cheaper than those in the west and central areas. The Charente-Maritime (Île de Ré, and Île d'Oléron) region is seen as a real alternative to Dordogne and it affords good value for buy-to-lets.

Although Île de Ré properties are expensive, pushed up by Parisian second-home purchasers, they offer excellent rental potential. The island's 500,000 younger visitors are willing to pay £600 a week during the summer season, but these rents are not sustainable year-long, and the island's northern stretch all but closes down in winter.

Slightly nearer to Dordogne, Angoulême's property price tags are higher than elsewhere in the region, but rental can be accrued year-long. Buyers get less value for money in Cognac and Saintes. Gîtes are speckled throughout the Charente-Maritime, and La Rochelle, Île de Ré, Angoulême and their environs are popular. Chadurie, near Angoulême, has a stream of visitors renting more or less throughout the year.

Social groups

Saintes, Angoulême and the Charente area are favourites with British relocators, and investment purchases here have excellent future sales potential. To the west of Poitiers, Chauvigny, Bellac, L'Isle Jordain, Saint-Savin, Montmorillon, and Bussière Poitevine are prime holiday-home locales, and especially popular with British tourists. ●

"Beautiful wooded valleys are dotted with vineyards that provide the grapes for the region's famous Cognac, which the French export mainly to the UK and Japan"

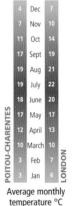

Average monthly temperature °C (Celsius)

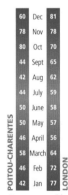

Average monthly rainfall mm (millimetres)

AVERAGE HOUSE SALE PRICES

Hotspot	2-bed	3-bed	4-bed	5-bed+
Île de Ré & La Rochelle	€191K (£133K)	€231K (£161K)	€355K (£246K)	€400K (£278K)
Charente	€80K (£56K)	€149K (£103K)	€221K (£153K)	€428K (£297K)
Poitiers	€98K (£72K)	€168K (£117K)	€228K (£158K)	€283K (£196K)
Châtelleraut	€68K (£47K)	€91K (£64K)	€140K (£97K)	€198K (£138K)

Focus on Charente

A fertile river valley that's home to rural villages as well as sophisticated towns, the Charente is the ideal relocation destination

POITOU-CHARENTES COMITÉ RÉGIONAL DU TOURISME

CHARENTE FACTS

■ Charente is home to the world-famous cognac which was first produced here

■ Angoulême houses a naval academy founded by Louis the Unavoidable (Louis XVIII) which is over 100 miles from the coast

■ In 1806 the 77-year-old General Resnier became the world first hanglider pilot, launching himself from the ramparts of Angoulême and soaring over the Charente river

THE CHARENTE VALLEY IS PATTERNED INTO FIELDS OF VERDANT FARMLAND and numerous vineyards that gracefully divide the rolling hills. Cognac originated here in a quieter, more rural time, but now the country idyll rubs shoulders with classy shops, restaurants and newly built villas that attest to the area's increasing wealth. Very popular with British buyers looking to relocate permanently instead of buying a second home, this western *département* between Bordeaux and the Loire Valley features miles of sandy Atlantic beaches while inland, several large rivers (including the Charente) run through peaceful wooded valleys.

The capital of Charente is the walled city of Angoulême, home to the annual World Music Festival. The city's most famous museum, the Centre national de la bande dessinée, celebrates cartoon characters from around the world – everything from Astérix to Peanuts. Housed in a former brewery elegantly modernised with contemporary glass extensions, the museum houses some 4,000 original drawings.

Prosperous Cognac is, predictably, the base of the main cognac houses. The oldest, Martell, was founded by a former smuggler. Although most attractions are connected with the drink, there are other interesting sites to visit. The château ruins are the birthplace of King François I while the town's museum contains an exhibition on the history of the region's wine-making industry. Cognac is also well-known for its annual detective thriller film festival.

House prices typically increase westwards in the region, although they are still cheaper than in Dordogne. The typical Charentaise house is made from stone and timber, with an ochre-tiled roof. Recently the *département* has seen a 7.3 per cent increase in prices, but despite this, a two-bedroom property will cost around €80,000. ●

ESSENTIALS

Population Angoulême 103,746, Cognac 27,042 ■ **Taxes** Taxe d'habitation: 6.62%, Taxe foncièrè: 14.11% ■ **Airport** Limoges/Bellegarde Airport, 87100 Limoges, Tel: +33 555 43 30 30

KEY FACTS

■ **Schools** Bordeaux International School, 53 Rue de Laseppe, 33000 Bordeaux Tel: +33 557 87 02 11

■ **Medical** Centre Hospitalier, Rue Montesquieu,16100 Cognac, Tel: +33 545 36 75 75

■ **Rentals** Good to average market, rental period up to four months a year ■ Demand is intermittent from Easter to end of October, but winter lets are possible ■ The average weekly rental price for a two-bedroom property is €470

■ **Pros** Cheap renovation properties, with a two-bedroom house costing from €80,210 ■ A wealthy area, and Angoulême is a lively town ■ Charente is the second sunniest region in France ■ A four-bedroom property is affordable at €221,000 but prices are expected to rise and have already done so by 7.3%

■ **Cons** Few habitable properties and poor employment prospects ■ Growing popularity means rising prices ■ Angoulême and south Angoulême are very expensive ■ Some prices have doubled due to foreign interest.

GETTING THERE

AIR Ryanair (08712 460000; www.ryanair.com) flies to La Rochelle and Tours from Stansted. Indirect flights can be taken from Paris to Poitiers on internal domestic flights.
ROAD Take a ferry to Cherbourg, St Malo or Le Havre with **Brittany Ferries** (08703 665333; www.brittanyferries.co.uk). From here take the A10 from Paris through to Saintes where the E603/N141 runs through to Angoulême and Charentes.
RAIL The **Eurostar** (08705 186 186; www.eurostar.com) travels to Paris and connects with TGV services available to Angoulême. From Angoulême there are local services in and around the Charente area. See **Rail Europe** (0870 830 2008; www.raileurope.co.uk) for more details.

HOTSPOTS

WHAT CAN YOU GET FOR YOUR EUROS?

€239,500

CHARENTE: A fully renovated property situated in the peaceful countryside of Charente, this house boasts five-bedrooms and a separate cottage within the grounds. Close to shops and amenities, this delightful property would make an ideal family holiday home.

€652,000

CHARENTE: An exceptional 16th-century manor house, this beautiful riverside property has nine bedrooms and 4,000m² of grounds. It boasts a 200m tall tower which requires renovation and is perfect for a tourist-based business. Close to the village and services of Aubeterre.

AVERAGE CHARENTE PROPERTY PRICES

	1-bed	2-bed	3-bed	4-bed	5-bed
Lettings	€350 (£243)	€470 (£326)	€680 (£472)	€840 (£583)	€1200 (£833)
House	€78,500 (£54,514)	€80,210 (£55,701)	€148,965 (£103,448)	€220,800 (£153,333)	€427,530 (£296,895)
Apartments	€53,000 (£36,806)	€95,000 (£65,972)	€145,100 (£100,764)	€169,800 (£117,917)	–

Property hotspots

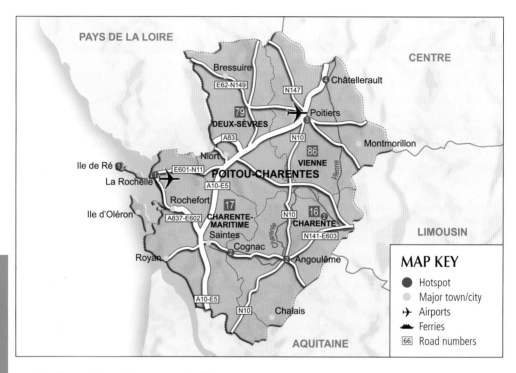

PAYS DE LA LOIRE

CENTRE

Bressuire

E62-N149

N147

Châtellerault

Poitiers

79

DEUX-SÈVRES

A83

N10

Montmorillon

Niort

VIENNE

Ile de Ré ①

E601-N11

POITOU-CHARENTES

La Rochelle

A10-E5

86

Rochefort

17

N10

16 ②

Ile d'Oléron

A837-E602

CHARENTE-
MARITIME

CHARENTE

LIMOUSIN

Saintes

N141-E603

Cognac

Royan

②

② Angoulême

MAP KEY

● Hotspot

○ Major town/city

✈ Airports

⛴ Ferries

66 Road numbers

A10-E5

N10

Chalais

AQUITAINE

1. Ile de Ré and La Rochelle

ESSENTIALS ■ **Population** 1999: 96,555 ■ **Taxes** Taxe d'habitation: 6.15%, Taxe foncière: 5.32% ■ **Airport** La Rochelle-Ile de Ré Airport, Rue du Jura, 17000 La Rochelle; Tel: +33 (0) 5 4642 3026

KEY FACTS

■ **Schools** Cité Scolaire Internationale Grand Air, Lycée et Collège de Grand Air, 77 Avenue du Bois d'Amour, 44500 La Baule Escoublac, Nantes; Tel: +33 (0) 2 4011 5800
■ **Medical** Centre hospitalier de La Rochelle, rue du Docteur Schweitzer, 1700 La Rochelle; Tel: +33 (0) 5 4645 5050 www.ch-larochelle.fr/
■ **Rentals** Ile de Ré: difficult to secure year-round rental ■ La Rochelle University ensures regular tenants ■ Tourism brings good short-term summer rentals ■ One-bedroom flats average at €360 per week, it costs around €980 for four-bedrooms
■ **Pros** Coastal resorts are popular with foreign second-home buyers ■ Property in Saint-Martin-de-Ré is also popular and La Rochelle has a busy, stable market ■ Ile de Ré enforces a two-storey height limit, plus white washed walls, green shutters and tiled roofs on all buildings ■ Good transport links
■ **Cons** Parisian second homes have raised prices, and both locations are expensive ■ Ile de Ré is quiet in winter, but very busy (500,000 visitors) in summer

La Rochelle is an unspoilt French Atlantic seaside town in Charente-Maritime, with a historic centre and waterfront protected from redevelopment and traffic. There are four distinct neighbourhoods: the 17th- to 18th-century centre; the innovative Les Minimes marina development, the residential and industrial inner suburbs, and to Ile de Ré Island.

Within the triangle of Place de Verdun, the Porte Royale and the Tour de la Lanterne is the historical centre where most of La Rochelle's architectural treasures lie, such as the military Tour Saint-Nicolas, providing a beautiful view of the Vieux Port. You'll also find the Musée du Nouveau Monde, the Musée des Beaux-Arts and Les Port des Minimes, one of Europe's biggest marinas.

Two miles away, the Ile de Ré, reached by a three-kilometre-long toll bridge, benefits from the Gulf Stream and year-round warmth. The north is a haven of oyster farms, salt marshes, wildlife sanctuaries and miles of unspoiled beaches. The east is more residential, with villages such as Saint-Martin or Sainte-Marie and their whitewashed cottages with brightly painted shutters. Here you can buy a maison de village to renovate, comprising five large rooms with walled garden and sea views for €350,000. A five-bedroom town house starts from €500,000. ●

2. Poitiers and area

ESSENTIALS ■ **Population** 1999: 83,500 ■ **Taxes** Taxe d'habitation: 6.08%, Taxe foncière: 7.10% ■ **Airport** Poitiers-Biard
Aeroport, Biard, 86000 Poitier;, Tel: +33 (0) 5 4930 0440

Overlooking the Clain and Boivre rivers, Poitiers was
seat to the dukes of Aquitaine and has tempted capture
by many past conquerors from Joan of Arc to Richard
the Lion Heart. It boasts a thriving University, stunning
Romanesque Notre-Dame Cathedral and lively
nightlife. Open spaces are plentiful, the 18th-century
Parc de Blossac with its elegant terraced limestone gardens is set on the
town's ramparts. Unusual events take place throughout the year with a
dog fair and the CollaVoce festival of music for organ and voice.

Six miles from the city is Futuroscope, the futuristic theme park set
in more than 130 acres devoted to giant screens, 3D cinemas, circular
cinemas and other state-of-the-art audio-visual spectacles. Space Station
3D recounts the daring in-orbit assembly of the International Space
Station. At night the finale is a fantastic laser light show with fireworks.

A two-bedroomed, semi-detached town house, close to the
cathedral, on four levels starts at €80,000. If you're looking for a home
to renovate, try Thénezay, a small market town just 30 minutes from
Poitiers. For €200,000 you can acquire a large house with exposed
beams and a private walled garden. In the quiet village of Vivonne, large
homes dating from 1880, in local hand-dressed stone with brick vaulted
ceilings and stained glass windows sell for €190,000. ●

KEY FACTS

■ **Schools** Cité Scolaire Internationale Grand Air,
Lycée et Collège de Grand Air, 77 Avenue du Bois
d'Amour, 44500 La Baule Escoublac, Nantes;
Tel: +33 (0) 2 4011 5800
■ **Medical** Centre Hospitalier Universitaire de
Poitiers, 2 Rue de la Miletrie, 86021Poitiers, Tel: +33
(0) 5 4944 4444
■ **Rentals** Average weekly rents for Poitiers and
environs are €540 for a two-bedroom place
(€1,400 for five bedrooms)
■ **Pros** Poitiers is attracting more foreign buyers ■
Good rail links and cheap flights from London
Stansted ■ Excellent climate ■ The Vendée coast is
just 90 minutes away and ski resorts two hours to
the west ■ Bellac, Montmorillon, Saint-Savin,
Chauvigny, L'Isle-Jordain and Bussière-Poitevine are
increasingly popular with foreign buyers ■ Good
potential returns on cheap renovation properties
■ **Cons** Once one of the cheapest property markets,
prices have more than doubled here in recent years

3. Châtellerault and area

ESSENTIALS ■ **Population** 1999: 36,026 ■ **Taxes** Taxe d'habitation: 6.08%, Taxe foncière: 7.10% ■ **Airport** Poitiers-Biard
Aeroport, Biard, 86000 Poitiers, Tel: +33 (0) 5 4930 0440

Founded in the 10th century, Châtellerault became a
favoured stopover for travellers and pilgrims while the
Henri IV bridge, constructed on order of Catherine de
Médici, opened the way to development as a major
river port. Visit the limestone underground caves at
nearby Availles-en-Châtellerault — legend says that they
were inhabited by gnomes in the 12th century. The Discovery Farm at
Thuré provides an introduction to local farming methods and to
gastronomy like honey and goats cheese.

A beautiful, busy spa town founded by the Romans in the 15th
century, la Roche-Posay is frequently visited for its healing waters, and
has an old town encircled by defence walls towering above the valley,
with donjon and fortified church. There are nine- and 18-hole golf
courses, a casino and horse racing, while the Tardes river is a favourite
for kayaking. The nearby Regional Park of the Brenne is one of the
largest wildlife sanctuaries in Europe, popular with bird-watchers.

Cheap properties are available in the area, and although there is not a
huge amount of foreign interest, demand still outstrips supply. French
buyers are the biggest group, and this is a good location in which to
invest. A typical country house built in limestone with clay roof tiles, a
courtyard garden and outbuildings costs from around €150,000. ●

KEY FACTS

■ **Schools** Cité Scolaire Internationale Grand Air,
Lycée et Collège de Grand Air, 77 Avenue du Bois
d'Amour, 44500 La Baule Escoublac, Nantes, Tel:
+33 (0) 2 4011 5800
■ **Medical** Hôpital Camille Guérin, Rocade Est,
86106 Châtellerault, Tel: +33 (0) 5 4902 9090
■ **Rentals** Not a tourist area; short-term rents are
not commonplace in Châtellerault ■ Average rent
for a two-bedroom property is €415 euros per week
■ A three-bedroom property costs €490 euros per
week ■ La Roche-Posay is a popular tourist
destination in summer, with a popular short-term
rental market
■ **Pros** Cheap properties are available, and it is still
possible to pick up a barn plus a piece of land for
around €10,000 euros ■ Steeped in history, this
area played a crucial role in the 100 Years' War
between France and England ■ There is still demand
for farm complexes, and demand for all property still
outstrips supply ■ This is still a good property
investment area
■ **Cons** Châtellerault is not really a tourist area ■
Few foreign buyers, and the market is primarily
French ■ There are limited employment
opportunities.

€50,000–€100,000
(£34,722–£69,444)

A good range of properties to suit those on a budget

€56,200   CODE VEF

NEAR LE DORAT

A quaint little house and barn in the countryside, requiring renovation

£39,028

🛏 – 🌼 *With a small garden* 🏞 *Situated near Le Dorat* 🛣 *Not located on a main road*
🏠 *Room for parking*

€63,600   CODE FPS

CHARENTE

A furnished holiday villa in a peaceful lakeside location, with communal pool

£44,167

🛏 2 🌼 *Private garden* 🏞 *Situated close to amenities* 🛣 *Not located on a main road*
🏠 *Room for parking*

€66,700   CODE PAP

BENEST

A renovation project with 9 rooms, water, electricity and lovely views

£46,319

🛏 – 🌼 *1,000m²* 🏞 *Situated at the edge of the hamlet* 🛣 *Not located on a main road*
🏠 *Room for parking*

€78,090   CODE VEF

NEAR BELLAC

An affordable holiday home just 30 minutes' drive from Limoges airport

£54,229

🛏 3 🌼 *Large garden* 🏞 *Situated 10 minutes from Bellac* 🛣 *Located on a main road*
🏠 *Room for parking*

€83,540   CODE VEF

NEAR BUSSIERE-POITEVINE

A charming stone cottage in habitable condition, with several outbuildings

£58,014

🛏 1 🌼 *Large garden* 🏞 *Situated in a quiet hamlet* 🛣 *Not located on a main road*
🏠 *Room for parking*

€100,000–€200,000
(£69,444–£138,889)

Well-positioned houses with good potential for development

€108,950

NEAR LA-MOTHE-ST-HERAY
A detached house and barn requiring some internal renovation
£75,659

🛏 2 ⚙ – 🏠 Situated in a small village 🚫 Not located on a main road
🏠 Room for parking

€111,200

CIVRAY
A former watermill requiring conversion and set over three floors, with a warehouse
£77,222

🛏 – ⚙ – 🏠 Situated on the outskirts of town 🚫 Not located on a main road
🏠 Room for parking

€148,400

NEAR MATHA
A traditional village house with 4 bedrooms and 2 attics, ripe for conversion
£103,055

🛏 4 ⚙ 1,100m² 🏠 Situated in the village centre 🚫 Not located on a main road
🏠 Room for parking

€162,000

NEAR BROSSAC, CHARENTE
A habitable 4-bedroom house set in wooded grounds, featuring 3 fishing lakes
£112,500

🛏 4 ⚙ 20,000m² 🏠 Situated close to Brossac 🚫 Not located on a main road
🏠 Room for parking

€178,624

LOULAY, CHARENTE-MARITIME
A large, detached house in excellent condition, with a garage and workshop
£124,044

🛏 5 ⚙ 300m² 🏠 Situated in the village centre 🚫 Not located on a main road
🏠 Room for parking, with a garage

€200,000–€300,000
(£138,889–£208,333)

Spacious houses and villas in quiet locations

€201,200   CODE PAP

LATILLE

A tidy detached villa with central heating and mains drainage
£139,722

🛏 3   ⊛ 1,100m²   🖼 Situated in a small town   🚫 Not located on a main road
🏠 Room for parking, with a double garage

€208,570   CODE PAP

CHARENTE-MARITIME

An attractive detached house requiring partial renovation, with a large barn
£144,840

🛏 3   ⊛ 4,000m²   🖼 Situated in a small hamlet   🚫 Not located on a main road
🏠 Room for parking

€225,220   CODE PAP

DAMPIERRE-SUR-BOUTONNE

A detached house with barns in excellent condition, plus attic conversion potential
£156,403

🛏 4   ⊛ 1,177m²   🖼 Situated in a quiet hamlet   🚫 Not located on a main road
🏠 Room for parking

€252,000   CODE PAP

PARTHENAY

A beautifully renovated medieval townhouse in a quiet market town
£175,000

🛏 4   ⊛ Courtyard garden   🖼 Situated in the town centre   🚫 Located on a main road
🏠 –

€299,000   CODE PAP

GENOUILLE

A lovely detached property set in large grounds in a quiet rural location
£207,639

🛏 4   ⊛ 1,925m²   🖼 Situated in a quiet hamlet   🚫 Not located on a main road
🏠 Room for parking

PRICE GUIDE

€300,000+
(£208,333+)

Distinctive properties with extensive grounds and facilities

€349,500   CODE PAP

LOUZAC-SAINT-ANDRE

A typical Charentaise house in good condition; plenty of potential, plus a distillery

£242,708

🛏 8 ⊛ 5,000m² Situated just outside the town Not located on a main road
Room for parking

€353,000   CODE FPS

SOUTH CHARENTE

A beautifully restored stone house with a large barn in a charming, historic town

£245,138

🛏 4 ⊛ 2,000m² Situated in the village centre Not located on a main road
Room for parking

€445,800   CODE SIF

RUFFEC, NORTH CHARENTE

A tastefully renovated watermill with old machinery incorporated into the living area

£309,583

🛏 4 ⊛ 74,120m² Situated close to the river Not located on a main road
Room for parking, with a large garage

€798,000   CODE SIF

CHARENTE

This attractive stone property includes a pool, 2 gîtes, stables and other outbuildings

£554,167

🛏 9 ⊛ 31,000m² Situated in the quiet location Not located on a main road
Room for parking

€1,000,000   CODE SIF

CHARENTE

This country property includes 6 gîtes, offering excellent business potential

£694,444

🛏 22 ⊛ 40,000m² Situated close to a pretty village Not located on a main road
Room for parking

PRICE GUIDE

Purchase foreign currency with confidence and ease when buying your home abroad

Exchange rate movements are unpredictable and volatile and can affect the cost of your overseas purchase. You can buy forward to eliminate this risk. It is easier than you think.

Currencies4Less offer you:
- **A personal and friendly service to guide you**
- **Specialist foreign exchange dealers**
- **Competitive rates**
- **No commission. No hidden costs.**

Talk to the specialists at Currencies4Less, a division of The 4Less Group plc. The 4Less Group is a publicly quoted company, offering a complete range of financial services for both private and corporate clients, including foreign exchange, overseas mortgages and overseas buildings and contents insurance. Call one of our dedicated dealers today on:

+44 (0)20 7594 0594
www.currencies4less.com

Currencies4less

Part of
The 4Less Group plc

Limousin & Auvergne

Beautiful medieval towns and glorious, unspoilt countryside

JACQUES MAFAITY

FACT BOX 2005

- ▥ **Population** 2,019,817
- ▥ **Migration** 108,902
- ▥ **Unemployment** 38,800
- ▥ **Median house price** €115,000
- ▥ **House price increase** Since 2002, house prices in Limousin have increased by 9.3%, while house prices in Auvergne have increased by 7.5%

Price Guide

GETTING THERE

AIR Air France (0845 084 5111; www.airfrance.co.uk) flies from London City, Heathrow, Bristol, Glasgow, Manchester, Southampton, Newcastle, Edinburgh, Glasgow and Aberdeen to Clermont-Ferrand and Limoges via Paris' Orly airport, while **Ryanair** (0871 246 0000, www.ryanair.com) offers direct flights from London Stansted to Limoges and Clermont-Ferrand.
ROAD Take the A10 from Paris, continuing on the A10-E5 and then the A71-E9 at the junction with the A71 for Limoges. At the junction for the A85, take the A20-E09 into Limousin and Limoges. For Clermont-Ferrand and the rest of Auvergne, follow the A10 from Paris to Orléans, taking the A71-E9 and then Junction 5 onto the A71-E11, then the N9 into Clermont-Ferrand.
RAIL A TGV service operates between Gare d'Austerlitz in Paris and Limoges. Gare de Lyon is linked with Clermont-Ferrand by an efficient, quick link.
Rail Europe (0870 830 2008; www.raileurope.co.uk) has further details.
COACH Eurolines (0870 514 3219; www.eurolines.com) operates services to Brive and Clermont-Ferrand.

Area profile

THE REGIONS OF LIMOUSIN AND AUVERGNE LIE ROUGHLY IN THE CENTRE of France. Limousin is one of the least explored areas of the country and it remains relatively unspoilt in comparison to the coast. The landscape is blessed with lakes, river valleys and rolling, tree-covered hills, and there are many beautiful medieval towns and villages.

The capital of Limousin is Limoges, which is home to almost 250,000 people. Fine porcelain and enamel have been produced in the city since the 1770s, and the city's museum houses an outstanding ceramic collection. Elsewhere, there's a beautiful old medieval quarter and a huge Gothic cathedral. East of Limoges, in the Creuse valley, lies Aubusson, a small town renowned for tapestry and carpet-weaving for over 500 years.

Further east is the Auverne region, which is in the heart of the Massif Central, a vast mountain range with spectacular gorges and more than 80 dormant volcanos. Allier in the north has the most gentle landscape and the impressive medieval town of Montluçon is its economic heart. Further south, the mountainous landscape is dotted with spa towns, which are built around the region's natural thermal springs. Le Puy-en-Velay, the capital of Haute-Loire, clings on to a selection of rocky outcrops, but most amazing is the Chapelle St-Michel d'Aiguilhe, which sits on the peak of a rocky spur.

Agriculture dominates much of the area and this is reflected in the cuisine – organic meat and foie gras are complemented with a wealth of berry fruits grown in Corrèze. Another popular local dish is *la Potée Auvergnate*, which is a stew made up of bacon, pork, potato and cabbage. Cantal cheese is another renowned local delicacy.

The economy and housing market

Both Limousin and Auvergne are popular with outdoor enthusiasts, including hikers, fishermen and windsurfers, and there are plenty of decent golf courses where you can enjoy the pleasant climate. As such, tourism

You'll find superb, unspoilt countryside in this beautiful area

dominates the Limoges economy, along the technological industry, including the production of electrical fittings. Clermont-Ferrand, near Vichy, is home to the Michelin tyre factory and Limagrain, one of the world's largest seed providers. Auvergne has a thriving blend of industry and commerce. The relocation of part of the French civil service to Limoges, and the positive attitude given to new business development by the regional capital's chamber of commerce, illustrates the developing economy.

Corrèze's economy is slowly changing from its tourism and agricultural roots to the production of Airbus components, which has provided the city with the nickname 'Mechanic Valley'.

House prices have risen rapidly in these regions, although they do offer good value for money compared to many others. Two-bedroom homes in Limoges sell for around £80,000, while La Creuse offers some of France's cheapest prices. Costs are competitive in Corrèze, and its proximity to Brive and planned improvements to the transport links give this area long-term investment potential. The villages around the Puy de Sancy mountain have a healthy rental season, with summer visitors drawn to the lakes and watersports while winter visitors enjoy the snow. The property market remains buoyant, despite a 50 per cent price increase in the last three years.

Properties in Besse-en-Chandesse are more expensive, with a renovated stone house costing around £260,000. Clermont-Ferrand is competitively priced and the rental market provides a good return for purchasers planning to let. Parisians favour it for second homes and its strong winter rental market is fuelled by the Mont Dore ski station. French, Dutch and Belgian tourists create excellent rental opportunities, while the Massif de Centrale has growing tourist popularity and good investment potential.

La Souterraine in La Creuse and Châlus to the southwest of Limoges offer excellent properties, and make for a good investment opportunity due to western Corrèze's high rental demand, which can generate a healthy rental income. Clermont-Ferrand offers good potential for relocation and short and long-term lets. New business is welcomed in Vichy, Limoges and Corrèze, while Brive and Tulle have good facilities for relocators to the area.

Property prices are increasing across this region and have risen by 18 per cent in 2004 because British and Dutch buyers are vying with French purchasers, creating a buoyant market. However, renovation properties in Corrèze are becoming harder to find and prices are continuing to rise. A large house requiring renovation generally costs over £100,000 here.

Social groups

Increased accessibility will bring in more foreign buyers, raising prices. An airport is planned for Brive in the next few years and a tram service is due for completion in Clermont-Ferrand in the next five years. More British buyers are moving here as prices rise even higher elsewhere. ●

> "Limousin is one of the least explored areas of France and it remains unspoilt in comparison to the coast. The landscape is blessed with lakes, river valleys and tree-covered hills"

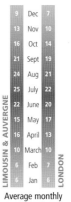

Average monthly temperature °C (Celsius)

Average monthly rainfall mm (millimetres)

AVERAGE HOUSE SALE PRICES

Hotspot	2-bed	3-bed	4-bed	5-bed+
Limoges	€114K (£79K)	€161K (£112K)	€184K (£128K)	€239K (£166K)
Clermont-Ferrand	€130K (£90K)	€180K (£125K)	€231K (£160K)	€277K (£192K)
Volcanic mountains & lakes	€102K (£71K)	€139K (£97K)	€167K (£116K)	€206K (£143K)
Corrèze	€99K (£69K)	€140K (£97K)	€176K (£122K)	€267K (£185K)
Vichy	€130K (£90K)	€190K (£132K)	€247K (£171K)	€417K (£290K)

Property hotspots

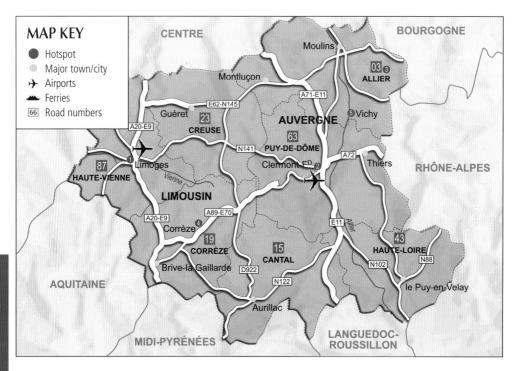

MAP KEY

- ● Hotspot
- ● Major town/city
- ✈ Airports
- ⏴ Ferries
- 66 Road numbers

CENTRE

BOURGOGNE

Moulins

Montluçon

03 ③
ALLIER

E62-N145

A71-E11

Guéret

23
CREUSE

A20-E9

AUVERGNE

⑤ Vichy

63
PUY-DE-DÔME

N141

Limoges

87

HAUTE-VIENNE

Vienne

Clermont-FD ②

A72

Thiers

RHÔNE-ALPES

LIMOUSIN

A20-E9

A89-E70

Corrèze ④

E11

Aller

43
HAUTE-LOIRE

19
CORRÈZE

15
CANTAL

N102

N88

Brive-la-Gaillarde

D922

N122

le Puy-en-Velay

AQUITAINE

Aurillac

MIDI-PYRÉNÉES

LANGUEDOC-
ROUSSILLON

1. Limoges

ESSENTIALS ■ **Population** 137,502 ■ **Taxes** Taxe d'habitation: 6.08%, Taxe foncière: 6.40% ■ **Airport** Limoges/Bellegarde Airport, 87100 Limoges, Tel: +33 555 43 30 30

KEY FACTS

■ **Schools** Bordeaux International School, 53 rue de Laseppe, 33000 Bordeaus, Tel: +33 557 87 02 11 ■ **Medical** CHU de Limoges, 2 avenue Martin-Luther-King, 87042 Limoges, Tel: +33 555 05 61 23 ■ **Rentals** Limoges offers the investor good rental potential ■ Mainly a long-term, local rental market, with approximately 16 weeks of summer rentals for short-term visitors ■ As it is relatively unknown, rental income may not be forthcoming in less-established areas ■ There are very few established agents ■ A two-bedroom house can be let from €450 a week
■ **Pros** Limoges is ideal for purchasers seeking a traditional French lifestyle ■ The city is packed with amenities and culture ■ The area has good transport links and there are good employment opportunities ■ This is an affordable city with a two-bedroom house costing €113,600
■ **Cons** The climate is cooler than the southern regions ■ Prices are rapidly rising, and the relocation of part of the Parisian civil service has driven property prices up ■ There isn't a big English-speaking community.

Located in northern Limousin, a region criss-crossed by rivers and lakes, Limoges offers good value for money and attractive surroundings. Initially built by the Romans, Limoges is not only at the heart of France's lake district and former home to Molière, but provides all the shopping, gastronomic and cultural attractions of a historic regional capital. The city's situation between the Loire and Bordeaux regions has resulted in a fertile soil ideal for vineyards, with wines aged in the sought-after Limoges oak, deriving from the nearby forests. By the Middle Ages, Limoges was known for its high-quality enamel work, and in the 18th century, the porcelain industry took off, making the city the world capital for ceramics and glass. The city boasts 12 miles of underground tunnels. First created as a subterranean network during Roman Times, the tunnels were made up of galleries used to supply the city with water, expanding to carry supplies into town from springs 3-4 miles away. On 28 December each year, Limoges hosts the Saint Innocent Fair, a winter extravaganza of *produits du terroir* in a tradition dating back to the 16th century.

Limoges is not an area renowned for its foreign property market, and it is dominated by the local French buyers. Prices are among the cheapest in France, with a three-bedroom property from €161,460. ●

2. Clermont-Ferrand ■

ESSENTIALS ■ **Population** 141,004 ■ **Taxe**s Taxe d'habitation: 7.47%, Taxe foncière: 10.76% ■ **Airport** Clermont-Ferrand Auvergne International Airport, Rue Youri Gagarine, 63510 Aulnat, Tel: +33 473 62 71 00

At the heart of Auvergne in the Massif Central, Clermont-Ferrand is one of France's oldest and most culturally dynamic cities. Clermont and Montferrand originally formed as two rival cities, until being merged under Louis XIV. Today's Clermont-Ferrand thrives as both a university city and the capital of the Puy de Dôme *département*. It is just half an hour's drive from Parc des Volcans, a natural, open air geological exhibition sculpted by volcanic eruptions and glaciers and made up of 80 dormant puys (volcanic chains). Many museums and attractions are dotted around this historic city, which is magically illuminated every Christmas with an open-air ice rink. The yearly Court Métrage Film Festival has become an international affair, showing cinema shorts from around the world. To the south lies the Mont-Dore massif, known for spa towns like La Bourbole, and the Super Besse ski resort.

Clermont-Ferrand is little known to the British and has been overlooked by buyers in favour of Provence and Côte d'Azur, despite property here costing half the price. The best value can be found in the suburbs, and as the city is undergoing redevelopment, property is likely to accrue value, with city centre property becoming expensive. Prices are competitive, with a three-bedroom house costing €179,960. ●

KEY FACTS

■ **Schools** École Internationale Michelin, 5 rue Bansac, 63000 Clermont-Ferrand, Tel: +33 473 98 09 70
■ **Medical** Centre Hospitalier Universitaire de Clermont-Ferrand, 58 rue Montalembert, 6300 Clermont-Ferrand, Tel: +33 473 75 07 50
■ **Rentals** There is interest both during summer and winter, due to the town's proximity to the Mont-Dore ski station ■ A two-bedroom house in Clermont-Ferrand starts at €480 a week ■ Lets are usually long term, and a one-bedroom apartment starts at €495 a month
■ **Pros** There are excellent transport links and budget flights serving the area ■ A three-bedroom property starts at an average €180,000 ■ The city has a large foreign population, and has a well-established and well-resourced international school ■ It is a place of cultural importance and national interest, with good job prospects
■ **Cons** Clermont-Ferrand is a university city and is lively and cosmopolitan, but may not suit those seeking a peaceful location ■ The city is very heavily industrialised in parts.

3. Volcanic Mountains and Lakes of Auvergne ■

ESSENTIALS ■ **Population** Moulins 21,100 ■ **Taxes** Taxe d'habitation: 8.11%, Taxe foncière: 9.05% ■ **Airport** Clermont-Ferrand Auvergne International Airport, Rue Youri Gagarine, 63510 Aulnat, Tel: +33 473 62 71 00

One of the cheapest places to buy property, the Allier *département* in North Auvergne is the birthplace of the Bourbon dukes, with 15th-century manor houses and châteaux available to buy. Criss-crossed by lakes and home to the Forest of Tronçais, this part of France is a true historic treasure. It is also referred to as 'the land of 1,001 châteaux,' 50 of which are open to the general public. Located on the Allier river north of Lyon, the agricultural town of Moulins is this region's capital.

Outdoor activities can be enjoyed on Lake Allier, a 300-acre expanse of water lined with open-air cafés and aquatic leisure centres. To the centre of Allier lies the Bocage Bourbonnais, a cattle-rearing area known for its monuments, castles and Romanesque churches. To the south of Moulins, the volcanic Montagne Bourbonnaise is a popular terrain favoured by hikers, mountain bikers, horse riders and skiers in winter.

This is a rural, undeveloped area that will not suit buyers looking for an active city life. As the area is popular with those on activity holidays, it is perfect for tourist-based businesses. The foreign buyer is beginning to be drawn to the area, so now is a good time to invest. Property is cheap, with a two-bedroom home costing from €102,250. ●

KEY FACTS

■ **Schools** École Internationale Michelin, 5 rue Bansac, 63000 Clermont-Ferrand, Tel: +33 473 98 09 70
■ **Medical** Centre Hospitalier Universitaire de Clermont-Ferrand, 58 rue Montalembert, 6300 Clermont-Ferrand, Tel: +33 473 75 07 50
■ **Rentals** Tourists quadruple the population in peak season, creating very high demand for rental properties for 20 weeks of the year
■ **Pros** The Massif du Sancy offers outdoor activities and watersports ■ Clermont-Ferrand is easily accessible, with a comprehensive transport network ■ The Massif du Sancy is an established tourist destination, with many foreign buyers rapidly recognising the area's merits ■ A two-bedroom property costs from €102,250
■ **Cons** A car is essential, otherwise it can be a very isolated place to live or stay ■ Apart from high season, the area is quiet and under-populated.

4. Corrèze

ESSENTIALS ■ **Population** 84,927 ■ **Taxes** Taxe d'habitation: 5.68%, Taxe foncière: 11.61% ■ **Airport** Limoges/Bellegarde Airport, 87100 Limoges, +33 555 43 30 30

KEY FACTS

■ **Schools** École Internationale Michelin, 5 rue Bansac, 63000 Clermont-Ferrand, Tel: +33 473 98 09 70
■ **Medical** Centre Hospitalier de Tulle, 3 Place du Dr Machat, 19000 Tulle, Tel: +33 555 29 79 68
■ **Rentals** Demand for properties to let is currently outstripping supply, but it is difficult to generate rental income ■ High season is predominantly June to August ■ Around 80 to 90 per cent of people relocating to this area wish to establish a tourist-based business ■ A good quality four-bedroom house in Corrèze could fetch around €780 per week
■ **Pros** Brive-la-Gaillarde is easily accessible, with good transport links ■ Brive and Tulle, the capital of Corrèze, both have good facilities and amenities ■ The area has a growing international community, with British and other foreign buyers ■ Property is cheap, the average two-bedroom home costing as little as €98,950
■ **Cons** The weather is similar to the Dordogne (see pages 235-5) but milder in the north ■ The bus service is irregular ■ Property is becoming hard to find in the most popular areas of Corrèze, particularly the Vallée de la Dordogne region and the southwest area of Turenne and Larche.

The Corrèze area has been popular for some time with holiday-makers and buyers who want better value for money than the Dordogne, without compromising on the quality of their destination. There is already a short-term lets market driven by the many tourists, who regularly visit the area, offering outstanding natural beauty, culture and gastronomy, as well as a good quality of life for its residents. Areas of interest in this region include Uzerche and Arnac-Pompadour, with their beautiful châteaux and romanesque churches, plus the picturesque villages of Turenne and Collonge-la-Rouge, with their spectacular views over ridges and valleys to the mountains of Cantal and Gimel-les-Cascades. The Vallée de la Dordogne, with its rivers, gorges and pretty villages, is also a very popular, with well-developed cycle and walking tracks in breathtaking surroundings making it popular in the summer months.

Besse-en-Chandesse has seen a 30 per cent growth in property prices during the past three years, and prices are rather steep in relation to the lack of facilities in the area. In northwestern Corrèze, however, property is more affordable. An average two-bedroom habitable property can be purchased for €99,000, while a four-bedroom home can be picked up for around €176,000. ●

5. Vichy

ESSENTIALS ■ **Population** 25,500 ■ **Taxes** Taxe d'habitation: 8.11%, Taxe foncière: 9.05% ■ **Airport** Clermont-Ferrand Auvergne International Airport, Rue Youri Gagarine, 63510 Aulnat, Tel: +33 473 62 71 00

KEY FACTS

■ **Schools** École Internationale Michelin, 5 rue Bansac, 63000 Clermont-Ferrand, Tel: +33 473 98 09 70
■ **Medical** Hôpital de Vichy, Bd Denière, 03201 Vichy, +33 473 98 09 70, www.ch-vichy.fr
■ **Rentals** A good rental season, lasting from May until September ■ A four-bedroom house costs from €580 per week, while a two-bedroom property costs from as little as €215 ■ The season for thermal spas is April to October, which attracts many tourists
■ **Pros** An established centre of tourism, Vichy has been relaunched as a major European centre for health, beauty and fitness ■ An increasing number of Dutch and French tourists have created a short-term rental market ■ Near to Clermont-Ferrand, it is an easily accessible town ■ There is an increasing number of foreign buyers, but 90 per cent of buyers are currently French retirees
■ **Cons** The area's rising popularity with semi-retired and retired couples has created a buoyant property market, and prices have increased by 30 per cent ■ Properties can be expensive.

Renowned for its cuisine and thermal spas, Vichy is a spa town and the birthplace of the Bourbon dynasty, as well as Pétain's 'Vichy France'. Over the past 10 years, Vichy has been revamped in an attempt to give the town international appeal. The city has invested in a spa, health farms and business tourism, and has undergone architectural renovation and a redevelopment of the town centre. Offering a relaxed cosmopolitan atmosphere, Vichy has a certain *belle époque* charm, and there is an abundance of cultural diversions.

Tourism is the biggest industry in the area, especially given that Vichy is central, and easily accessible from Clermont-Ferrand and its airport. The town has begun to attract an increasing number of Dutch and French buyers, and demand for property is on the increase. As the property market becomes increasingly buoyant, property prices have risen by approximately 30 to 40 per cent. The international market is split between those who are buying to retire and those who are permanently relocating to the area, and although there is an ever-increasing number of British buyers, 90 per cent of those who buy in Vichy are French; most British buy in the Ébreuil area, 28 kilometres away. Property is affordable, with a two-bedroom house costing an average of €130,000 and a four-bedroom home from €247,000. ●

USEFUL CONTACTS

PRÉFECTURES

Préfecture de la Région Auvergne
18 Boulevard Desaix
63033 Clermont-Ferrand Cedex
Tel: +33 473 98 63 63
Fax: +33 473 98 61 03
www.auvergne.pref.gouv.fr

Préfecture de la Région Limousin
Rue de la Préfecture
87031 Limoges Cedex
Tel: +33 555 44 18 00
Fax: +33 555 79 86 58
www.haute-vienne.pref.gouv.fr

Préfecture de l'Allier
2 Rue Michel de l'Hospital
BP 1649
03016 Moulins Cedex
Tel: +33 470 48 30 00
Fax: +33 470 20 57 72
Email: webmestre@
allier.pref.gouv.fr
www.allier.pref.gouv.fr

Préfecture de Haute–Loire
6 Avenue Charles-de-Gaulle
43000 Le Puy-en-Velay
Tel: +33 471 09 43 43
Fax: +33 471 09 78 40
Email: centre.doc.prefecture
@wanadoo.fr
www.haute-loire.pref.gouv.fr

Préfecture de Cantal
Cours Monthyon
BP 529
15005 Aurillac
Tel: +33 471 46 23 00
Fax: +33 471 64 88 01
www.cantal.pref.gouv.fr

Préfecture de Creuse
Place Louis Lacrocq
23011 Gueret Cedex
Tel: +33 555 51 58 00
Fax: +33 555 52 48 61

Email: info@creuse.pref.gouv.fr
www.creuse.pref.gouv.fr

Préfecture de Corrèze
1 Rue Souham
BP 250
19012 Tulle Cedex
Tel: +33 555 20 55 20
Email: prefcorreze@
correze.pref.gouv.fr
www.correze.pref.gouv.fr

LEGAL

Chambre des Notaires du Puy-de-Dôme
10 Rue du Maréchal Foch
63000 Clermont-Ferrand
Tel: +33 473 29 16 66
www.chambre-puy-de-
dome.notaires.fr

Chambre des Notaires de la Corrèze
3 Place Winston-Churchill
87000 Limoges
Tel: +33 555 77 15 91
www.chambre-
limousin.notaires.fr

Chambre des Notaires de l'Allier
19 Rue Diderot
03000 Moulins
Tel: +33 470.44.10.30
Email: c.allier@notaires.fr
www.chambre-allier.notaires.fr

Chambre des Notaires de la Haute Loire
9 Impasse Michelet
BP 158
43004 Le Puy-en-Velay
Tel: +33 4.71.02.11.29
www.chambre-haute-
loire.notaires.fr

FINANCE

Direction des Impôts du Centre

70 Rue de la Bretonnerie
BP 2457
45032 Orléans Cedex 1
Tel: +33 238 74 55 25
Fax: +33 238 74 55 62

Direction des Impôts du Sud-Ouest
2 Rue des Piliers de Tutelle
BP 45
33025 Bordeaux Cedex
Tel: +33 557 14 21 00

BUILDING & PLANNING

Chambre Régionale de Métiers d'Auvergne
Centre Victoire
1 Avenue de Cottages BP 358
63010 Clermont-Ferrand
Cedex 1
Tel: +33 473 29 42 00
Email: crma@crm-auvergne.fr

Chambre Régionale de Métiers du Limousin
14 Rue de Belfort
87100 Limoges
Tel: +33 555 79 45 02
www.crm-limousin.fr

Caue de Haute-Vienne
1 Rue des Allois
87000 Limoges
Tel: +33 555 32 32 40

Caue du Puy-de-Dôme
Hôtel du Département
30 Rue Saint Esprit
63000 Clermont-Ferrand
Tel: +33 473 42 21 20

EDUCATION

Rectorat de l'Académie de Clermont-Ferrand
3 Avenue Vercingétorix
63033 Clermont-Ferrand
Tel: +33 473 99 30 00
Fax: +33 473 99 30 01
www.ac-clermont.fr

Rectorat de l'Académie de Limoges
13 Rue François-Chénieux
87031 Limoges Cedex
Tel: +33 555 11 40 40
Fax: +33 555 79 82 21
www.ac-limoges.fr

Caue de l'Allier
14, Rue Jean Jaurès
03000 Moulins
Tel: +33 470 20 11 00
Email: caue03@wanadoo.fr

Caue du Cantal
20, Rue Guy de Veyre
15000 Aurillac
Tel: +33 471 48 50 22
Fax: +33 471 48 24 71
Email: caue.cantal@wanadoo.fr

Caue de Haute-Loire
Hôtel du département
1 Pl. Mgr de Galard BP 310
43011 Le Puy-en-Velay Cdx
Tel: +33 471 07 41 76

Caue de la Corrèze
1 Rue Félix Vidalin
19000 Tulle
Tel: +33 555 26 06 48
Fax: +33 555 26 61 16
Email: caue.19@wanadoo.fr

HEALTH

Caisse Primaire d'Assurance
Maladie de la Haute-Vienne
22 Avenue Jean Gagnant
87037 Limoges
Tel: +33 820 90 41 31
Fax: +33 555 45 88 29

Caisse Primaire d'Assurance
Maladie du Puy-de-Dôme
Rue Pélissier
63000 Clermont-Ferrand
Tel: +33 820 90 41 45
www.cpam-clermont-
ferrand.ameli.fr

HOTSPOTS

205

€25,000–€100,000
(£17,361–£69,444)

There are plenty of bargain projects to be found in some of the smaller villages

€25,900 — CODE PAP

ST-HILAIRE-LA-TREILLE, LIMOUSIN

A quaint village house requiring considerable renovation to make it habitable
£17,986

🛏 1 ❀ Small, enclosed yard 🖼 Situated in the village centre 🚗 Located on a main road 🏠 Room for parking

€47,400 — CODE PAP

CHAMBORAND, LIMOUSIN

A lovely little village house with a small patio garden. Requires some renovation
£32,917

🛏 2 ❀ 40m² 🖼 Situated in the village centre 🚗 Located on a main road 🏠 Room for parking

€75,200 — CODE PAP

SACIERGES-ST-MARTIN, LIMOUSIN

This converted barn has great potential and could become a lovely family home
£52,222

🛏 – ❀ 10,110m² 🖼 Situated in quiet cul-de-sac 🚗 Not located on a main road 🏠 Room for parking

€83,850 — CODE FRA

AMBERT, AUVERGNE

An attractive 2-bedroom house with an adjoining barn that has conversion potential
£58,229

🛏 2 ❀ – 🖼 Situated in a quiet rural area 🚗 Not located on a main road 🏠 Room for parking

€97,200 — CODE FPS

NEAR ROCHECHOUART, HAUTE-VIENNE

A habitable, detached stone house requiring some renovation
£67,500

🛏 4 ❀ 1,000m² 🖼 Situated a short walk from the village 🚗 Not located on a main road 🏠 Room for parking, with a garage

€100,000–€200,000
(£69,444–£138,889)

Most of these large properties offer plenty of potential for expansion

€100,000   CODE FRA

NEAR RANDANNE, PUY-DE-DÔME

An attractive old village house with 3 outbuildings and lots of potential

£69,444

🛏 3   ✦ 5,150m²   🏠 Situated in a peaceful hamlet   🚗 Not located on a main road

🏠 Room for parking, with a garage

€129,600   CODE PAP

ST-GERMAIN-BEAUPRÉ, LIMOUSIN

A nicely restored village house with great potential for expansion

£90,000

🛏 4   ✦ 1,600m²   🏠 Situated in a peaceful hamlet   🚗 Not located on a main road

🏠 Room for parking, with a garage

€138,750   CODE PAP

ST-PRIEST-LA-PLAINE, LIMOUSIN

A lovely and surprisingly large village house, with a barn for possible conversion

£96,354

🛏 4   ✦ 1,582m²   🏠 Situated in a quiet rural area   🚗 Not located on a main road

🏠 Room for parking, with a garage

€178,600   CODE PAP

NAILLAT, LIMOUSIN

A carefully restored farmhouse with great potential, set in lovely rural surroundings

£124,028

🛏 3   ✦ 1,529m²   🏠 Situated in a quiet cul-de-sac   🚗 Not located on a main road

🏠 Room for parking

€188,400   CODE PAP

FURSAC, LIMOUSIN

The neglected garden in front of this large house belies the light and spacious interior

£130,833

🛏 6   ✦ 2,500m²   🏠 Situated in a small hamlet   🚗 Not located on a main road

🏠 Room for parking

PRICE GUIDE

€200,000–€300,000
(£138,889–£208,333)

A selection of large family homes in idyllic rural settings

€210,000   CODE FRA

ALLIER, AUVERGNE

An incredible 3-bedroom house in large grounds, with a vaulted wine cellar

£145,833

🛏 3   ❀ 30,000m²   🏞 *Situated in the north of Allier*   🛣 *Not located on a main road*   🏠 *Room for parking, with a double garage*

€244,200   CODE FRA

ALLIER, AUVERGNE

An attractive 1930s property with plenty of character and splendid views

£169,583

🛏 6   ❀ 1,870m²   🏞 *Situated on the outskirts of town*   🛣 *Not located on a main road*   🏠 *Room for parking*

€265,000   CODE FPS

HAUTE-VIENNE, LIMOUSIN

A licensed bar/restaurant with a barn and garden in a small, lively village

£184,028

🛏 5   ❀ *Garden with barn*   🏞 *Situated in the village centre*   🛣 *Located on a main road*   🏠 *Room for parking*

€270,000   CODE FRA

NEAR AMBERT, AUVERGNE

A very attractive property in a small hamlet, with superb mountain views

£187,500

🛏 3   ❀ 6,100m²   🏞 *Situated 5km from Ambert*   🛣 *Not located on a main road*   🏠 *Room for parking, with a garage*

€285,650   CODE PAP

DOMPIERRE-LES-EGLISES, LIMOUSIN

Set in idyllic rural surroundings, this house has been thoughtfully renovated

£198,368

🛏 3   ❀ 8,000m²   🏞 *Situated in a quiet rural area*   🛣 *Not located on a main road*   🏠 *Room for parking*

€300,000+
(£208,333+)

These beautiful properties represent a great investment opportunity

€301,800   CODE PAP

LA SOUTERRAINE, LIMOUSIN

This modern but traditionally styled house requires absolutely no work

£209,583

🛏 5   ✦ 1,500m²   🏞 Situated on the outskirts of town   🚫 Not located on a main road   🏠 Room for parking, with a garage

---

€338,000   CODE FPS

HAUTE-VIENNE, LIMOUSIN

A well-restored house with a gîte, barn and garage, set in large grounds

£234,722

🛏 7   ✦ 4,000m²   🏞 Situated in a quiet hamlet   🚫 Not located on a main road   🏠 Room for parking, with a garage

---

€389,000   CODE DEM

ALLIER, AUVERGNE

A huge farm with a 19th Century Maison de Maître to restore and three outbuildings

£270,139

🛏 –   ✦ 32 hectares   🏞 Situated close to Montluçon   🚫 Not located on a main road   🏠 Room for parking

---

€405,000   CODE FPS

CORRÈZE, LIMOUSIN

A beautifully renovated farmhouse with large cellars and an indoor pool

£281,250

🛏 4   ✦ 34,000m²   🏞 Situated in a peaceful area   🚫 Not located on a main road   🏠 Room for parking, with a private driveway

---

€590,000   CODE FPS

HAUTE-VIENNE, LIMOUSIN

A fully-renovated 17th-century watermill with a guest house and large outbuildings

£409,722

🛏 4   ✦ 92,000m²   🏞 Situated in an idyllic rural location   🚫 Not located on a main road   🏠 Room for parking

Rhône Alps

Glorious Beaujolais, gastronomic Lyon and stunning mountains

OFFICE DU TOURISME DE COURCHEVEL

FACT BOX 2005

- **Population** 5,645,407
- **Migration** 625,753
- **Unemployment** 115,092
- **Median house price** €154,335
- **House price increase** Since 2002, house prices in the Rhône Alps have increased by 18.2%, which is the second-largest increase of any French region

Price Guide

GETTING THERE

AIR British Airways (0870 850 9850; www.britishairways.com) flies to Lyon Airport from Birmingham, Heathrow and Manchester; **Ryanair** (0871 246 0000; www.ryanair.com) operates flights to Saint Etienne from Stansted; **easyJet** (0871 750 0100; www.easyjet.com) flies to Lyon and Grenoble from Stansted, and Geneva International Airport from all across the UK; **Air France** (0845 084 5111; www.airfrance.co.uk) operates from Heathrow to Lyon Airport. In addition, **BMI Baby** (0870 264 2229; www.bmibaby.com), **Virgin Express** (0870 730 1134; virgin-express.com), **Aer Lingus** (0845 084 4444; www.aerlingus.com), **Air France** and **British Airways** all fly to nearby Geneva International Airport.

ROAD From Paris, take the A6 to Lyon and then the A43, which takes a fairly direct route to Chambéry and Grenoble. For Lake Annecy and its environs, take the A6-E15 (with toll booths) from Lyon. This links to the A40-E21 at the junction with the A40, then take the N508 to Annecy. For Megève and the Trois Vallées, break off the A40-E21 at the A401 'Genève-centre' junction. From here take the A40-E25 via its junction with the A411. This leads to the N205, then the N212.

COACH National Express Eurolines operates to Lyon (08705 143219; www.eurolines.com).

RAIL Fast TGV trains run from Gare de Lyon in Paris to Lyon and Grenoble, which provides convenient access to Annecy, Megève, Evian-les-Bains and all the town/ski resort hotspots (www.sncf.fr, www.voyages-sncf.com or www.tgv.com). Taxis operate from Chambéry, Lyon, Annecy and Geneva stations to the Courchevel, Val d'Isère, Les Menuires, Val Thorens and Tignes ski stations. **Eurostar** (0870 518 6186; www.eurostar.co.uk) offers a direct route (twice a week in the skiing season; one overnight and one in daytime) to Bourg-Saint-Maurice or Moutiers in the centre of the ski resorts from London Waterloo or Ashford in Kent (08705 353535; www.eurotunnel.com).

Area profile

THE RHÔNE ALPS REGION ENCOMPASSES SOME OF EUROPE'S MOST spectacular scenery, fabulous ski resorts, France's second city Lyon, and the rolling vineyards of Beaujolais. In the east of the region, the Alps serve as a natural border with Switzerland in the north and Italy in the south.

The Rhône Valley cuts through the mid-western section of the region and it's here you discover the lush, fertile hills and vineyards of Beaujolais. A few miles south is Lyon, the nation's gastronomic capital and a city that has prospered for many hundreds of years. Its wealth was originally built on printing and weaving, and today it has four UNESCO World Heritage sites as well as many of the country's finest restaurants. Seventy miles southeast of Lyon is Grenoble, the capital of the French Alps, which is home to more than 40,000 students and numerous high-tech research companies. With lots of museums and yearly festivals, the city is a great cultural centre and a good location from which to explore the nearby mountain ranges.

Further east, along the border with Switzerland and Italy, are some of Europe's finest winter resorts including Chamonix, Megève, Méribel, Courchevel and Val d'Isère. Many of these towns are exclusive and hugely expensive, particularly during the skiing season. In the summer months the Alps are generally quieter, but they still attract hikers and mountaineers. Summers are generally dry and very warm but, of course, the Alps see a tremendous amount of snow between December and February.

As mentioned, Rhône Alps is home to France's gastronomic capital and the variety of food and wine is fabulous. Although there are lots of restaurants with Michelin stars, you can eat cheaply at the many *bouchons*, small bistros that serve hearty fare for little money. Specialities include *quenelle de brochet* (poached pike mousse), *boudin noir* (salty blood sausage often served with potatoes in butter) and *cervelle de canut* (cream cheese mixed with garlic and chives). Charcuterie is also very popular. Fine wines include Châteauneuf du Pape, Côtes du Rhône and, of course, Beaujolais.

The Alps have warm summers, as well as snowy winters

The economy and housing market

The Rhône Alps resorts around Mont Blanc have tourism-based economies. This extends to the Lake Annecy villages and the popular resorts of Annecy, Talloires and Thonon-les-Bains. Very much the ski locale's capital and historically an industrial town, Grenoble offers less glitz and more substance, with four large universities as well as a thriving industrial sector. Lyon, the major commercial centre, is big on banking and commerce. Wine production, tourism and, to the southwest of Villefranche, one of France's premier wine routes, are mainstays of the Beaujolais economy.

Megève's lower position on the slopes and resulting poor snow record should, at first glance, make this international resort an insecure investment, but thanks to its golf course, hotels and restaurants, it's a year-round rental proposition. Val d'Isère's ski season and good snow record ensure that's it's a sure-fire hit for buying to let.

A rising star for relocators, the western side of the Beaujolais, stretching from La Clayette in the north of the region to Tarare in the south, is very different from the vineyard region between Lyon and Mâcon. Its remoteness from these big cities makes its properties cheaper to buy than the former wine-growers' homes around Mâcon overlooking the Saône valley and built of the characteristic *pierre dorée* stone.

Village houses around Chamonix, Annecy, and Chambéry are sound investments, as the long-term rental potential is good. A shortage of building land and increasing land prices in the winter ski resorts of Chamonix, Morzine, Val d'Isère and Chambéry, plus a current ban on building permits in Les Gets point to demand outstripping supply, and increasing prices on the horizon.

Social groups

Grenoble and Chambéry are both home to small British communities, while the exclusive skiing resorts attract the glitterati from all over the continent. Talloires and Annecy boast some excellent all-year-round amenities, and many British buyers make use of the pistes around La Clusaz and Grand Bornard. ●

"The Rhône Alps region encompasses some of Europe's most spectacular scenery, fabulous ski resorts and the glorious vineyards of Beaujolais"

Average monthly temperature °C (Celsius)

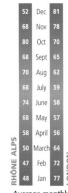

Average monthly rainfall mm (millimetres)

AVERAGE HOUSE SALE PRICES

Hotspot	2-bed	3-bed	4-bed	5-bed+
Lake Annecy	€207K (£144K)	€330K (£229K)	€380K (£264K)	€525K (£365K)
Lake Geneva	€215K (£149K)	€289K (£201K)	€400K (£278K)	€484K (£336K)
Megève	€209K (£145K)	€319K (£222K)	€513K (£356K)	€651K (£452K)
Chamonix	€311K (£216K)	€522K (£362K)	€615K (£427K)	€1,033K (£717K)
Méribel	€241K (£167K)	€418K (£290K)	€540K (£375K)	€720K (£500K)
Courchevel	€269K (£187K)	€384K (£267K)	€451K (£313K)	€913K (£639K)
Les Menuires	€168K (£117K)	€305K (£212K)	€316K (£220K)	€426K (£296K)
Val d'Isère	€297K (£206K)	€431K (£299K)	€725K (£503K)	€1,050K (£729K)
Grenoble	€196K (£136K)	€365K (£253K)	€365K (£253K)	€558K (£388K)
Les Portes du Soleil	€180K (£125K)	€290K (£201K)	€402K (£279K)	€590K (£410K)
Lyon	€241K (£167K)	€265K (£184K)	€420K (£292K)	€591K (£410K)
Beaujolais	€160K (£111K)	€223K (£155K)	€349K (£242K)	€448K (£311K)

Property hotspots

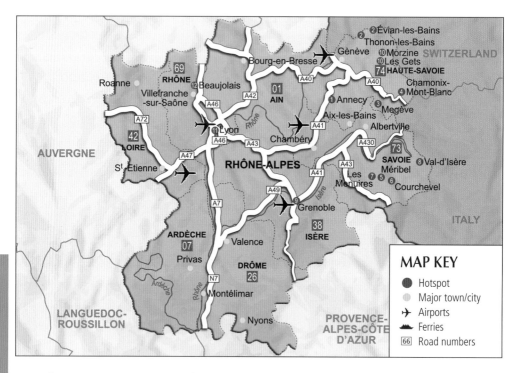

Map labels: Évian-les-Bains, Thonon-les-Bains, Genève, Morzine, Les Gets, SWITZERLAND, HAUTE-SAVOIE, Bourg-en-Bresse, Roanne, RHÔNE 69, Beaujolais, Chamonix-Mont-Blanc, Villefranche-sur-Saône, AIN 01, Annecy, Megève, Aix-les-Bains, Albertville, AUVERGNE, LOIRE 42, Lyon, Chambéry, RHÔNE-ALPES, SAVOIE 73, Val-d'Isère, St Etienne, Méribel, Les Menuires, Courchevel, Grenoble, ITALY, ARDÈCHE 07, Valence, ISÈRE 38, Privas, DRÔME 26, Montélimar, LANGUEDOC-ROUSSILLON, Nyons, PROVENCE-ALPES-CÔTE D'AZUR

MAP KEY
- ● Hotspot
- ◐ Major town/city
- ✈ Airports
- ⛴ Ferries
- 66 Road numbers

1. Lake Annecy

ESSENTIALS ■ **Population** 53,571 ■ **Taxes** Taxe d'habitation: 5.33%, Taxe foncière: 7.65% ■ **Airport** Annecy Metz Airport, 8 route de Côte Merle, 74370 Metz-Tessy, Tel +33 450 27 30 06, www.annecy.aeroport.fr

KEY FACTS

■ **Schools** Nearest: Albertville, Megève and Ferney Voltaire
■ **Medical** Centre Hospitalier, av Trésum 1, 74000 Annecy, Tel: +33 450 88 33 33
■ **Rentals** Foreign buyers choose Talloires for year-round stays ■ Average rental for a two-bedroom house in Talloires is €920 a week ■ Winter is peak season in this popular tourist resort ■ Annecy's average rental fees are from €600 to €1,800 per week for a two-bedroom villa
■ **Pros** Plenty of tourist amenities, including shops and art exhibitions ■ Excellent transport links ■ On a par with the Côte d'Azur for French retirees ■ Annecy Old Town is very attractive ■ Golfing facilities are nearby
■ **Cons** Annecy's Old Town is very crowded in summer ■ Limited winter rentals; skiers prefer resorts closer to the slopes.

Annecy is a charming alpine town with a medieval quarter, canals, flower-covered bridges and narrow streets. In the 19th century, European nobility rediscovered it and built lavish palaces on the lake, which at nine miles long and framed by woodland, is reputedly Europe's cleanest. Outdoor pursuits such as swimming, sailing, and cycling give it a standing on a par with the Côte d'Azur, and there are many ski resorts within a 90-minute drive.

Villas with swimming pools, chalets and apartments in and around the lakeside villages are much cheaper than in the mountain resorts. Some villages can be reached by steamer, and many have their own beaches. Talloires lies eight miles south, on the eastern side of the Tournette, Annecy's highest surrounding mountain. It houses the Michelin-starred Auberge du Père-Bise restaurant and an 11th-century Benedictine abbey, now the luxurious Hôtel de l'Abbaye (Cézanne and Churchill were famous residents). In August, French families come to hike and camp. A studio apartment with private garden in Talloires is around €110,000, with larger properties priced from around €300,000. Properties with lake views are especially pricey – a three-bedroom, renovated chalet with lake views is around €660,000. A shortage of building land has also pushed up prices. ●

2. Lake Geneva ■

ESSENTIALS ■ **Population** 37,480 ■ **Taxes** Taxe d'habitation: 5.33%, Taxe foncière: 7.65% ■ **Airport** Geneva Airport, PO BOX 100, CH-1215 Geneva 15, Switzerland, Tel: + 41 227 17 71 11

Popular with aristocrats during the *Belle Époque*, Thonon–les–Bains spa lies in the lower Chablais region, north of Haute-Savoie on Lake Geneva. Constructed on three levels between lake and mountains in a naturally arched bay, it offers magnificent views of Lake Geneva from the upper part of town, while the spa centre of Les Thermes overlooks the waterfront.

The Versoie spring was first discovered by the Romans and opened to the public in the 19th century. Thonon–les–Bains is also the first stage on the Route-des-Alpes, covering the main alpine passes and several nature reserves from Lake Geneva to the Mediterranean.

Attractions include the Eco Fishing Museum, the Chablais Museum, and Gorges du Pont du Diable, a partly submerged network of jagged, grey marble eroded into spectacular shapes over time. Thonon's fishing port, tucked behind Rives castle, is active throughout the year, and a large market sells produce every Monday and Thursday.

The average cost of a two-bedroom home in the region is €215,000, rising to €400,000 if you want four bedrooms. For a waterfront location, a four-bedroom house at Port Ripaille costs around €500,000. This is a prime tourist rental locale, excellently positioned for tourists drawn to the French Alps and Annecy. ●

KEY FACTS

■ **Schools** Nearest: Albertville, Megève and Ferney Voltaire
■ **Medical** Annecy Centre Hospitalier, av Trésum 1, 74000 Annecy, Tel: +33 450 88 33 33 ■ Hôpitaux du Léman, avenue de la Dame 3, 74 200 Thonon-les-Bains, Tel: +33 450 83 20 00, www.ch-leman.fr
■ **Rentals** Good for four to six months in Thonon-les-Bains ■ Average rental for a one-bedroom apartment is €600 per week in Thonon-les-Bains ■ Short-term average rental for a studio apartment in high season is €400 per week
■ **Pros** Amenities include a golf course and nearby skiing in La Clusaz and Grand Bornand ■ Excellent transport links to the area
■ **Cons** Not really a winter spot, Thonon is a 40-minute journey from Morzine and Portes du Soleil, and cannot compete with the ski resorts ■ Nearby Evian-les-Bains has a reputation as Lake Geneva's tourist trap, attracting hordes of visitors in summer.

3. Megève ■

ESSENTIALS ■ **Population** 4,509 ■ **Taxes** Taxe d'habitation: 5.33%, Taxe foncière: 7.65%
■ **Airport** Chambéry/Aix-les-Bains Airport, Chambre de Commerce, 73420 Viviers du Lac, Tel +33 479 54 49 54

West of Mont Blanc, the medieval Savoyard town of Megève is ultra-chic. 'Discovered' by the Baroness de Rothschild in 1921, it still attracts the rich out of season from the French Riviera, and most of its visitors are French. More than 70 farms make regional specialities like *Tomme de Savoie* cheese.

The 290 kilometres of ski-runs are a skier's paradise. Chamonix is less than 30 minutes away and is included on the Mont Blanc ski pass, which accesses 13 other resorts. This World Cup ski venue is a good choice for non-skiers too, who can easily access Michelin mountain restaurants and enjoy a first-class spa or lively, varied après-ski.

Property is expensive but high-quality, with a choice of large luxury chalets rather than new apartments. The main hotspots of Mont d'Arbois (an area on the golf course, above the resort) and villages like Ormaret, with views of Mont Blanc, also attract a premium.

Centrally located chalets start from €1,000,000 and new chalets, built in original materials to add old Savoyard cachet, are priced from €2,000,000 to €5,000,000. Le Hameau des Ours may offer the best value, with two-bedroom apartments from €500,000, three-bedrooms from €500,000, and new chalets from €1,000,000. Properties in the villages of Combloux and Saint-Gervais are more reasonably priced. ●

KEY FACTS

■ **Schools** Nearest: Megève
■ **Medical** Centre Hospitalier, rte Pèlerins 509, 74400 Chamonix Mont Blanc, Tel: +33 450 53 84 00
■ **Rentals** Excellent, with plenty of demand, the rental season lasts more than 15 weeks ■ Peak is December through to April ■ The average rental price per week is €1,050 for a two-bedroom chalet ■ Average short-term rentals for high season are €500 per week for a studio, €660 per week for a one-bedroom apartment, €880 per week for a two-bedroom apartment
■ **Pros** Hailed as the most beautiful of the French ski resorts, it combines the modern jet-set feel with an old-world charm ■ Top international resort with winter and summer appeal ■ Good golf course, restaurants and hotels ■ Easy to access. with excellent transport links
■ **Cons** Roads are congested during the winter months; chains for your wheels are mandatory ■ The snow record is poor as Megève lies at a low altitude, so is not for the most advanced skier ■ A huge tourist influx for the winter sports.

Property hotspots

4. Chamonix

ESSENTIALS ■ **Population** 9,830 ■ **Taxes** Taxe d'habitation: 5.33%, Taxe foncière: 7.65% ■ **Airport** Chambéry/Aix-les-Bains Airport, Chambre de Commerce, 73420 Viviers du Lac, Tel: +33 479 54 49 54

KEY FACTS

■ **Schools** Nearest: Megève
■ **Medical** Centre Hospitalier, rte Pèlerins 509, 74400 Chamonix Mont Blanc,
Tel: +33 450 53 84 00
■ **Rentals** Excellent, with a season lasting for more than 15 weeks (December to April) ■ A fashionable, cosmopolitan resort, with international rental appeal ■ The average rental price per week is between €300 off-season to €1,000 in peak season for a two-bedroom property ■ A two-bedroom standard property costs €420 to €840 per week
■ **Pros** Budget easyJet flights into Geneva Airport have made travelling to a second home here cheap ■ An upmarket Italian development, Résidence-les-Alpes, has sold well, and more buildings are due for completion in 2005 ■ Best in the region for advanced skiers, despite its accessibility problems ■ Low availability of land for build makes property purchase a sound investment ■ Popular second and permanent homes ■ Dog sledding, mountain biking, paragliding, helicopter trips, an ice-rink, and a climbing centre are available here
■ **Cons** Much traffic and people ■ Difficult access; skiers rely on shuttle buses or cars to reach the slopes ■ Dramatic price increases in recent years ■ An almost seven-hour car journey from Paris.

Situated at the foot of Mont Blanc and at the crossroads of France, Italy and Switzerland, with easy access to Italy via the Mont Blanc tunnel, Chamonix is much sought after for both its sporting and scenic qualities. Although developed as a summertime mountaineering centre, the resort is renowned as a destination for expert skiers, so there's a demand for quality property.

Throughout the year the town is busy, but it has retained its charm, with narrow streets lining the car-free centre and a river flowing through the valley floor. Visitors choose primarily to ski at high altitude, taking in a circuit from the main town to the valley across Le Brévent, La Flégère, Les Grand Montets, and Le Tour, including seven glaciers and the world's biggest lift-served vertical drop of 2,807 metres.

New, traditionally constructed apartments are good-value buys and often have superior mountain views and a concierge. Three and four-bedroom apartments start at around €310,000, rising to €1,000,000 for larger ones. Smaller one and two-bedroom apartments are from €200,000, while a three-bedroom chalet costs around €520,000.

With precious little building land available and a strong demand from wealthy buyers across the world – despite the already-high prices – Chamonix remains one of the region's most exclusive resorts. ●

5. Méribel

ESSENTIALS ■ **Population** 1,850 ■ **Taxes** Taxe d'habitation: 4.78%, Taxe foncière: 7.24% ■ **Airport** Chambéry/Aix-les-Bains Airport, Chambre de Commerce, 73420 Viviers du Lac, Tel: +33 479 54 49 54

KEY FACTS

■ **Schools** Nearest: Albertville
■ **Medical** Nearest: Hôpital de Moutiers, rue École des Mines, 73 600 Moutiers Toulentaise, Tel: +33 479 09 60 60
■ **Rentals** Excellent rental season from December to April ■ Popular international location with bags of potential for permanent and second homes ■ A low availability of land to build has made property a premium investment ■ A standard, two-bedroom apartment can fetch from €850 per week off season to €2,100 in peak season, while a more luxurious apartment can cost from €1,350 to €2,400
■ **Pros** Budget easyJet flights and excellent transport networks make for easy access ■ Méribel is the most British-dominated of all the resorts in the Alps ■ Plenty of après-ski amenities
■ **Cons** Busy tourist location and slightly less sophisticated than other resorts in the region ■ Almost seven hours from Paris by road.

High up in the Alps at 1,450 metres, in the centre of the Trois Vallées, Méribel has access to 720 kilometres of pistes, both nursery slopes and off-piste for the more experienced skier. Méribel's night life revolves largely around British-run bars with live music. Restaurants specialise in Savoyard dishes like *raclette*, *tartiflette* and pizza savoyarde, made with Beaufort, Comté and Emmental cheese over dried meats. Méribel-les-Allues is 10 minutes from the lift station at Chaudanne, and a quieter base from which to explore the Trois Vallées.

La Chaudanne Olympic Park has a swimming pool, sauna, ice rink, parapenting, snowbiking, ice karting and dog sledding. Almost everything built since development started in 1931 has been traditional in style, using pinewood, slate-covered roofs and local stone, making Méribel one of the most tasteful French purpose-built resorts. Chalets are rarely available and can cost more than €1,500,000, though some of the region's cheapest prices can be found here as well.

Buyers prefer newer properties, particularly apartments, as they have larger rooms and are of better quality, but the dearth of such properties in Val d'Isère and Méribel sends buyers to cheaper areas like Sainte Foy, less than 30 minutes away, where high-quality, detached, new-build chalets are built to blend with 100-year-old chalets. ●

6. Courchevel

ESSENTIALS ■ **Population** 1,850 ■ **Taxes** Taxe d'habitation: 4.78%, Taxe foncière: 7.24% ■ **Airport** Annecy Metz Airport, route de Côte Merle, 74370 Metz-Tessy, Tel: +33 450 27 30 06, www.annecy.aeroport.fr

Courchevel is located in the Trois Vallées ski area, along with Méribel, Les Menuires and Val Thorens. With 640 kilometres of piste and superb skiing, this area constitutes the largest interconnected ski resort in France. Here, the world's largest cable car and numerous ski lifts carry 52,000 skiers per hour.

Four hours from Geneva, the resort is built on four levels, named according to their elevation in metres: 1300, 1550, 1650, and 1850. All have luxury private villas or chalets that are ski-in, ski-out, but Courchevel 1850 is the most upmarket, drawing royalty and celebrities. Extensive and varied terrain suits everyone from beginners to experts, though some slopes get very crowded. Courchevel 1650 has an extra hour's sunlight per day. The two lower areas are Le Praz (1300m), a traditional Savoie hamlet; and family-friendly La Tania (also at 1300m), where it is possible to find a village house or small chalet for under €3,000,000. Chalets are built in the traditional Savoyard style of architecture, featuring exposed stone, large roof beams and handcrafted wooden doors. A decreasing amount of land to build on has meant a competitive market, with ski companies chasing chalets to run as winter rentals. However, small two-bedroom apartments in less-exclusive areas can be picked up for less than €300,000. ●

KEY FACTS

■ **Schools** Nearest: Albertville
■ **Medical** Hôpital de Moutier, rue Ecole des Mines, 73600 Moûtiers Tarentaise, Tel: +33 479 09 60 60
■ **Rentals** Excellent in the high-season winter months ■ A 15 week+ rental season ■ The average rental price per week varies from €2,100 to €2,550 during peak season ■ Good winter rentals ■ Average short-term, high-season rental prices: €630 per week for a studio and €1,200 per week for a two-bedroom apartment
■ **Pros** Budget airline easyJet flies into Geneva Airport and has made travelling to a second home quick, easy and cheap ■ Courchevel exudes luxury and glamour, both on and off the piste, and has a tried-and-tested tourist market ■ Luxury shops, gourmet restaurants, an active après-ski life and illuminated sledge run
■ **Cons** The town gets taken over by tourists in the winter months and can have a crowded feel; the population increases 17-fold during the winter and the town is occupied by 30,000 people each week ■ Slightly off the beaten track, the resort does not offer easy access ■ The top resort hotels only open in winter.

7. Les Menuires

ESSENTIALS ■ **Population** 2,532 ■ **Taxes** Taxe d'habitation: 4.78%, Taxe foncière: 7.24% ■ **Airport** Annecy Metz Airport, route de Côte Merle, 74370 Metz-Tessy, Tel: +33 450 27 30 06

Many consider Les Menuires the least attractive resort in the Alps, with few woodland slopes. Located in the Belleville Valley at the head of the Trois Vallées ski area, it remains in demand as a purpose-built resort, offering immediate access to the challenging pistes of La Masse, and is rarely used by visitors from the other valleys.

The main intermediate and beginner slopes benefit from a lot of sun while Allemands, the red run twisting from the top of Roc des Trois Marches into Les Menuires, is one of the finest. Split into three main levels, the resort is composed of Reberty (the highest section with most visual charm); the main resort of Croisette; and low-lying Preyerand.

While Les Menuires is less renowned for its après-ski than other alpine resorts, the first-class restaurant of La Mercée is rated as one of the best eateries by those in the know. You cannot ski directly to it, but the restaurant shuttle bus takes diners back to the ski lifts.

Reberty is made up of two parts – 1850 and 2000; the latter is slightly higher up. In 1850, you can acquire a north-facing, furnished studio for two people from a starting price of €185,000. A family could choose a southwest-facing three-bedroom apartment, equipped for six with living room, corner kitchen, separate bathroom and lift access for around €305,000. Limited land has helped the rental market. ●

KEY FACTS

■ **Schools** Nearest: Albertville
■ **Medical** Hôpital de Moutier, rue Ecole des Mines, 73600 Moûtiers Tarentaise, Tel: +33 479 09 60 60
■ **Rentals** Excellent, year-round potential ■ Being a base for second and permanent homes, and having a shortage of land to build new homes on, has fuelled the rental market ■ The peak season during winter is from December to April ■ Summer months offer activity holidays ■ The average rent for this area per week is from €950 to €1,900 ■ A timber chalet costs €330 to €710 per week ■ Average, short-term rental costs for high season are €450 a week for a studio apartment and €630 per week for a one-bedroom apartment
■ **Pros** Nearly 650 kilometres of pistes make up the Trois Vallées area, plus a snow park for snowboarders and three snow-makers, which ensure snow ■ A family-orientated resort with some cheap hotels ■ Convenient link to Val Thorens, the highest ski resort in Europe ■ Many small apartments, good for low budget skiers
■ **Cons** Many unattractive apartments ■ An unsightly resort ■ More than seven hours by road from Paris.

Property hotspots

8. Val d'Isère

ESSENTIALS ■ **Population** 45,000 ■ **Taxes** Taxe d'habitation: 4.78%, Taxe foncière: 7.24% ■ **Airport** Annecy Metz Airport, route de Côte Merle 8, 74370 Metz-Tessy, Tel: +33 450 27 30 06

KEY FACTS

■ **Schools** Nearest: Albertville
■ **Medical** Nearest is Hôpital, rue Nantet 139, 73700 Bourg Saint-Maurice, Tel: +33 479 41 79 79
■ **Rentals** Excellent winter resort ■ Val d'Isère has international, year-round appeal with a five-month-long winter season ■ The average rental price for a property is approximately €1,000 a week ■ Average rental prices for short-term rental are €730 a week for a studio apartment in high season and €1,350 per week for a two-bedroom apartment
■ **Pros** One of the best resorts in the region and a favourite with skiers ■ Covers a massive area and has more than 100 lifts with numerous ski runs, (some reaching 3,200m) ■ A must for the sociable skier ■ Après-ski for serious party-goers, with lots of bars and more than 70 restaurants offering a huge range of food at all price levels ■ Long ski season and good snow record ■ Masses of winter sports and the shortage of building land contribute to its soundness for investment
■ **Cons** Lack of available property ■ A demand for larger apartments and chalets.

Located at high altitude, with the peaks of La Grande Motte and La Grande Casse in the background, Val d'Isère enjoys frequent snowfalls and is one of France's finest skiing resorts. It is not a picturesque resort, with unattractive high-rise apartment blocks at La Daille, but the town centre has a more upmarket feel and look. Over the years the resort has proved popular with the British.

Val d'Isère's slopes are divided into three sectors: Bellevarde, which can be accessed from the centre; La Daille, Solaise, which is accessed directly from the centre; and Col de L'Iséran which is reached from Le Fornet. The Pissaillas glacier is open from late June to mid-August.

In summer, there are few facilities for the non-skier, so the Trois Vallées is a better choice for buyers sourcing a property for both summer and winter seasons, while still having access to a large ski area. Apartments sell very quickly, especially those recently built. Prices start at a rather hefty €1,000,000 , but if you have a more modest budget, consider the nearby resort of Sainte-Foy. It has retained it original charm, yet is only 30 minutes by car from Val d'Isère. Here, new chalets are blended in with existing homes, some of which are more than a century old. Prices start at around €400,000 for a linked three-bedroom chalet. Smaller apartments start at just under €300,000. ●

9. Grenoble

ESSENTIALS ■ **Population** 156,203 ■ **Taxes** Taxe d'habitation 6.44%, Taxe foncière 10.71% ■ **Airport** Grenoble Saint-Geois Airport, 38590 Saint-Etienne-de-Saint-Geois, Tel: +33 476 65 48 48

KEY FACTS

■ **Schools** Nearest: Grenoble
■ **Medical** Mutuelle Générale de l'Éducation Nationale, rue Félix Poulat 38000 3, Grenoble, Tel: +33 476 86 63 63
■ **Rentals** Excellent, with a huge international appeal ■ A university town with more than 50,000 students a year needing rental properties
■ Purchases are less common here, more common in the ski resorts ■ Average long-term rental prices are €800 per month for a one-bedroom apartment, €1,000 per month for a two-bedroom apartment
■ **Pros** Perfectly placed for Switzerland, Italy and the Mediterranean; hiking, mountain climbing, skiing, snowboarding, rafting, kayaking and canoeing are available ■ The city is surrounded by three famous Alpine ranges
■ **Cons** Approximately 10,000 visitors a month pour into Grenoble between December and January, so it can get crowded.

Grenoble has the distinction of being the capital of the French Alps, with strong international appeal. It is a beautiful, highly advanced city with numerous industrial and technological sites, and many research laboratories. A university city with 50,000 students making up 10 per cent of its suburban population, Grenoble has some wonderful heritage sites, such as the Dauphinois museum and the Fort de la Bastille, accessible by cable car over the river. Helping to keep Italian heritage alive are 200 pizzerias.

Capital of the Dauphiné – a former province – Grenoble has an exceptional geographic setting, with the skiing season beginning from mid-November. Close to Switzerland, Italy, and the Mediterranean, it offers a fast gateway to Les Deux Alpes and Alpes d'Huez, which are just half an hour away. It is not generally a hotspot area, but as the ski resorts are more popular, a lack of new developments makes property a premium investment and prices are climbing.

For superb rural views and a peaceful haven, try Saint-Pierre-de-Chartreuse, a medieval mountain village in the heart of the Chartreuse Regional Park, famous for the Chartreuse liqueur, made in its monastery. Two-bedroom apartments can be picked up for under €200,000, while five-bedroom homes average at just over €500,000. ●

10. Les Portes du Soleil

ESSENTIALS ■ **Population** 1,369 ■ **Taxes** Taxe d'habitation: 5.33%, Taxe foncière: 7.65% ■ **Airport** Annecy Metz Airport, route de Côte Merle 8, 74370 Metz-Tessy, Tel: +33 450 27 30 06, www.annecy.aeroport.fr

Set on a sunny mountain pass, just over the border from Switzerland in Haute-Savoie, family-friendly Les Gets is a traditional alpine village that is also one of the most popular smaller ski resorts. Part of the Portes du Soleil network that links 12 resorts on either side of the French/Swiss border, Les Gets is not acclaimed for its nightlife, but appeals instead to the many families who want to sample the great outdoors rather than après-ski. The skiing area spreads to both sides of Les Gets with the smaller, but less crowded, Mont Chéry offering more challenging skiing, while Les Chavannes is a much more suitable area for families and beginners or intermediates.

In Les Gets, brand new locations near the Chavannes ski slope, close to the village centre, are highly desirable. Prices are rising and stringent property laws have clamped down on the square metrage of land permitted to build on. Planning permission is now only given for 'filling in' existing hamlets, or if a property fronts a main road. Further building in Les Gets is banned for two years. Chalet builders are snapping up blocks of land to ensure their businesses keep running, so recent builds have been bought 'off-plan'. In the area as a whole, two-bedroom apartments average under €200,000, but you can pay much more in exclusive blocks. Four-bedroom homes average at €400,000. ●

KEY FACTS

■ **Schools** Nearest: Megève and Ferney Voltaire
■ **Medical** Hôpitaux du Léman, avenue de la Dame 3, 74200 Thonon-Les-Bains, Tel: +33 450 83 20 00, www.ch-leman.fr
■ **Rentals** Excellent winter rental season from December to April ■ A traditional three-bedroom property off-season costs between €600 to €1,500 ■ A two-bedroom apartment costs from €200 to €900 per week
■ **Pros** Budget flights into Geneva airport ■ Lots of family-friendly outdoor activities are available, including swimming in hill-top lakes, horse riding, canyoning and alpine boarding ■ A mecca for the sporty, there are 19 mountain walks (served by an efficient lift service) and cross-country cycle routes
■ **Cons** Purchasers are competing with French, Swiss, Italian and Dutch buyers ■ Les Gets is quite low (1,175 metres), the top reaching 2,350 metres with access to high-level skiing areas ■ It is unknown to many British as a summer resort ■ Buyer demand outstrips supply.

11. Lyon

ESSENTIALS ■ **Population** 453,187 ■ **Taxes** Taxe d'habitation: 5.73%, Taxe foncière: 5.47% ■ **Airport** Lyon-Exupéry Aéroport, BP113, 69125 Lyon, Tel: +33 772 22 72 21, www.lyon.aeroport.fr

With more restaurants per square metre than any other city in the world, Lyon is justifiably the gastronomic capital of France, with a lively night scene and cultural life. Top Michelin restaurants sit alongside *bouchons* (bistros, which owe their name to medieval times when the bill for wine was calculated by the number of corks on the table) serving Lyonnais specialities in a picturesque setting.

The city is graced with Roman amphitheatres, Renaissance architecture and a silk-weaving tradition, found in the district of Croix Rousse. The *traboules*, or secret passageways, link streets and houses and were used by the Resistance during World War II. The Basilique Notre-Dame de Fourvière is the old town's landmark, its interior adorned with ornate stone carvings and gilded mosaics, and its exterior affording panoramic views of the city. In 2000, four of Lyon's neighbourhoods were designated World Heritage sites, including Croix Rousse, Fourvière, the Presqu'île peninsula and Vieux Lyon.

A double-glazed, fully-furnished art deco-style apartment by the 260-acre Parc de la Tête d'Or starts at €475,000, with concierge. Half an hour away, overlooking the Saône Valley, an eight-bedroom home with 16th/17th-century frontage, is around the same price. There are not many foreign buyers here and there is not a big tourist scene. ●

KEY FACTS

■ **Schools** Cité scolaire internationale, place de Montréal 2, 69361 Lyon Cedex, Tel: +33 478 69 60 00
■ **Medical** Hôpital de l'Hôtel Dieu, place de l'Hôpital, 69288 Lyon Cedex, Tel: +33 472 41 30 24, www.chu-lyon.fr
■ **Rentals** Average rentals throughout the year for two bedrooms is €480 per week; for three bedrooms it's €680 per week ■ This is a working city with a long-term rental market
■ **Pros** A centre of commercial activity, with great employment opportunity ■ Well-served by TGV trains, it has a convenient link to Paris for commuters, and its own international airport ■ The 6ème is an expensive *arrondissement*, as is the Croix Rousse, but cheaper properties can be bought in the 8ème ■ The large population of university students provides an annual pool of tenants ■ A thriving array of amenities, including slick shopping centres
■ **Cons** You may need to be willing to learn French to relocate here.

HOTSPOTS

Property hotspots

12. Beaujolais

ESSENTIALS ■ **Population** 31,213 ■ **Taxes** Taxe d'habitation: 5.73%, Taxe foncière: 5.47% ■ **Airport** Lyon-Exupéry Aéroport, BP113, 69125 Lyon, Tel: +33 772 22 72 21, www.lyon.aeroport.fr

KEY FACTS

■ **Schools** Cité Scolaire Internationale, place de Montréal 2, 69361 Lyon Cedex 07, Tel: +33 478 69 60 06
■ **Medical** Centre Hospitalier de Villefranche-sur-Saône, Quilly Gleizé BP 436, 69655 Villefranche-sur-Saône Cedex, Tel: +33 474 09 29 29, www.ch-villefranche.fr
■ **Rentals** A one-bedroom apartment costs €480 per week, the average weekly cost for a four-bedroom place is €1,225
■ **Pros** Within 30 kilometres of Lyon, it has cheaper properties than the region's capital ■ An area full of rivers, tributaries, granite peaks, farms and forests ■ Full of gastronomic delights, olive oil and fine wines ■ Villefranche has an excellent choice of restaurants and shops along its Rue Nationale ■ Amenities include the Nicéphore Niépce Museum, which includes the first colour photographs, holograms and audio-visual exhibits
■ **Cons** Incredibly appealing, hence properties in the Lyon to Mâcon area are expensive ■ Properties are cheaper in the area from La Clayette to Tarare.

The Beaujolais is a region of lush, fertile hills, picturesque villages and rolling vineyards in the southeast of France. Perched above the valley of the River Saône and surrounding the town of Villefranche-sur-Saône, with numerous vineyards in which to sample the area's wines, the Beaujolais offers a glimpse of the traditional vineyard lifestyle and local life. The vineyard region stretches from Lyon in the south to Mâcon, and properties are often former winegrowers' homes built of stone with the typical pierre dorée colour. There are nearly 100 square kilometres of vineyards.

The east of Beaujolais is the best known part, and Villefranche-sur-Saône has become the economic hub of this area of the Rhône, succeeding Beaujeu, the historic capital. Villefranche-sur-Saône's church dates back to the 12th century and there are fine Renaissance houses and a 17th-century hospital. A 17th-century house can be bought for around €450,000. Two-bedroom homes average at just under €250,000, but it will cost you around €600,000 for five bedrooms.

This area is rich in history and architecture, with many of the tiny, wine-producing villages containing some architectural gems. Properties are generally slightly cheaper from La Clayette to Tarare, an area with 500 to 1,000-metre high mountains. ●

The Rhône Alps is home to some of France's best ski resorts, Courcheval is among the best

COURCHEVAL TOURIST BOARD

BUYING ABROAD?

Save up to 20% when you buy a Property Buying Guide today!

- An unrivalled blend of expertly researched, up-to-the-minute information and authoritative practical advice
- Step-by-step guides to the legal and financial stages of buying a property
- Inspirational real-life stories reveal how to turn a dream into reality
- Illustrated price guides show you what to expect for your money, with photographs of hundreds of sample properties
- Fact-filled regional profiles highlight top hotspots, key facilities and taxes
- Comparative price charts provide an at-a-glance guide to properties in all the hotspots
- Extensive listings of useful contacts and addresses, from estate agents and solicitors to tradesmen and surveyors
- Detailed analysis of each country's economy and property market from our panel of experts

NEW! RED GUIDE TO PROPERTY IN EASTERN EUROPE

...YING, SELLING AND LETTING IN ...E, TURKEY & CYPRUS

FREE Pocket Map Inside!

ORDER NOW AND SAVE UP TO 20%!

CALL OUR ORDER HOTLINE TODAY ON
01225 786850
Please quote order code FR05 when ordering

€150,000–€400,000
(£104,167–£277,778)

A range of charming country houses and apartments on the slopes

€163,000   CODE FPS

SAINT-GENEST-MALIFAUX, LOIRE

This traditional detached stone-built house is located in a pretty little hamlet

£113,194

🛏 4   🌼 Small garden   🏡 Situated in a quiet hamlet   🚫 Not located on a main road
🏠 Room for parking, with a garage

€168,000   CODE FPS

YSSINGEAUX, LOIRE

A renovated farmhouse with a part-converted stable and outbuildings

£116,667

🛏 4   🌼 5,000m²   🏡 Situated in the village centre   🚫 Not located on a main road
🏠 Room for parking

€252,000   CODE FPS

COURCHEVEL, SAVOIE

A beautiful apartment in the famous ski area, with a large south-facing terrace

£175,000

🛏 2   🌼 Large terrace   🏡 Situated in the ski resort   🚫 Not located on a main road
🏠 Room for parking, with a garage

€254,400   CODE LAT

NEAR BELLEY, AIN

A beautifully restored farmhouse with outbuildings, a courtyard and a garden

£176,667

🛏 2   🌼 650m²   🏡 Situated in a peaceful location   🚫 Not located on a main road
🏠 Room for parking

€256,200   CODE FPS

CROZANT, CREUSE

A fully licensed 9-bedroomed hotel and restaurant with separate lodging for owner

£177,916

🛏 9   🌼 No garden   🏡 Situated in a tourist area   🚫 Located on a main road
🏠 Room for parking

€275,500   CODE LAT

NEAR BELLEY, AIN

A pretty stone country house with large outbuildings to convert

£191,319

🛏 5   ❀ 10,000m²   📷 Situated in a peaceful location   🚫 Not located on a main road
🏠 Room for parking

€295,000   CODE LAT

NEAR PASSY, HAUTE-SAVOIE

A charming second-floor apartment in a four-storey house with exceptional views

£204,861

🛏 3   ❀ 300m²   📷 Situated near the ski resort   🚫 Not located on a main road
🏠 Room for parking, with a garage

€318,200   CODE FPS

SAINT-MAURICE-EN-GOURGOIS, LOIRE

A 1970s villa with excellent fixtures and fittings and an enclosed garden

£220,972

🛏 3   ❀ Small garden   📷 Situated in the village centre   🚫 Not located on a main
road   🏠 Room for parking, with 2 garages

€352,000   CODE FPS

COURCHEVEL, SAVOIE

A well-appointed renovated chalet with a large terrace and a veranda

£244,444

🛏 4   ❀ 70m² terrace   📷 Situated near the ski resort   🚫 Not located on a main road
🏠 Room for parking, with 2 garages

€353,000   CODE LAT

SAINT-GERVAIS-LES-BAINS, HAUTE-SAVOIE

A first-floor apartment facing Mont Blanc, with garage, balcony and ski store

£245,139

🛏 2   ❀ No garden   📷 Situated near the ski slopes   🚫 Not located on a main road
🏠 Room for parking, with a garage

€365,000   CODE FPS

MONISTROL, LOIRE

A contemporary villa with outbuildings set in large grounds with superb views

£253,472

🛏 4   ❀ 2,000m²   📷 Situated in a small village   🚫 Not located on a main road
🏠 Room for parking, with a large garage

SuperTickets™ the most unique offer for cross-Channel ferry tickets ever.

Book your SuperTickets™ now to secure fully flexible super low cost ferry crossings for next year.

Cheap tickets for Channel crossings normally offer cheap conditions. All sorts of restrictions apply and usually the traveller's money is lost if the sailing is missed or if any changes have to be made in relation to a planned trip.

This has never been the case at SpeedFerries where tickets are always amendable for a fee of £10. Now we are pushing the limits for low cost ferry tickets even further by offering SuperTickets™ at no extra cost for our customers.

All tickets for travel until the end of 2005 will automatically be issued as SuperTickets™ if booked before 31 December 2004.
The SuperTicket™ offers great value for all, at the same time as being a unique offer for frequent travellers:

Fixed price £50 Return for standard car + 6
• The fastest Channel crossing – just 50 minutes - at high quality and low cost, bringing the traveller closer to France via a superior destination.

Fully amendable
• Tickets can always be amended for a £10 fee, giving e.g. a price of £60 if a SuperTicket™ is changed once to any sailing including peak season sailings.

Valid from now and all through 2005
• SuperTickets™ can be amended to any departure (which is not sold out), irrespective of the future price of the new selected sailing, including peak sailings.

No restrictions on the duration of stay
• Valid for all lengths of trips

No restrictions on the available sailing
• Valid on all not sold out departures, including high season peak sailings
Book your SuperTicket™ on-line at www.speedferries.com

SpeedFerriesHolidays

SpeedFerries is now also offering Short Breaks in France from only £31 per person, including cross-Channel travel!
Visit www.speedferriesholidays.com to benefit from a selection of short breaks throughout France and Belgium, including Le Touquet, Boulogne, Calais, St Omer, Paris and Brugge. All short breaks include accommodation on a B&B basis and return travel from Dover – Boulogne with SpeedFerries.
All short breaks are offered by the Travel Market Ltd, ABTOT bonded, no.5028. All short breaks can be booked via www.speedferriesholidays.com or tel: 0870 2642644.

Dover Departure	Boulogne Arrival	Boulogne Departure	Dover Arrival	
07:45	09:35	10:30	10:20	■ All year schedule
11:15	13:05	14:00	13:50	
14:45	16:35	17:30	17:20	■ Additional sailings April to September
18:15	20:05	21:00	20:50	Schedule in local time,
21:45	23:35	00:30	00:20	subject to change.

Check the price and book on-line at www.speedferries.com or through our call centre* – Tel: +44 (0) 870 22 00 570

*a call centre supplement of £10 pounds will be applied

€400,000–€500,000
(£277,778–£347,222)

A selection of large rural properties and small apartments near the slopes

€419,240   CODE FPS

BOZEL, SAVOIE

A superb detached chalet, built in 1997, with a lovely open-plan kitchen

£291,139

🛏 4   800m²   *Situated in the village centre*   *Not located on a main road*   *Room for parking, with double garage*

€440,000   CODE FPS

NEAR COURCHEVEL, SAVOIE

A lovely chalet with a jacuzzi, in a village just outside Courchevel

£305,556

🛏 3   *No garden*   *Situated in a small village*   *Not located on a main road*   *Room for parking*

€460,000   CODE LAT

SAINT-DIDIER-SUR-CHALARONNE, AIN

A magnificent character house overlooking the river with a pontoon and mooring

£319,444

🛏 4   200m²   *Situated close to the village centre*   *Not located on a main road*   *Room for parking*

€490,000   CODE LAT

NEAR ÉVIAN-LES-BAINS, HAUTE-SAVOIE

A pretty detached house with a large garden, swimming pool and garage

£340,278

🛏 4   892m²   *Situated between Évian and Thonon-les-Bains*   *Not located on a main road*   *Room for parking, with a garage*

€495,000   CODE FPS

COURCHEVEL 1300, SAVOIE

A beautifully kept apartment in this chic ski resort with a large, south-facing terrace

£343,750

🛏 3   *Large terrace*   *Situated in the ski resort*   *Not located on a main road*   *Room for parking*

€500,000–€700,000
(£347,222–£486,111)

These large chalets are a short drive from the main ski resorts

€529,000   CODE LAT

NEAR SALLANCHES, HAUTE-SAVOIE
A charming chalet set in large wooded gardens with lovely mountain views
£367,361

🛏 3 ❀ 1,500m² 🏞 Situated in the Mont Blanc valley 🚧 Not located on a main road 🏠 Room for parking, with a garage

€550,000   CODE LAT

LAKE ANNECY, HAUTE-SAVOIE
A lovely detached house with pool and garage and superb views over the lake
£381,944

🛏 4 ❀ 1,000m² 🏞 Situated in a quiet location 🚧 Not located on a main road 🏠 Room for parking, with a garage

€550,000   CODE LAT

NEAR ANNECY, HAUTE-SAVOIE
A beautifully renovated stone farmhouse within easy reach of the ski resorts
£381,944

🛏 3 ❀ 1,500m² 🏞 Situated 10 minutes from Annecy 🚧 Not located on a main road 🏠 Room for parking, with a double garage

€678,000   CODE LAT

NEAR ANNECY, HAUTE-SAVOIE
This lovely south-facing detached chalet with pool enjoys breathtaking views
£470,833

🛏 6 ❀ 1,258m² 🏞 Situated 10 minutes from Annecy 🚧 Not located on a main road 🏠 Room for parking, with a double garage

€693,000   CODE LAT

LAKE ANNECY, HAUTE-SAVOIE
A beautiful chalet with a gym, sauna and summer kitchen. Lovely lake views
£481,250

🛏 3 ❀ 1,450m² 🏞 Situated near the town of Sévrier 🚧 Not located on a main road 🏠 Room for parking

€700,000–€1,000,000
(£486,111–£694,444)

From beautiful wooden chalets to renovated farmhouses with amazing views

€730,000   CODE SIF

DRÔME

This property consists of two houses, one to restore, with a pool and lovely views

£506,944

🛏 4 ❋ 10,000m² 🖼 Situated in a small hamlet 🚫 Not located on a main road 🏠 Room for parking

€735,000   CODE LAT

ANNECY, HAUTE-SAVOIE

An attractive detached house within easy reach of the major ski resorts

£510,416

🛏 5 ❋ 1,500m² 🖼 Situated in a quiet position 🚫 Not located on a main road 🏠 Room for parking, with a double garage

€760,000   CODE LAT

LAKE ANNECY, HAUTE-SAVOIE

A south-facing detached house with terrace, summer kitchen and barbecue area

£527,778

🛏 3 ❋ 3,450m² 🖼 Situated on the banks of the lake 🚫 Not located on a main road 🏠 Room for parking, with a double garage

€864,000   CODE SIF

NEAR ST-JALLE, DRÔME

This charming 17th-century farmhouse is set in immense grounds

£600,000

🛏 3 ❋ 1,400,000m² 🖼 Situated just outside the village 🚫 Not located on a main road 🏠 Room for parking

€910,000   CODE FPS

COURCHEVEL, SAVOIE

A large detached chalet with a garden in this most exclusive of ski resorts

£631,944

🛏 5 ❋ 810m² 🖼 Situated in the ski resort 🚫 Not located on a main road 🏠 Room for parking, with a garage

€1,000,000+
(£694,444+)

An assortment of deluxe rural properties and a chalet right on the piste

€1,000,000   CODE LAT

VACHERESSE, HAUTE-SAVOIE
This huge chalet and gîte are set in large grounds with magnificent views
£694,444

🛏 15   ❋ 3,000m²   🏞 Situated in a quiet location   🛣 Not located on a main road
🏠 Private parking

€1,100,000   CODE SIF

NEAR SUZE-LA-ROUSSE, DRÔME
A large restored property in pretty grounds with a separate caretaker's house
£763,889

🛏 8   ❋ 15,000m²   🏞 Situated near the village   🛣 Not located on a main road
🏠 Room for parking

€1,272,000   CODE SIF

DRÔME
This lovely old fortified stone farmhouse is in great condition, if slightly isolated
£883,333

🛏 10   ❋ 70,000m²   🏞 Situated 10km from amenities   🛣 Not located on a main road
🏠 Room for parking

€1,365,000   CODE LAT

CHÂTEL, HAUTE-SAVOIE
A traditional chalet comprising 9 apartments in need of renovation
£947,916

🛏 9   ❋ Balconies   🏞 Situated in the centre of town   🛣 Located on a main road
🏠 14 parking spaces

€11,000,000   CODE SIF

COURCHEVEL 1850, SAVOIE
This substantial chalet is right next to the piste in Courchevel 1850, hence the price
£7,638,889

🛏 8   ❋ No garden   🏞 Situated on the piste   🛣 Not located on a main road
🏠 Room for parking, with a garage for 3 cars

French Alps & Côte d'Azur

Builders of High Quality Properties

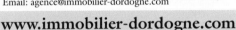

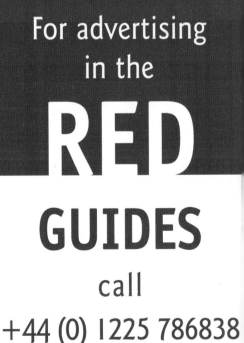
230

Aquitaine

Bordeaux wines, the beautiful Dordogne and fashionable Biarritz

TOURISME D'AQUITAINE

FACT BOX 2005

■ **Population** 2,908,359
■ **Migration** 250,939
■ **Unemployment** 68,111
■ **Median home price** €190,000
■ **House price increase** Since 2002, house prices have increased by 15.4%

Price Guide

Area profile

GETTING THERE

AIR Bordeaux-Merignac receives **British Airways** flights (0870 850 9850; www.britishairways.co.uk) from major UK airports and **Ryanair** (0871 246 0000) flies direct from Stansted to Biarritz and Pau. **Flybe** (0871 700 0535; www.flybe.com) operates flights into Bergerac (from London and Bristol) and Bordeaux, and in addition, **Air France** (0845 084 5111; www.airfrance.co.uk) flies direct to Bordeaux.

ROAD The region's main motorway is the A10, which connects Paris and Poitiers with Bordeaux and Toulouse, before continuing into Spain. For Biarritz, take the A63. As the A10 is often highly congested, you may prefer to travel on smaller roads. From Paris the A71/A20 leads to Limoges, from where the N20 takes you to Toulouse. For Pau, take the A64. The A20 for Limoges provides access to Dordogne and Quercy, while the Autoroute des Deux Mers (A62-A61) links Bordeaux, the Atlantic coast and the Mediterranean.

COACH Eurolines (0870 514 3219; www.eurolines.com) offers services to Agen, Arcachon. Bayonne, Bergerac, Biarritz, Bordeaux and Périgueux.

RAIL The TGV takes just 3.25 hours from Gare Montparnasse in Paris to Bordeaux, on the Paris-Poiters-Angoulême-Bordeaux line. The Toulouse, Biarritz and Bayonne areas are served by the TGV service from the Gare d'Austerlitz in Paris. There is a direct TGV service to Bordeaux from the Eurostar interchange at Lille. **Rail Europe** provides full details of services in France (0870 830 2008; www.raileurope.co.uk).

AQUITAINE STRETCHES ALONG THE SOUTHWEST OF FRANCE FROM Poitou-Charentes in the north, down to the Pyrénées and the border with Spain. Home to the world's largest wine-growing region and 200km of unspoilt Atlantic coast, it's a very popular area with British homebuyers.

The capital is Bordeaux, France's fifth largest city, a bustling, cosmopolitan port with a population of 750,000. Its 18th-century classical architecture bears testament to its past as a major centre for trade with Europe and the Americas. Of course, the Bordeaux region is most renowned for its fine wines, such as those from the vineyard of the famous Mouton-Rothschild. Northwest of Bordeaux, the Dordogne *département* (known as *Périgord* by the French) is one of the most popular areas for British homebuyers, so much so it's been dubbed 'Little Britain' by locals. Split into four colour-defined territories, the Dordogne offers everything from protected parks and fortified towns, to 30,000 cave paintings.

In the far southwest of the region is the seaside resort of Biarritz. In the 19th century it became a fashionable place for rich Europeans to congregate, and the grand architecture from that period is still very much in evidence. A few miles east is the capital of the French Basque country, Bayonne, where the majestic Cathédrale Ste-Marie dominates the skyline. The local speciality served in the centre's many cafés is frothy hot chocolate.

Aquitaine's diverse landscape attracts visitors both from France and abroad. The fabulous Atlantic beaches are far less crowded than their Côte d'Azur counterparts, though the two prominent resorts, Biarritz and Arcachon, are very busy in the summer months. Naturally, the Bordeaux vineyards are a major attraction and the Pyrénées provide great hiking country as well as skiing in the winter. The region's gastronomic pleasures are equally diverse: seafood paellas and oysters proliferate in the Basque country (Bayonne produces lots of fine chocolates), while further north, *foie gras*, black truffles, confit of duck and game stews are popular.

The Dordogne has been dubbed 'Little Britain' by its locals

TOURISME D'AQUITAINE

The economy and housing market

Renowned for producing some of France's finest wines, the region owes its immense wealth to vineyards and pine forests. The area has diversified into the aerospace industry, agri-foodstuffs and the wood pulp industry, while the strikingly beautiful coastline has contributed to the development of the tourist industry. Lot-et-Garonne, one of France's largest fruit producers, is known as the 'granary of France' and is particularly famous for its truffles.

Known as 'the Alternative South', the Southwest region of France is more expensive than most regions in the country, and yet its increasing ease of access has been attracting the foreign buyer. However, except for the Dordogne, most of Aquitaine is still relatively unknown in spite of a substantial increase in property purchases. Southwest Dordogne has become so popular, that it's in danger of being spoiled by tourism. Demand in southern Dordogne has caused prices to skyrocket, and there are few areas that represent really good value for money. Lot-et-Garonne has always been expensive due to its position midway between Bordeaux and Toulouse. Properties on the southwest coast, from Arcachon to Biarritz and Bayonne, are very pricey, with demand from both the French and foreign markets. Both Biarritz and Arcachon are very popular, with many French and Britons buying there. The exclusive and expensive resorts of Biarritz and Bayonne, are frequently compared to Nice on the Côte d'Azur.

The refuge of retirees and families alike, Dordogne is fast becoming the permanent home of an array of foreign and French buyers who are flooding the market. Those who are drawn to the area enjoy easy access to both the coast and the Pyrenean ski resorts, while its attractive rolling landscape and the ever-increasing number of British expats offer familiarity and comfort to many who seek to buy here.

The Pyrénées-Atlantiques area is already popular with the French and is forecast as the next up-and-coming foreign market; even though prices are rising, it's still the cheapest part of the region. It's only here that there are cheaper properties available for renovation, and these are all to be found inland. Generally, Aquitaine is not an ideal area in which to seek a renovation property because of the cost.

As access to the Aquitaine region has improved, areas other than Dordogne have become increasingly popular with foreign buyers. With Pau as a new destination for Ryanair flights from Stansted, the last 18 months have witnessed a real explosion of interest. Although price rises for the region as a whole are slowing slightly, the southwest saw a rise of 17.6 per cent in the first three-quarters of 2004.

Social groups

The Dordogne is popular with British buyers, as well as Dutch and German. Some of the area's towns and villages are dominated by foreign residents. Cosmopolitan Bordeaux has a large North African and student population. ●

"Properties on the southwest coast, from Arcachon to Biarritz and Bayonne are very expensive, with demand from both the French and foreign markets"

Average monthly temperature °C (Celsius)

Average monthly rainfall mm (millimetres)

AVERAGE HOUSE SALE PRICES

Hotspot	2-bed	3-bed	4-bed	5-bed+
Cap Ferret & Bay of Arcachon	€225K (£156K)	€352K (£244K)	€358K (£249K)	€529K (£368K)
Dordogne	€116K (£80K)	€203K (£141K)	€254K (£176K)	€341K (£237K)
Agen	€127K (£88K)	€233K (£161K)	€290K (£201K)	€328K (£228K)
Bordeaux	€217K (£151K)	€282K (£196K)	€324K (£225K)	€438K (£304K)
Biarritz & Bayonne	€258K (£179K)	€314K (£218K)	€465K (£323K)	€589K (£409K)

233

Focus on the Dordogne

Known as 'Dordogneshire', France's most stunning *département* is home to many expats who have lived the dream of relocating to France

TOURISME D'AQUITAINE

DORDOGNE FACTS

■ Outside Paris, the Dordogne boasts more monuments and historic artefacts than anywhere else in France

■ The Dordogne is famous for the Lascaux caves, decorated with prehistoric art

■ The Dordogne is actually referred to as 'Périgord' by the French, and is divided into four regions: Périgord vert (green); Périgord blanc (white); Périgord pourpre (purple); and Périgord noir (black)

SITUATED IN THE HISTORIC DORDOGNE, WHICH BOASTS MORE THAN 1,000 castles, Bergerac and Périgueux are within easy reach of superb châteaux, fortified towns crowning precipitous hills, and gentle countryside. The Dordogne is one of the oldest inhabited regions of France, with some of the world's greatest prehistoric cave settlements.

Devastated during the Wars of Religion, Bergerac is the main market centre for the surrounding maize, vine and tobacco farms. Its prosperity is founded on the success of the tobacco trade and the Musée du Tabac pays homage to this. The old quarter has lots of charm, with numerous late-medieval houses, and in the square there's a statue of Cyrano de Bergerac, the town's literary hero. Try sampling the local sweet wine of *Château Monbazillac*, or enjoy a coffee in the timeless Café des Tilleuls.

To the east is Sarlat, the capital of Périgord Noir, which avoids the traditional image of a 'home away from home' for the British buyer. Boasting an alluring medieval *quartier*, packed with houses of historical interest, Sarlat has been protected from the overdevelopment that has plagued parts of the Dordogne since the 1960s, and as such remains a traditional and attractive town. Périgueux, the old capital city of Dordogne, boasts one of the largest clusters of ancient Roman ruins outside Rome itself, and a colourful Wednesday market.

Cheap flights into Bergerac have helped to sustain the continued appreciation in prices that the region has seen. Prices have risen annually by roughly 15 per cent over the past few years, and this trend is set to continue. The Dordogne is popular with the international and French buyer so demand has soared, as have prices. Owing to the vast numbers of British people who move to the area, prices are high for rural France. The average cost of a four-bedroom home is around €250,000, but you can pay a lot more. ●

ESSENTIALS

■ **Population** 1999: 212,494 ■ **Taxes** Taxe d'habitation: 5.96%, Taxe foncière: 15.73% ■ **Airport** Bergerac-Rouman Aéroport, Route d'Agen, 24100 Bergerac, Tel: +33 553 22 25 25 ■ Limoges Airport, 87100 Limoges, Tel: +33 555 43 30 30

KEY FACTS

■ **Schools** Bordeaux's international school is the only one in the area and is 95 kilometres from Bergerac ■ Bordeaux International School, 53 Rue de Laseppe, 33000 Bordeaux, Tel: +33 557 87 02 11, www.bordeaux-school.com

■ **Medical** Medical Centre Hospitalier, 80 Av Georges Pompidou, 24000 Périgueux, Tel: +33 553 45 25 25

■ **Rentals** One of the most popular holiday areas in France ■ Southwest Dordogne, the most popular part, is scattered with holiday rental properties ■ The area generates a huge amount of rental income and guarantees a rental season from June to September ■ Rentals become long-term in winter

■ **Pros** The climate in southwest Dordogne is warmer than the north ■ Low-cost flights to the region have developed the foreign market

■ **Cons** This area is becoming overcrowded, and risks becoming spoiled and overrun by tourists ■ Massive price rises have forced many buyers to seek property in damper north Dordogne ■ The area is heavily colonised by British buyers.

GETTING THERE AND AROUND

AIR Bergerac is the region's only airport and there are flights from Stansted with **Ryanair** (0871 246 0000; www.ryanair.com), and with **flybe** (0871 700 0535; www.flybe.com) from Bristol and Southampton
ROAD You can take the **Eurotunnel** (www.eurotunnel.com) to Calais, or a ferry to Calais, Cherbourg, Le Havre or Saint-Malo. From here the E05, A16 or A1 takes you on to Paris. From Paris, the A10 runs down to Orléans, and from there the A71/A20 runs south to Brive, while the N89 runs west into the Dordogne. Once in the Dordogne, the N21 runs from north to south, and the A20 runs from east to west.
RAIL The **Eurostar** (08705 186 186; www.eurostar.com) travels to Paris, from where there are services to Bordeaux. From Bordeaux there are local services in and around the Dordogne area. See **Rail Europe** (0870 830 2008; www.raileurope.co.uk) for more details.

HOTSPOTS

WHAT CAN YOU GET FOR YOUR EUROS?

€147,780

West Dordogne: This habitable, detached property has a unique character, with a large garden and spectacular views. Close to two thriving market towns, this renovation property is typical of the kind of home to be found throughout the Dordogne area.

€481,500

Dordogne valley: This restored stone house with a converted barn shows just what can be achieved through property renovation. Boasting a swimming pool and spacious grounds, this three-bedroom house has a traditional interior design and separate apartment.

AVERAGE DORDOGNE PROPERTY PRICES

Hotsppt	1-bed	2-bed	3-bed	4-bed	5-bed
Lettings	€375 (£260)	€620 (£431)	€965 (£670)	€1,170 (£813)	€1,350 (£938)
House	€73,400 (£50,972)	€116,000 (£80,555)	€202,500 (£140,625)	€253,833 (£176,273)	€341,000 (£236,805)
Apartments	€72,500 (£50,347)	€122,000 (£84,722)	€175,000 (£121,528)	€206,000 (£143,055)	–

Property hotspots

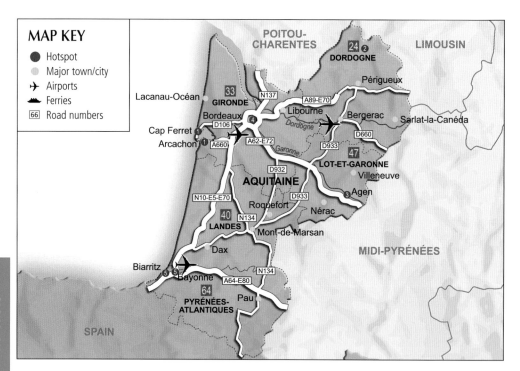

MAP KEY

- ● Hotspot
- ○ Major town/city
- ✈ Airports
- ⚓ Ferries
- 66 Road numbers

1. Cap Ferret/Bay of Arcachon

ESSENTIALS ■ **Pop** Arcachon: 1,800, Cap Ferret: 6,307 ■ **Taxes** Taxe d'habitation: 6.49%, Taxe foncière: 8.33%
■ **Airport** Bordeaux/Merignac Airport, Cedex 40, 33700 Merignac, Tel: +33 (0) 5 5634 5000

KEY FACTS

■ **Schools** The nearest international school is in Bordeaux, which is 70.5 km, 50 minutes, from Arcachon: Bordeaux International School, 53 Rue de Laseppe, 33000 Bordeaux, Tel: +33 (0) 5 5787 0211, www.bordeaux-school.com
■ **Medical** Medical Centre De Secteur, 68 boulevard Deganne, 33120 Arcachon, Tel: +33 (0) 5 5752 5590
Hôpital Saint-André, 1 Rue Jean Burguet, Centre Ville, Bordeaux, Tel: +33 (0) 5 5679 5679
■ **Rentals** The area is very popular for rentals, particularly with the French market ■ The location of Arcachon makes it very popular for holiday rentals and guarantees a good income ■ The season lasts from June to September
■ **Pros** The preserve of the wealthy and a highly exclusive resort ■ Located on the northern headland of the Bassin d'Arcachon, this is a protected area with stunning beaches
■ **Cons** During the high season, Arcachon tends to become extremely overcrowded ■ Certain bay areas, particularly Lacanau-Ocean, can be overpriced ■ Outside of the tourist season, a lack of tourist attractions can give the area a relatively deserted feel.

Cap Ferret and the Bay of Arcachon are situated on the Aquitaine peninsula, where sand dunes stretch west, scattered with breathtaking bays, 7,000 hectares of forest and many oyster-farming villages. Arcachon has a mild climate, with the Atlantic lapping the west coast.

Built during the 19th century, the town has long enjoyed a reputation as an exclusive holiday resort. It was visited by the Rothschilds, who came to take its mineral-rich marine curatives.

The town presents two varied styles. La Ville d'Hiver (winter town) is perched on a sand dune overlooking the community and is constructed like a labyrinth to avoid blustery sea weather. The whole neighbourhood reflects 19th-century architecture, with Swiss chalets and châteaux symbolising decadent bourgeois leisure.

Arcachon's most appealing attraction is its vivid and lively Saturday market, where you will find a good range of local cuisine, including fresh oysters and Bayonne ham. Visit the nearby heritage-listed, oyster-farming harbours of Gujan-Mestras and Biganos, or take a trip to the natural salt marshes of Arès. A popular area with French and international buyers alike, there is great demand for holiday homes in the area. The average cost of a two-bedroom property on the Aquitaine peninsula is €225,000 rising to €530,000 for five bedrooms. ●

2. Dordogne – see Aquitaine special on p 234-5

3. Agen

ESSENTIALS ■ **Pop** 1999: 32,180 ■ **Taxes** Taxe d'habitation: 7.55%, Taxe foncière: 14.61% ■ **Airport** Bergerac-Roumaniere Aeroport, Route d'Agen, 24100 Bergerac, Tel: +33 (0) 5 5322 2525

The westerly region of Lot-et-Garonne is the agricultural heartland of Aquitaine, rich in orchards, vines and scenic villages. Its prosperous capital, Agen, has earned culinary praise for its famous prunes and plums. Rue Beauville, with its beautifully restored medieval houses, leads through to Rue Voltaire, which has many ethnic restaurants. The Musée Municipal des Beaux-Arts, housed in four 16th and 17th-century mansions, displays archaeological finds, medieval furniture and paintings which include five by Goya.

Despite periodic flooding, the Garonne is one of France's most attractive inland waterways. You can cross the river by footbridge close to the gardens at Le Gravier. This former island became the site of one of the area's most important medieval fairs, which is now protected by a flood-proof esplanade. Agen's canal bridge is the second longest in France, offering panoramic views of the town from a height of 10 metres, or you may prefer to gaze upwards at it from a river boat.

The Lot-et-Garonne *département* has always been expensive, even in the days before Dordogne became popular. A large, stone farmhouse with a pool and terracing cost around €500,000. In Agen, a two-bedroom home averages at roughly €125,000. ●

KEY FACTS

■ **Schools** Bordeaux's international school is the only one in the area and is 94.5 km from Bergerac Bordeaux International School, 53 Rue de Laseppe, 33000 Bordeaux, Tel: +33 (0) 5 5787 0211, www.bordeaux-school.com
■ **Medical** Medical Centre Hospitalier d'Agen, RN 21/route de Villeneuve, 47000 Agen, Tel: +33 (0) 5 5369 7071
■ **Rentals** Agen itself is not renowned for its rental market, but the areas surrounding it and throughout the Lot-et-Garonne countryside are guaranteed a June to September rental season
■ **Pros** This is the capital of the Garonne, a 'rural unhurried town', located on the river Garonne
■ It is well-located, halfway between Bordeaux and Toulouse ■ Reliant upon agriculture, Agen is known for its production of prunes and plums ■ The Place Goya is the centre of Agen's most interesting district, featuring the Musée Municipal des Beaux-Arts and the 13th-century church of Notre-Dame
■ **Cons** The Lot-et-Garonne département was always very expensive, even before Dordogne became popular ■ Very few renovation properties still exist, and property is not good value for money here.

4. Bordeaux

ESSENTIALS ■ **Pop** 1999: 735,000 ■ **Taxes** Taxe d'habitation: 6.49%, Taxe foncière: 8.33% ■ **Airport** Bordeaux/Merignac Airport, Cedex 40, 33700 Merignac, Tel: +33 (0) 5 5634 5000

KEY FACTS

■ **Schools** Bordeaux International School, 53 rue de Laseppe, 33000 Bordeaux, Tel: +33 (0) 5 5787 0211, www.bordeaux-school.com
■ **Medical** Medical Hôpital Saint-André, 1 rue Jean Burguet, Centre Ville, Bordeaux, Tel: +33 (0) 5 5679 5679
■ **Rentals** Rentals are targeted at the long-term French market, rather than the foreign holiday market ■ Britons tend to focus on the areas outside of Bordeaux
■ **Pros** As a city of wealth, Bordeaux is an expensive place in which to live and stay ■ Home to the Bordeaux wine trade and one of the oldest trading ports in France, Bordeaux produces more than 44 million cases of wine each year ■ Bordeaux is a dynamic city with a university that boasts 60,000 students ■ Easily accessible and the centre of transport for the region
■ **Cons** Apart from its small 18th-century city centre, Bordeaux is a relatively shabby city with some less attractive areas ■ As Bordeaux is primarily a city in which the French live and work, it is not geared towards foreign buyers ■ Most activity in the foreign property market takes place in areas outside of the city

Bordeaux has been a wealthy city since Roman times, and has recently received millions of euros for urban regeneration. Yet apart from its 18th-century centre, graced by buildings constructed from limestone and adorned by ornate cast-iron balconies, this urban sprawl of more than half a million people is, in parts, notably shabby. The city centre is easily explored on foot and its attractions include restaurants selling the region's world-renowned wines. The Palais de la Douane et de la Bourse, and the residences of well-renowned merchants display window arches adorned with bunches of grapes and sculptures of Bacchus. The opulent 18th-century Grand Théâtre is surrounded by Corinthian-style columns and is said to possess perfect acoustics to match a near-perfect interior.

This is primarily an area in which the French live and work. It has encouraged long-term property lets and generated interest from the local, rather than international property market. International interest is centred on Bordeaux's surrounding countryside which attracts many Britons, and property prices having soared in recent years as a result. The most seductive landscape is the vast pine-covered expanse of Les Landes, to the south, or the huge Atlantic beaches. Prices are lower around the city itself; four-bedroom homes cost around €325,000 ●

5. Biarritz and Bayonne

ESSENTIALS ■ **Pop** 1999: 72,000 ■ **Taxes** Taxe d'habitation: 7.30%, Taxe foncière: 8.38% ■ **Airport** Biarritz-Bayonne-Anglet Aeroport, 7 Esplanade de l'Europe, 64600 Anglet, Tel: +33 (0) 5 5943 8383

KEY FACTS

■ **Schools** Bordeaux International School, 53 rue de Laseppe, 33000 Bordeaux, Tel: +33 (0) 5 5787 0211, www.bordeaux-school.com
■ **Medical** Medical Centre Hospitalier de la Côte Basque, 13 Avenue de lInterne J Loëb, 64100 Bayonne, Tel +33 (0) 5 5944 3535
■ **Rentals** Situated in a well-known resort area, these towns have always been popular with the international market ■ The area's exclusivity is guaranteed to produce rental income in a season lasting from June to September ■ More appealing to the French market, the two resorts are very expensive
■ **Pros** Located very close to the Spanish border, an area popular for relocation ■ Enjoying a warm winter climate, this is an attractive, comfortable area n Close to the coast and also easily accessible
■ **Cons** This popular area can become very busy and overrun ■ Almost exclusively a French resort; international buyers buy more in the surrounding area ■ Property is poor value for money and few renovation properties exist ■ Lying between Toulouse and Bordeaux, the area is expensive

Once christened 'the Monte Carlo of the Atlantic coast' after being transformed by Napoleon III in the 19th century into a playground for the affluent, Biarritz was overshadowed by the rise of the Côte d'Azur. Now rediscovered by Parisians, surfers and celebrities, the town is a showcase of impressive Victorian buildings, alongside traditional Basque homes and modern apartments. Blessed with a long sandy beach, a casino, a promenade and numerous restaurants, Biarritz also has a quieter side, with lots of sheltered beaches next to the Plage du Vieux Port. Place Clémenceau is the main shopping area and there is a good selection of museums; the Bonnat Museum displays works by Rubens, Titian and Raphaël.

A few miles inland from Biarritz at the Adour-Nives river junction, lies Bayonne, the region's capital. More commercial than Biarritz, its Basque essence is, however, reflected in the tall, half-timbered colombage houses with woodwork painted in the traditional Basque colours of green and red. The Basque people are proud of their distinct, lively culture, their language and their sport of pelota. Bayonne is very popular with the affluent French market. A south-facing three-bedroom maison de ville starts at €315,000, while a five-bedroom house is priced at €590,000. ●

€90,000–€150,000
(£62,500–£104,166)

Traditional French properties available at bargain prices

€99,000

NEAR BEAUVILLE, LOT-ET-GARONNE
A spacious old *boulangerie* in the heart of a pretty village

£68,750

🛏 4 ❀ 250m² 🏘 *Situated in the village centre* 🛣 *Located on a quiet street*
🏠 *Room for parking, with a garage*

€100,000

NEAR BEAUVILLE, LOT-ET-GARONNE
This huge, stone barn has excellent potential for renovation

£69,444

🛏 – ❀ *Small garden* 🏘 *Situated in the village centre* 🛣 *Located on a quiet village street* 🏠 *Room for parking*

€138,450

NEAR MARVAL, DORDOGNE
A renovated farmhouse in a peaceful setting at the heart of a regional park

£96,146

🛏 2 ❀ 7,600m² 🏘 *Situated in a quiet rural area* 🛣 *Not located on a main road*
🏠 *Room for parking*

€146,805

PIEGUT-PLUVIERS, DORDOGNE
An attractive detached property with a large cellar, set in a mature park

£101,948

🛏 2 ❀ 4,800m² 🏘 *Situated in a quiet rural location* 🛣 *Not located on a main road* 🏠 *Room for parking, with 2 garages*

€148,000

NEAR BEAUVILLE, LOT-ET-GARONNE
A traditional stone and *colombage* village house with a courtyard

£102,777

🛏 3 ❀ *Courtyard* 🏘 *Situated in the village centre* 🛣 *Located on a quiet village street* 🏠 *Room for parking*

Builders of new properties
in south west France

NEW BUILD IN SOUTH WEST FRANCE
CHARENTES – AQUITAINE – MIDI-PYRENEES

Maisons SIC have been building personalised homes for over 30 years.
From the plot search to handing over the keys our aim is to provide satisfaction and peace of mind.
How reassuring to know you can have a house designed to your requirements, with a ten-year guarantee and at fixed price.
Modern homes are built to a very high standard and Maisons SIC offer you an extensive range of interior fixtures and finishings, tiling and materials.
If you don't feel up to renovating, or just want a maintenance free home, why not consider new build.

**Maisons SIC are present in the UK every fortnight,
please contact us for a meeting**
Maisons SIC - 11, rte de Bordeaux
47400 Tonneins – France
Tel:(0033)553841616 Fax:(0033)553841612
E-mail: contact@maisons-sic.com

www.maisons-sic.com

UNCMI
Union Nationale des Constructeurs
de Maisons Individuelles

€150,000–€300,000
(£104,166–£208,333)

A selection of larger cottages, farmhouses and modern homes

€198,000   CODE VIA

NEAR BEAUVILLE, LOT-ET-GARONNE
An attractive stone cottage with a walled garden and swimming pool

£137,500

🛏 2   ⚙ 50m²   🏘 Situated in the village centre   🛣 Located on a quiet village street

🅿 Room for parking

€242,000   CODE LAT

BERGERAC AREA, DORDOGNE
A detached stone country house with a garage, outbuildings and lovely views

£168,056

🛏 2   ⚙ 8,000m²   🏘 Situated in the Bergerac area   🛣 Not located on a main road

🅿 Room for parking, with a garage

€261,000   CODE VIA

NEAR PUJOLS, LOT-ET-GARONNE
An 18th-century stone farmhouse and barn, set in large grounds

£181,250

🛏 4   ⚙ 28,000m²   🏘 Situated in a quiet rural area   🛣 Not located on a main road

🅿 Room for parking, with a garage

€268,000   CODE VIA

NEAR BEAUVILLE, LOT-ET-GARONNE
A charming stone farmhouse in large grounds, with a stone barn

£186,111

🛏 4   ⚙ 13,760m²   🏘 Situated 6km from the village   🛣 Not located on a main road

🅿 Room for parking, with a garage

€291,000   CODE LAT

NEAR DAX, LANDES
A modern house set in large grounds, just 40 minutes from the beach

£202,083

🛏 4   ⚙ 1,627m²   🏘 Situated 2km from the village   🛣 Not located on a main road

🅿 Room for parking

PRICE GUIDE

€300,000–€600,000
(£208,333–£416,667)

Superb houses with lots of land and all mod-cons

€304,000   CODE HDG

CHARENTE BORDER, DORDOGNE

A completely restored, natural stone village house with a large garden

£211,111

🛏 3 🌼 2,200m² 🏞 Situated on a river bank 🛣 Not located on a main road

🏠 Room for parking

€404,000   CODE FRA

RIBERAC, DORDOGNE

A substantial property with outbuildings and large grounds. Lots of potential

£280,556

🛏 6 🌼 5,340m² 🏞 Situated in the village centre 🛣 Not located on a main road

🏠 Room for parking

€420,000   CODE FRA

PERIGUEUX, DORDOGNE

A lovely old property set in a meadow, with a pool and guest accommodation

£291,667

🛏 4 🌼 Courtyard 🏞 Situated in the village centre 🛣 Not located on a main road

🏠 Room for parking

€457,000   CODE VIA

NEAR MONFLANQUIN, LOT-ET-GARONNE

An impressive stone residence in a rural setting with large grounds

£317,361

🛏 4 🌼 30,000m² 🏞 Situated 5km from the village 🛣 Not located on a main road

🏠 Room for parking, with a garage

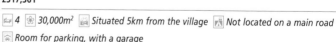

€585,000   CODE VIA

NEAR BEAUVILLE, LOT-ET-GARONNE

A superbly renovated stone farmhouse, including a barn with planning permission

£406,250

🛏 4 🌼 8,000m² 🏞 Situated 6km from the village 🛣 Not located on a main road

🏠 Room for parking, with a garage

€600,000+
(£416,667+)

Gorgeous châteaux and historical buildings with plenty of character

€653,000   CODE VIA

NEAR VILLENEUVE-SUR-LOT, LOT-ET-GARONNE
A stunning art deco château with plenty of original features, set in large grounds
£453,472

🛏 5 ⚙ 30,000m² 🖼 *Situated close to the village* 🚫 *Not located on a main road*
🏠 *Room for parking*

€764,000   CODE VIA

TOURNON-D'AGENAIS, LOT-ET-GARONNE
An ancient millhouse set in large grounds, with a lake and 3 gîtes
£530,556

🛏 12 ⚙ 233,000m² 🖼 *Situated 5km from the village* 🚫 *Not located on a main
road* 🏠 *Room for parking, with a garage*

€765,000   CODE HDG

PERIGUEUX, DORDOGNE
A beautifully restored 17th-century property with outbuildings and large grounds
£531,250

🛏 7 ⚙ 60,000m² 🖼 *Situated in the village centre* 🚫 *Not located on a main road*
🏠 *Room for parking, with a garage*

€1,500,000   CODE FRA

RIBERAC, DORDOGNE
A beautiful château that dates back to the 15th century; with 6 outbuildings
£1,041,667

🛏 15 ⚙ 720,000m² 🖼 *Situated in a peaceful area* 🚫 *Not located on a main road*
🏠 *Room for parking*

€1,579,000   CODE DEM

WESTERN DORDOGNE, AQUITAINE
A stunning 18-century château that underwent complete restoration in 2000
£1,096,528

🛏 11 ⚙ 55,000m² 🖼 *Situated close to the village* 🚫 *Not located on a main road*
🏠 *Room for parking*

Find the house of your dreams among the wide choice available through our *daily updated site*

www.*blueHOMES*.com

Our office base in France

Our international multilingual team welcomes you in the picturesque little village of Simorre. We share with you our availability, our efficiency and we help you to find your dream house among our numerous properties.
Present in the whole France with an extensive, professional network of partners and excellent customers care, blueHOMES is becoming the internet's fastest moving website for southern European real estate.

Agence Immobilière de Simorre
Rue du Midi
32420 Simorre/France
phone   +33 5 62 65 35 10
email   kossel@blueHOMES.com

Our *multilingual network* *of agents* are ready to assist you!

blueHOMES
discover your dream real(i)ty..

Midi-Pyrénées

High peaks, world-famous Lourdes, and France's Basque country

JUSTIN POSTLETHWAITE

FACT BOX 2005

- **Population** 2,552,687
- **Migration** 265,220
- **Unemployment** 60,166
- **Median house price** €160,350
- **House price increase** Since 2002, house prices in the Midi-Pyrénées have risen by 13%

Price Guide

GETTING THERE

AIR British Airways (0870 850 9850; www.britishairways.com) flies to Toulouse, as does **Air France** (0845 084 5111; www.airfrance.co.uk). **Ryanair** (0871 246 0000; www.ryanair.com) flies from London Stansted into Rodez, **BMI Baby** (0870 264 2229; www.bmibaby.com) flies from Cardiff and the East Midlands into Toulouse, while **Flybe** (0871 700 0535; www.flybe.com) flies to Toulouse from Bristol, Birmingham and Southampton.
ROAD The A71/A20 runs from Paris through Limoges and from there the N20 continues on to Toulouse. The D938/7 runs to Lourdes and the N21 continues from there to Cauterets. From the Channel ports, travel to Le Mans and then follow the N138 and N143, then the A20 at Châteauroux, to get to Toulouse.
COACH The **Eurolines** bus service (0870 514 3219; www.eurolines.com) travels from various cities in the UK to Cahors, Lourdes, Tarbes and Toulouse.
RAIL The TGV service runs from the Gare d'Austerlitz in Paris through to Toulouse. Contact **Rail Europe** (0870 584 8848; www.raileurope.co.uk) for all the details of local services. There is a comprehensive network of local services from Toulouse that operates throughout the Midi-Pyrénées region.

Area profile

THE MIDI-PYRÉNÉES REGION IS HOME TO THE HIGHEST PEAKS IN THE famous mountain range that towers along the border with Spain, and its diverse landscape also encompasses great valleys, national and regional parks, and beautiful fortified towns and châteaus.

Toulouse is the fourth-largest metropolis in the country and the capital of the Midi-Pyrénées. Home to the second-largest student population in France (over 100,000), it has a wealth of bars, restaurants and clubs. It also houses a number of high-tech industries and has a large aerospace industry.

One of the world's most famous pilgrimage sites lies in the far southwest of the Midi-Pyrénées. Lourdes attracts more than five million visitors from across the globe every year. The nearby town of Tarbes is one of the region's largest commercial centres and it provides a lot of accommodation for visiting pilgrims. North of Tarbes is Auch, a beautiful small city with a UNESCO-recognised cathedral in the heart of Gascony. Albi, 70 miles northeast of Toulouse, is dominated by a huge, impressive Gothic cathedral built from reddish bricks, and it's also home to the largest collection of the work of artist Henri de Toulouse-Lautrec, the town's most famous son.

The Midi-Pyrénées is perfect for those who enjoy outdoor activities. From mountain climbing to gentle river cruising, the region has something for everyone.

Food and wine

Like most regions of France, gastronomy plays a huge part in the lives of the Midi-Pyrénées inhabitants. *Foie gras* is a speciality in Gers and Lot, and *le cassoulet de Toulouse* is a stew of white beans, kidney beans and confit of duck sausage cooked in goose fat. Gers is also the home of France's oldest brandy, the fragrant and complex *Armagnac*. Naturally, there are lots of vineyards producing distinctive wines ranging from dry, fruity whites to full-bodied reds; there are more than 15 AOC (guarantee of region) wines in the Midi-Pyrénées.

Agriculture is important in the mountainous Midi-Pyrénées region

The economy and housing market

Traditionally an agricultural area, the region has seen its ecomony expand in recent years, despite depopulation. Toulouse is the centre for the French aerospace industry (it employs more than 60,000 people), and there are now many high-tech concerns centred in the Midi-Pyrénées. Agriculture remains one of the region's economic drivers, though. Apples, melons, prunes and grapes are all grown in a region which also provides around 60 per cent of France's garlic. Tourism, particularly in Rocamadour and Cahors, has also added hugely to the economy of the region, and has grown in recent years due to the increase in budget flights to the area.

The whole region has experienced an increase in property prices over the last few years, and the least you can now expect to pay for a habitable property is about £110,000. Gers is the most expensive and in-demand *département*, with interest beginning to expand into the Hautes-Pyrénées. However, there are still renovation projects to be found, and many good investments. Toulouse is a very expensive, French-centred market, while Aveyron has been opened up to the foreign buyer by budget flights to Rodez and the new A20 motorway. Auch is the capital of Gers, and offers access into the Midi-Pyrénées, but can be pricey. Although in demand, Gers is still a source of reasonably priced period homes, and offers large stone properties with a lot of land and outbuildings.

Aveyron is an up-and-coming *département* with a rugged landscape and fairly cheap properties, while Toulouse is ideal for the buyer seeking a metropolis. British buyers have been purchasing property in Toulouse's suburban areas along the *autoroute*. The Hautes-Pyrénées (like the Gers) still offers renovation properties and spacious stone farmhouses, while Cauterets, La Mongie and the northern Hautes-Pyrénées region are the areas to target if you are seeking a property close to the ski resorts.

With improved access into the Midi-Pyrénées has come increased interest and an inevitable growth in prices. The Lot, Tarn and Tarn-et-Garonne *départements* have experienced a boom in foreign property sales, and are dominated by families and those seeking retirement homes.

Huge demand in neighbouring Languedoc-Roussillon has driven property seekers inland, so the Midi-Pyrénées is enjoying increasing interest from international buyers. It has a hugely varied landscape, which offers easy access to both the coast and the ski resorts, and is still reasonably priced. However, prices are likely to rise over the next few years.

Social groups

British buyers are discovering the mountainous beauty and Gascon countryside in ever-increasing numbers. British buyers also proliferate in and around Toulouse. Part of the Midi-Pyrénées is Basque, which has its own language and customs. The French Basques are generally less separatist in nature than their Spanish counterparts, though only about 10 per cent of the Basque region is in France. ●

"Lourdes, one of the world's most famous pilgrimage sites, lies in the far southwest of the region and attracts more than five million people every year"

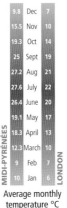

MIDI-PYRÉNÉES		LONDON
9.8	Dec	7
15.5	Nov	10
19.3	Oct	14
25	Sept	19
27.2	Aug	21
27.6	July	22
26.4	June	20
19.1	May	17
18.3	April	13
12.3	March	10
9	Feb	7
10	Jan	6

Average monthly temperature °C (Celsius)

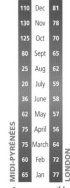

MIDI-PYRÉNÉES		LONDON
110	Dec	81
130	Nov	78
125	Oct	70
80	Sept	65
25	Aug	62
20	July	59
36	June	58
62	May	57
75	April	56
75	March	64
60	Feb	72
65	Jan	77

Average monthly rainfall mm (millimetres)

AVERAGE HOUSE SALE PRICES

Hotspot	2-bed	3-bed	4-bed	5-bed+
Cahors & Rocamadour	€126K (£87K)	€166K (£115K)	€208K (£144K)	€387K (£269K)
Gascony/Gers	€168K (£117K)	€162K (£113K)	€244K (£169K)	€448K (£311K)
Toulouse	€186K (£129K)	€230K (£160K)	€347K (£241K)	€482K (£335K)
Bagnères de Bigorre	€161K (£112K)	€196K (£136K)	€240K (£167K)	€384K (£267K)

Focus on Gascony

With a number of fortified villages, spectacular agricultural land and pretty villages, Gascony has long been popular with the British buyer

MIDI-PYRÉNÉES COMITÉ REGIONAL DU TOURISME

GASCONY FACTS

■ Brave and skilled Gascon soldiers were the inspiration for Alexander Dumas's *d'Artagnan* and Edmond Rostand's *Cyrano de Bergerac*

■ Gers is France's biggest producer of *foie gras*, which has been a Gascon speciality since the 16th century

■ *Armagnac* originates from Gascony, where it was first produced in 1411

TRADITIONALLY AN AGRICULTURAL AND WINE-PRODUCING AREA blessed with fertile soils, Gascony – now known as Gers – is the most rural *département* in France, famed for its preserves, pâtés and particularly *foie gras*. One of France's most 'French' areas despite an invasion of British buyers, Gascony still remains unspoilt and retains much of its characteristic charm.

The capital Auch is an outstanding Gallo-Roman city on the Saint James of Compostela route, and retains its medieval style, with ochre stone and rose-coloured tiles gracing many old houses around the centre. The cathedral of Saint Mary's was one of the last to be built in France, with its unusual choir stalls and stained glass created by a Gascon artist, Arnaud de Moles. Immediately south of the cathedral, in the tree-filled Place Salinis, is the 40-metre-high Tour d'Armagnac, which served as an ecclesiastical court and prison in the 14th century. Descending from here to the river is a monumental stairway of 234 steps, boasting a statue of d'Artagnan of *Three Musketeers* fame.

Outside Auch there are a handful of peaceful towns, offering a genuine taste of French rural life. Condom in the north has an impressive cathedral, the Armagnac museum and some attractive winding streets, while Fleurance and Lectoure are both attractive hillside towns with medieval houses, town halls and central squares.

Auch is the focal point of the Gascony property market and is regarded as the gateway into the region. Gascony is very popular with the foreign buyer, the majority of whom are British, and a standard property is a spacious stone-built farmhouse. While there is little cheap property available in Gascony, better value homes can be found away from Auch in the surrounding rural areas, and a two-bedroom property can be picked up for €168,200. ●

ESSENTIALS

Population 1999: 172,300 ■ **Taxes** Taxe d'habitation 25.36%, Taxe foncière 62.13% ■ **Airport** Toulouse-Blagnac, BP 103, 31703 Blagnac Cedex, Tel: +33 561 42 44 00, Fax: +33 561 42 45 55

KEY FACTS

■ **Schools** Contact the Rectorat de l'Académie de Toulouse, Place Saint-Jacques, 31073 Toulouse, Cedex, Tel: +33 561 36 40 00, Fax: +33 561 52 80 27 for advice on education

■ **Medical** Centre Hospitalier, rte Tarbes, 32000 Auch, Tel: +33 562 61 32 32

■ **Rentals** Gascony has always been popular with the British market, and is a popular tourist area ■ The rental season is guaranteed to last from June to September, with 10 weeks of rentals being the least you can expect ■ More people are moving to the area, seeking to set up a holiday rentals business

■ **Pros** Easily accessible from Toulouse, the major airport in the region ■ Property in Gascony is spacious and includes a lot of land, with homes often being extremely luxurious

■ **Cons** Renovation properties do exist, but take longer and more organisation to complete, due to a shortage of artisans and high demand.

GETTING THERE AND AROUND

AIR There are regular flights to Toulouse with **British Airways** (08708 509850; www.britishairways.co.uk) from Gatwick. **easyJet** (08717 500100; www.easyjet.com) flies to Toulouse from Gatwick, while **Flybe** (08717 000535; www.flybe.com) goes from Birmingham, Bristol and Southampton. **ROAD** Take a ferry to Cherbourg, Saint-Malo or Le Havre with **Brittany Ferries** (08703 665333; www.brittanyferries.co.uk). Join the A71 at Orléans and then take the A20 to Toulouse. From here the N124 leads towards Auch and Gascony. **RAIL** The Eurostar (08705 186 186; www.eurostar.com) travels to Paris, from where there are TGV services to Toulouse. From Toulouse there are local services in and around the Gascony area. See **Rail Europe** (0870 830 2008; www.raileurope.co.uk) for more details.

HOTSPOTS

WHAT CAN YOU GET FOR YOUR EUROS?

€112,450

GERS: A rare property at this price, this stunning waterside mill comes complete with original millstone. Set amidst gorgeous countryside, the mill is close to a town boasting all the necessary services and facilities. A real find, this home is a bargain at £78,100.

€275,600

GERS: This charming property boasts a lake set in three acres of land. Situated on a quiet lane, the building is in immaculate condition and offers two bedrooms plus a separate wooden chalet. Close to the town of Casteljaloux, this house has a traditional interior design.

AVERAGE GASCONY PROPERTY PRICES

	1-bed	2-bed	3-bed	4-bed	5-bed
Lettings	€410 (£285)	€575 (£399)	€760 (£528)	€870 (£604)	€975 (£677)
House	€105,600 (£73,333)	€168,200 (£116,805)	€162,400 (£112,778)	€243,667 (£169,213)	€447,600 (£310,833)
Apartments	€68,000 (£47,222)	€125,000 (£86,806)	€158,000 (£109,722)	€195,000 (£135,417)	–

Property hotspots

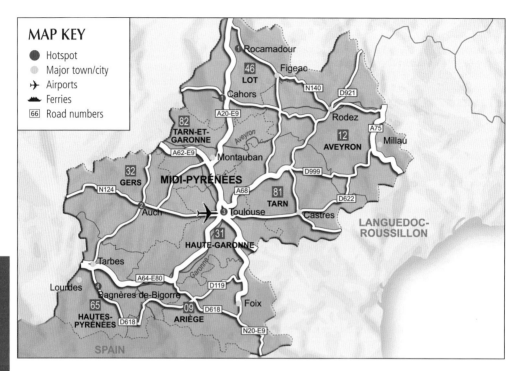

MAP KEY

● Hotspot
○ Major town/city
✈ Airports
⛴ Ferries
66 Road numbers

1. Cahors and Rocamadour

ESSENTIALS ■ **Population** Cahors 23,128, Rocamadour 46,500 ■ **Taxes** Taxe d'habitation 6.20%, Taxe foncière 13.12% ■ **Airport** Toulouse-Blagnac, BP 103, 31703 Blagnac Cedex, Tel: +33 561 42 44 00, Fax: +33 561 42 45 55

KEY FACTS

■ **Schools** International School of Toulouse SA, Route de Pibrax, 31770 Colomiers, Tel: +33 562 74 26 74, www.intst.net
■ **Medical** Centre Hospitalier Cahors 335 rue Président Wilson, 46000 Cahors, Tel: +33 565 20 50 50, Fax: +33 565 20 50 51
■ **Rentals** Hugely popular for tourists, the areas surrounding Cahors and Rocamadour have great rental potential ■ The rental season is guaranteed to last from June to September, with longer-term lettings becoming popular in the winter months ■ A two-bedroom property rents for €575 and a three-bedroom property for €800 per week
■ **Pros** The Lot area has a mild climate during the winter months, and has stunning rural surroundings ■ This is an ideal area for a family home and those seeking rental income ■ The area has a strong market where property is continuing to appreciate
■ **Cons** Rocamadour is inundated with coach tours and tourists, which are damaging the natural beauty of the area ■ This is a sellers' market, with rising prices ■ Industry here is almost non-existent and jobs are based in the service sector.

Capital of the Lot *département* and built on a rocky peninsula, Cahors dates back to 1BC, and was also an important centre during the Middle Ages. Pope John XXII, who was born here, founded the University of Cahors in the early 14th century, which later became the University of Toulouse. Interesting sites include the 12th-century cathedral of Saint-Étienne; the Roman aqueduct ruins; and the Pont Valentré, a fortified stone bridge with three towers.

Also known for its deep ruby-red wines (the vineyard trail can be followed west of town), Cahors has the biggest property market in the Lot and draws a huge amount of international interest. Prices increased by 13 per cent in the Midi-Pyrénées area last year, and Cahors experiences a high turnover of properties. Nevertheless, the more luxurious properties have not been as popular in recent years. Despite this, if you are seeking a more exclusive property, prices range from €100,000 to €1,000,000.

Prices in the Lot are slightly above the national average, but it is possible to find a range of homes with land in and around Cahors. Prices start at around €120,000 for a renovated two-bedroom property, although there are still one or two ruins available for renovation from €50,000. A typical four-bedroom house will cost €208,000. ●

2. Auch – see Focus on Gascony on pp. 248-9

COMITÉ RÉGIONAL DU TOURISME TOULOUSE MIDI PYRÉNÉES

3. Toulouse

ESSENTIALS ■ **Population** 390,350 ■ **Taxes** Taxe d'habitation 7.88%, Taxe foncière 11.45% ■ **Airport** Toulouse-Blagnac, BP 103, 31703 Blagnac Cedex, Tel: +33 561 42 44 00, Fax: +33 561 42 45 55

One of the most vibrant and metropolitan provincial cities in France, Toulouse is dubbed La Ville Rose, thanks to its pink-brick buildings constructed from local clay. Transformed since World War II into a centre for high-tech industry, the city leads the way in aeronautics, being home to *Aérospatiale*, the dynamics behind Concorde, Airbus, and the Ariane space rocket. The National Space Centre and European Shuttle programme are also based here, and Toulouse has the biggest university outside Paris.

Old Toulouse is split by two 19th-century streets: the long north-south rue d'Alsace-Lorraine/rue du Languedoc, and the east-west rue de Metz. The Dominican church of Les Jacobins, which inspired Dali's painting, and the resplendent Renaissance town houses, known as *hôtels particuliers*, are worth a look. Parks include the formal gardens of the Grand-Rond and Jardin des Plantes.

Being a large city dominated by French buyers, Toulouse is expensive, although cheaper properties are available in the surrounding area. A traditional, fully renovated five-bedroom house, 30 minutes from Toulouse, costs from €175,000, while in the city the average price for a three-bedroom apartment is €173,000, and, for a three-bedroom house, expect to pay around €230,000. ●

KEY FACTS

■ **Schools** International School of Toulouse SA, Route de Pibrax, 31770 Colomiers, Tel: +33 562 74 26 74, www.intst.net
■ **Medical** Centre Hospitalier Universitaire de Toulouse, Place du Docteur Baylac, 31059 Toulouse, Cedex 3, Tel: +33 561 77 82 03, www.chu-oulouse.fr
■ **Rentals** Toulouse's rental market is not directed at foreign holiday-makers ■ There are are long-term rentals aimed at the local French market ■ Typically, a one-bedroom property will rent for €435 per week, while a property with five or more bedrooms can fetch an average of €1,400 per week
■ **Pros** Toulouse is a dynamic and vibrant city, ideal for those who are seeking a metropolitan lifestyle ■ Toulouse enjoys good road and rail connections
■ **Cons** Primarily an area dominated by the local French market ■ Most foreign buyers live in the suburbs around Toulouse, especially along the autoroutes ■ Property prices have increased dramatically throughout the Toulouse area.

4. Bagnères-de-Bigorre ▬▬▬▬▬▬▬▬▬

ESSENTIALS ■ **Population** 8,423 ■ **Taxes** Taxe d'habitation 7.97%, Taxe foncière 13.73% ■ **Airport** Pau-Pyrénées, 64230 Lescar, Tel: +33 559 33 33 00

KEY FACTS

■ **Schools** International School of Toulouse SA, Route de Pibrax, 31770 Colomiers,
Tel: +33 562 74 26 74, www.intst.net
■ **Medical** Hôpital de Bagnères-de-Bigorre, 15 rue Gambetta, 65200 Bagnères-de-Bigorre,
Tel: +33 562 91 41 11
■ **Rentals** The close proximity of the town to the expensive ski areas guarantees good rental potential ■ The ski season is guaranteed to generate interest from at least December through to April, and the summer sees activity breaks ■ A two-bedroom property here will rent for €460 per week, whilst a property with five or more bedrooms will usually attract €1,260 per week
■ **Pros** Bagnères-de-Bigorre is an excellent location, only 20 minutes away from the ski resorts ■ Barèges la Mongie is the main ski resort in the Pyrénées, easily accessible from Bagnères-de-Bigorre ■ Residents benefit from a more peaceful lifestyle outside the main resorts ■ The town has not been spoiled by modern development
■ **Cons** The area itself is fairly remote and access can be a problem ■ If you do not speak French, communicating with the locals may prove problematic.

At an altitude of 2,877 metres, this elegant spa town in the heart of the Pyrénées owes its wealth to local grey marble, used to construct the Paris Opera House and the National Assembly. Today, Bagnères–de–Bigorre produces high-tech railway equipment and has recently seen a boost in slate quarrying. While enjoying a mild climate, Bagnères–de–Bigorre draws homebuyers with an interest in the nearby intermediate ski resort of Barèges La Mongie, which offers access to 64 pistes at lower prices than resorts in the Alps. To the south, the Pic du Midi has splendid panoramas and hiking opportunities over the Pyrénées. Every June the *Fête de la Transhumance* is celebrated with folk singing, films and pageantry, while in July cyclists try their luck on the legendary Tour de France passes of Col de Tourmalet and Col d'Aspin. Outdoor activities include an 18-hole golf course; fly fishing in the Adour river; or visits to the Grottes de Medous.

It is much cheaper to buy in Bagnères–de–Bigorre than in the ski resorts, with a five-bedroomed chalet at the base of the Pyrénées costing an average of €384,400. Although the market tends to be a mainly French, it is up and coming with the foreign buyer. A traditional villa with three double bedrooms is priced from €234,300, while a smaller house with two bedrooms can be found from €120,000. ●

It is much cheaper to buy in Bagnéres-de-Bogorre than it is in the nearby ski resorts

JUSTIN POSTLETHWAITE

€100,000–€200,000
(£69,444–£138,889)

Great smaller houses and renovation projects with lots of potential

€116,000
CODE VIA

NEAR LAUZERTE, TARN-ET-GARONNE
Farmhouse and outbuildings to renovate, set in 12 acres of land
£80,556

🛏 4 ❀ 50,000m² Situated 6km from the village Not located on a main road
Room for parking, with a garage

€129,300
CODE FRA

NEAR CAZAUBON, GERS
Pretty farmhouse and barns for renovation, set in 2.5 acres
£89,792

🛏 4 ❀ 10,000m² Situated in a peaceful location Not located on a main road
Room for parking

€143,000
CODE VIA

NEAR MOISSAC, TARN-ET-GARONNE
Spacious, fully renovated house with garden in a central village location
£99,306

🛏 3 ❀ 200m² Situated in a quiet village Located on a main road
Room for parking

€196,000
CODE FRA

NEAR CAHORS, LOT
Main house with 3 bedrooms and a further two buildings with pretty gardens
£136,111

🛏 3 ❀ – Situated in a quiet village Not located on a main road
Room for parking

€198,000
CODE VIA

NEAR LAUZERTE, TARN-ET-GARONNE
A spacious old stone farmhouse to renovate, with outbuildings and splendid views
£137,500

🛏 4 ❀ 2,000m² Situated 2km from the village Not located on a main road
Room for parking, with a garage

€200,000–€400,000
(£138,889–£277,778)

Magnificent properties, from cottages to country châteaux

PRICE GUIDE

€226,000   CODE FRA

NEAR GOURDON, LOT

A delightful 2-bedroom cottage with a new pool and terrace views
£156,944

🛏 2 ✸ 2,000m² 🖼 Situated near Gourdon 🚫 Not located on a main road
🏠 Room for parking

€244,700   CODE FPS

NEAR SAINT ANTONIN, TARN-ET-GARONNE

Grand, well-restored village house that's currently operating as a bed and breakfast
£169,930

🛏 5 ✸ – 🖼 Situated near Saint Antonin 🚫 Not located on a main road
🏠 Room for parking

€248,000   CODE FRA

NEAR AURIGNAC, HAUTE-GARONNE

A lovely character farmhouse with a barn, set in an acre of land
£172,222

🛏 4 ✸ 4,000m² 🖼 Situated near Aurignac 🚫 Not located on a main road
🏠 Room for parking

€285,000   CODE FRA

NEAR CAZÈRES, HAUTE-GARONNE

A pretty farmhouse with many outbuildings; requires some restoration
£197,917

🛏 3 ✸ 10,000m² 🖼 Situated 10 minutes from the motorway 🚫 Not on a main road
🏠 Room for parking

€285,690   CODE FRA

NEAR GRAMAT, LOT

A renovated 3-bedroom farmhouse with plenty of character and a pool
£198,396

🛏 3 ✸ – 🖼 Situated in a quiet hamlet 🚫 Not located on a main road
🏠 Room for parking

€320,000

SAINT ANTONIN, TARN-ET-GARONNE

A large house in need of renovation in a quiet hamlet with views over the valley

£222,222

🛏 5 ❋ 4,000m² 🖼 *Situated in a peaceful location* 🚫 *Not located on a main road*
🏠 *Room for parking*

€326,000 CODE SIF

GERS

A completely renovated farmhouse with period features and 2 hectares of land

£226,389

🛏 2 ❋ 20,000m² 🖼 *Situated in peaceful countryside* 🚫 *Not located on a main road*
🏠 *Room for parking, with a garage*

€337,830 CODE FRA

AVEYRON

A classic 4-bedroom house with outbuildings, set in nearly an acre of land

£234,604

🛏 4 ❋ 3,800m² 🖼 *Situated near local amenities* 🚫 *Not located on a main road*
🏠 *Room for parking*

€370,000 CODE SIF

ARIÈGE

A superb 18th–century *maison de maître* in a peaceful village, with all amenities

£256,944

🛏 6 ❋ 400m² 🖼 *Situated just west of Saverdun* 🚫 *Not located on a main road*
🏠 *Room for parking, with a garage*

€399,000 CODE VIA

LAUZERTE, TARN-ET-GARONNE

A lovely renovated farmhouse with a barn, a guest wing and a swimming pool

£277,083

🛏 6 ❋ 30,000m² 🖼 *Situated 5km from the village* 🚫 *Not located on a main road*
🏠 *Room for parking, with a garage*

€400,000 CODE SIF

ARIÈGE

A 17th–century *maison de maître* with outbuildings, including a gîte

£277,778

🛏 5 ❋ 11,840m² 🖼 *Situated in a protected area* 🚫 *Not located on a main road*
🏠 *Room for parking*

PRICE GUIDE

€400,000+
(£277,778+)

Fantastic properties with their own land and all modcons

€420,000   **CODE** FPS

CAYLUS, TARN-ET-GARONNE
Well-renovated rural farmhouse with a large detached stone barn
£291,667

🛏 3   ✳ 8,000m²   🖼 Situated in a quiet village   🖼 Not located on a main road
🏠 Room for parking, with a garage

€477,000   **CODE** DAK

NEAR CONDOM, GERS
A traditional Gascon mill with a gîte, a lake and a swimming pool
£331,250

🛏 6   ✳ –   🖼 Situated in a peaceful rural location   🖼 Not located on a main road
🏠 Room for parking

€482,000   **CODE** VIA

MONTCUQ, LOT
2 stone houses, 1 to renovate, in an acre of gardens with a swimming pool
£334,722

🛏 5   ✳ 4,409m²   🖼 Situated 5km from the village   🖼 Not located on a main road
🏠 Room for parking, with a garage

€496,000   **CODE** FPS

SAINT PROJET, TARN-ET-GARONNE
A charming farmhouse with annexes, a covered terrace and a swimming pool
£344,444

🛏 6   ✳ 25,000m²   🖼 Situated in a quiet location   🖼 Not located on a main road
🏠 Room for parking

€499,000   **CODE** FRA

NEAR RODEZ, AVEYRON
A lovely secluded property on nearly 2.5 acres, with a swimming pool and 2 terraces
£346,528

🛏 3   ✳ 9,880m²   🖼 Situated in a peaceful location   🖼 Not located on a main road
🏠 Room for parking

€643,000   CODE VIA

MONTCUQ, LOT

A beautifully renovated stone farmhouse with stables and a pool

£446,528

🛏 4 ❋ 130,000m² 🖼 Situated 5km from the village 🛤 Not located on a main road
🏠 Room for parking, with a garage

€696,000   CODE VIA

MONTAIGU-DE-QUERCY, TARN-ET-GARONNE

A beautiful country house with a guest cottage and swimming pool, set in 30 acres

£483,333

🛏 7 ❋ 120,000m² 🖼 Situated 5km from the village 🛤 Not located on a main road
🏠 Room for parking, with a garage

€735,000   CODE VIA

BOURG-DE-VISA, TARN-ET-GARONNE

Impressive country residence set in 43 acres; ideal for a bed and breakfast

£510,417

🛏 6 ❋ 170,000m² 🖼 Situated 3km from the village 🛤 Not located on a main road
🏠 Room for parking, with a garage

€757,900   CODE FRA

NEAR CAHORS, LOT

A superb character property with 5 bedrooms and an immense habitable area

£540,972

🛏 5 ❋ 350m² 🖼 Well positioned 🛤 Not located on a main road
🏠 Room for parking

€980,000   CODE LAT

GAILLAC AREA, TARN

A beautiful former watermill with a stone barn, set in 180 acres of grounds

£680,555

🛏 5 ❋ 720,000m² 🖼 Situated in a peaceful rural area 🛤 Not located on a main road
🏠 Room for parking, with a garage

€1,200,000   CODE DAK

NEAR CONDOM, GERS

A fine period château with 8 bedrooms, set in large grounds

£833,333

🛏 8 ❋ 24,000m² 🖼 – 🛤 Not located on a main road
🏠 Room for parking

PRICE GUIDE

Languedoc-Roussillon

Mediterranean coast, medieval cities and vineyards galore

VEF

FACT BOX 2005

- ■ **Population** 2,295,648
- ■ **Migration** 338,308
- ■ **Unemployment** 81,432
- ■ **Median house price** €163,000
- ■ **House price increase** Since 2002, house prices in Languedoc-Roussillon have risen by 28.4%, which is the largest increase in the whole country

GETTING THERE

AIR Languedoc-Roussillon has an international airport in Montpellier, and three smaller but extremely active airports in Nîmes, Perpignan and Carcassonne. **Ryanair** (0871 246 0000; www.ryanair.com) flies directly from London Stansted into Montpellier, Carcassonne, Nîmes and Perpignan airports. **GB Airways** (0870 551 1155; www.gbairways.com) also flies into Montpellier from Gatwick, while **British Airways** (0870 850 9850; www.britishairways.com) operates from a variety of UK airports to Montpellier and Perpignan (via Paris).

ROAD The A9 runs along the coastline of Languedoc-Roussillon from Nîmes through Montpellier and down to Perpignan. From Paris the A10 leads on to the A20 from Orléans to Toulouse, while the A61 motorway provides access from the west, and the A75 enters from the north. The smaller road networks are well-maintained, making for easy access throughout the region.

COACH Eurolines (0870 514 3219; www.eurolines.com) provides coach travel from the UK to Béziers, Carcassonne, Narbonne, Nîmes and Perpignan.

RAIL The **TGV** runs a service between Paris Gare de Lyon and Nîmes, Montpellier and Perpignan, while Motorail operates from Calais to Narbonne. There are **Eurostar** services between Lille Europe and Perpignan. For more details on local services, contact **Rail Europe** (0870 830 2008; www.raileurope.co.uk).

Area profile

THE LANGUEDOC-ROUSSILLON RÉGION ARCHES BETWEEN THE MIDI-Pyrénées and Provence, and then along the Mediterranean coast through the heart of French Catalonia to the border with Spain. The coast offers great beaches and inland, much of the spectacular scenery, which encompasses mountains and lakes, is protected within national and regional parks. As well as hiking, cycling and fishing, the Pyrénées offers great skiing in the winter months.

The capital is Montpellier, a city home to more than 200,000 people, almost a quarter of them students. Much of its centre is pedestrianised and its wide boulevards, open squares and fountains ensure it's a very pleasant city in which to stroll. Montpellier's medical school is the oldest in Europe, dating back 900 years. Nîmes has some spectacular Roman architecture, particularly Les Arènes, an amphitheatre modelled on the the Colosseum in Rome. Just outside the city is the Pont du Gard, a three-tiered Roman aqueduct built to provide the city with water. This UNESCO World Heritage Site attracts millions of visitors every year.

Carcassonne in the southwest is quite simply one of the world's most visually stunning cities. A medieval hilltop fortress fortified by walls and turrets, it looks positively Disney-esque. Much of La Cité, as the walled centre is called, was rebuilt in the latter part of the 19th century, and today it attracts hundreds of the thousands of visitors.

Travel southeast of Carcassonne and you discover Perpignan, a city of cultural contrasts. Just over 10 miles from the border with Spain, it has strong Catalan roots and its signs are written in both French and Catalan – it is actually Catalonia's third largest city.

The diverse terrain provides for a varied local cuisine. Roquefort cheese, a local speciality, is made from ewe's milk and then left to mature in caves, while other popular dishes include game stews and charcuterie. There is a strong Mediterranean influence and seafood is abundant.

Languedoc is predicted to soon become as popular as the Cote d'Azur

The economy and housing market

Languedoc-Roussillon is the largest wine-producing area in France with the highest concentration of vineyards. It is also a leading centre for the scientific and medical industries, as well as for biotechnology. Tourism is a major contributor to the economy.

The large cities in the region are extremely expensive to live. Perpignan and Montpellier are very exclusive and in demand, and are ideally situated for those seeking a dynamic city environment. French Basque city, Perpignan, is fashionable and therefore very costly, and Montpellier – the priciest city in the region – has experienced a growth of more than 40 per cent in the last six years. The Gard and Hérault *départements* are also expensive and popular, while renovation properties along the coast can cost upwards of £150,000. Cheaper properties do exist further inland, particularly in the Pyrénées-Orientales *département*, in the far south. Better value can also be found in Aude, which is cheaper than Gard and Hérault.

Céret and Banyuls are attractive towns on the Spanish border offering a Mediterranean climate, and Céret is renowned for being an 'English' town. It should be remembered that the South of France is very expensive and consequently there are very few towns and cities within the Languedoc area that offer cheap property. Those who wish to relocate to the coast will find a wealth of coastal resorts to choose from, but you must be prepared to pay a premium for this, as there is a huge demand for coastal villas.

The popularity of the Côte d'Azur has led to spiralling prices within the area and has driven people to search for other retreats on the western coast. Not yet as popular as the Côte d'Azur, it is predicted that Languedoc will eventually catch up.

The problem with the Languedoc-Roussillon region is the scarcity of property in general, and cheap property in particular. With much of the region being covered in vineyards, there is no room for expansion and property development, but as demand for property is growing continuously, prices are being driven up. Renovation properties are practically non-existent, but throughout Languedoc-Roussillon the real estate market is developing, making this a good time to invest. On the Vermillion Coast, the purpose-built resorts are rather less picturesque than the traditional coastal towns.

In terms of transport, there has been an increase in budget flights to the region in recent years and this has greatly aided the development the property market.

Social groups

In the last five years an expansion in the property market has been witnessed with prices doubling, along with increased interest from the British, German and Swiss markets, amongst others. Notably, Uzef on the outskirts of Nîmes, is now effectively a British suburb. ●

> "The coast offers great beaches and inland, much of the spectacular scenery, which encompasses mountains and lakes, is protected within national parks"

LANGUEDOC-ROUSSILLON		LONDON
13.5	Dec	7
16	Nov	10
21	Oct	14
26	Sept	19
28	Aug	21
28.5	July	22
26.5	June	20
20	May	17
17.5	April	13
12.5	March	10
12.5	Feb	7
12.5	Jan	6

Average monthly temperature °C (Celsius)

LANGUEDOC-ROUSSILLON		LONDON
61	Dec	81
50	Nov	78
68	Oct	70
48	Sept	65
31	Aug	62
12	July	59
33	June	58
50	May	57
50	April	56
40	March	64
40	Feb	72
61	Jan	77

Average monthly rainfall mm (millimetres)

AVERAGE HOUSE SALE PRICES

Hotspot	2-bed	3-bed	4-bed	5-bed+
Perpignan	€163K (£113K)	€214K (£149K)	€260K (£180K)	€407K (£282K)
Southern Roussillon	€170K (£118K)	€277K (£193K)	€404K (£280K)	€629K (£437K)
Montpellier	€190K (£132K)	€235K (£163K)	€369K (£256K)	€540K (£375K)
Carcassonne	€170K (£118K)	€250K (£173K)	€460K (£320K)	€489K (£340K)
Beziers-Narbonne	€137K (£95K)	€186K (£129K)	€236K (£164K)	€287K (£199K)

Property hotspots

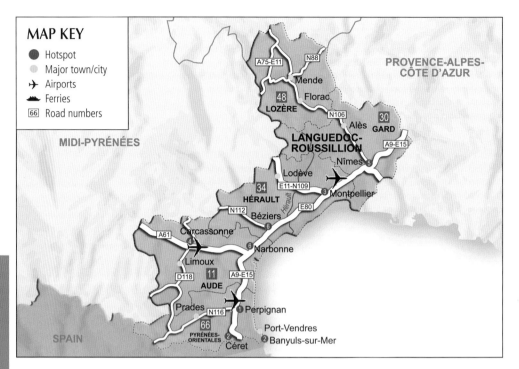

MAP KEY
- ● Hotspot
- ● Major town/city
- ✈ Airports
- ⛴ Ferries
- 66 Road numbers

1. Perpignan

ESSENTIALS ■ **Population** 108,000 ■ **Taxes** Taxe d'habitation 7.36%, Taxe foncière 9.91% ■ **Airport** Aéroport Perpignan, Avenue Maurice Bellonte, 66000 Perpignan, Tel: +33 468 52 60 70, Fax: +33 468 51 31 03

KEY FACTS

■ **Schools** Rectorat de l'Académie de Montpellier, 31 rue de l'Université, 34064 Montpellier, Cedex 02, Tel: +33 467 91 47 00
■ **Medical** Hôpital Maréchal Joffre, 20 Avenue du Languedoc, BP 4052, 66046 Perpignan, Tel: +33 468 61 66 33
■ **Rentals** Perpignan is not a main resort and, with very little to offer tourists, has little short-term rental potential ■ The main market is long-term rentals for French workers ■ A one-bedroom property will rent for €380 per week in high season
■ **Pros** Offering a real variety of surroundings, the city offers proximity to both the coast and the ski slopes ■ Located only 15 minutes from the Spanish border ■ The area experiences good weather and very warm winters ■ Property here is cheaper than on the Côte d'Azur
■ **Cons** Perpignan's coastal position makes it vulnerable to bombardment by winds from Tunisia, on a similar scale to the Marseille mistral ■ Primarily an industrial city, parts of it are not attractive ■ House prices are rising here.

Catalonia's third largest city and the capital of Roussillon, Perpignan lies just 12 miles from Spain's northern border and offers an intriguing blend of French and Spanish lifestyles. With a significant part of the population claiming Spanish ancestry to pre-Civil War times, Catalan culture is dominant, with road signs and street names displayed in Spanish alongside the vernacular French.

The Place de la Loge, in the renovated and pedestrianised old town, is dominated by the stock exchange building, the Gothic Loge de Mer with Venetian arches, Catalan archways and gargoyles. To the south, the two-storey Palais des Rois de Majorque, with its 13th-century Moorish courtyard, offers the best views of Perpignan. Sip a glass of locally produced muscat from one of the cafés lining the banks of the Basse.

The Languedoc-Roussillon region is not as expensive as the Côte d'Azur, although demand for property here rose more sharply than in any other region last year at 28.4 per cent. Perpignan is primarily a French town where the French live and work, and does not represent a huge market for international buyers. A five-bedroom villa in Perpignan would cost from €350,000, and a traditional three-bedroom villa approximately €215,000. Apartments here are increasingly popular, and a two-bedroom flat will cost €175,000 on average. ●

2. Southern Roussillon

ESSENTIALS ■ **Population** 13,000 ■ **Taxes** Taxe d'habitation 7.36%, Taxe foncière 9.91% ■ **Airport** Aéroport Perpignan, Avenue Maurice Bellonte, 66000 Perpignan, Tel: +33 468 52 60 70, Fax: +33 468 51 31 03

To the southwest of Perpignan, the Roussillon settlements of Céret and Banyuls both enjoy a Mediterranean climate. An ancient town on the river Aude with a Catalan flavour, Céret is known for producing the first cherries in France. The trees traditionally blossomed in January and cherries were sent to the French President each spring. The pink and russet houses of the old town are grouped around the small, colourful bay, with its many boats. Said to be the birthplace of Cubism, Céret was a favourite with Picasso, whose works are on display at the local museum of modern art.

Ten miles from Perpignan, Banyuls is a pretty village on the Roussillon plain, set amid vine-clad hills, palms and eucalyptus. A quiet place with no through traffic, Banyuls has its own wine-making establishment, and has long been noted for its sweet port-like red. The inhabitants claim that Banyuls is the sunniest village in Roussillon.

Properties in the area are stone-built and Céret is dominated by the English market. Prices have shown a 20 per cent increase in 2004. Cheaper properties are still available in the more rural areas, although these are becoming scarce. A modern villa with three bedrooms close to Céret starts at €320,000, while a traditional property with five bedrooms will sell for €629,000 on average. ●

KEY FACTS

■ **Schools** Rectorat de l'Académie de Montpellier, 31 rue de l'Université, 34064 Montpellier, Cedex 02, Tel: +33 467 91 47 00
■ **Medical** Centre Hospitalier Spécialisé Léon Jean Grégory, Centre de jour La Tuilerie, 7 chem Vivès, 66400 Céret, Tel: +33 468 87 38 87
■ **Rentals** A well-known area with a steady influx of British holiday-makers that should ensure a good rental income ■ The rental season lasts from June to September, as the weather is mild and the surroundings attractive ■ Buying to rent in this area is a sound investment ■ A property with three bedrooms will rent for €750 per week on average
■ **Pros** Typical properties in the area are built of stone and generally come with a good deal of land ■ The area is located close to the border, making Spain easily accessible ■ There are good road connections to the rest of France
■ **Cons** An expensive area, with renovation properties costing from €200,000, while a habitable property with four bedrooms starts at €400,000 ■ Banyuls can be very isolated in winter, being some 40 minutes from Perpignan.

3. Montpellier

ESSENTIALS ■ **Population** 250,000 ■ **Taxes** Taxe d'habitation 8.24%, Taxe foncière 11.69% ■ **Airport** Aéroport Montpellier Méditerranée, Ch. de Commerce et Industrie de Montpellier, 34035 Montpellier Cedex 4, Tel: +33 467 20 85 00

The capital of the Languedoc-Roussillion region is a stunning city, sparkling with modern stylish buildings, open squares and fountains. Dating back to the 13th century, Montpellier University is internationally acclaimed for its Faculty of Medicine, which was France's first teaching hospital, counting Nostradamus among its students. From its 17th-century mansions with inner courtyards to its new Antigone quarter, and from its neo-classical development of futuristic flats, offices and hotels to its Olympic swimming pool, Montpellier is a must-see location.

The vast 18th-century marble Place de la Comédie is the most lively part of town, nicknamed 'L'Oeuf' owing to its curved central roundabout. The ornately sculpted Fontaine des Trois-Graces is at its centre, while cafés and the well-known statue, Les Trois Graces, face the Opéra Théâtre – an exact copy of the Paris Opera House.

Demand for property in the Montpellier area is ever-increasing. An apartment with three bedrooms will cost upwards of €230,000, while a townhouse with four bedrooms will cost €368,000. Villas to renovate are rare in Montpellier, and if you do find one, expect to pay more than €90,000. Try looking in one of the villages just outside the city where a renovated house with three bedrooms can be found for €175,000. ●

KEY FACTS

■ **Schools** Rectorat de l'Académie de Montpellier, 31 rue de l'Université, 34064 Montpellier, Cedex 02, Tel: +33 467 91 47 00
■ **Medical** Centre Hospitalier Universitaire, 39 Avenue Charles Flahault, 34000 Montpellier, Tel: +33 467 33 58 17
■ **Rentals** Montpellier's coastal location and the fact that Parisians are increasingly drawn to the area guarantees a good rental income ■ Rentals are most likely between June and September ■ A four-bedroom property will rent for €880 per week
■ **Pros** This is a lively and forward-thinking city, with a quarter of its population under the age of 25 ■ Montpellier is an international city, which draws a good number of foreign buyers and students alike ■ Properties are rising in value and are expected to continue to do so
■ **Cons** It is estimated that the population of Montpellier will have doubled by 2015, due to its popularity ■ The area has seen a lot of modern new developments.

HOTSPOTS

Property hotspots

4. Carcassonne

ESSENTIALS ■ **Population** 44,400 ■ **Taxes** Taxe d'habitation 8.64%, Taxe foncière 19.39% ■ **Airport** Aéroport de Salvaza, Route de Montréal, 11000 Carcassonne Cedex, Tel: +33 468 71 96 46

KEY FACTS

■ **Schools** Rectorat de l'Académie de Montpellier, 31 rue de l'Université, 34064 Montpellier, Cedex 02, Tel: +33 467 91 47 00
■ **Medical** Hôpital de Carcassonne, Route Saint-Hilaire, 11000 Carcassonne, Tel: +33 468 24 24 24
■ **Rentals** This is an extremely popular tourist area, with a rental season lasting from June to September ■ Demand for holiday rentals in the Carcassonne area is very high, and long-term winter lets are an option ■ A property with three bedrooms in Carcassonne will rent for €700 per week
■ **Pros** Carcassonne's fortress is the second most visited attraction in France, with six million tourists a year ■ The town has many good hotels and restaurants ■ Carcassonne is close to Toulouse, which is easily accessed by flights from the UK
■ **Cons** The climate in Carcassonne is slightly chillier than in other parts of Languedoc because of its proximity to the Black Mountains, and the fact that it is located midway between the Atlantic and Mediterranean climates ■ During the winter months there is very little activity.

As the administrative centre of the Aude *département*, medieval Carcassonne has long enjoyed a reputation as one of the most beguiling UNESCO World Heritage cities in France. Inhabited since the sixth century BC, by the Middle Ages it was the site for the 13th-century Cathar uprising. It then became heavily fortified, its architecture dominated by pointed roofs and double ramparts.

Under the 19th-century architect Viollet-le-Duc, the city's 52 towers and two immense walls were restored to their former glory. In summer the walls and whole courtyards are covered with vines, a perfect place to rest from the sun, surrounded by houses, shops, restaurants and cafés.

Across the river Aude lies the *Ville Basse* (lower town), a typical 13th-century fortified *bastide*. From June to September, Carcassonne celebrates its rich heritage, with a month-long festival in July, crowned with spectacular fireworks on Bastille Day.

Carcassonne boasts a vibrant foreign property market, with prices dictated by the town's excellent location, good weather, and proximity to Toulouse. The price of an average three-bedroom town house is €249,800, while a villa with four bedrooms will cost €460,000. Best-value properties can be found in the areas north of Carcassonne, where a house with three bedrooms can be found for €160,000. ●

5. Nîmes

ESSENTIALS ■ **Population** 133,424 ■ **Taxes** Taxe d'habitation 8.89%, Taxe foncière 13.18% ■ **Airport** Nîmes-Garons Aéroport, 30800 Saint-Gilles, Tel: +33 466 70 49 49, Fax: +33 466 70 91 24

KEY FACTS

■ **Schools** Rectorat de l'Académie de Montpellier, 31 rue de l'Université, 34064 Montpellier, Cedex 02, Tel: +33 467 91 47 00
■ **Hospitals** Hôpital Caremeau, Place du Professeur Robert Debré, 30029 Nîmes Cedex 9, Tel: +33 466 68 68 68
■ **Rentals** Nîmes offers easy access to the coast and Montpellier, making it good for rental income ■ This is a popular area for holiday-makers and families ■ The most in-demand properties with three bedrooms will rent for €900 per week
■ **Pros** Nîmes's proximity to Avignon draws a lot of buyers and tourists to the area ■ Nîmes is one of the biggest tourist attractions in the south of France ■ The city has recently undergone a facelift, with various high-profile architects and designers flocking to offer it vibrancy and modernity ■ There is a healthy demand for property, and many British buyers are moving to this area
■ **Cons** There have been major price hikes due to high demand.

On the border between Provence and Languedoc, Nîmes is capital of the Gard *département* and is best known as the home of denim and for the influence of ancient Rome. The latter's impact is visible in some of the most spectacular ancient remains in Europe.

Recently given a hi-tech look by various architects and designers, including Philippe Starck and Norman Foster, Nîmes is bidding to be the city of innovation in today's southern France.

There are many prized ancient landmarks, such as Diana's Temple in La Fontaine Gardens, the Jardin de la Fontaine and the Arènes amphitheatre, now covered with a retractable roof and used to stage bullfights. Twenty minutes from Nîmes lies the Pont du Gard aqueduct, and surrounding Nîmes is the Rhône valley, with its gently rolling hills.

Nîmes' proximity to Avignon draws many buyers, as well as those seeking a rental property in the area. The international demand is great, with the British being particularly drawn to Uzès on the outskirts of Nîmes. Recent price hikes have pushed prices up close to Côte d'Azur levels. A villa with three bedrooms costs €250,000, while an apartment with three bedrooms will sell for €230,000. Just beyond town you can purchase a *mas*, set in over an acre of land with a pool for €670,000, or a large modern property with all mod-cons for €380,000. ●

6. Béziers-Narbonne

ESSENTIALS ■ **Population** Béziers 77,996, Narbonne 46,510 ■ **Taxes** Taxe d'habitation 8.24%, Taxe foncière 11.69%
■ **Airport** Aéroport Montpellier Méditerranée, Ch. de Commerce et Industrie de Montpellier, Tel: +33 467 20 85 00

Located in the Hérault *département*, Béziers was already a thriving city when the Romans arrived in 36BC, and is still an important trade centre for wines and liqueurs. The 18th-century arena, known for its bullfights, was designed initially as an opera house, and in August now hosts the four-day, Spanish-style *feria*, a spectacular pageant of music, dancing and fine food. Near the Cathedral is the 19th-century esplanade, and Allées Paul-Riquet, specifically created and planted with ponds, palm and lime trees to give it an English flavour.

Narbonne is a medium-sized town which has benefited greatly from tourism, chiefly from the interest in canal holidays which pass through the town's heart. The old town is dominated by its Gothic Cathédrale de Saint-Just et Saint-Saveur. The north tower has spectacular views.

Béziers is one of the cheapest areas in the region, but with the recent completion of the A75 motorway, property prices have started to rise. The minimum price for a villa is now €160,000, and this rises steeply with the addition of land. A few renovation properties are available from €55,000, and the average two or three bedroom townhouse costs from €80,000 to around €180,000. Just outside Béziers a renovated village house with two bedrooms costs €95,000, while a renovated mill close to a river and with a pool is available for €379,000. ●

KEY FACTS

■ **Schools** Rectorat de l'Académie de Montpellier, 31 rue de l'Université, 34064 Montpellier, Cedex 02, Tel: +33 467 91 47 00
■ **Medical** Centre Hospitalier, 2 rue Valentin Hauy, 34500 Béziers, Tel: +33 467 35 70 35
■ **Rentals** Béziers is well located, close to the sea and in a popular part of Hérault ■ Béziers and Narbonne are important destinations for the French, and have started to attract the interest of international holiday-makers ■ Prices here are cheaper than elsewhere in Languedoc-Roussillon; a property with two bedrooms will typically rent for €495 per week
■ **Pros** Béziers is currently one of the cheapest areas in which to purchase property ■ It is a developing area that is popular with the foreign market ■ Narbonne is an attractive and peaceful area, close to Béziers and the coast
■ **Cons** The development of the new A75 motorway has inevitably pushed up property prices in the area ■ Béziers is primarily a French city and is developing into a major logistical centre ■ Most British buyers focus on the outskirts, such as Saint-Chinian, Roquebrun, Clermont-l'Hérault and Lamalou-les- Bains ■ Narbonne is renowned for being excessively windy.

HOTSPOTS

The Languedoc is home to many picturesque villages such as Campagne Pont Riviere

BARRY SMITH

€10,000–€100,000
(£6,944–£69,444)

Within this budget you will find small stone houses in need of renovation

€10,300   CODE FPS

MAGALAS, HÉRAULT

A tiny terraced house with three floors for renovation. Ideal for storage purposes
£7,152

🛏 1   ✾ No garden   🖼 Situated in the village centre   🚗 Located on a main road
🏠 No private parking

€53,307   CODE FPS

PUISSALICON, HÉRAULT

A charming terraced house that requires the installation of a bathroom and kitchen
£37,018

🛏 1   ✾ No garden   🖼 Situated in the village centre   🚗 Located on a main road
🏠 No private parking

€57,200   CODE VEF

NEAR FLORAC, CÉVENNES

A stone barn built into the hillside requiring total renovation to make it habitable
£39,722

🛏 –   ✾ With a garden   🖼 Situated in small hamlet   🚗 Not located on a main road
🏠 Room for parking

€79,480   CODE VEF

NEAR ST-AMBROIX, CÉVENNES

A small terraced house in need of some work, with lovely views over the valley
£55,194

🛏 2   ✾ Small terrace   🖼 Situated in the village centre   🚗 Not located on a main road
🏠 Room for parking

€83,600   CODE FPS

NEAR MAZAMET, AUDE

A terraced village house requiring some renovation, in a mountainous location
£58,056

🛏 2   ✾ Small garden   🖼 Situated just outside the village   🚗 Not located on a main road
🏠 Room for parking

Souillac COUNTRY CLUB
SUR DORDOGNE

Come for a Holiday –
You May Decide to Stay...

I f you are contemplating a second home purchase, planning an action-packed family holiday or just organising a winter golf break, Souillac Country Club in the Dordogne, is perfectly positioned and uniquely resourced to provide you with an unrivalled facility from which to enjoy the many sporting, cultural, social and gastronomic attractions of this stunning yet accessible area of South West France.

The resort's luxury, 2, 3 and 4 bedroom lodge-style properties are available to purchase or rent year round and are situated around a challenging 18 hole golf course that meanders through 120 acres of ancient oak forest. Other on-site facilities include swimming pools, tennis courts, an excellent restaurant and bar with terrace, putting green, volleyball, clubhouse and driving range.

The properties have been specifically designed to complement this area of outstanding natural beauty. Arranged in small 'hamlets' around a centralised pool, each property is located to maximise the stunning golf course or countryside views.

So join us for a visit and let us tempt you to stay.

FINAL PHASE OF RESORT DEVELOPMENT
NEW PROPERTIES NOW FOR SALE
FROM **€235,000**˙   *including recuperation of French government TVA tax

LET US INTRODUCE YOU TO OUR WAY OF LIFE

To find out more about Souillac Country Club, call the UK on 0871 7801 444 or France on +33(0)5 65 27 56 00 or e-mail us at sales@souillaccountryclub.com
www.souillaccountryclub.com

€100,000–€200,000
(£69,444–£138,889)

Habitable houses and apartments with plenty of potential for expansion

€113,700   CODE VEF

NEAR NÎMES, GARD

A smart apartment in a lovely old town to the south of Nîmes

£78,958

🛏 1   ❀ Communal garden   🏙 Situated in the town centre   🛣 Located on a main road
🏠 Room for parking

€140,000   CODE FPS

NEAR PÉZENAS, HÉRAULT

A lovely little village house with a new roof and a sunny courtyard

£97,222

🛏 3   ❀ 40m² courtyard   🏙 Situated in a quiet village   🛣 Not located on a main road
🏠 Room for parking

€141,750   CODE VEF

NEAR ST-AMBROIX, CÉVENNES

This large detached property could be converted to add another two bedrooms

£98,437

🛏 2   ❀ With a garden   🏙 Situated on the edge of the village   🛣 Located on a main road
🏠 Room for parking, with a garage

€143,000   CODE LAV

NEAR PERPIGNAN, PYRÉNÉES-ORIENTALES

A small terraced village house just 20 minutes from the city of Perpignan

£99,305

🛏 2   ❀ Terrace   🏙 Situated in the village centre   🛣 Not located on a main road
🏠 Room for parking, with a garage

€156,830   CODE VEF

NEAR ST-AMBROIX, CÉVENNES

A lovely old farmhouse in need of modernisation, with numerous outbuildings

£108,909

🛏 4   ❀ 4,000m²   🏙 Situated in a quiet hamlet   🛣 Not located on a main road
🏠 Room for parking

€200,000–€300,000
(£138,889–£208,333)

A range of pretty stone houses in beautiful historic villages

€209,000   CODE FRA

NEAR ST-PONS-DE-THOMIÈRES, HÉRAULT

This lovely village house has been entirely renovated and enjoys superb views

£145,138

🛏 3   🌼 *With a garden*   *Situated in a pretty hamlet*   *Not located on a main road*

🏠 *Room for parking, with a garage*

€243,000   CODE DAK

NEAR NÎMES, GARD

A restored stone village house with many original features

£168,750

🛏 2   🌼 *Terrace*   *Situated in the village centre*   *Not located on a main road*

🏠 *Room for parking*

€243,000   CODE FRA

NEAR NÎMES, GARD

A large terraced village house in an excellent position with great views

£168,750

🛏 4   🌼 *Terrace*   *Situated in the village centre*   *Not located on a main road*

🏠 *Room for parking*

€243,500   CODE FPS

NEAR NÎMES, GARD

A lovely village house with large rooms and plenty of character

£169,097

🛏 2   🌼 *$25m^2$ courtyard*   *Situated in the village centre*   *Not located on a main road*

🏠 *Room for parking*

€299,750   CODE FPS

FANJEAUX, AUDE

This detached stone house is set in large grounds with a swimming pool and garage

£208,159

🛏 4   🌼 *$2,800m^2$*   *Situated on the outskirts of the village*   *Not located on a main road*

🏠 *Room for parking, with a garage*

PRICE GUIDE

€300,000–€400,000
(£208,333–£277,778)

Larger family homes in lovely locations, often with pools and outbuildings

€320,000   CODE SIF

SAUVE, GARD

This old converted mill is set on the banks of the river, enjoying lovely views
£222,222

🛏 2 ❀ 900m² 🖼 Situated in the centre of town 🛣 Not located on a main road
🏠 Room for parking

€320,070   CODE VEF

ALÈS, GARD

A lovely property in a private position with cast-iron entrance gates
£222,270

🛏 5 ❀ Large garden 🖼 Situated in the village centre 🛣 Not located on a main road
🏠 Room for parking

€336,000   CODE SIF

NEAR OMS, PYRÉNÉES-ORIENTALES

This south-facing property has been used as a bed and breakfast in the past
£233,333

🛏 6 ❀ 1,500m² 🖼 Situated on the road to Oms 🛣 Not located on a main road
🏠 Room for parking

€363,490   CODE VEF

ST-HIPPOLYTE-DU-FORT, GARD

This attractive modern villa is set in well kept gardens with a large swimming pool
£252,423

🛏 4 ❀ With a garden 🖼 Situated in a quiet hamlet 🛣 Not located on a main road
🏠 Room for parking

€378,000   CODE FPS

LUNAS, HÉRAULT

An 18th-century mill and separate detached house in landscaped grounds, with a pool
£262,500

🛏 4 ❀ Large garden 🖼 Situated in the village centre 🛣 Not located on a main road
🏠 Room for parking, with a double garage

€400,000–€700,000
(£277,778–£486,111)

For this sort of money you can expect something really special

€406,450   CODE VEF

ALÈS, GARD

A typical old village house built on several levels on the hillside, with a large terrace

£282,257

🛏 5   ❀ Courtyard   🏞 Situated in the village centre   🚫 Not located on a main road

🏠 Room for parking, with a garage

€411,480   CODE FPS

PUISSERGUIER, HÉRAULT

A recently-built detached villa in large grounds, with a pool and lovely views

£285,750

🛏 4   ❀ 1,200m²   🏞 Situated in the village centre   🚫 Not located on a main road

🏠 Room for parking, with a garage

€428,200   CODE SIF

NEAR ANDUZE, GARD

A beautiful *bastide*-style house set in the hills behind the market town of Anduze

£297,361

🛏 4   ❀ 2,300m²   🏞 Situated just outside the town   🚫 Not located on a main road

🏠 Room for parking

€455,000   CODE DAK

ST-GILLES, GARD

This lovely renovated farmhouse is set in beautiful countryside with great views

£315,972

🛏 4   ❀ Large grounds   🏞 Situated in a rural location   🚫 Not located on a main road

🏠 Room for parking

€493,000   CODE SIF

LOZÈRE

A large stone-built property in an idyllic setting beside the river. Partially renovated

£342,361

🛏 4   ❀ 3,000m²   🏞 Situated beside the river   🚫 Not located on a main road

🏠 Room for parking

PRICE GUIDE

€499,220

CASTELNAUDARY, AUDE

A beautiful villa built in the traditional style with a large swimming pool

£346,680

🛏 3 ❋ With a garden 🖼 Situated in the village centre 🚫 Not located on a main road
🏠 Room for parking, with a garage

€512,400

NEAR NÎMES, GARD

A spacious 18th-century property with outbuildings, including stables

£355,833

🛏 3 ❋ 4,500m² 🖼 Situated in a rural location 🚫 Not located on a main road
🏠 Room for parking

€584,830

NEAR ALÈS, GARD

A truly unique property, lovingly presented with taste and style

£406,132

🛏 9 ❋ With a garden 🖼 Situated in the village centre 🚫 Not located on a main road
🏠 Room for parking

€605,000

CORNEILHAN, HÉRAULT

A large 18th-century property with an independent three bedroom apartment

£420,138

🛏 8 ❋ 1,100m² 🖼 Situated in the village centre 🚫 Not located on a main road
🏠 Room for parking, with a garage

€649,000

NEAR UZÈS, GARD

A gorgeous old stone-built village house with a pool and courtyard garden

£450,694

🛏 5 ❋ Courtyard 🖼 Situated in the village centre 🚫 Not located on a main road
🏠 Room for parking

€695,000

NEAR PERPIGNAN, PYRÉNÉES-ORIENTALES

This delightfully-restored property offers spacious family accommodation with a pool

£482,638

🛏 4 ❋ 2,000m² 🖼 Situated on the outskirts of Perpignan 🚫 Not located on a main road
🏠 Room for parking

€700,000+
(£486,111+)

Your chance to own a real piece of French history

PRICE GUIDE

€735,510   CODE VEF

NEAR ALÈS, GARD

An enormous old stone house set on the side of a hill with wonderful views

£510,770

🛏 6   ✻ Large garden   🖼 Situated in the village centre   🛣 Not located on a main road

🏠 Room for parking, with a garage

€750,000   CODE FPS

MONTAGNAC, HÉRAULT

A fully-modernised farm complex comprising two independent houses and a pool

£520,833

🛏 8   ✻ 40,000m²   🖼 Situated 15 minutes from the sea   🛣 Not located on a main road

🏠 Room for parking, with a garage

€800,000   CODE SIF

NEAR CASTELNAUDARY, AUDE

A traditional-styled house dating from 1985, set in large wooded grounds with a pool

£555,555

🛏 5   ✻ 21,454m²   🖼 Situated 3 kms from amenities   🛣 Not located on a main road

🏠 Room for parking

€848,000   CODE FRA

ST-PONS-DE-THOMIÈRES, HÉRAULT

This 19th-century *maison bourgeoise* includes two converted gîtes and a pool

£588,889

🛏 13   ✻ 3,427m²   🖼 Situated in the village centre   🛣 Not located on a main road

🏠 Room for parking, with a large garage

€850,000   CODE SIF

AUDE

A fine *maison de maître* set in large enclosed grounds with a pool

£590,277

🛏 14   ✻ 18,900m²   🖼 Situated 40 minutes from Toulouse   🛣 Not located on a main road

🏠 Room for parking

€856,000   CODE FPS

CASTELNAUDARY, AUDE

A large *maison bourgeoise* with artist's studio set in large mature grounds
£594,444

🛏 16 🌼 20,000m² 🖼 *Situated in the village centre* 🚫 *Not located on a main road*
🏠 *Room for parking*

€980,000   CODE SIF

NEAR CARCASSONNE, AUDE

An attractive *maison de maître* in good condition with a caretaker's house and pool
£680,556

🛏 8 🌼 260,000m² 🖼 *Situated in the village centre* 🚫 *Not located on a main road*
🏠 *Room for parking, with a garage*

€1,337,500   CODE FPS

NEAR NÎMES, GARD

A modern detached house with pool, tennis court and a small caretaker's house
£928,819

🛏 4 🌼 10,000m² 🖼 *Situated in the village centre* 🚫 *Not located on a main road*
🏠 *Room for parking*

€1,578,950   CODE FRA

NEAR MONTPELLIER, HÉRAULT

A charming *maison de maître* in perfect condition with a swimming pool
£1,096,493

🛏 5 🌼 2,000m² 🖼 *Situated 20 minutes from the beach* 🚫 *Not located on a main road*
🏠 *Room for parking, with a large garage*

€5,300,000   CODE DEM

NEAR NÎMES, GARD

A genuine 12th-century castle, beautifully-restored and set in massive grounds
£3,680,556

🛏 27 🌼 47,000m² 🖼 *Situated in a rural area* 🚫 *Not located on a main road*
🏠 *Room for parking*

€5,335,716   CODE FPS

NEAR NÎMES, GARD

A beautiful 10th-century château with many partially-renovated outbuildings
£3,705,358

🛏 12 🌼 40,000m² 🖼 *Situated in the village centre* 🚫 *Not located on a main road*
🏠 *Room for parking*

Rest easy about Inheritance Tax

Rising house prices have meant that many homeowners could be affected by inheritance tax.

But there are things you can do to reduce potential inheritance tax liability simply by talking to the Financial Adviser at your local Bristol & West Branch.

Pop into your local branch now for more information or call **0117 943 2003**

Bringing financial solutions to life

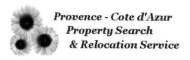

Côte d'Azur, Provence and Corsica

Beautiful scenery, idyllic beaches and exciting nightlife. It's all here

OMT AJACCIO; JC ATTARD

FACT BOX 2005

- ∎ **Population** 4,766,347 (+4.8% from 1990)
- ∎ **Foreign residents** 308,262
  Provence, Alpes, Côte d'Azur: 282,589, Corsica: 25,673
- ∎ **Migration** 819,582 international migrants
  Provence, Alpes, Côte d'Azur: 779,330, Corsica: 40,252
- ∎ **Unemployment** 154,955
- ∎ **Median house price** €330,000
- ∎ Since 2002 prices in the Côte d'Azur have increased by 11.4% and the market remains strong and popular with expats

AIR Ryanair (0871 246 0000; www.ryanair.com) offers flights from Stansted to Nîmes. **British Airways** (0870 850 9850; www.britishairways. co.uk) flies to Marseille and Nice via Heathrow. **easyjet** (0871 750 0100; www.easyjet.com) serves Nice, Marseille and Toulon from Gatwick. Flights are available with **British Midland** (0870 607 0555; www.britishmidland.com) to Nice from East Midlands. **GB Airways** (0870 850 9850; www.gbairways.com) flies to Toulon from Gatwick. **Flybe** (0870 889 0908; www.flybe.com) serves Nice, Toulouse and Bergerac from Southampton. **Jet2** (0870 737 8282; www.jet2.com) operates flights to Nice from Leeds-Bradford. **Air France** (0845 359 1000; www.airfrance.co.uk) flies into Figari and Calvi on Corsica via Orly Airport.

SEA Southern Ferries/SNCM (0207 491 4968; www.sncm.fr) operates between Nice and Marseille to Calvi, Bastia, Ajaccio and Propriano in Corsica.

ROAD The A6 passes through Paris, Lyon, then the A7 to Orange and Avignon links to the A8 for Cannes and Nice. On leaving Paris, the A1 joins the A6, via the N412/A1 junction. At junction A9, the A6 joins the A6/E15 to Villefranche. At the Villefranche junction, join the A46, and the A42/E611 at the A42 junction. This links back to the A46, via the A43 junction. Take the A7/E15 to Aire de Mornas-Village from the A46. Then take its junction with the A9 on to the A7/E714, then the A8/E80 via the junction with the A8 at A8-E80. This road leads into Nice-centre.

COACH Eurolines (0870 580 8080; www.eurolines.com) operates services to Toulon, Cannes, Marseille, Antibes, Fréjus, Grasse, Nîmes, St Tropez and Nice.

RAIL TGVs (www.tgv.com) operate from Paris and Lille to Aix-en-Provence and Marseille, and **Rail Europe** (0870 584 8848; www.raileurope.co.uk) runs lines from London Waterloo to Aix-en-Provence, Cannes, Antibes, Marseille, Nice, Nîmes and Toulon.

Area profile

THE ASTONISHING NATURAL BEAUTY OF PROVENCE AND THE CÔTE D'AZUR has inspired numerous artists and writers, from Van Gogh and Cézanne to F. Scott Fitzgerald. It's a tremendously varied region, encompassing the sophisticated resorts of the French Riviera, the wildlife-rich wetlands of the Camargue, sunbaked fields of lavender, and the Alpes Maritimes, with their gorges, rivers, and unspoiled villages.

In the north of the region the city of Avignon teems with culture and history, and the beautiful palace of 'King Philippe the Handsome' is one of the highlights of all Provence. Other highlights include Aix-en-Provence with its elegant avenues and fountains, and Arles with its magnificent Roman amphitheatre.

Those who seek more excitement should take a look at nearby Marseille. This is France's second-biggest city and a thriving port with a cosmopolitan atmosphere, a renowned fish market and superb museums. The stretch of coast between Marseille and Toulon offers the region's most underdeveloped coastline, along with spectacular cliffs and views.

Further up the coast is Cannes, most famous for its annual film festival which attracts the cream of the Hollywood industry, while Grasse is the perfume capital of the world. The French Riviera itself has many lively beach resorts, golf courses and casinos, most famously in Monte Carlo, which attract tourists and celebrities alike.

In contrast, the remoteness of Corsica is one of its main attractions. The birthplace of Napoleon, it's one of the Mediterranean's largest islands, and is an area of unspoiled beauty, with huge areas of uninhabited forest, snowy mountains and over 600 kilometres of beaches, coves and villages to explore. Half the population resides in the towns of Ajaccio and Bastia.

Dry, fruity, rosé wines, especially *Côtes de Provence*, are popular jug wines in Provence. While rosé isn't generally seen as a 'serious' wine, the *Bandol* brand is superb, and is available in a full-bodied spicy red variety. Other popular reds include *Châteauneuf-du-Pape* and *Côtes du Rhone*.

Food in the area is based around olive oil, basil, olives, fish and shellfish while a generous use of thyme and rosemary gives a genuine Mediterranean flavour. One speciality is *tapenade*, which is made of mashed black olives, anchovies, garlic and olive oil, eaten on toasted bread. Corsican food is heavily influenced by Italian cookery, with a great

Much of beautiful Corsica is remote and remains unexplored

OMT AJACCIO; JC ATTARD

selection of sausages and hams, while goat and lamb are also popular. On the island of Corsica fish and shellfish dishes abound, while cheese and dishes made with sweet chestnuts are also a local delicacy.

The economy and housing market

The Côte d'Azur's Mediterranean climate, beaches and international kudos have created a tourist-based economy in Cannes, St Tropez and Nice, which in turn has encouraged a thriving property buying and rental market, both for permanent movers and second-home buyers. Fuelled by international investment, a seemingly boundless property market has grown up, world renowned for famous rental tenants during Cannes' International Film Festival. A proven success story for buying to let, Cannes has a year-round rental markets. Foreign and French purchasing power has pushed prices up, and local first-time buyers have been priced out of the market. Cheaper properties exist in Nice's Riquier borough, a favourite with locals, and a long-term rental market exists. St Tropez's market has plateaued, and though property will hold its value, prices do not have the same potential to rise as in Cannes.

Corsica, too, is reliant on its idyllic position and beaches for a tourist-based economy, while engaging in some agricultural activity as well. Provence's coastal villages and vineyards provide a mix of tourism and industry, while Marseille is home to France's biggest port. Maussane, Pont Royal and Les Baux form a popular tourist triangle with high prices, but the busy rental market can justify a costly investment. Mougins, Menton and Juan-les-Pins offer less space for more money. High changeover fees asked by locals for the upkeep of holiday properties in Saint-Rémy can make an unprofitable rental market for one-home, buy-to-let owners.

Social groups

Many British residents are moving to this area, and its popularity has been boosted by the success of Peter Mayle's book and subsequent TV series *A Year in Provence*. There's a genuine mix of people moving here, from those seeking second homes with a view to retiring, to younger, more career-driven people who take advantage of the fast train to Paris and the accessibility of Nice airport. However, the area is popular with buyers from all around Europe, as well as America and the Middle and Far East. ●

> "Corsica's clement climate and the appeal of its seeming exclusivity guarantee a rental season from May until the end of October"

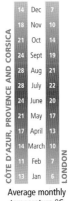

Average monthly temperature °C (Celsius)

CÔTE D'AZUR, PROVENCE AND CORSICA / LONDON

	Côte d'Azur	London
Dec	14	7
Nov	18	10
Oct	21	14
Sept	24	19
Aug	28	21
July	28	22
June	24	20
May	21	17
April	17	13
March	14	10
Feb	11	7
Jan	13	6

Average monthly rainfall mm (millimetres)

CÔTE D'AZUR, PROVENCE AND CORSICA / LONDON

	Côte d'Azur	London
Dec	78	81
Nov	120	78
Oct	100	70
Sept	60	65
Aug	20	62
July	10	59
June	30	58
May	80	57
April	86	56
March	90	64
Feb	80	72
Jan	100	77

AVERAGE HOUSE SALE PRICES

Hotspot	2-bed	3-bed	4-bed	5/6-bed
Aix-en-Provence	€331K (£230K)	€467K (£324K)	€539K (£374K)	€760K (£528K)
Antibes	€430K (£300K)	€490K (£340K)	€621K (£431K)	€890K (£618K)
Briançon	€257K (£175K)	€280K (£194K)	€437K (£304K)	€590K (£410K)
Cannes	€397K (£276K)	€696K (£483K)	€1.6M (£1 million)	€2M (£1.5 million)
Marseille	€269K (£188K)	€378K (£262K)	€447K (£311K)	€658K (£457K)
Nice	€388K (£269K)	€518K (£360K)	€655K (£455K)	€888K (£617K)
Porto Vecchio (Corsica)	€295K (£205K)	€427K (£296K)	€595K (£413K)	€628K (£436K)
St Tropez	€646K (£449K)	€1.2M (£855K)	€2M (£1.3 million)	€3M (£1.8 million)
Toulon	€261K (£181K)	€311K (£216K)	€352K (£244K)	€482K (£335K)
Var département	€189K (£131K)	€337K (£234K)	€548K (£380K)	€530K (£368K)
Vaucluse	€167K (£116K)	€220K (£153K)	€379K (£263K)	€562K (£391K)

Property hotspots

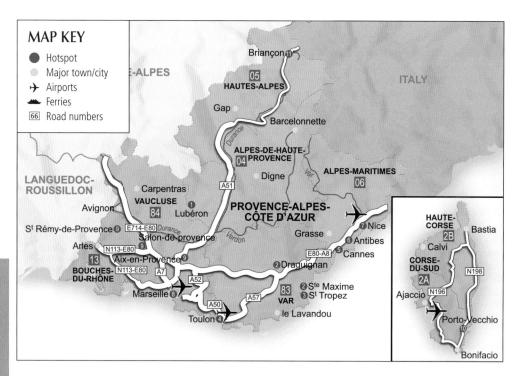

MAP KEY
- ● Hotspot
- ● Major town/city
- ✈ Airports
- ⛴ Ferries
- 66 Road numbers

1. Vaucluse (Lubéron)

ESSENTIALS ■ **Population** 1999: 499,685 ■ **Taxes** Taxe d'habitation: 6.08%, Taxe foncière: 7.85% ■ **Airport** Avignon/Caumont Airport, RN7, Route de Marseille, 84140 Montfavet, Tel: +33 (0) 4 9081 5151

KEY FACTS

■ **Schools** École Val Saint-André, 19 Avenue Malacrida, 13100 Aix-en-Provence, Tel: +33 (0) 4 4227 1447, International School of Provence, Domaine des Pins, 55 Route Bouc Bel Air, Luynes, 13080, Aix-en-Provence, Tel: +33 (0) 4 4224 0340
■ **Medical** Centre Hospitalier du Pays d'Apt, Route de Marseille, 84400 Apt, Tel: +44 (0) 4 9004 3400; Centre Hospitalier de Cavaillon, 119 Avenue Georges Clémenceau, 84300 Cavaillon, Tel: +33 (0) 4 9078 8500
■ **Rentals** Rental income in Lubéron is in the region of €1,500 per week during July and August
■ The average rental price for a long-term let throughout the year for a two-bedroom apartment is €580 per month ■ On average a three-bedroom house costs €710 per month to rent
■ **Pros** The region is easily accessed by the A7 motorway. Cavaillon connects to the N7 and Marseille is directly served ■ There is a growing community of British and other foreign nationals
■ **Cons** Houses are very expensive: from Cavaillon to Gordes they cost about €1,500 per square metre.

This region has long been an escape for well-to-do Parisians, Dutch and Britons, with buyers attracted by the older properties that are frequently found within easy reach or walking distance of villages. Visitors and incomers are drawn by traditional Provençal houses, or *mas*, with beguiling views, and by the abundant Provençal architecture with its arches, exposed stone walls, open fireplaces, spacious rooms, warm colours and terracotta. Mediterranean vegetation and olive trees add to the attraction. Village houses with balconies, terraces and small courtyards invite the residents to dine *al fresco* and enjoy the Mediterranean climate.

The best-value properties are to be found to the north of the Vaucluse at Bollène (a town famous for its troglodyte antecedents) and the Côtes du Rhône villages of Visan and Sault to the east. Although these areas are supposedly less chic, with a less developed infrastructure, they are a gateway to the serene beauty of the high plateau.

The whole *département* is extremely expensive, but there are certainly cheaper properties to be found in the north of the area. Lubéron, with its mountain villages, offers spectacular views of the countryside, and good-sized renovation properties cost from €300,000. However, basic two-bedroom apartments start at under €170,000. ●

HOTSPOTS

2. Inland Var (Draguignan, Sainte-Maxime)

ESSENTIALS ■ **Population** 1999: Sainte-Maxime 12,000, Draguignan 30,183 ■ **Taxes** Taxe d'habitation: 5.29%, Taxe foncière: 6.40% ■ **Airport** St Tropez Aéroport du Golfe, Le Mole, Aerodrome de St Tropez, 83310 La Mole, Tel: +33 (0) 4 9449 5729

One of the areas first discovered by the British, the Var region remains a very popular area, offering prices under €190,000, although renovation properties are relatively rare. Inland Var is blessed with vineyards and olive groves, spectacular lavender plantations and acres of beautiful sunflowers.

This *département* is well-situated between the mountains and the sea, with medieval hilltop villages offering a quieter lifestyle than St Tropez. The superb climate, with more than 300 days of sunshine each year, is another bonus. Skiers are within easy reach of Les Arcs, with its TGV station providing a good connection to the rest of Europe.

Draguignan, the former capital, is a large commercial town with many museums, while the towns of Lorgues and Brignoles have excellent markets. The village of Fayence is the hang-gliding capital of Europe, while Le Muy, a traditional Provençal town, has a huge selection of food shops and one of the best markets in Southern France.

Prices have stabilised, with best value buys found far north around Aups, a town on the edge of the Alps which is famous for its truffle market. Other areas to consider include Lac Saint-Croix, the largest man-made lake in Europe, at the foot of the Gorges du Verdon. The average cost of a four-bedroom house is €550,000. ●

KEY FACTS

■ **Schools** Mougins School, 615 Avenue Dr. Maurice Donat, Font de l'Orme, BP 401, 06251 Mougins Cedex, Tel: +33 (0) 4 9390 1547
The International School of Nice, 15 Avenue Claude Debussy, 06200 Nice, Tel: +33 (0) 4 9321 0400
■ **Medical** Centre Hospitalier de Draguignan, route Montferrat, 83300 Draguignan, Tel: +33 (0) 4 9460 5000
■ **Rentals** Very good in the summer ■ The average rental price for a one-bedroom apartment per week is €440 ■ A three-bedroom house costs about €930 per week ■ Houses are more popular for lets, with a two-bedroom house costing €640 per week
■ **Pros** Affordable prices. This is not a touristy town, and the inhabitants are local ■ The town is pretty, with Provençal architecture and atmosphere, and situated 50 miles from Nice ■ A good climate.
■ **Cons** Not directly on the coast ■ Property prices have increased.

3. St Tropez

ESSENTIALS ■ **Population** 1999: 5,542 ■ **Taxes** Taxe d'habitation: 5.29%, Taxe foncière: 6.40% ■ **Airport** St Tropez Aéroport du Golfe, Le Mole, Aerodrome de St Tropez, 83310 La Mole, Tel: +33 (0) 4 9449 5729

Nestling at the foot of the Massif de Maures, St Tropez still retains its tiny squares and rich pastel-coloured houses that first beguiled Guy de Maupassant in the 19th century. It remained relatively unspoiled throughout the first half of the 20th century until it provided the setting for the movie *And God Created Woman* starring Brigitte Bardot, which was released in 1956.

Today, although tourists cause the town to suffer traffic congestion in the summer, it has not deterred the international jet-set, who take up residence in multi-million dollar yachts along the restaurant-lined waterfront. There is an excellent fruit, vegetable and fish market at the Place aux Herbes, and the famous brasseries Le Gorille and Sénéquier are unmissable. Just outside the town are some magnificent sandy beaches where you can escape from the tourist hordes.

As St Tropez is in great demand, there is the potential for many buyers to make a handsome profit from renting out their properties. Because property in the town is phenomenally expensive – more so than other areas of the Côte d'Azur – you need to be quite wealthy to buy here. Two-bedroom homes average at around €650,000, while an extra bedroom costs almost double. Five-bedroom homes start at over €2, 500,000 but, of course, you can pay much, much more than this. ●

KEY FACTS

■ **Schools** Mougins School, 615 Avenue Dr. Maurice Donat, Font de l'Orme, BP 401, 06251 Mougins Cedex, Tel: +33 (0) 4 9390 1547
The International School of Nice, 15 Avenue Claude Debussy, 06200 Nice, Tel: +33 (0) 4 9321 0400
■ **Medical** Centre Hospitalier de St Tropez, 12 Avenue Foch 83990, St Tropez, Tel: +33 (0) 4 9447 5808
■ **Rentals** Average to excellent (short-term), depending on location and furnishings ■ More of a summer/short-term letting market ■ Average prices are €620 per week for a one-bedroom apartment and €850 for a two-bedroom apartment
■ **Pros** If you buy a property here it will hold its value ■ Many private villas are available ■ Sainte-Maxime is in a quiet location, right next to St Tropez, and has a traditional harbour ■ Extensive golfing facilities are available at Sainte-Maxime
■ **Cons** You cannot buy property here unless you're wealthy ■ Without a huge bank balance it will not be possible to spread your investment, as in Cannes, and have the potential for cross-letting a property ■ Some think St Tropez has been overrun by tourists and is tawdry.

4. Toulon

ESSENTIALS ■ **Population** 1999: 166,442 ■ **Taxes** Taxe d'habitation: 5.29%, Taxe foncière: 6.40% ■ **Airport** Toulon/Hyères Aéroport, Boulevard de la Marine, 83400 Hyères, Tel: +33 (0) 4 9400 8383

KEY FACTS

■ **Schools** Mougins School, 615 Avenue Dr. Maurice Donat, Font de l'Orme, BP 401, 06251 Mougins Cedex, Tel: +33 (0) 4 9390 1547 ■ The International School of Nice, 15 Avenue Claude Debussy, 06200 Nice, Tel: +33 (0) 4 9321 0400 ■ **Medical** Hôpital Font-Pré, 1208 avenue Colonel Picot, Toulon, Tel: +33 (0) 4 9461 6161 ■ Hôpital Chalucet, Rue Chalucet, Toulon, Tel: +33 (0) 4 9422 7777 ■ Hôpital Georges Clemenceau, 421 Avenue Infanterie de Marine du Pacifique, La Garde, Tel: +33 (0) 4 9408 8686 ■ **Rentals** The average rental price for a one-bedroom apartment is €420 per week ■ A two-bedroom house costs an average of €680 per week ■ For five or more bedrooms expect to pay €940 ■ **Pros** Ouerse and Pierre-Sieu are excellent locations to buy a vineyard, which can be bought for less than the price of a flat in London ■ Calculated in terms of the size and privacy of their property, vineyards begin at around €1.5 million ■ Toulon has a fine Mediterranean climate ■ **Cons** Destroyed in World War II, Toulon has been rebuilt and is not an authentic Provençal town ■ There is no price ceiling for vineyards.

While Toulon centre is not considered a hotspot, the Mont Faron area offers impressive views of the city's port and bay. Expect to find houses painted in pastel shades, with the stone door and window frames integrated into the façades. Close by, the fortified town of Hyères is considered a desirable location thanks to its position at the foot of the Maures hills, bordered by the Mediterranean. Offering 14,000 hectares of protected scenery and watersports facilities, Hyères is consistently awarded the European Blue Flag for its beaches. The old town has fine examples of 12th-century architecture, including the Château Saint-Bernard and the Tour de Saint-Blaise, built by the Knights Templar. Toulon's naval legacy remains a draw for visitors, and the National Maritime Museum celebrates its seafaring past. The bustling market is one of the largest in the region.

Toulon is not regarded as the most desirable area by foreign property buyers, predominantly catering for its local inhabitants. Expect Toulon to be a typical French city rather than displaying the glitz and glamour found further south. In consequence, the market experiences a rapid turnover of property driven by the local French population. Prices are reasonable when compared with those on the French Riviera. An average three-bedroom property in the area costs around €310,000. ●

5. Cannes

ESSENTIALS ■ **Population** 1999: 67,304 ■ **Taxes** Taxe d'habitation: 5.29%, Taxe foncière: 6.40% ■ **Airport** Cannes Airport, Aéroport Cannes-Mandelieu, 06150 Cannes la Bocca, +33 (0) 4 8988 9828

KEY FACTS

■ **Schools** CIV International School of Sophia Antipolis, BP 097, 06902 Sophia Antipolis, Tel: +33 (0) 4 9296 5224 ■ **Medical** Centre Hospitalier de Cannes, 13 avenue des Broussailles, Cannes, Tel: +33 (0) 4 9369 7000, www.hopital-cannes.fr ■ **Rentals** Rentals, both short and long-term, are highly lucrative ■ For short-term lets, the excellent weather gives Cannes excellent rental potential ■ During the Cannes Film Festival those who own property have no limits on what they can charge ■ One-bedroom apartments average at €620 to €2,900 for five or more bedrooms ■ **Pros** Nice's posh relation, so there are many more amenities on offer ■ The rarity of new building developments enables a property to retain its value, creating a thriving rental market ■ Excellent weather ■ **Cons** Properties are extremely expensive, selling from €1,500 to €20,000 per square metre ■ There are not many native, first-time buyers because of tight planning regulations ■ Villas can range from €700,000 plus; there is no ceiling.

Glitzy Cannes combines history, beautiful architecture, ornate palace-style hotels, well-heeled holiday-makers and its world-renowned film festival. The price of property in Cannes has been rising fast, but that hasn't deterred British buyers, who are prepared to shell out for a place with sunshine and sophistication. In terms of the European summer rental market, the French Riviera is the most popular area for holidaymakers – even more than Spain, Greece and Italy – so buying to rent on the Riviera is an excellent investment.

Summer rental prices on the Riviera are very expensive due to the limited length of the season, with prices varying from €620 per week for a one-bedroom apartment to around €3,000 per week for a five-bedroom house. Undoubtedly, Cannes is phenomenally expensive and you won't be able to pick much up for under €400,000, bar the odd small apartment. Four-bedroom homes cost in the region of €1,500,000. A decent-sized villa with terracing and a swimming pool will set you back around €2,500,000.

Three miles inland from Cannes lies the hilltop village of Mougins, where Picasso made his home. It's famous for its picturesque narrow lanes, gastronomy and superb coastal views; a renovated three-bedroom 18th-century village house costs around €400,000. ●

6. Antibes

ESSENTIALS ■ **Population** 1999: 72,412 ■ **Taxes** Taxe d'habitation: 5.29%, Taxe foncière: 6.40% ■ **Airport** Nice/Côte d'Azur Airport, Chambre de Commerce et d'Industrie,06281 Nice, Cedex 3, Tel: +33 (0) 4 9321 3030

Antibes has proved an attractive location to buyers mesmerised by its setting, its stunning views and long hours of sunshine. It is famous for its jazz festival, the military citadel Fort Carré, and the lovely old town, where artists and writers including Picasso and Graham Greene have long chosen to live. Residents can enjoy the international flavour created by visitors, who have their pick of 48 beaches, from small coves to sheltered, family–friendly bays.

These foreign buyers are not expressing a preference for any particular style, although the traditional Provençal villa is still selling strongly. The secluded area of Cap d'Antibes, set just outside the centre of town, which has retained some woodland despite the rise in property development, is extremely expensive. A luxuriously appointed villa here, with private swimming pool and six bedrooms or more, can cost upwards of €4,000,000.

Property prices are rising faster in Cap than anywhere else in the Côte d'Azur. The best value properties are to be found inland towards Mougins, Valbonne and Biot, where it is less expensive. Due to its proximity to Nice and the A8, the town of Villeneuve-Loubet has proved particularly successful with the overseas property market, and for a one-bedroom studio here buyers can expect to pay €170,000. ●

KEY FACTS

■ **Schools** Mougins School, 615 Avenue Dr. Maurice Donat, Font de l'Orme, BP 401, 06251 Mougins Cedex, Tel: +33 (0) 4 9390 1547 The International School of Nice, 15 Avenue Claude Debussy, 06200 Nice, Tel: +33 (0) 4 9321 0400
■ **Medical** Hospitalier Centre d'Antibes Juan les Pins, 7 Route Nationale, 06600 Antibes, Tel: +33 (0) 4 9291 7777, www.ch-antibes.fr
■ **Rentals** Most rentals are short-term ■ An average rental price for a one-bedroom apartment is €540 per week ■ On average, a two-bedroom apartment can command €1,000 per week during peak season ■ A house with five bedrooms costs approximately €2,600 per week
■ **Pros** A real town with a strong community, there is always activity here ■ The property market is stable, making for a safe investment ■ Popular with yachting enthusiasts, Antibes has an extensive infrastructure, and the N98, A8 motorway and D5 roads run directly into town
■ **Cons** The property market has a high rate of turnover, while villas and houses are only ever on the market for a very short length of time ■ Prices for a four-bedroom villa in a good locale can start from €2,000,000.

7. Nice and area

ESSENTIALS ■ **Population** 1999: 345,892 ■ **Taxes** Taxe d'habitation: 5.29%, Taxe foncière: 6.40% ■ **Airport** Nice/Côte d'Azur Airport, Chambre de Commerce et d'Industrie, 06281 Nice, Cedex 3, Tel: +33 (0) 4 9321 3030

In Nice location is paramount, with Nice West being a popular choice due to its proximity to the airport, and more available land to build on. Other hotspots include the green and tranquil Mont Boron, one of the most exclusive areas on the Côte d'Azur. Situated to the east of the old town, away from the crowds, this area offers spectacular views and a wealth of Belle Epoque buildings. The area to the north of the main station, 1km from the seafront, is home to the cheapest properties in Nice, while old Nice is favoured because its flower markets, restaurants and pedestrian zones create an attractive environment within the centre of town.

Nice is an expensive area, yet the boroughs can yield cheaper properties. Potential buyers are mostly interested in second homes, choosing properties with a swimming pool and sea views. Brand new homes are in demand, and villas frequently offer a choice of colours, tiles and layout before being finished – many feature art deco interiors and balconies. There is an increasing number of new-building projects, and almost half of these are bought as weekend or second homes.

Two-bedroom homes cost on average just under €400,000, although it's possible to pick up apartments a little cheaper. However, you will often have to pay more than €700,000 for four bedrooms. ●

KEY FACTS

■ **Schools** Mougins School, 615 Avenue Dr. Maurice Donat, Font de l'Orme, BP 401, 06251 Mougins Cedex, Tel: +33 (0) 4 9390 1547 The International School of Nice, 15 Avenue Claude Debussy, 06200 Nice, Tel: +33 (0) 4 9321 0400
■ **Medical** Centre Hospitalier Universitaire de Nice, Hôpital de Cimiez, 4 avenue Reine Victoria, BP 1179, 06003 Nice, Cedex 1, Tel: +33 (0) 4 9203 7777
■ **Rentals** Excellent for long and short-term lets, rental is big business for the native population, and this is an ever-popular summer destination ■ A one-bedroom apartment costs on average €410 per week ■ A three-bedroom apartment costs an average of €1,160 per week ■ The average cost for a five-bedroom house per week in peak season is around €2,200
■ **Pros** Nice has excellent transport networks ■ As an international hotspot, Nice has undeniable glamour ■ Mild, sunny winters and gentle summer breezes
■ **Cons** The area is packed during summer ■ Very expensive and unlikely to generate huge rental yields as villas are expensive.

8. Marseille

ESSENTIALS ■ **Population** 1999: 807,071 ■ **Taxes** Taxe d'habitation: 8.70%, Taxe foncière: 7.15% ■ **Airport** Marseille/Provence Airport, BP7 Aéroport, 13727 Marignane, Tel: +33 (0) 4 4214 1414

KEY FACTS

■ **Schools** École Val Saint-André, 19 Avenue Malacrida, 13100 Aix-en-Provence, Tel: +33 (0) 4 4227 1447 ■ EPIM – Marseille International School, 156-178 Bd Perier, 13008 Marseille, Tel: +33 (0) 4 9153 0000 ■ International School of Provence, Domaine des Pins, 55 Route Bouc Bel Air, Luynes, 13080, Aix-en-Provence, Tel: +33 (0) 4 4224 0340
■ **Medical** Centre Hospitalier Universitaire La Timone, 264 rue Saint Pierre, 13005 Marseille, Tel: +33 (0) 4 9138 6000
■ **Rentals** Excellent, year-round rental potential ■ There is a very good student rentals market, while July and August attract holiday-makers ■ The average rental price for a one-bedroom apartment per week is €565 ■ The average weekly price for a two-bedroom place is €850, and €930 per week week for three bedrooms
■ **Pros** Marseille's image is much improved ■ Money spent on improvements has attracted foreign buyers ■ Toulon is within easy reach of the city.
■ **Cons** Marseille used to have a rather unflattering image and this can linger; the city has only recently managed to shake off this image inland.

A melting pot of nationalities with a rich cultural heritage, Marseille is associated with the golden age of maritime prosperity in the late 19th century. The city is now being revitalised thanks to regeneration and investment projects in many of its districts, with the aim of creating a gateway to Europe. The second largest city in France, Marseille offers fine architecture, museums and the greatest concentration of theatres per head of population. Along the Vieux Port at Place Thiars are trendy bars and restaurants, while early risers can visit the fish market to source ingredients for the local speciality, *bouillabaisse*. Ferries run between the Vieux Port and Château d'If, the island prison setting for the film, *The Count of Monte Cristo*.

Marseille's regeneration has helped the foreign property market prosper. There are more than 100 *quartiers*, many with their own village life, while the upmarket 8th district offers modern 18 metre square two-bedroom studios in a modern apartment block from €100,000. If you're looking for a coastal village try Ensuès-la-Redonne, 12 miles west of Marseille. Looking out over the sea, this combines beautiful bays and deep rocky inlets which extend all along the coast, with the city forming a backdrop. A modern, three-bedroom villa here has a starting price of €1,600,000. ●

9. Aix-en-Provence and Saint-Rémy-de-Provence

ESSENTIALS ■ **Population** Aix-en-Provence 134,222, Saint-Rémy-de-Provence 9,429 ■ **Taxes** Taxe d'habitation: 8.70%, Taxe foncière: 7.15% ■ **Airport** Marseille/Provence Airport, BP7 Aéroport, 13727 Marignane, Tel: +33 (0) 4 4214 1414

KEY FACTS

■ **Schools** École Val Saint-André, 19 Avenue Malacrida, 13100 Aix-en-Provence, Tel: +33 (0) 4 4227 1447 International School of Provence, Domaine des Pins, 55 Route Bouc Bel Air, Luynes, 13080, Aix-en-Provence, Tel: +33 (0) 4 4224 0340
■ **Medical** Centre Hospitalier du Pays d'Aix, Avenue des Tamaris, 13616 Aix-en-Provence, Cedex 1, Tel: +33 (0) 4 3223 5650, www.ch-aix.fr
■ **Rentals** Offers excellent rental potential ■ A one-bedroom apartment can be let for around €590 per week ■ In Le Thalonet, a house costing around €400,000 can be let for about €30,000 a month
■ The average rental price for the long-term let of a two-bedroom apartment is €660 per week
■ **Pros** The large student population makes for healthy rentals ■ Aix-en-Provence is more desirable than the Var, as all amenities are found in the town ■ An average two-bedroom home costs around €330,000
■ **Cons** Studio apartments are in very short supply ■ Fewer vineyards available than in the Var ■ The Saint-Rémy triangle is a very expensive area to buy in.

Dating back to Roman times and loved by the painter Paul Cézanne, Aix-en-Provence is well-known for its impressive monuments and cultural heritage. The old town is ringed by a circle of boulevards and squares, while the main street, Cours Mirabeau, is lined with trees, cafés, bookshops and spectacular fountains, earning it a reputation as the most beautiful city in Southern France. Some 45 miles from Aix and surrounded by lush green, perfumed valleys, Saint-Rémy's ancient streets – such as Rue Carnot, which is an ideal stop for local crafts – are lined with beautifully restored houses.

This area is very expensive and there is a restricted amount of land available for development. In the village of Venelles, perched on a rock four miles from Aix, quality properties and beautiful scenery have attracted buyers to homes. A typical four-bedroom south-facing property costs over €500,000. Saint-Victoire offers a more rural environment in which a renovated property costs about €480,000.

The market town of Saint-Rémy-de-Provence is much sought after for its properties, particularly by celebrities and others who appreciate its unhurried pace of life. Naturally, it's very expensive: in Saint-Rémy prices start at €900,000 for a *maison de maître,* while a luxury four-bedroom, 19th-century stone farmhouse starts at €1,700,000. ●

10. Porto-Vecchio (Corsica)

ESSENTIALS ■ **Population** 1999: 10,326 ■ **Taxes** Taxe d'habitation: 9.74%, Taxe foncière: 6.32% ■ **Airport** Ajaccio Airport, 20090 Ajaccio Cedex, Tel: +33 (0) 4 9523 5656, www.ajaccio.aeroport.fr

Blessed with breathtaking mountain scenery, lakes and more than 600 miles of dramatic coastlines, Corsica is frequently described as the 'Scented Isle' as the aroma of its forests perfumes the air. The principal towns are Ajaccio (where Napoleon was born in 1769), Bastia, Sartène and Bonifacio. French is the official language of Corsica, but many native locals speak Corsican (Corsu).

Located at the end of a sheltered gulf, the port of Porto-Vecchio is the most popular area of Corsica, and its marina is one of the island's most prominent ferry links, connecting the city to mainland France and Italy. Porto-Vecchio has a maze of narrow streets lined with exclusive shops and stylish boutiques, fashionable restaurants and lively bars. The resort is best known for its beaches, such as the Palombaggia and Cala Rossa, which are some of the best-known in the whole of Corsica.

While short-term holiday rentals dominate the island's property market, many locals cash in on the busy summer months and invest in rental properties. Property is expensive, and this reflects the island's exclusive nature and atmosphere. Traditional properties vary from white stone villas with red-roof tiling, to the Provençal terracotta-based villa. Expect to pay around €150,000 for a two-bedroom apartment, and around €350,000 for a two-bedroom villa with swimming pool. ●

KEY FACTS

■ **Schools** The International School of Nice, 15 Avenue Claude Debussy, 06200 Nice, Tel: +33 (0) 4 9321 0400
■ **Medical** Centre Hospitalier Général, Route Impériale, 20200 Bastia, Tel: +33 (0) 4 9559 1111
■ **Rentals** Rental income is excellent in the summer months, ranging from €670 to €1,600 a week depending on a property's facilities ■ A property with an outside pool has a season from May until the end of October
■ **Pros** The area round Porto Vecchio has beautiful beaches and is close to Bonifacio and Bastia
■ **Cons** The main pitfall of living or buying to let in Corsica is the difficulty and expense in reaching the island ■ Limited access and flight times have an obvious impact on rental potential ■ To preserve the island's beautiful lush greenery, direct flights are limited. Paris, Nice and Marseille offer direct flights.

11. Briançon and surrounding Alpine resorts

ESSENTIALS ■ **Population** 1999: 17,023 ■ **Taxes** Taxe d'habitation: 4.65%, Taxe foncière: 12.56% ■ **Airport** Turin International Airport, Strada San Maurizio 12, 10072 Caselle Torinese, Tel: +39 (0) 11 567 6361/2

Europe's highest town, Briançon, is the largest settlement in the Serre Chevalier area, a grouping of Hautes-Alpes ski resorts in the Guisane valley linked by 77 lifts and 155 miles of runs. The area has a great climate, offering 300 days of sunshine per year, as well as excellent skiing. Serre Chevalier has 111 runs, and popular villages include Chantemerle and Villeneuve, both located near the ski lifts. Villeneuve is a 10-minute ride from Chantemerle, the largest of the villages, which has an attractive centre.

Le Monêtier-les-Bains (1,200 metres) has more rustic charm, being a typical Savoyard village with minimum development, in keeping with local styles. It has also been a hot spa for hundreds of years, and you can still take the waters. The villages are not very far apart and are well-served by the local bus service.

Briançon enjoys a beautiful setting, with hilltop fortifications and a pleasant old town. Its steep streets, shops and restaurants create a lively ambience. However, the town is not fully served by ski buses, which can result in long walks for skiers to and from the ski lifts. Two-bedroom homes in Briançon average at just over €250,000, although small apartments are cheaper. If you're looking to buy a four-bedroom home in the region, you'll need a budget of around €400,000. ●

KEY FACTS

■ **Schools** Mougins School, 615 Avenue Dr. Maurice Donat; Font de l'Orme, BP 401, 06251 Mougins Cedex; Tel: +33 (0) 4 9390 1547
The International School of Nice, 15 Avenue Claude Debussy, 06200 Nice, Tel: +33 (0) 4 9321 0400
■ **Rentals** Excellent rental potential, with the season lasting all year ■ There is potential for four months' ski rental and three months' summer rental ■ On average, a two-bedroom apartment is €410 per week ■ Four-bedroom homes cost on average €725 per week
■ **Pros** Aspres and Serres village houses range massively from €100,000 to €1,000,000 ■ Property is excellent value for money and many French are opting to buy in this area, instead of purchasing a ski lodge and summer home ■ The South coast is only two hours' drive away ■ Opportunity for almost year-round rental
■ **Cons** The cold climate can be discouraging.

USEFUL CONTACTS

PRÉFECTURE
Préfecture de la Région
Provence-Alpes-Côte d'Azur
Boulevard Paul-Peytral 2
13282 Marseille Cedex 20
Tel: +33 491 15 60 00
Fax: +33 491 15 61 90
www.paca.pref.gouv.fr

Préfecture de Corse
Parc Belvédère 9
BP 229
20179 Ajaccio Cedex
Tel: +33 495 29 99 29
Fax: +33 495 21 32 70
www.corse.pref.gouv.fr

LEGAL
**Chambre des Notaires des
Bouches-du-Rhône**
Boulevard Périer 77
13008 Marseille
Tel: +33 491 53 49 67
Fax: +33 491 53 49 75
www.chambre-
bouchesdurhone.notaires.fr

**Chambre des Notaires des
Alpes-Maritimes**
Rue du Congrès 18
06000 Nice
Tel: +33 497 03 02 02
Fax: +33 493 03 02 09
www.chambre-
alpesmaritimes.notaires.fr

**Chambre des Notaires de la
Corse du Sud**
Cours Grandval 2
20000 Ajaccio
Tel: +33 495 51 31 36
Fax: +33 495 21 04 24
Email: chambre.corse-du-
sud@notaires.fr

FINANCE
Direction des Impôts
Sud-Est Réunion
Rue Roux de Brignoles 23

13281 Marseille Cedex 6
Tel: +33 491 13 82 01
Fax: +33 491 37 92 69

BUILDING AND PLANNING
**Chambre Régionale de
Métiers Provence-Alpes-
Côte d'Azur**
87 Boulevard Perier
13008 Marseille
Tel: +33 496 10 05 40
Fax: +33 496 10 05 49
www.crm-paca.fr

**Chambre Régionale de
Métiers de Corse**
Chemin de la Sposata
20090 Ajaccio
Tel: +33 495 23 53 00
Fax: +33 495 23 53 03

**Caue des Bouches-du-
Rhône**
Rue Montgrand 35
13006 Marseille
Tel: +33 491 33 02 02
Fax: +33 491 33 42 49

Email: caue13@free.fr

Caue de Haute-Corse
Bis Rue de l'Annonciade 2
20200 Bastia
Tel: +33 495 31 80 90
Fax: +33 495 31 54 80
Email: caue-2b@wanadoo.fr

EDUCATION
**Rectorat de l'Académie
d'Aix-Marseille (Bouches-
du-Rhône, Vaucluse, Alpes-
Haute-de-Provence, Hautes-
Alpes)**
Place Lucien-Paye
13621 Aix-en-Provence
Tel: +33 442 91 70 00
Fax: +33 442 26 68 03
www.ac-aix-marseille.fr

**Rectorat de l'Académie de
Nice (Alpes-Maritimes, Var)**
Avenue Cap-de-Croix 53
06181 Nice Cedex
Tel: +33 493 53 70 70
Fax: +33 493 53 72 44

www.ac-nice.fr

**Rectorat de l'Académie de
Corse**
Boulevard Rossini BP 808
20192 Ajaccio Cedex
Tel: +33 495 50 34 08
Fax: +33 495 51 27 06
www.ac-corse.fr

HEALTH
**Caisse Primaire d'Assurance
Maladie des Alpes-
Maritimes**
Rue Roi Robert Comte 48 de
Provence
06100 Nice
Tel: +33 492 09 40 00
Fax: +33 492 98 02 42

**Caisse Primaire d'Assurance
Maladie d'Ajaccio**
Boulevard Abbé Recco BP 910
Quartier Les Padules
20702 Ajaccio Cedex 9
Tel: +35 495 23 52 00
Fax: +33 495 20 64 74

Corsica's stunning coastline generates a huge amount of tourist interest

LISA MCGEE

HOTSPOTS

€100,000–€400,000
(£69,444–£277,778)

A range of lovely apartments are available to suit all budgets

€188,950   CODE VEF

CÔTE D'AZUR

A newly renovated apartment in the heart of the city, with its own private garden

£131,215

🛏 *2* ❀ *With a small garden* 🖼 *Local amenities* 🚦 *Located on a main road*

🏠 *Room for parking*

€194,000   CODE DAK

PORT GRIMAUD, NEAR ST TROPEZ

A delightful 1-bed studio flat with a private garden

£134,722

🛏 *1* ❀ *–* 🖼 *Situated near fashionable St Tropez* 🚦 *Not located on a main road*

🏠 *–*

€234,165   CODE SIF

BOUCHES-DU-RHÔNE, AIX-EN-PROVENCE

A beautiful ground-floor apartment in the restored former stables of a castle

£162,615

🛏 *2* ❀ *–* 🖼 *Situated 20 minutes from Avignon* 🚦 *Not located on a main road*

🏠 *–*

€300,000   CODE AZP

ST TROPEZ

A lovely, recently renovated apartment with a splendid harbour view

£208,333

🛏 *2* ❀ *12m² terrace* 🖼 *Situated in the historic port* 🚦 *Located on a main road*

🏠 *Room for parking, with a garage*

€385,000   CODE AZP

ST TROPEZ

A superb south-facing apartment with breathtaking panoramic views

£267,361

🛏 *1* ❀ *–* 🖼 *Situated close to the beach* 🚦 *Not located on a main road*

🏠 *Room for parking*

€400,000–€550,000
(£277,778–£381,944)

A prime selection of city apartments, village properties and villas

€406,000   CODE DAK

NEAR LACOSTE, VAUCLUSE
An 18th-century stone village house with an attractive courtyard garden
£281,944

🛏 2   ❀ Courtyard garden   Situated near Lacoste   Not located on a main road

🏠 Room for parking

€460,000   CODE LAV

VAUCLUSE, PROVENCE
A large, south-facing Provençal villa with spectacular mountain views
£319,444

🛏 5   ❀ 5,000m²   Situated in a quiet, rural location   Not located on a main road

🏠 Room for parking, with a double garage

€495,000   CODE DAK

LA-GARDE-FREINET, VAR
An idyllic former mill set in a rural location just 7km from the village
£343,750

🛏 3   ❀ –   Situated 7km from the village   Not located on a main road

🏠 Room for parking

€517,920   CODE VEF

NICE
A wonderfully designed top-floor apartment in the suburbs to the west of Nice
£359,667

🛏 2   ❀ 220m² terrace   Situated in the city   Located on a main road

🏠 Room for parking, with a garage

€540,000   CODE AZP

CAVALAIRE
A beautiful villa with a covered terrace, swimming pool and enviable panoramic views
£375,000

🛏 4   ❀ 2,800m²   Situated in a quiet rural area   Not located on a main road

🏠 Parking for 3 cars

PRICE GUIDE

From: Clinton Rogers
Sent: 19 November 2003 12:17
To: info@hifx.co.uk
Subject: THANKS

Dear All at HIFX

Just wanted to drop you a quick note to say a big thank you for your help
recently in organising currency for the purchase of a property abroad.
The whole experience was painless, efficient and PLEASANT!

Real people answer the phones!

And when I did have a couple of headaches,
Stephen Lemon was better than an aspirin.

Well done to all - and big thanks.

Clinton Rogers

Excellent exchange rates, excellent service

When sending large amounts of currency to France its not just the exchange
rate that matters. We understand that the process can be daunting.
Our service doesn't stop once you have bought the euros; our dedicated team
are here to ensure that you have total peace of mind until the money arrives in
the notaires's account.

UK office: +44(0)1753 859 159

 HIFX PLC   mpa@hifx.co.uk

€550,000–€750,000
(£381,944–£520,833)

In this price range, you'll find larger properties with their own gardens and land

€550,000   CODE LAV

VAUCLUSE, PROVENCE

A stone farmhouse in a shared domain, with a swimming pool and tennis court
£381,944

🛏 5 🌸 – 🖼 *Situated in a small, shared domain* 🚧 *Not located on a main road*
🏠 *Room for parking, with a garage*

€609,000   CODE SIF

SAUSSET-LES-PINS, BOUCHES-DU-RHÔNE

A 19th-century, 3-storey property with a pool that's only minutes from the sea
£422,917

🛏 4 🌸 360m² 🖼 *Situated in a lovely coastal village* 🚧 *Not located on a main road*
🏠 *Room for parking, with a garage*

€685,000   CODE DAK

DRAGUIGNAN, VAR

A newly-built *bastide* under 1 hour from Nice airport and 2km from the town
£475,694

🛏 4 🌸 4,800m² 🖼 *Situated close to the town* 🚧 *Not located on a main road*
🏠 *Room for parking*

€688,000   CODE SIF

VAR

A charming property in one of the hilltop villages of the upper Var
£477,778

🛏 6 🌸 – 🖼 *Situated in the village centre* 🚧 *Located on a main road*
🏠 *Room for parking*

€735,000   CODE LAV

VAUCLUSE

A renovated 18th-century house with a landscaped garden and incredible views
£510,417

🛏 5 🌸 *Landscaped garden* 🖼 *Situated in quiet location* 🚧 *Not located on a main road*
🏠 *Room for parking*

PRICE GUIDE

€750,000–€1 million
(£520,833–£694,444)

Larger properties with superb features in attractive areas

€770,000   CODE AZP

ST TROPEZ

A magnificent Provençal-style villa with a large terrace, pool and tennis court
£534,722

🛏 6   🌱 6,700m²   🏖 Situated 15 minutes from the beach   🛣 Not located on a main road
🏠 Room for parking

€770,000   CODE SIF

ST CÉZAIRE

A spacious property occupying a privileged position in the hills above St Cézaire
£534,722

🛏 4   🌱 4,100m²   🏖 Situated 4km from the village   🛣 Not located on a main road
🏠 Room for parking, with a garage

€795,000   CODE AZP

CANNES, ALPES-MARITIMES

A superb apartment in glitzy Cannes, with parking and an incredible sea view
£552,083

🛏 3   🌱 250m²   🏖 Situated 5 minutes from La Croisette   🛣 Not located on a main road
🏠 Room for parking, with a garage

€840,000   CODE SIF

VAR

A lovely south-facing villa with swimming pool, tennis court and a private apartment
£583,333

🛏 4   🌱 4,313m²   🏖 Situated close to Les Arcs   🛣 Not located on a main road
🏠 Room for parking, with a garage

€960,000   CODE SIF

VAR

A beautiful property set in large wooded grounds, with a heated pool
£666,667

🛏 6   🌱 10,851m²   🏖 Situated in a quiet, rural area   🛣 Not located on a main road
🏠 Room for parking, with a garage

€1 million–€1.5 million
(£694,444–£1,041,667)

Gorgeous properties for both city and country living

€1,100,000   CODE LAV

VAUCLUSE

A large *chambre d'hôtes* with a swimming pool and lovely views

£763,889

🛏 7   ❀ 1,650m²   🖼 *Situated in the village centre*   🛤 *Not located on a main road*
🏠 *Room for parking, with a garage*

€1,200,000   CODE DAK

NEAR VILLEFRANCHE-SUR-MER

A traditional stone property with 3 bedrooms and a guest flat

£833,333

🛏 3   ❀ –   🖼 *Situated close to the village*   🛤 *Not located on a main road*
🏠 *Room for parking*

€1,300,000   CODE SIF

VENCE, ALPES-MARITIMES

A spacious, renovated, south-facing villa with a heated pool and tennis court

£902,778

🛏 7   ❀ 3,300m²   🖼 *Situated 15 minutes from Nice airport*   🛤 *Not located on a main road*
🏠 *Room for parking, with a garage*

€1,500,000   CODE AZP

CANNES, ALPES-MARITIMES

A truly desirable south-facing apartment with incredible sea views

£1,041,667

🛏 2   ❀ 25m² terrace   🖼 *Situated in the village centre*   🛤 *Not located on a main road*
🏠 *No parking*

€1,500,000   CODE DAK

LA-GARDE-FREINET, VAR

A quality stone house with fine views and a pool, set in wooded grounds

£1,041,667

🛏 4   ❀ Large garden   🖼 *Situated in the village centre*   🛤 *Not located on a main road*
🏠 *Room for parking*

€1.5 million–€2 million
(£1,041,667–£1,388,889)

There are some fantastic properties available in this price range

€1,596,000   CODE AZP

ST TROPEZ-ST RAPHAEL
A prestigious seafront property between Cannes and St Tropez
£1,108,333

🛏 2   ⬡ 574m²   🖼 Situated in a peaceful area   🚫 Not located on a main road
🏠 Room for parking

€1,616,000   CODE DAK

VIDAUBAN, VAR
A traditional Provençal house with a vineyard, overlooking a lake
£1,122,222

🛏 4   ⬡ 128,000m²   🖼 Situated in a rural location   🚫 Not located on a main road
🏠 Room for parking

€1,750,000   CODE LAV

ALPES-MARITIMES, PROVENCE
A recently restored villa with large, mature gardens and stunning mountain views
£1,215,278

🛏 3   ⬡ Large garden   🖼 Situated in a quiet location   🚫 Not located on a main road
🏠 Room for parking

€1,800,000   CODE SIF

MOUANS-SARTOUX, ALPES-MARITIMES
A magnificent property with a pool, set in large grounds planted with olive trees
£1,250,000

🛏 4   ⬡ 4,000m²   🖼 Situated in a peaceful location   🚫 Not located on a main road
🏠 Room for parking

€1,920,000   CODE SIF

CARRY-LE-ROUET, BOUCHES-DU-RHÔNE
An attractive coastal property with spectacular sea views, a pool and a summer house
£1,333,333

🛏 6   ⬡ 2,500m²   🖼 Situated in a quiet location   🚫 Not located on a main road
🏠 Room for parking, with a garage

€2 million–€3 million
(£1,388,889–£2,083,333)

Gorgeous, larger properties, from monasteries to villas

€2,090,000   CODE SIF

CANNES, ALPES-MARITIMES
An attractive villa in the Californie region of Cannes, with superb sea views
£1,451,389

🛏 6 🌸 1,000m² 🖼 *Situated in the city* 🚫 *Not located on a main road*
🏠 *Room for parking, with a double garage*

€2,200,000   CODE AZP

ST TROPEZ
A stylish, south-facing villa with a pool in a beautiful part of St Tropez
£1,527,778

🛏 4 🌸 1,500m² 🖼 *Situated close to the beach* 🚫 *Not located on a main road*
🏠 *Room for parking, with a garage*

€2,700,000   CODE SIF

CANNES, ALPES-MARITIMES
A superbly renovated house with a swimming pool and sea views, set in large grounds
£1,875,000

🛏 7 🌸 1,150m² 🖼 *Situated in the city* 🚫 *Not located on a main road*
🏠 *Room for parking, with a garage*

€2,950,000   CODE SIF

NEAR GRASSE, ALPES-MARITIMES
This recently renovated property was once a monastery
£2,048,611

🛏 6 🌸 9,892m² 🖼 *Situated in a peaceful setting* 🚫 *Not located on a main road*
🏠 *Room for parking*

€3,000,000   CODE LAV

ALPES-MARITIMES, PROVENCE
A beautiful stone château next to the river Brague, featuring many ancient walls
£2,083,333

🛏 6 🌸 30,000m² 🖼 *Situated in quiet location* 🚫 *Not located on a main road*
🏠 *Room for parking, with a 4-6 car garage*

€3 million+
(£2,083,333+)

You can enjoy French living at its best with these fantastic properties

€3,300,000   CODE AZP

CANNES, ALPES-MARITIMES

A beautiful villa in fashionable Cannes with large grounds, a pool and a sea view
£2,291,667

🛏 5   ✳ 2,200m²   *Situated in a quiet location*   *Not located on a main road*
Room for parking, with a garage for 3 cars

€3,600,000   CODE AZP

ST TROPEZ

A splendid villa with plenty of character and facilities, set within a secure compound
£2,500,000

🛏 6   ✳ 7,000m²   *Situated in a private compound*   *Not located on a main road*
Room for parking, with a garage for 2 cars

€5,000,000   CODE AZP

ST TROPEZ

A fantastic property in one of the most exclusive parts of St Tropez
£3,472,222

🛏 8   ✳ 3,600m²   *Situated in a desirable region*   *Not located on a main road*
Room for parking, with a garage for 2 cars

€5,400,000   CODE SIF

BOUCHES-DU-RHÔNE, AIX-EN-PROVENCE

A substantial property in beautiful landscaped grounds planted with cypress and pine
£3,750,000

🛏 7   ✳ 51,360m²   *Situated in protected parkland*   *Not located on a main road*
Room for parking, with a garage for 2 cars

€12,000,000   CODE AZP

CANNES, ALPES-MARITIMES

A magnificent renovated château with sea views, set in gorgeous landscaped grounds
£8,333,333

🛏 8   ✳ 15,000m²   *Situated very close to La Croisette*   *Not located on a main road*
Room for parking, with a garage for 5 cars

PRICE GUIDE

Move with confidence

MOVE WITH

COLES Ltd

OVERSEAS REMOVALS

CALL

020 8800 3315

VISIT

www.colesremovals.co.uk

UNIT 1, NORMAN ROAD,
RANGEMOORE INDUSTRIAL ESTATE,
LONDON N15 4ND

JUSTIN POSTLETHWAITE

Buyer's Reference

All the information the French house hunter could need, from price matrices to essential contact information

House price matrix

	2-bed	3-bed	4-bed	5+ bed
Brittany				
Dinard/Dinan/St Malo	€109,500 (£76,076)	€152,500 (£105,903)	€232,750 (£161,632)	€294,975 (£204,844)
Lorient	€117,630 (£81,688)	€185,210 (£128,618)	€253,825 (£176,267)	€268,800 (£186,667)
Golfe du Morbihan	€147,310 (£102,299)	€199,150 (£138,299)	€275,160 (£191,083)	€444,700 (£308,820)
Brest	€114,000 (£79,167)	€142,000 (£98,611)	€198,190 (£137,632)	€253,500 (£176,042)
Quimper	€103,000 (£71,528)	€118,500 (£82,292)	€167,000 (£115,972)	€250,000 (£173,611)
Guingamp	€82,000 (£56,944)	€116,950 (£81,215)	€189,000 (£131,250)	€257,500 (£178,820)
Rennes	€106,300 (£73,820)	€161,875 (£112,413)	€194,100 (£134,792)	€237,100 (£164,653)
Normandy				
Deauville	€193,950 (£134,688)	€275,070 (£191,020)	€350,262 (£243,237)	€527,631 (£366,410)
Trouville	€158,412 (£110,008)	€213,090 (£147,980)	€422,564 (£293,447)	€391,087 (£271,588)
Honfleur	€185,700 (£128,958)	€209,083 (£145,197)	€305,000 (£208,904)	€407,520 (£283,000)
Rouen	€135,455 (£94,066)	€144,245 (£100,170)	€240,130 (£166,757)	€368,830 (£256,132)
Caen	€132,912 (£92,300)	€178,472 (£123,939)	€257,565 (£178,865)	€401,067 (£278,519)
Avranches	€99,639 (£69,194)	€140,861 (£97,820)	€194,636 (£135,164)	€278,702 (£193,543)
Dieppe	€112,400 (£78,055)	€185,450 (£128,785)	€166,850 (£115,868)	€354,970 (£246,507)
Nord Pas-de-Calais & Picardy				
Le Touquet	€230,100 (£159,792)	€466,690 (£324,090)	€574,670 (£399,076)	€703,845 (£488,780)
Amiens	€116,073 (£80,606)	€147,982 (£102,765)	€257,723 (£178,975)	€321,868 (£223,519)
Lille	€108,340 (£75,236)	€177,300 (£123,125)	€218,444 (£151,697)	€343,750 (£238,715)
Somme Valley	€102,175 (£70,955)	€133,700 (£92,847)	€243,620 (£169,180)	€283,292 (£196,730)
Montreuil & Hesdin	€110,140 (£76,486)	€156,867 (£108,935)	€162,279 (£112,693)	€328,900 (£228,403)
Ile-de-France				
Arrondissement 1	€550,000 (£381,944)	€760,000 (£527,770)	€1,100,000 (£764,236)	€1,780,000 (£1,236,110)
Arrondissement 2	€475,000 (£329,861)	€825,000 (£572,917)	€1,128,000 (£845,833)	€2,430,000 (£1,687,500)
Arrondissement 3	€434,000 (£301,389)	€753,000 (£522,917)	€1,032,750 (£717,189)	€1,317,000 (£914,583)
Arrondissement 4	€473,300 (£328,680)	€730,000 (£506,944)	€1,375,000 (£954,861)	€1,773,000 (£1,231,250)
Arrondissement 6	€525,000 (£364,583)	€714,000 (£495,833)	€1,075,000 (£746,527)	€1,916,000 (£1,330,555)

	2-bed	3-bed	4-bed	5+ bed
Arrondissement 7	€560,000 (£388,889)	€860,000 (£597,222)	€980,000 (£680,555)	€1,423,000 (£988,000)
Arrondissement 8	€360,000 (£250,000)	€835,000 (£579,861)	€1,123,000 (£779,861)	€2,000,000 (£1,388,889)
Arrondissement 16	€595,000 (£413,195)	€975,000 (£677,083)	€1,426,000 (£990,278)	€2,663,000 (£1,849,305)
Arrondissement 17	€550,500 (£382,292)	€785,000 (£545,139)	€1,158,750 (£804,688)	€3,143,250 (£2,182,813)
Versailles	€535,000 (£371,527)	€607,000 (£421,527)	€803,000 (£557,639)	€1,753,000 (£1,217,361)
Champagne-Ardenne				
Charleville-Mézières	€93,600 (£65,000)	€121,800 (£84,583)	€183,500 (£127,430)	€563,400 (£391,250)
Reims & Epernay	€152,800 (£106,111)	€181,100 (£125,764)	€192,200 (£133,472)	€272,700 (£189,375)
Châlons-en-Champagne	€138,800 (£96,389)	€185,300 (£128,680)	€205,400 (£142,639)	€312,800 (£217,222)
Alsace, Lorraine & Franche-Comté				
Strasbourg	€176,000 (£122,222)	€277,700 (£192,847)	€360,200 (£250,139)	€555,600 (£385,833)
Metz & Nancy	€161,300 (£112,014)	€200,750 (£139,410)	€229,000 (£159,028)	€321,600 (£223,333)
The Vosges	€149,800 (£104,028)	€181,200 (£125,833)	€257,000 (£178,472)	€348,000 (£241,667)
Besançon	€161,250 (£111,980)	€236,000 (£163,889)	€336,720 (£233,833)	€394,750 (£274,132)
Lons-le-Saunier, Haut-Jura & Vallée des Lacs	€79,800 (£55,417)	€120,000 (£83,333)	€182,800 (£126,945)	€294,000 (£204,167)
The Loire				
Vendée coast	€176,000 (£122,222)	€218,000 (£151,389)	€270,200 (£187,639)	€293,100 (£203,542)
Saumur & Angers	€153,900 (£106,875)	€171,350 (£118,993)	€232,500 (£161,458)	€312,500 (£217,014)
Nantes	€167,000 (£115,972)	€241,000 (£167,361)	€290,000 (£201,389)	€361,900 (£251,319)
Le Mans	€130,500 (£90,625)	€152,900 (£106,180)	€207,800 (£144,305)	€342,250 (£237,674)
Orléans	€166,800 (£115,833)	€168,700 (£117,153)	€259,200 (£180,000)	€309,000 (£214,583)
Tours & the Touraine	€136,600 (£94,861)	€186,690 (£129,646)	€271,650 (£188,646)	€336,150 (£233,458)
Burgundy				
Côte d'Or	€132,400 (£91,944)	€176,400 (£122,500)	€318,220 (£220,986)	€578,300 (£401,597)
Saône-et-Loire (Cluny & Mâcon)	€120,000 (£83,330)	€185,000 (£128,472)	€229,000 (£159,027)	€302,000 (£209,722)
Morvan Regional Park	€109,000 (£75,694)	€162,700 (£112,986)	€196,250 (£136,285)	€297,300 (£206,458)
Auxerre	€97,200 (£67,500)	€158,200 (£109,861)	€209,800 (£145,694)	€274,000 (£190,278)

	2-bed	3-bed	4-bed	5+ bed
Châtillon-sur-Seine	€126,000 (£87,318)	€216,000 (£150,000)	€250,000 (£173,611)	€431,000 (£299,305)
Poitou-Charentes				
Ile de Ré & La Rochelle	€191,100 (£132,708)	€231,200 (£160,555)	€354,600 (£246,250)	€400,000 (£277,777)
Charente	€80,210 (£55,701)	€148,965 (£103,448)	€220,800 (£153,333)	€427,530 (£296,895)
Poitiers	€97,534 (£72,488)	€168,000 (£116,666)	€227,800 (£158,194)	€282,600 (£196,250)
Châtelleraut	€67,560 (£46,916)	€91,450 (£63,507)	€139,600 (£96,944)	€198,480 (£137,833)
Limousin & Auvergne				
Limoges	€113,600 (£78,889)	€161,460 (£112,125)	€184,000 (£127,778)	€238,960 (£165,944)
Clermont-Ferrand	€130,250 (£90,451)	€179,960 (£124,972)	€230,740 (£160,236)	€277,000 (£192,361)
Volcanic mountains and lakes	€102,250 (£71,010)	€138,975 (£96,510)	€166,500 (£115,625)	€205,750 (£142,882)
Corrèze	€98,950 (£68,715)	€139,500 (£96,875)	€175,750 (£122,050)	€266,600 (£185,139)
Vichy	€129,920 (£90,222)	€190,250 (£132,118)	€246,725 (£171,337)	€417,030 (£289,604)
Rhône Alps				
Lake Annecy	€207,000 (£143,750)	€329,600 (£228,889)	€380,100 (£263,958)	€525,000 (£364,583)
Lake Geneva	€214,600 (£149,028)	€288,960 (£200,667)	€400,000 (£277,778)	€483,500 (£335,764)
Megève	€208,500 (£144,792)	€319,000 (£221,528)	€512,750 (£356,076)	€651,000 (£452,083)
Chamonix	€311,250 (£216,145)	€521,500 (£362,153)	€615,400 (£427,361)	€1,032,500 (£717,014)
Meribel	€241,000 (£167,361)	€418,000 (£290,278)	€540,000 (£375,000)	€720,000 (£500,000)
Courchevel	€268,800 (£186,667)	€384,300 (£266,875)	€450,500 (£312,847)	€912,500 (£633,680)
Les Menuires	€168,000 (£116,667)	€305,250 (£211,979)	€316,150 (£219,549)	€426,250 (£296,010)
Val d'Isère	€296,667 (£206,019)	€431,000 (£299,305)	€725,000 (£503,472)	€1,050,000 (£729,167)
Grenoble	€196,000 (£136,111)	€364,750 (£253,299)	€364,750 (£253,299)	€558,000 (£387,500)
Les Portes du Soleil	€180,000 (£125,000)	€290,000 (£201,389)	€402,000 (£279,167)	€590,000 (£409,722)
Lyon	€241,000 (£167,361)	€265,000 (£184,028)	€420,000 (£291,667)	€591,000 (£410,417)
Beaujolais	€160,000 (£111,111)	€223,250 (£155,035)	€348,500 (£242,014)	€448,000 (£311,111)
Aquitaine				
Cap Ferret & Bay of Arcachon	€225,000 (£156,250)	€352,000 (£244,444)	€358,200 (£248,750)	€529,200 (£367,500)
Dordogne	€116,000 (£80,555)	€202,500 (£140,625)	€253,833 (£176,273)	€341,000 (£236,805)

	2-bed	3-bed	4-bed	5+ bed
Agen	€127,200 (£88,333)	€232,520 (£161,472)	€289,500 (£201,042)	€327,750 (£227,604)
Bordeaux	€217,400 (£150,972)	€281,800 (£195,694)	€324,200 (£225,139)	€437,500 (£303,819)
Biarritz & Bayonne	€258,040 (£179,194)	€313,800 (£217,917)	€464,500 (£322,569)	€588,800 (£408,889)
Midi-Pyrénées				
Cahors & Rocamadour	€125,800 (£87,361)	€165,880 (£115,194)	€208,060 (£144,486)	€387,200 (£268,889)
Gascony/Gers	€168,200 (£116,805)	€162,400 (£112,778)	€243,667 (£169,213)	€447,600 (£310,833)
Toulouse	€186,000 (£129,167)	€230,000 (£159,722)	€346,667 (£240,740)	€481,800 (£334,583)
Bagnères-de-Bigorre	€161,400 (£112,083)	€196,000 (£136,111)	€240,500 (£167,014)	€384,400 (£266,944)
Languedoc-Roussillon				
Perpignan	€162,980 (£113,180)	€214,330 (£148,840)	€259,600 (£180,278)	€406,750 (£282,465)
Southern Roussillon	€169,800 (£117,917)	€277,400 (£192,639)	€403,600 (£280,278)	€629,200 (£436,944)
Montpellier	€190,400 (£132,222)	€234,600 (£162,917)	€368,600 (£255,972)	€539,600 (£374,722)
Carcassonne	€170,000 (£118,055)	€249,800 (£173,472)	€460,400 (£319,722)	€488,500 (£339,236)
Nîmes	€146,710 (£101,882)	€247,220 (£171,680)	€310,600 (£215,694)	€372,520 (£258,694)
Béziers-Narbonne	€136,600 (£94,861)	€185,660 (£128,930)	€235,600 (£163,611)	€286,600 (£199,028)
Côte d'Azur, Provence & Corsica				
Vaucluse	€167,100 (£116,042)	€219,950 (£152,743)	€379,400 (£263,472)	€562,400 (£390,555)
Inland Var	€188,800 (£131,111)	€336,600 (£233,750)	€547,800 (£380,417)	€529,930 (£368,007)
Saint Tropez	€646,250 (£448,785)	€1,230,600 (£854,583)	€1,815,000 (£1,260,417)	€2,539,200 (£1,763,333)
Toulon	€260,550 (£180,937)	€311,000 (£215,972)	€352,000 (£244,444)	€481,800 (£334,583)
Cannes	€397,000 (£275,694)	€695,500 (£482,986)	€1,557,600 (£1,081,667)	€2,105,500 (£1,462,152)
Antibes	€430,000 (£298,611)	€490,000 (£340,278)	€620,800 (£431,111)	€890,000 (£618,055)
Nice & area	€388,000 (£269,444)	€517,833 (£359,606)	€654,800 (£454,722)	€888,1200 (£616,805)
Marseille	€268,600 (£186,528)	€377,800 (£262,361)	€447,200 (£310,555)	€658,0200 (£456,944)
Aix-en-Provence & Saint-Rémy-de-Provence	€331,150 (£229,965)	€466,500 (£323,958)	€538,8220 (£374,180)	€760,167 (£527,893)
Corsica-Porto-Vecchio	€295,000 (£204,861)	€426,600 (£296,250)	€595,300 (£413,403)	€628,000 (£436,111)
Briançon	€256,800 (£175,139)	€279,800 (£194,305)	€437,000 (£303,472)	€590,000 (£409,722)

Apartment price matrix

	1-bed	2-bed	3-bed	4-bed
Brittany				
Dinard/Dinan/St Malo	€120,000 (£83,330)	€139,900 (£97,153)	€214,000 (£148,610)	€266,000 (£184,720)
Lorient	€83,000 (£57,638)	€106,000 (£73,610)	€150,000 (£104,167)	€192,000 (£133,330)
Golfe du Morbihan	€84,600 (£58,750)	€125,000 (£86,805)	€130,000 (£90,278)	€202,000 (£140,278)
Brest	€42,000 (£29,167)	€102,200 (£70,970)	€135,800 (£94,305)	€188,000 (£130,555)
Quimper	€72,000 (£50,000)	€100,800 (£70,000)	€138,000 (£95,830)	€217,000 (£150,695)
Guingamp	€60,900 (£42,292)	€110,000 (£76,389)	€80,000 (£55,555)	€152,000 (£105,555)
Rennes	€90,200 (£62,639)	€120,000 (£83,330)	€137,000 (£95,139)	€176,600 (£122,639)
Normandy				
Deauville	€93,000 (£64,583)	€205,000 (£142,361)	€286,000 (£198,610)	€335,000 (£232,639)
Trouville	€85,400 (£59,305)	€150,000 (£104,167)	€235,000 (£163,195)	€316,000 (£219,444)
Honfleur	€133,000 (£92,361)	€158,000 (£109,722)	€230,000 (£159,722)	€337,000 (£234,028)
Rouen	€77,000 (£53,472)	€95,750 (£66,493)	€130,000 (£90,278)	€279,000 (£193,750)
Caen	€63,000 (£43,750)	€115,000 (£79,861)	€150,000 (£104,167)	€201,000 (£139,583)
Dieppe	€160,000 (£111,110)	€178,000 (£123,611)	€230,000 (£159,722)	€275,000 (£190,972)
Nord Pas-de-Calais & Picardy				
Le Touquet	€121,000 (£84,028)	€231,000 (£160,417)	€394,000 (£273,611)	€420,000 (£291,667)
Amiens	€99,000 (£68,750)	€152,000 (£105,555)	€193,000 (£134,028)	€255,000 (£177,083)
Lille	€78,000 (£54,167)	€119,000 (£82,639)	€209,000 (£145,139)	€271,000 (£188,194)
Ile-de-France				
Arrondissement 1	€508,000 (£352,778)	€690,000 (£479,167)	€1,008,000 (£700,000)	€2,921,000 (£2,028,472)
Arrondissement 2	€312,000 (£216,667)	€554,000 (£384,722)	€731,000 (£507,639)	€1,157,500 (£803,319)
Arrondissement 3	€302,000 (£209,722)	€571,000 (£396,527)	€959,000 (£665,972)	€1,025,000 (£711,805)
Arrondissement 4	€335,000 (£232,639)	€574,000 (£398,611)	€917,000 (£636,805)	€1,210,000 (£840,277)
Arrondissement 6	€313,000 (£217,361)	€586,000 (£406,944)	€862,000 (£598,611)	€1,493,000 (£1,036,805)
Arrondissement 7	€331,000 (£229,861)	€762,000 (£529,167)	€1,083,000 (£752,083)	€1,426,000 (£990,278)
Arrondissement 8	€323,000 (£224,305)	€662,000 (£459,722)	€1,003,000 (£696,527)	€1,656,000 (£1,150,000)
Arrondissement 16	€320,000 (£222,222)	€518,000 (£359,722)	€767,000 (£532,639)	€1,406,000 (£976,389)
Arrondissement 17	€307,000 (£213,194)	€541,000 (£375,000)	€655,000 (£454,861)	€1,016,000 (£705,555)
Versailles	€212,000 (£147,222)	€335,200 (£232,639)	€602,000 (£418,055)	€740,000 (£513,889)

	1-bed	2-bed	3-bed	4-bed
Champagne-Ardenne				
Reims & Epernay	€95,600 (£66,389)	€147,000 (£102,083)	€236,000 (£163,889)	€325,000 (£225,695)
Châlons-en-Champagne	€72,000 (£50,000)	€103,000 (£71,527)	€119,600 (£83,055)	€180,000 (£125,000)
Alsace, Lorraine & Franche-Comté				
Strasboug	€83,000 (£57,639)	€140,000 (£97,222)	€188,000 (£130,555)	€372,000 (£258,333)
Metz & Nancy	€89,000 (£61,805)	€157,000 (£109,027)	€216,000 (£150,000)	€228,000 (£158,333)
The Vosges	€91,000 (£63,195)	€107,000 (£74,305)	€163,000 (£113,195)	€220,000 (£152,777)
Besançon	€72,000 (£50,000)	€98,000 (£68,055)	€177,000 (£122,916)	€250,000 (£173,611)
The Loire				
Vendée Coast	€63,500 (£44,097)	€98,700 (£68,542)	€148,000 (£102,777)	€222,000 (£154,167)
Nantes	€107,000 (£74,305)	€127,000 (£88,195)	€202,000 (£140,278)	€274,000 (£190,278)
Le Mans	€113,000 (£78,472)	€118,000 (£81,945)	€176,000 (£122,222)	€173,000 (£120,139)
Burgundy				
Côte d'Or	€84,000 (£58,333)	€116,200 (£80,695)	€154,000 (£106,945)	€259,200 (£180,000)
Auxerre	€76,000 (£52,778)	€124,000 (£86,111)	€176,000 (£122,222)	€224,000 (£155,555)
Poitou-Charentes				
Ile de Ré & La Rochelle	€121,300 (£84,236)	€169,000 (£117,361)	€308,000 (£213,889)	€363,000 (£252,083)
Poitiers	€55,000 (£38,115)	€105,000 (£72,917)	€168,000 (£116,667)	€253,000 (£175,695)
Limousin & Auvergne				
Limoges	€75,000 (£52,083)	€97,000 (£67,361)	€125,800 (£87,361)	€249,000 (£172,917)
Clermont-Ferrand	€78,000 (£54,167)	€110,000 (£76,389)	€212,000 (£147,222)	€270,000 (£187,500)
Volcanic Mountains and Lakes	€47,000 (£32,639)	€62,000 (£43,055)	€121,600 (£84,445)	€222,000 (£154,167)
Rhône-Alps				
Lake Annecy	€185,000 (£128,472)	€265,000 (£184,027)	€253,000 (£175,695)	€355,000 (£246,528)
Lake Geneva	€98,000 (£68,055)	€163,000 (£113,195)	€254,000 (£176,389)	€390,000 (£270,833)
Megève	€135,000 (£93,750)	€292,000 (£202,778)	€395,000 (£274,305)	€445,000 (£309,028)
Chamonix	€135,000 (£93,750)	€355,000 (£246,528)	€448,000 (£311,111)	€553,000 (£384,028)
Méribel	€298,000 (£206,944)	€565,000 (£392,361)	€811,000 (£563,195)	€1,260,000 (£875,000)
Courchevel	€218,000 (£151,389)	€285,000 (£197,917)	€457,000 (£317,361)	€506,000 (£351,389)
Val d'Isère	€265,000 (£184,028)	€418,000 (£290,278)	€556,000 (£386,111)	€1,160,000 (£805,555)

	1-bed	2-bed	3-bed	4-bed
Grenoble	€125,000 (£86,865)	€157,000 (£109,028)	€238,000 (£165,278)	€392,000 (£272,222)
Les Portes du Soleil	€161,000 (£111,805)	€265,000 (£184,028)	€320,000 (£222,222)	€423,000 (£293,750)
Lyon	€163,000 (£113,195)	€211,000 (£146,528)	€278,000 (£193,055)	€469,000 (£325,695)
Aquitaine				
Cap Ferret & Bay of Arcachon	€129,000 (£89,397)	€213,000 (£147,917)	€295,000 (£204,861)	€432,000 (£300,000)
Agen	€71,600 (£49,722)	€110,000 (£76,389)	€163,000 (£113,195)	€263,000 (£182,639)
Bordeaux	€150,000 (£104,167)	€154,000 (£106,945)	€254,000 (£176,389)	€285,000 (£197,917)
Biarritz & Bayonne	€125,000 (£86,805)	€225,000 (£156,250)	€341,000 (£236,805)	€411,000 (£285,417)
Midi-Pyrénées				
Cahors & Rocamadour	€65,000 (£45,139)	€106,000 (£73,611)	€148,000 (£102,778)	€226,000 (£156,945)
Toulouse	€100,000 (£69,445)	€142,000 (£98,611)	€173,000 (£120,139)	€272,000 (£188,889)
Languedoc-Roussillon				
Perpignan	€127,000 (£88,195)	€175,000 (£121,528)	€167,000 (£115,972)	€258,000 (£179,167)
Montpellier	€146,000 (£101,389)	€168,000 (£116,667)	€235,000 (£163,195)	€276,000 (£191,667)
Nîmes	€119,000 (£82,639)	€130,000 (£90,278)	€229,750 (£159,549)	€263,500 (£182,986)
Béziers-Narbonne	€70,000 (£48,611)	€78,000 (£54,167)	€127,000 (£88,195)	€172,000 (£119,445)
Côte d'Azur, Provence & Corsica				
Vaucluse	€122,000 (£84,722)	€179,000 (£124,305)	€208,000 (£144,445)	€288,000 (£200,000)
Inland Var	€122,000 (£84,722)	€191,000 (£132,639)	€246,000 (£170,833)	€409,000 (£284,028)
Saint-Tropez	€212,000 (£147,222)	€378,000 (£262,500)	€493,000 (£342,361)	€525,000 (£364,583)
Toulon	€142,000 (£98,611)	€242,000 (£168,055)	€267,000 (£185,417)	€369,000 (£256,250)
Cannes	€216,000 (£150,000)	€411,700 (£285,903)	€520,000 (£361,111)	€750,000 (£520,833)
Antibes	€201,000 (£139,583)	€244,000 (£169,445)	€384,000 (£266,667)	€614,000 (£426,389)
Nice & area	€153,000 (£106,250)	€242,000 (£168,055)	€395,000 (£274,305)	€543,800 (£377,639)
Marseille	€111,000 (£77,083)	€168,200 (£166,805)	€226,800 (£157,500)	€316,000 (£219,445)
Aix-en-Provence & Saint-Rémy-de-Provence	€179,200 (£124,445)	€290,000 (£201,389)	€386,800 (£268,611)	€461,800 (£320,695)
Corsica-Porto-Vecchio	€122,300 (£84,930)	€231,000 (£160,417)	€340,000 (£236,111)	€440,000 (£305,555)
Briançon	€95,000 (£65,972)	€136,000 (£94,445)	€202,000 (£140,278)	€303,500 (£210,764)

Letting price matrix (weekly)

	1-bed	2-bed	3-bed	4-bed	5+ bed
Brittany					
Dinard/Dinan/St Malo	€440 (£305)	€460 (£320)	€580 (£403)	€750 (£520)	€1,600 (£1,111)
Lorient	€350 (£243)	€490 (£340)	€540 (£375)	€650 (£451)	€800 (£555)
Golfe du Morbihan	€550 (£382)	€610 (£424)	€620 (£430)	€940 (£653)	€1,620 (£1,125)
Brest	€360 (£250)	€520 (£361)	€650 (£451)	€700 (£486)	€880 (£611)
Quimper	€350 (£243)	€545 (£378)	€720 (£500)	€810 (£562)	€1,170 (£813)
Guingamp	€300 (£208)	€410 (£285)	€500 (£347)	€615 (£427)	€810 (£562)
Rennes	€340 (£236)	€560 (£389)	€670 (£465)	€950 (£660)	€1,050 (£730)
Normandy					
Deauville	€365 (£253)	€430 (£299)	€740 (£514)	€980 (£680)	€1,100 (£764)
Trouville	€420 (£292)	€485 (£337)	€720 (£500)	€605 (£420)	€1,085 (£753)
Honfleur	€370 (£257)	€485 (£337)	€750 (£521)	€925 (£642)	€1,350 (£938)
Rouen	€360 (£250)	€580 (£403)	€725 (£503)	€840 (£583)	€1,180 (£819)
Caen	€305 (£212)	€560 (£389)	€770 (£535)	€1,010 (£701)	€1,200 (£833)
Avranches	€345 (£240)	€450 (£313)	€530 (£368)	€1,100 (£764)	€930 (£646)
Dieppe	€280 (£194)	€450 (£313)	€600 (£417)	€900 (£625)	€1,470 (£1,021)
Nord Pas-de-Calais & Picardy					
Le Touquet	€470 (£326)	€730 (£510)	€1,100 (£764)	€1,480 (£1028)	€1,820 (£1,264)
Amiens	€385 (£267)	€610 (£424)	€660 (£458)	€820 (£569)	€950 (£660)
Lille	€440 (£305)	€750 (£521)	€690 (£479)	€1,025 (£712)	€1,345 (£934)
Somme Valley	€310 (£215)	€495 (£344)	€565 (£392)	€625 (£434)	€840 (£583)
Montreuil & Hesdin	€260 (£180)	€320 (£222)	€530 (£368)	€680 (£472)	€800 (£555)
Ile-de-France					
Arrondissement 1	€760 (£528)	€1,395 (£969)	€2,100 (£1,458)	€2,760 (£1,917)	€3,000 (£2,083)
Arrondissement 2	€680 (£472)	€1,170 (£812)	€1,360 (£944)	€2,250 (£1,562)	€2,680 (£1,861)
Arrondissement 3	€850 (£590)	€1,411 (£980)	€1,800 (£1,250)	€2,280 (£1,583)	€2,780 (£1,930)
Arrondissement 4	€980 (£680)	€1,740 (£1,208)	€2,575 (£1,788)	€3,180 (£2,208)	€3,480 (£2,417)
Arrondissement 6	€800 (£555)	€1,120 (£778)	€1,980 (£1,375)	€2,000 (£1,389)	€2,400 (£1,667)

	1-bed	2-bed	3-bed	4-bed	5+ bed
Arrondissement 7	€880 (£611)	€1,170 (£812)	€2,660 (£1,847)	€2,180 (£1,514)	€3,100 (£2,153)
Arronsissement 8	€990 (£687)	€1,700 (£1,180)	€2,280 (£1,583)	€2,600 (£1,805)	€3,335 (£2,316)
Arrondissement 16	€710 (£493)	€935 (£650)	€2,000 (£1,389)	€2,115 (£1,469)	€2,300 (£1,597)
Arrondissement 17	€515 (£358)	€1,390 (£965)	€1,310 (£910)	€1,850 (£1,285)	€2,440 (£1,694)
Versailles	€500 (£347)	€1,275 (£885)	€1,750 (£1,215)	€1,980 (£1,375)	€2,500 (£1,736)
Champagne-Ardenne					
Charleville-Mézières	€200 (£139)	€270 (£187)	€360 (£250)	€445 (£309)	€480 (£333)
Reims & Epernay	€225 (£156)	€305 (£212)	€450 (£312)	€515 (£358)	€535 (£372)
Châlons-en-Champagne	€270 (£188)	€330 (£229)	€550 (£382)	€555 (£385)	€590 (£410)
Alsace, Lorraine & Franche-Comté					
Strasbourg	€320 (£222)	€490 (£340)	€610 (£424)	€720 (£500)	€1,010 (£701)
Metz & Nancy	€260 (£180)	€330 (£229)	€630 (£438)	€745 (£518)	€1,350 (£938)
The Vosges	€350 (£243)	€510 (£354)	€650 (£451)	€740 (£514)	€860 (£597)
Besançon	€295 (£205)	€475 (£330)	€610 (£424)	€865 (£601)	€1,000 (£694)
Lons-le-Saunier, Haut-Jura & Vallée des Lacs	€265 (£184)	€325 (£226)	€475 (£330)	€565 (£392)	€805 (£559)
The Loire					
Vendée coast	€490 (£340)	€710 (£493)	€605 (£420)	€1,120 (£778)	€1,000 (£694)
Saumur & Angers	€365 (£253)	€415 (£288)	€615 (£427)	€1,050 (£730)	€990 (£687)
Nantes	€400 (£278)	€660 (£458)	€855 (£594)	€900 (£625)	€1,210 (£840)
Le Mans	€360 (£250)	€560 (£389)	€650 (£451)	€1,000 (£694)	€1,400 (£972)
Orléans	€300 (£208)	€545 (£378)	€600 (£417)	€825 (£573)	€1,020 (£708)
Tours & the Touraine	€350 (£243)	€520 (£361)	€700 (£486)	€1,200 (£833)	€1,430 (£993)
Burgundy					
Côte d'Or	€260 (£180)	€450 (£312)	€600 (£417)	€715 (£497)	€1,015 (£705)
Saône-et-Loire (Cluny & Mâcon)	€350 (£243)	€430 (£299)	€590 (£410)	€890 (£618)	€1,200 (£833)
Morvan Regional Park	€230 (£160)	€330 (£229)	€425 (£295)	€530 (£368)	€870 (£604)
Auxerre	€375 (£260)	€640 (£444)	€690 (£479)	€900 (£625)	€1,060 (£736)

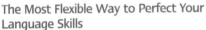

	1-bed	2-bed	3-bed	4-bed	5+ bed
Châtillon-sur-Seine	€255 (£177)	€295 (£205)	€375 (£260)	€540 (£375)	€630 (£440)
Poitou-Charentes					
Ile de Ré & La Rochelle	€360 (£250)	€540 (£375)	€800 (£555)	€980 (£680)	€1,210 (£840)
Charente	€350 (£243)	€470 (£326)	€680 (£472)	€840 (£583)	€1,200 (£833)
Poitiers	€350 (£243)	€540 (£375)	€730 (£507)	€1,260 (£875)	€1,400 (£972)
Châtellerault	€270 (£188)	€415 (£288)	€490 (£340)	€680 (£472)	€750 (£521)
Limousin & Auvergne					
Limoges	€340 (£236)	€450 (£313)	€500 (£347)	€730 (£507)	€975 (£677)
Clermont-Ferrand	€340 (£236)	€480 (£333)	€660 (£458)	€895 (£621)	€1,125 (£781)
Volcanic mountains and lakes	€230 (£160)	€430 (£299)	€510 (£354)	€730 (£507)	€715 (£497)
Corrèze	€395 (£274)	€680 (£472)	€750 (£521)	€780 (£542)	€1,100 (£764)
Vichy	€215 (£149)	€295 (£205)	€360 (£250)	€580 (£403)	€750 (£521)
Rhône Alps					
Lake Annecy	€450 (£313)	€750 (£521)	€970 (£674)	€1,345 (£934)	€1,750 (£1,215)
Lake Geneva	€600 (£417)	€770 (£535)	€1,090 (£757)	€1,400 (£972)	€1,830 (£1,271)
Megève	€610 (£424)	€1,050 (£729)	€1,620 (£1,125)	€1,990 (£1,382)	€2,420 (£1,681)
Chamonix	€495 (£344)	€760 (£528)	€1,270 (£882)	€2,000 (£1,389)	€3,100 (£2,153)
Méribel	€640 (£444)	€710 (£493)	€1,100 (£764)	€1,520 (£1,055)	€2,500 (£1,736)
Courchevel	€550 (£382)	€760 (£528)	€960 (£667)	€1,860 (£1,292)	€2,600 (£1,805)
Les Menuires	€400 (£278)	€670 (£465)	€750 (£521)	€925 (£642)	€1,030 (£715)
Val d'Isère	€795 (£552)	€1,010 (£701)	€1,400 (£972)	€2,030 (£1,410)	€2,850 (£1,979)
Grenoble	€465 (£323)	€610 (£424)	€790 (£549)	€990 (£688)	€1,155 (£802)
Les Portes du Soleil	€460 (£319)	€710 (£493)	€900 (£625)	€1,230 (£854)	€1,810 (£1,257)
Lyon	€480 (£333)	€680 (£472)	€925 (£642)	€1,225 (£851)	€1,880 (£1,306)
Beaujolais	€410 (£285)	€645 (£448)	€855 (£594)	€1,040 (£722)	€1,160 (£805)
Aquitaine					
Cap Ferret & Bay of Arcachon	€410 (£285)	€650 (£451)	€905 (£628)	€1,420 (£986)	€1,825 (£1,267)
Dordogne	€375 (£260)	€620 (£431)	€965 (£670)	€1,170 (£813)	€1,350 (£938)

	1-bed	2-bed	3-bed	4-bed	5+ bed
Agen	€330 (£229)	€500 (£382)	€600 (£417)	€750 (£521)	€875 (£608)
Bordeaux	€405 (£281)	€745 (£517)	€955 (£663)	€1,250 (£868)	€1,600 (£1,111)
Biarritz & Bayonne	€440 (£306)	€620 (£431)	€1,025 (£712)	€1065 (£740)	€1,165 (£809)
Midi-Pyrénées					
Cahors & Rocamadour	€465 (£323)	€575 (£399)	€800 (£555)	€1,120 (£778)	€1,280 (£889)
Gascony/Gers	€410 (£285)	€575 (£399)	€760 (£528)	€870 (£604)	€975 (£677)
Toulouse	€435 (£302)	€680 (£472)	€810 (£53)	€950 (£660)	€1,440 (£1,000)
Bagnères-de-Bigorre	€410 (£285)	€460 (£319)	€605 (£420)	€840 (£583)	€1,260 (£875)
Languedoc-Roussillon					
Perpignan	€380 (£264)	€630 (£438)	€760 (£528)	€1,030 (£715)	€1,230 (£854)
Southern Roussillon	€500 (£347)	€580 (£403)	€750 (£521)	€940 (£653)	€1,005 (£698)
Montpellier	€470 (£326)	€720 (£500)	€800 (£555)	€880 (£611)	€1,010 (£701)
Carcassonne	€405 (£281)	€560 (£389)	€700 (£486)	€775 (£538)	€935 (£649)
Nîmes	€375 (£260)	€675 (£469)	€900 (£625)	€855 (£594)	€985 (£684)
Béziers-Narbonne	€380 (£264)	€495 (£344)	€640 (£444)	€735 (£510)	€760 (£528)
Côte d'Azur, Provence & Corsica					
Vaucluse	€420 (£292)	€580 (£403)	€710 (£493)	€830 (£576)	€980 (£681)
Inland Var	€440 (£306)	€640 (£444)	€930 (£646)	€1,075 (£747)	€1,315 (£913)
St Tropez	€620 (£431)	€850 (£590)	€960 (£667)	€1,270 (£882)	€1,690 (£1,174)
Toulon	€420 (£292)	€680 (£472)	€960 (£667)	€840 (£583)	€940 (£653)
Cannes	€620 (£431)	€975 (£677)	€1,600 (£1,111)	€2,210 (£1,535)	€2,900 (£2,014)
Antibes	€540 (£375)	€970 (£674)	€1,620 (£1125)	€1,560 (£1,083)	€2,600 (£1,806)
Nice & area	€410 (£285)	€820 (£569)	€1,160 (£806)	€1,480 (£1,028)	€2,170 (£1,507)
Marseille	€565 (£392)	€850 (£590)	€930 (£646)	€1,830 (£1,271)	€1,840 (£1,277)
Aix-en-Provence & Saint-Rémy-de-Provence	€590 (£410)	€660 (£458)	€1,030 (£715)	€1,750 (£1,215)	€2,360 (£1,639)
Corsica – Porto-Vecchio	€670 (£465)	€600 (£417)	€1,050 (£729)	€1,100 (£764)	€1,600 (£1,111)
Briançon	€310 (£215)	€410 (£285)	€510 (£354)	€725 (£503)	€855 (£594)

Raising the standard of removals since 1982

BURKE BROS

WORLDWIDE MOVING GROUP

- ◆ Collection throughout the UK

- ◆ Guaranteed weekly services -
  we serve the following
  regions: Aquitaine, Auvergne,
  Burgundy, Brittany, Centre,
  Languedoc-Rouissillon,
  Limousin, Midi-Pyrenees,
  Normandy, Pay de la Loire,
  Picardy, Poitou-Charentes,
  Provence-Alpes-Côte d'Azur,
  Rhône-Alpes

- ◆ Part Load/Return Loads

- ◆ Storage in the UK and France

- ◆ Contact our head office for a
  free survey and quotation

FREEPHONE: **0800 413256**

www.burkebros.co.uk

Email: **sales@burkebros.co.uk**   Fax: **01902 427837**

Glossary

nm = masculine noun
nf = feminine noun

A

acompte (nm)
deposit
acte (nm)
deed
  acte authentique deed -
  conveyance
  acte authentique de vente -
  conveyance
  acte de vente - conveyance
agent immobilier (nm)
estate agent
architecte (nmf)
architect
artisan (nm)
builder; skilled craftsman
assurance multirisques habitation (nf)
comprehensive household
insurance

B

bail (nm)
lease
bastide (nf)
Provençal country house
bâtiment (nm)
building

C

caisse (nf)
office; fund
  caisse primaire d'assurance
  maladie - state health
  insurance centre
carte (nf)
card; permit
  carte de séjour - residence
  permit
  carte grise - car registration
  document
  carte professionelle -
  professional licence
cave (nf)
cellar
caveau (nm)
small cellar
centre des impôts (nm)
local tax office
certificat (nm)

certificate
  certificat de conformité -
  certificate of compliance
  certificat d'urbanisme -
  planning permission certificate
chambre (nf)
bedroom; chamber
  chambre des notaires -
  chamber of notaries
  chambre de(s) métiers -
  chamber of trade
  chambres d'hôte - bed and
  breakfast; bed and breakfast
  rooms
chauffage (nm)
heating
clause (nf)
clause
  clause pénale - penalty clause
  clause suspensive - get-out
  clause
  clause tontine - survivorship
  clause
colombage (nm)
half-timbering
compromis de vente (nm)
sales contract
conservation des hypothèques (nf)
land registry
contrat (nm)
contract
  contrat de réservation -
  reservation contract for a
  property still to be constructed
cotisation (nf)
contributions
contribution sociale (nf)
social charge
copie authentique (nf)
certified copy
copropriété (nf)
co-ownership
  charges de copropriété -
  maintenance/service charges
  immeuble en copropriété -
  block of flats
cuisine (nf)
kitchen

D

demande de prêt (nf)
loan application

département (nm)
administrative area
dépendance (nf)
outbuilding
dépôt de garantie (nm)
deposit
domicile (nm)
place of residence;home
droit (nm)
right; duty; law
  droit de préemption - right of
  first refusal
  droits de succession -
  inheritance tax
  droit de timbre - stamp duty
duplex (nm)
maisonette

E

eau de la ville (nf)
mains water
en propriété libre (adverb)
freehold
expert immobilier (nm)
valuer
expertise (nf)
valuation; survey

F

ferme (nf)
farm; farmhouse
fermette (nf)
small farmhouse
fosse septique (nf)
septic tank

G

gendarmerie (nf)
police station
géomètre (nm)
land surveyor
grange (nf)
barn
grenier (nm)
attic

H

hypothèque (nf)
mortgage; remortgage

I

immobilier (nm)

property
impôt (nm)
tax
  impôt sur les plus-values -
  capital gains tax
  *impôt sur le revenu des
  personnes physiques (IRPP)* -
  income tax
indivision (nf)
joint ownership

L

location (nf)
letting; rented accommodation
longère (nf)
longhouse or long barn

M

mairie (nf)
town hall
maison (nf)
house
  maison bourgeoise - upmarket
  period house
  maison de campagne - country
  cottage
  maison individuelle - detached
  house
  maison jumelée - semi-
  detached house
  maison de maître - classic
  mansion-style house
mandat (nm)
power of attorney
manoir (nm)
country manor
mas (nm)
stone farmhouse

N

notaire (nm)
notary (the lawyer who oversees
the conveyancing)

O

occupant (nmf)
occupier
offre (nf)
offer; bid

P

parcelle de terre (nf)

plot of land
pavillon (nm)
typical modern house
permis de construire (nm)
planning permission
pierre (nf)
stone
  en pierre - built of stone
  pierre de taille - sandstone;
  limestone
pigeonnier (nm)
dovecote
plan (nm)
plan; outline
  plan cadastral - official record
  of site boundaries
  plan d'occupation des sols -
  local authority plan outlining
  the area's planning restrictions
préfecture (nf)
administrative offices of the local
state representative
prélèvement automatique (nm)
direct debit
prêt (nm)
loan
  prêt immobilier
  mortgage
  prêt immobilier à taux fixe
  fixed-rate mortgage
  prêt immobilier à taux variable
  variable-rate mortgage
  *prêt immobilier sans capital
  différé*
  repayment mortgage
promesse de vente (nf)
sales agreement

R

rectorat (nm)
local education authority

S

salle (nf)
room
  salle à manger - dining room
  salle de bain - bathroom
  salle d'eau - shower room
salon (nm)
sitting room
séjour (nm)
living room

société civile immobilière (SCI) (nf)
property-holding company
sous-seing privé (nm)
private agreement
surface habitable (nf)
living space
système d'écoulement des eaux (nm)
drainage

T

taxe (nf)
tax
  taxe d'habitation - residential
  tax
  taxe foncière - property
  ownership tax
  taxe sur la valeur ajoutée (TVA)
  VAT; *toutes taxes comprises
  (TTC)* - VAT included
titre (nm)
title deed
toit (nm)
roof
toiture (nf)
roofing
tout-à-l'égout (nm)
mains drainage
type (T) (nm)
(followed by a number) a
property with a given number of
main rooms
  T4 - four-room flat

U

usufruit (nm)
lifetime interest

V

villa (nf)
detached modern house
vendre (verb)
to sell
  à vendre - for sale
vendeur (nm)
seller
vente (nf)
sale
  vente aux enchères - auction
versement (nm)
payment
volet (nm)
shutter

Directory of Useful Contacts

Accountants

A E A Antipolis Experts Associés
(French equivalent to Chartered
Accountant)
Les Bastides de la Mer, Bâtiment C,
60–62 Route de Nice,
06600 Antibes
Tel: +33 4 92 91 87 81
www.antipolis-experts.com

Arthur D Little France
50 avenue Gauteur
75017 Paris
Tel: +33 1 55 74 29 00
www.adl.com

Blevins Franks Group Limited
Barbican House
26-34 Old Street
London EC1V 9QQ
Tel: 020 7336 1000
www.blevinsfranks.com

Coopers & Lybrand
32 rue Guersant
75017 Paris
Tel: +33 1 45 72 80 80

Ernst & Young
Tour Ernst & Young
11 allée de l'Arche
92037 Paris la Défense Cedex
Tel: +33 1 46 93 60 00

GE Factofrance
Tour Facto
18 rue Hoche
92988 Paris La Défense Cedex
Tel: +33 1 46 35 70 00

Inter Audit
21 bis rue Lord Byron
75008 Paris
Tel: +33 1 43 59 58 73

PKF (Guernsey) Limited
PO Box 296,Suites 13 & 15,
Sarnia House
Le Truchot, St Peter Port
Guernsey GY1 4NA
Tel: 01481 727927

Price Waterhouse
Tour AIG
34 place des Corolles
92908 Paris la Défense Cedex
Tel: +33 1 56 57 58 59

Architects

A4 Architects Associés
64 Cours le Rouzic
33100 Bordeaux
Tel: +33 5 56 32 33 66

Adrian Barrett
(Design and Construction Consultant)
Lower Road, Churchfields
Salisbury SP2 7PN
Tel: 01722 333583
www.adrian-barrett.co.uk

Cedric Mitchell
22a Hill Street
Haverfordwest
Pembrokeshire SA61 1QE
Tel: 01437 762244

David Martyn Architects
rue des Martyrs
24210 La Bachellerie
Tel: +33 5 53 50 57 82

French Architectural Services
Le Maine Arnaud
Perignac
Tel: +33 545 24 08 25
www.french-architectural-
services@netfirms.com

Graham Price
16 Place Mazarin
53500 Ernée
Tel: +33 2 43 05 40 06
pricegraham@aol.com

Iain Stewart
8 rue Pailleron
69004 Lyon
Tel: +33 4 78 30 01 92

James Matthews
71 Hornsey Lane Gardens
London N6 5PA
Tel: 020 8347 5970

Louis Sorridente
808 rue de la Colle
06570 Saint Paul de Vence
Tel: +33 4 93 32 58 26

Pierre M Weingaertner
Le Mas des Couestes
Route de St Canadet
13100 Aix en Provence
Tel: +33 6 60 55 29 74

PSI Sarl
(Chartered Building Surveyor)
Mas Agora
Place Jules Ferry
84440 Robion
Tel: +33 4 90 76 60 65

Robert Lyell Architects
4 Allée des Maronniers
11300 Limoux
Tel: +33 4 68 31 25 66

Banks and Financial Advisors

Abbey National
Les Arcades de Flandre
70 rue Saint Sauveur
59800 Lille
Tel: +33 3 20 18 18 18
www.abbey-national.fr

Anthony & Company
(Overseas Tax Advisors)
11 Villantipolis
473 route des Dolines
06560 Valbonne
Tel: +33 4 93 65 76 24

AXA Mutuelles Unis
William Gérard
5 avenue Tournelli
06600 Antibes
Tel: +33 4 93 34 64 10

Banque Scalbert Dupont
85 Boulevard La Fayette
62100 Calais
Tel: +33 3 21 19 16 30

Barclays France Champs Elysées
6 Rond Point des
Champs Elysées
75008 Paris
Tel: +33 1 56 69 43 43
www.barclays.fr

BML Alain Montagnon
6 Rue Kitchener
22102 Dinan
Tel: +33 2 96 39 04 49
www.bml.fr

Britline Crédit Agricole
5 esplanade Brillaud de Lujardière
14050 Caen Cedex
Tel: +33 2 31 55 67 89

Charles Hamer
87 Park Street
Thame
Oxfordshire OX9 3HX
Tel: 01844 218 956

Conti Financial Services
204 Church Road
Hove, East Sussex, BN3 2DJ
Tel: 0800 970 0985
www.mortgagesoverseas.com

Dun & Bradstreet International
55 avenue de champs pierreux
92012 Nanterre
Tel: +33 141 37 50 00

Eurogroup
Tour Areva
92400 Paris la Défense Cedex
Tel: +33 1 47 96 64 00
www.eurogroup.fr

Fralex
4 Wimpole Street
London W1G 9SH
Tel: 020 7323 0103

French Mortgage Connection
(French Legal Advisors)
20 Park Road Fordingbridge
Hampshire SP6 1EQ
Tel: 01425 653408

HSBC
Private Bank France
117 Ave Champs Elysées
F-75008 Paris
Tel: +33 1 44 86 18 61
www.hsbc.com

John Siddall International
(Financial/Investment Advice)
Parc Innolin, 3 rue du Golf
33700 Bordeaux-Mérignac
Tel: +33 5 56 34 75 51

Kevin Sewell Mortgages
(Investments/Mortgages)
7a Bath Road Business Park
Devizes
Wiltshire SN10 1XA
Tel: 01380 739198

MFS Partners
(Independent Financial Advisers)
Grosvenor House
47 Alma Road
Plymouth
Devon PL3 4HE
Tel: 01752 664777

Porter & Reeves
5 rue Cambon
75001 Paris
Tel: +33 1 42 61 55 77

Siddalls
Lothian House, 22 High Street
Fareham, Hampshire
Tel: 01329 281 157
www.siddalls.net

Templeton Associates
(Mortgage Brokers)
3 Gloucester Street
Bath
BA1 2SE
Tel: 01225 422282

The Spectrum Group (TSG)
43 Rue de Provence
Paris
Tel: +33 1 44 83 64 65
www.spectrum-ifa.com

Builders and Decorators

A Neal
Ombrabols
12700 Capdenac Gare
Tel: +33 5 65 64 81 54

Brit Consulting
29 Rue de Verdun, Tregueux
Cotes d'Armor
Tel: +33 6 23 86 30 21
www.britconsulting.com

Brittany Renovations
(Renovation, Heating,
Construction, Decorating)
4 Langedraou
22580 Plouha
Tel: +33 2 96 20 38 11

Central Construction
115 City Road
Norwich NR1 2HL
Tel: 01603 762804

D Cheeseman
(Carpentry & joinery)
Rouffignac
46600 Montvalent
Tel: +33 5 65 32 56 11

Espace Immobilier
15 bld de La Liberté
BP 51 34701 Lodève Cedex
Tel: +33 4 67 96 42 32

Gedimat
Brunel Frères
ZA La Petrole
127 rue Curie BP116
34400 Lunel
Tel: +33 4 67 71 16 22

James Everett SARL
La Roblinais, Langourla,
Côtes d'Armor
Tel: +33 2 96 30 49 70
james.everett@wanadoo.fr

John Rainforth
Les Puits Neufs
84300 Cavaillon
Tel: +33 4 90 76 28 01

Keith Beaseley & Associates
Les Moellons
4 rue des Noyers
La Bonnière
17250 Geay
Tel: +33 5 46 95 37 02

Le Sabot Bleu
Place de la République
11260 Esperanza
Tel:+33 4 68 74 23 60

Magon Home Improvements
(Interior Decoration and Renovation
Work)
12 rue Corneille
78220 Viroflay
Fax: +33 1 30 24 71 48

Heritage Renovation
(Septic Tanks, General Building,
Sandblasting, Electrics)
1 rue de Moulin
17470 Contré
Tel: +33 5 46 33 32 04

First Realty
(Property Developers)
111 Avenue Victor Hugo
75784 Paris Cedex 16
Tel: +33 1 46 26 23 26

Mark LaTour
11220 Rieux-en-Val
France
Tel: +33 4 68 24 02 94
www.diyinfrance.com

Propriété a la Campagne Ltd
La Poujade,
Vidillace
Tel: +33 5 65 24 37 53
andylow@wanadoo.fr

Société Cévenole de Travaux Publics
(Ground Works)
Cartels
34700 le Bosc
Tel: +33 4 67 44 13 18

Welby
La Bénardais
22100 Léhon
France
Tel: +33 2 96 87 57 37

Building supplies

Brico Lots
Le Jonco
16400 La Couronne
Tel:+33 5 45 67 42 84

CICO Chimney Linings
The Street
Westleton
Saxmundham
Suffolk IP17 3AG
Tel: 01728 648608

Car Hire

Alamo
Brassmill Lane
Bath
BA1 3JE
Tel: 0870 599 3000

Autos Abroad
Weldon House
Corby Gate Business Park
Priors Haw Road
Corby Northants NN17 5JG
Tel: 0870 066 7788

Avis
The Victoria Building
Harbour City
Salford Quays
Manchester M5 2SP
Tel: 0870 6060100

Car Hire Ware House
11 Snowball Road
Kingsnorth
Ashford
Kent TN23 3NF
Tel: 01233 500464

Eurodrive Car Rental
Navigation Yard
Chantry Bridge
Wakefield
WF1 5PQ
Tel: 0870 160 9060

Europcar UK Ltd
Europcar House
Aldenham Road
Bushey
Watford WD23 2QQ
Tel: 01923 811000

Hertz Car Hire
23 Broadwater Road
Welwyn Garden City Hertfordshire
AL7 3BQ
Tel: 01707 331433

Holiday Wheels
Flightform House
Halifax Road
Cressex Business Park
High Wycombe
Bucks
HP12 3SN
Tel: 01494 751515

Nova Rent-a-Car
1 Castle Street
Portaferry
BT22 1NZ
Tel: 028 4272 8189

Regent Car Rental
Tel: 01273 821777
Fax: 01273 821999
res@regent-res.demon.co.uk

Skycars International
Monument House
215 Marsh Road
Pinner
Middlesex HA6 3A
Tel: 0870 789 7789

The Car Hire Group
Weldon House
Corby Gate Business Park
Priors Haw Road
Corby
Northamptonshire N17 5JG
Tel: 0870 758 9945

Carpenters

Dinan Renovation
Le Plessis
22350 Plumaudan
Tel: +33 2 96 86 00 44
www.dinanrenovation.com

Robin Pacey
Leur Vras
2 Heut Pennar Guer
29620 Guimaec
Tel: +33 2 98 67 67 50

Stuart Cook
Valley House
Burne
Bickington
Devon TQ12 6PA
Tel: 01626 824749

Chambers of Commerce

Assemblée des Chambres Françaises de Commerce et d'Industrie (ACFCI)
45 avenue d'Iléna
BP 3003
7573 Paris Cedex 16
Tel: +33 1 40 69 37 00
www.acfci.cci.fr

Paris Chamber of Commerce and Industry
Bourse de Commerce
2 Rue de Viarmes
75001 Paris
Tel: +33 1 53 40 48 05
www.ccip.fr

Currency Exchange

CA Britline
15 esplanade Brillaud
de Laujardière
14050 Caen Cedex
Tel: +33 2 31 55 67 89

Caxton FX
2 Motcomb Street
London
Tel: 0870 751 5048
www.caxtonfx.com

Currencies4Less
160 Brompton Road
Knightsbridge
London SW3 1HW
Tel: 020 7228 7667

Currencies Direct
73-74 High Holborn
London
Tel:0207 813 0332
www.currenciesdirect.com

Currency UK
1 Battersea Bridge
London SW11 3BZ
Tel:020 7738 0777

Escape Currency Plc
Escape House
45 Buckingham Street
Aylesbury, Bucks
Tel: 08000 342 600
www.escapecurrency.com

DIRECTORY

FX Solutions
FX Solutions House
86 High Street
Orpington, Kent, BR6 0JZ
Tel: 0870 900 7007
www.fxsol.com

HIFX
59-60 Thames Street
Windsor
Berkshire SL4 1TX
Tel: 01753 859159

MoneyCorp
2 Sloane Street
Knightsbridge
London SW1X 9LA
Tel: 020 7235 4200

SGM FX
Prince Rupert House
64 Queen Street, London EC4R 1AD
Tel: 020 7778 0123
www.sgm-fx.com

Tom Wells
Le Moulin à Vent
16380 Charras
Tel: +33 5 45 23 05 09

Estate Agents and Developers

Agences-immobilieres.com
www.agences-immobilieres.com

Fédération Nationale des Agents Immobiliers (FNAIM)
129 rue du faubourg Saint-Honoré
75047 Paris Cedex 08
Tel: +33 1 44 20 77 00
www.fnaim.fr

Fédération Nationale des Promoteurs Constructeurs
106 rue de l'Université
75007 Paris
Tel: +33 1 47 05 44 36
www.fnpc.fr

Fédération of Overseas Property Developers, Agents and Consultants (FOPDAC)
Lacey House
St Clare Business Park
Holly Road
Hampton Hill
Middlesex TW12 1QQ
Tel: 020 8941 5588
www.fopdac.com

Exhibitions and Seminars

Buying Your Dream Home in France
(Seminars in the South West)
20 High Street, Honiton
Devon EX14 1PU
Tel: 01404 47830
www.homebuyingfrance.co.uk

Homes Overseas Exhibitions
(28 exhibitions each year, held in the UK, Scandinavia and Ireland)
207 Providence Square
Mill Street
London SE1 2EW
Tel: 020 7939 9888

UNIBAEL
(Office space)
5 Boulevard Malesherbes
75008 Paris
Tel: +33 1 53 43 73 05

Vive La France
(Annual Show; 21 – 23 Jan, 2005)
Grand Hall, London Olympia
Tel: 0870 902 0444

World of Property/ Focus on France
(Three exhibitions each year in the UK)
1 Commercial Rd
Eastbourne
East Sussex BN21 3XQ
Tel: 01323 726040

Government Bodies

Department of Social Services Overseas Branch
EU Office
Benton Park Road
Longbenton
Newcastle-Upon-Tyne NE98 1ZZ

France Embassy
58 Knightsbridge
London SW1X 7JT
Tel: 020 7073 1000
www.ambafrance-uk.org

French Chamber of Commerce
21 Dartmouth Street
London SW1
Tel: 020 7304 4040
www.ccfgb.co.uk

House Inspection, Gardening and Cleaning

Azur Security
497 route de Nice
06560 Valbonne
Tel: +33 4 93 12 18 79

Brittany Home Care Service
4 Oakfields
Walton-on-Thames
Surrey KT12 1EG
Tel: 01932 247681

Charente Caretakers
Chemin de la Perche
16170 Vaux-Rouillac
Tel: +33 5 45 96 56 41

Chevalier Conservation
(Cleaning and Restoring Carpets and Rugs and Antiques)
64 bld de la Mission-Marchand
92400 Courbevoie
Tel: +33 1 47 88 41 41

Entreprise Christian Audibert
La Selle d'Andon
06750 Andon
Tel: +33 4 93 60 20 01

Les Jardins Verts
Garden Maintenance & Landscaping
Tel: +33 2 96 82 73 65
richardneol@wanadoo.fr

Marine Security
41 Burnley Road
Newton Abbott
Devon TQ12 1YD
Tel: 01626 365282

Vendée Rendez-vous
Le Vicariat
32 rue de la Venise Verte
85420 Oulmes
Tel: +33 2 51 52 49 09

Insurance

Agence Eaton
(Continent Assurances)
BP 30 1 Parc Doarel Molac
56610 Arradon
Tel: +33 2 97 40 80 20

Agence Tredinnick
(Household, Health, Travel, Mortgage)
12 Rue Dupy
16100 Cognac
Tel: +33 5 45 82 42 93

Andrew Copeland Group
230 Portland Rd
London SE25 4SL
Tel: 020 8656 2544

Anglo-French Underwriters
25 rue de Liège
75008 Paris
Tel: +33 1 44 70 71 00

DIRECTORY

Cabinet F X Bordes
11 rue des Desportes
BP 05, 24150 Lalinde
Tel: +33 5 53 61 03 50

Chubb Insurance Company of Europe
16 avenue Matignon
75008 Paris
Tel: +33 1 45 61 73 00

Eric Blair
33 Bld Princesse Charlotte
BP 265 MC
98005 Monaco Cedex
Tel: +37 7 93 50 99 66 (Monaco)

European Benefits Administrators
28 rue Momogador
75009 Paris
Tel: +33 1 42 81 97 00

HIFX Insurance Services Ltd
59-60 Thames Street
Windsor, SL4 1TX
Tel: 01753 859159
www.hifxinsure.com

Insurance for Homes Abroad
28 Waterloo Street
Weston-super-Mare
Tel: 01934 424 040
www.insuranceforhomesabroad.co.uk

**Lark Insurance Broking Group
(Home Insurance)**
Wigham House,
Wakering Road
Barking,
Essex IG11 8PJ
Tel: 020 8557 2300

Lloyds of London
4 rue des Petits Pères
75002 Paris
Tel: +33 1 42 60 43 43

**London & European Title Insurance
Services Ltd**
5th Floor Minerva House
Valpy Street
Reading RG1 1AQ
Tel: 0118 957 5000

MMA Assurance
29 Ave Victor Hugo
29270 Carhaixt
Tel: +33 2 98 93 04 03
johan.ollivier@mma.fr

Property Plus
La Tour du Guet
28/30 Place d'Armes
Calais
Tel: +33 3 21 967 777
info@propertyplusinsurance.com

**Saga Services Ltd
(Holiday Home Insurance)**
The Saga Building
Middelburg Square
Folkestone, Kent CT20 1AZ
Tel: 01303 771111

Schofield's Holiday Home Insurance
Trinity House, 7 Institute Street
Bolton, Lancs
Tel: 01204 365 080
www.schofields.ltd.uk

Tyler and Co
12 rue de la Paix
75002 Paris
Tel: +33 1 42 61 63 31

Woodham Group Ltd
Plas Kenrhos, Burry Port
Carmarthenshire SA16 0DG
Tel: 01554 835252

Interior Design

A S Décor
Plélan le Petit
Tel: +33 6 79 21 93 99
aevans@wanadoo.fr

Chaix Décoration
8 rue Paul Deroulède
06000 Nice
Tel: +33 4 93 88 52 02

Home Comforts
Chez Deschamps
Route de Medillac
16210 Chalais
Tel: +33 5 45 98 00 97

Hestia-Domus Decoration
11 boulevard Carnot
06000 Nice
Tel: +33 4 93 56 10 43

Ikea (Marseille)
Tel: +33 8 25 82 68 26

Ikea (Paris)
Tel: +33 8 25 82 68 26

LLa Poterie Sourdive
Le Village
26270 Cliousclat
Tel: +33 4 75 63 05 69

Les Toiles de Mayenne
(Interior Decoration, Fabrics)
9 rue Mézière
75006 Paris
Tel: +33 1 45 48 70 77

Loft
(Interior Designers)
25-27 rue de la Buffa
06000 Nice
Tel: +33 4 93 16 09 09

Madame Taillardat
44 avenue Marceau
75008 Paris
Tel: +33 1 47 20 1712

Manuel Canovas
(Interior Decoration, Fabrics)
223 rue Saint-Honoré
75001 Paris
Tel: +33 1 58 62 33 50

Manufacture des Lauriers
Avenue de la Foux
83670 Varages
Tel: +33 4 94 77 64 79

Mondo
(Japanese mattress specialist)
85 bld Beaumarchais
75003 Paris
Tel: +33 1 48 04 04 02

Raineri Décoration
16 rue Biscarra
06000 Nice
Tel: +33 4 93 80 27 89

Shogun
71 avenue des Ternes
75017 Paris
Tel: +33 1 40 68 07 61

Société des Ocres de France
BP 18
526 avenue Victor Hugo
84401 Apt Vaucluse Cedex
France
Tel: +33 4 90 74 63 82

Souleiado
39 rue Proudhon
13150 Tarascon
Tel: +33 4 90 91 08 80

Spearpoint Interior Design
45 Northumberland Place
London
Tel: 0207 221 5339

Urban Home Design (CINNA)
Angle 123 rue d'Antibes
06400 Cannes
Tel: +33 4 93 68 32 20

Woodstock Fires Ltd
3 Station Road
Heathfield
East Sussex
TN21 8LD
Tel: 01435 868686

Kitchen Supplies

Cuisine & Cuisinier
1570 chemin Saint Bernard
06220 Vallauris
Tel: +33 4 92 95 37 37

Godin
(Stoves & Hobs)
Sarl Bauris & Fils
764 route de Grenoble
06200 Nice
Tel: +33 4 93 08 11 08

Mr Pine
The Old Sorting Office
Maple Road
Bramhall
Stockport SK7 2DH
Tel: 0161 439 0055

Old Image
451 Gloucester Road
Horfield
Bristol BS7 8TZ
Tel: 0117 975 4434

Woodstock Fires Ltd
(Delivers to FR/UK)
3 Station Road
Heathfield
East Sussex TN21 8LD
Tel: 01435 868686

Language Services

Accelerated Learning Systems
50 Aylesbury Road
Aston Clinton, Aylesbury
Bucks HP22 5AH
Tel: 01296 631177

Accent Français
7 rue de Verdun
34000 Montpellier
Tel: +33 4 67 58 12 68

Accord
14 bld Poissonnière
75009 Paris
Tel: +33 1 55 33 52 33

Actilangue
2-4 rue Alexis Mossa
06000 Nice
Tel: +33 4 93 96 33 84

Alliance Française
101 bld Raspail
75270 Paris Cedex 06
Tel: +33 1 42 84 90 00

British Institute in Paris
9-11 rue de Constantine
75007 Paris
Tel: +33 1 44 11 73 73

Centre de Pratique de Langues Étrangères
58 rue de l'Hôpital Militaire
59000 Lille
Tel: +33 3 28 53 00 28

Clac
10 Shelford Park Avenue
Great Shelford
Cambridgeshire CB2 5LU
Tel: 01223 240340
www.clac.org.uk

Département des Étudiants Étrangers
Université Charles-de-Gaulle-Lille 3 BP
59653 Villeneuve-d'Ascq Cedex
Tel: +33 3 20 41 60 00
www.univ-lille3.fr

Documentation and Translation Services
Oakmeade
St Michael's Road, Myerscough
Preston, Lancs
Tel: 01995 640 002

École des 3 Ponts
Château de Matel
42300 Roanne
Tel: +33 4 77 71 53 00

École Yvelines Langues
2a rue Ducastel
78100 Saint Germain en Laye
Tel: +33 1 30 61 02 08

Eurotalk Limited
315-317 New Kings Road
London SW6 4RF
Tel: 020 7371 7711

French Language Courses
Alexandra and John Waddington
16110 La Rochefoucauld
Tel: +33 5 45 63 53 07

ICT (Intermédiare Consultante Traduction)
Castel Briasse
La Briasse
19310 Ayen
Tel: +33 5 55 25 21 66

IDIOM
4 Boulevard de Cimiez
Nice
Tel: +33 4 93 92 60 90
www.idiom.fr

Janet O'Brian
La Croix Lagrise
35120 Cherrueix
Tel: +33 2 99 80 86 55

La Cardère
Institut de la Langue Française
71580 Frontenaud
Tel: +33 3 85 74 83 11

Language in Provence
L'Oustalet
Fontaine de Guby
84490 Saint Saturnin
Tel: +33 4 90 75 56 47

Lutece langue
31 rue Etienne Marcel
75001 Paris
Tel: +33 1 42 36 31 51

OISE Intensive Language Schools
(French courses in Paris)
OISE House
Binsey Lane
Oxford OX2 OEY
Tel: 0845 601 1157

Promolangues
8 rue Blanche
75009 Paris
Tel: +33 1 42 85 19 45

Legal Experts

Conseil Supérieur du Notariat
31 rue du Général Foy
75008 Paris
Tel: +33 1 44 90 30 00
www.notaires.fr

Letting Specialists

French Magazine
Merricks Media Ltd
3/4 Riverside Court
Lower Bristol Rd
Bath BA2 3DZ
Tel: 01225 786800

French Life
Kerry House, Kerry Street
Horsforth Leeds LS18 4AW
Tel: 0870 444 8877

Meon Villas
Meon House
College Street
Petersfield GU32 3JN
Tel: 01730 230200

Quality Villas
46 Lower Kings Road
Berkhamsted
Hertfordshire HP4 2AA
Tel: 01442 870055

Something Special
Field House
Station Approach
Harlow, Essex CM20 2EW
Tel: 020 8939 5137

Vacances en Campagne
Manor Courtyard
Bignor, Pulborough
West Sussex RH20 1QD
Tel: 01798 869461

Est Paul Gee
(Kitchens, Cookers Central Heating)
Centre Commercial
32410 Castera-Verduzan
Tel: +33 5 62 68 12 48

Pet Transportation

Airpets Oceanic
Willowslea Farm
Spout Lane
Stanwell Moor
Staines
Middlesex
TW19 6BW
01753 685571

Animal Airlines
35 Beatrice Avenue
Manchester
Lancashire
M18 7JU
0161 2234035

Animal Inn
Dover Road
Ringwould
Deal
Kent
CT14 8HH
01304 373597

Chilworth Pet Exports/Chilworth Kennels
Lordswood Lane
Chilworth
Southampton SO16 7JG
02380 766876

Pet Travel Services
24 Cruston Street
Dunfermline
Fife, KY12 7QW
01383 722819

Skymaster Air Cargo
Room 15
Building 305
Cargo Terminal, Manchester Airport
M90 5PY
0161 4362190

The Dog House International Kennels and Cattery
Camino De La Sabatera 5
Teulada/Moraira
Alicante, Spain
+34 965 741302

Transfur
19 Dean Close
Salisbury Green
Southampton SO31 7TT
01489 588072

Property Search

Brittany Properties
2 rue de la Boissière
22810 Belle
Isle en Terre
Brittany
Tel: +33 2 96 43 09 94
e-mail: sales@brittanyproperties.com

Charente-Maritime French-Home-Service
Tel: +33 5 46 94 48 59
rsayner@club-internet.fr

French Discoveries
92 Oxford Road
Mosely B13 9SQ
Tel: 0121 4491155

Homes in Real France
3 Delgany Villas
Plymouth PL6 8AG
Tel: 01752 771777
sales@hirf.co.uk

La Foncière Charentaise Sarl
14 bis Grande Rue
16140 Aigre
Tel: +33 5 45 21 78 38

Live France Group
Pavail
32100 Condom
Tel: +33 5 62 28 02 64
www.livefrancegroup.com

Property Centre
42 California Road
Longwell Green
Bristol BS30 9XL
Tel: 0870 444 2078
www.overseasproperties.com

The Mediterranean Property Agent
26 High Street
Sevenoaks Kent TN13 1HX
Tel: 01732 451144
www.tmpa.co.uk

South Loire Property Search
La Gouarie
Bossay sur Claise 37290
Indre et Loire
Tel: +33 2 47 94 44 20
www.southloire
propertysearch.com

Removals and Haulage

Anglo French Removals
Invicta Works
Farleigh Lane
Barming, Maidstone
Kent ME16 9LX
Tel: 01622 679004

Armishaws
3 Alfred's Way
Wincanton Business Park
Wincanton
Somerset BA9 9RT
Tel: 01963 34065

Associated Moving Services
1,2 & 3 Pelham Yard
High Street
Seaford
East Sussex BN25 1PQ
Tel: 01323 892934

Bishop's Move Group
Harcourt Street
Off Southern Street
Manchester
Lancashire M28 3GN
Tel: 0845 666 3322

Bradshaw International
Centrepoint
Marshall Steven's Way
Westing House Road
Trafford Park
Manchester M17 1PP
Tel: 0161 877 5555

Brookfields
Cesncoch
Nr Welshpool
Powys SY21 OAQ
Tel: 01938 810 649

Burke Brothers
Foxs Lane
Wolverhampton
West Midlands WV1 1PA
Tel: 01902 714555

Callington Carriers International Removers
Valentine Road
Callington
Cornwall PL17 7DF
Tel: 0157 938 3210

D Todd Removals
Mills Road
Chiltern Industrial Estate
Sudbury, Suffolk
Tel: 01787 319 777
www.todd-removals.co.uk

David Dale Removals
Dale House
Forest Moor Road
Harrogate HG5 8LT
Tel: 01423 867788

Eardley's Removals and Storage
Unit 2 First Avenue
Crewe CW1 6BG
Tel: 01270 588225

Farrer & Fenwick Removals
Bridge House
Bridge Street
Walton-on-Thames
Surrey KT12 1AL
Tel: 01932 253737

F&N Worldwide Removals
Unit 14, Autumn Park
Dysart Road Grantham
Lincolnshire NG31 7DD
Tel: 01476 579210

Franklins Removals Ltd
112 Streetly Lane
Sutton Coldfield
B74 4TB
Tel: 0121 353 7263
www.franklinsremovals.com

French Connexion
The Old Vicarage
Leigh, Sherborne
Dorset DT9 6HL
Tel: 01935 872222

Greens Removals Ltd
Tomo Industrial Estate Creeting Road
Stowmarket
Suffolk IP14 5AY
Tel: 01449 613053

H AppleYard & Sons
Denby Way
Hellaby Industrial Estate
Rotherham, Yorkshire S66 8HR
Tel: 01709 549718

Hambleton Removals and Storage
Capp House, 96d South End
Croydon CRO 1DQ
Tel: 020 8686 1197

Henry's Table
Newnham Court Farm
Bearsted Road
Maidstone
Kent ME14 5LH
Tel: 01622 734211

Home to Home
Units W1 & W2, Hazel Road Woolston
Southampton
SO19 7GB
Tel: 0800 783 4602

Henry Johnson Ltd
(Customs and Shipping Agent)
5 rue Jacques Kablé
75018 Paris
Tel: +33 1 46 07 94 39

Kidds Services
International House
Kidd Park Cliff Road
Hornsea, Hull
East Yorkshire
HU18 1JB
Tel: 0800 252220

David Powell
The Elephant House
Deykin Avenue
Birmingham B6 7BH
Tel: 0121 326 6008

Langdon Removals Bristol
163 South Liberty Lane
Bristol
BS3 2TL
Tel: 0117 963 7404

Martell's International Removers
Charlwood Road
East Grinstead RH19 2HG
Tel: 01342 321303

Metro Removals
Orion Way
Kettering
Northants N15 6NL
Tel: 01536 519696

Monarch UK & International Movers
Grove Barns
North Road
South Ockendon RM15 6SR
Tel: 0800 954 6474

The Personal Moving Service Ltd
Tel: +33 2 33 35 31 80
barry@tpmsl.com
www.tpmsl.com

Reflex Move
Castlegate Business Park
Old Sarum
Sailsbury SP4 6QX
Tel: 01722 414350

Richman-Ring Ltd
Eurolink Way
Sittingbourne
Kent ME10 3HH
Tel: 01795 427151

Simpsons of Sussex
Units 1-3 Ditchling Common
Industrial Estate
Burgess Hill, Hussocks
Sussex BN6 8SL
Tel: 0800 027 1958

TBA
2 Strawberry Hill
Bloxham, Banbury
Oxon OX15 4NW
Tel: 01295 720902

Trans Euro Worldwide Movers
47 Route Principal du Port
92238 Gennevilliers Cedex
Tel: +33 1 34 48 97 97

White and Company
23 Invincible Road
Farnbrough
Hampshire GU14 7QU
Tel: 01252 541674

Solicitors and Legal Advisors

James Bennett & Co Solicitors
Nightingale House
Brighton Road, Crawley
West Sussex RH10 6AE
TEL: 01293 544044

Blake Lapthorn
(Solicitors)
Holbrook House
14 Great Queen Street
London WC2B 5DG
Tel: 020 7430 1709

France Legal
Chalkland, The Heath
Tattingstone, Ipswich, Suffolk
Tel: 01473 327 759
www.french-lawyers.com

French Lawyers
1 Place du Palais
Nice
Tel: 0870 808 0079
www.french-lawyers.com

French Mortgage Connection
20 Park Road, Fordingbridge
Hampshire SP6 1EQ
Tel: 01425 653408

French Property Law
69 Wright Way
Bristol
Tel: 07949 588 856
www.frenchpropertylaw.com

John Howell & Co
(International Lawyers)
The Old Glassworks
22 Endell Street, Covent Garden
London WC2H 9AD
Tel: 020 7420 0400

Kingsfords
(Solicitors)
5/7 Bank Street
Ashford
Kent TN23 1BZ
Tel: 01233 624545

Liliane Levasseur-Hills
69 Pullman Lane
Godalming
Surrey GU7 IYB
Tel: 01483 424303

MB Law
King Charles House
King Charles Croft
Leeds LS1 6LA
Tel: 0113 242 4444

Mortgages for Business
London Office
53-55 High Street
Sevenoaks TN13 1JF
Tel: 01732 471600

Pannone & Partners
(Solicitors)
123 Deansgate
Manchester M3 2BU
Tel: 0161 909 3000

Pretty Solicitors
Elm House
25 Elm Street, Ipswich
Suffolk IP1 2AD
Tel: 01473 232121

Russell-Cooke
2 Putney Hill
London SW15 6AB
Tel: 020 8789 9111

Sean O'Connor & Co
(Bilingual Solicitors)
2 River Walk
Tonbridge, Kent TN9 1DT
Tel: 01732 365 378
seanoconnorco@aol.com327

Simone Paissoni
(In France for France)
22 avenue Notre Dame
06000 Nice
Tel: +33 4 93 62 94 95
spaissoni@magic.fr

Stephen Smith Solicitors
(France Limited)
161 Cemetery Road
Ipswich IP4 2HL
Tel: 01473 437186

Taylors
The Red Brick House
28-32 Trippet Lane
Sheffield S1 4EL
Tel: 0114 276 6767

Thrings Townsend
(Solicitors)
Midland Bridge
Bath BA1 2HQ
Tel: 01225 340000

Turner & Co
(Solicitors)
59 Charlotte Street
St Paul's Square
Birmingham
B3 1PX
Tel: 0121 200 1612

TVEF (UK) Ltd.
(Legal services & French Property
services)
4 Raleigh House
Admirals Way
London E14 9SN
Tel: 020 7515 8660

Surveyors

AlpineSpace Ltd
BP 43
74400 Argentière
Tel: +33 4 50 54 22 81

Burrows-Hutchinson
11 rue du Parc
56160 Ploerdut
Tel: +33 2 97 39 45 53

Curchod & Co.
54 Church Street
Weybridge, Surrey KP13 8DP
Tel: 01932 823630

James Latter
(Expert Immobilier)
Couvrigny
14700 Saint Pierre du Bû
Tel: +33 2 31 90 17 70

PSI Sarl
Mas Agora
Place Jules Ferry
84440 Robion
Tel: +33 4 90 76 60 65

Red Field Property Care
Le Champ Rouge, Bion
Mortain
www.red-field.co.uk
Tel: +33 233 49 57 89

Smith-Woolley & Perry
Chartered Surveyors
130 Sandgate Road
Folkstone CT20 2BW
Tel: 01303 226622

Swimming Pools

A B Piscines Ltd
11 Rue André Pichon
24340 Mareuil
Tel: +33 5 53 56 68 87

Bakewell Pools Ltd.
38 Bagley Wood Road
Kennington
Oxford OX1 5LY
Tel: 01865 735205

Claire Pernod-Fantini
119 bd Sadi Carnot
06110 Le Cannet
Tel: +33 4 92 99 01 00

Clearwater Swimming Pools Ltd
The Studio
81 Langley Close
Headington
Oxford OX3 7DB
Tel: 01865 766112

Christal Pools
139 Enville Street
Stourbridge
West Midlands DY8 3TD
Tel: 01384 440990

JW Green Swimming Pools Ltd
Regency House
88a Great Brick Kiln Street Graiseley
Wolverhampton WV3 0PU
Tel: 01902 427709

London Swimming Pool Company
138 Replingham Road
London SW18 5LL
Tel: 020 8874 0414

Peter Joyce Poolstore UK Ltd
Monks Brook House
Nutburn Road
North Baddesly
Southampton
SO52 9BG
Tel: 0845 128 4373

Piscines du Canal
Michel Roques
56 av Foch
34500 Béziers
Tel: +33 4 99 43 08 69

Transaqua
60 Couers Reverseaux
1700 Saintes
Tel: +33 5 46 97 25 84
www.transaqua-piscines.com
transaqua@wanadoo.fr

Televisions

Big Dish Satellite
Mouriol Milhaguet
87440 Marvel
Tel: +33 5 55 78 72 98
www.bigdishsat.com

French-Help
32140 Chelan
Tel: +33 5 62 66 08 25

Susat UK
37 Spencer Mews
London W6 8PB
Tel: 0845 451 3133

TV5 (UK) Medialink
King's House
Bristol BS99 5HR
Tel: 0117 954 9189

TV5 (France)
19 rue Cognacq-Jay
75007 Paris Cedex 07
Tel: +33 1 44 18 55 55

UBALDI
272 avenue de la Californie
06002 Nice
Tel: +33 4 93 18 80 88

Tourism

Maison de la France
178 Piccadilly
London W1J 9AL
Tel: 090 6824 4123
www.franceguide.com

Travel – Air

Air France
Terminal 2, London Heathrow Airport
Hounslow
Middlesex TW6 1ET
Tel: 0845 0845 111
Tickets: 10 Warwick Street
London W1B 5LZ

Aurigny Air Services
Southampton International Airport
Southampton
Hampshire SO18 2NL
Tel: 01481 822886
www.aurigny.com

DIRECTORY

Britannia Airways Ltd
London Luton Airport
Luton
Bedforshire LU2 9ND
Tel: 0870 6076757/
01582 424155

British Airways Travel Shops
213 Piccadilly
London W1J 9HQ
Tel: 0845 6060747

British Midland
Cargo Building
552 Shoreham Road East Hounslow
Middlesex TW6 3EU
Tel: 0870 2400203
www.bmicargo.com

EasyJet Airline Plc
Easyland
London Luton Airport
Bedfordshire LU2 9LS
Tel: 0870 600 0000
www.easyjet.com

FlyBe
Jack Walker House
Exeter International Airport
Exeter EX5 2HL
Tel: 0871 7000123

Genie Travel
60 Lansdowne Street
Hove Sussex
Tel: 01273 770453

LyddairLondon Ashford Airport
Lyddair, Kent TN29 9QL
Tel: 01797 320000

Ryanair
Dublin Airport
County Dublin
Tel: 0871 246 0000

Travel – Coach

Eurolines
52 Grosvenor Gardens
Victoria
London SW1W OAU
Tel: 0870 808080

Travel – Rail

Euro Tunnel
Contacts Centre
St Martin's Plain
Cheriton Parc
Folkestone
Kent CT19 4QD
Tel: 0870 5353535

Eurostar (Customer Services)
3rd Floor, Kent House
81 Station Road
Ashford, Kent TN23 1AP
Tel: 0870 518 6186

Eurostar (Head Office)
Eurostar House
Waterloo Station,12 Lower Road
London SE1 8SE
Tel: 0870 518 6186

Rail Europe Ltd
34 Tower View
Kings Hill
West Malling
Kent ME19 4ED
Tel: 0870 584 8848
www.raileurope.co.uk

SNCF
23 avenue de la Porte d'Aubervilliers
75018 Paris
Tel: +33 8 91 36 20 20

Travel – Sea

Brittany Ferries
Milbay Docks
Plymouth
Devon PL1 3EW
Tel: 0870 536 0360

Condor Ferries Ltd
Condor House
New Harbour Road
South Hamworthy
Poole
Dorset BH15 4AJ
Tel: 0845 345 2000

Ferry Savers
International Life
Leisure Ltd
Kerry House
Kerry Street
Horsforth
Leeds LS18 4AW
Tel: 0870 990 8492

France Canterbury
29/30 Palace Street
Canterbury
Kent CT1 2DZ
Tel: 01227 454508

Hoverspeed Ltd
International Hoverport
Dover, Kent, CT17 9TG
Tel: 0870 524 0241

Irish Ferries
Corn Exchange Building
Brunswick Street
Liverpool, L2 7TP
Tel: 0870 5171717

Norfolkline
Norfolk House
South Osborne Way
Off Western Access Road
Immingham Dock
North East Lincs DN40 2QA
Tel: 01469 570900

P&O Ferries
Channel House
Channel View Road
Dover Kent CT17 9TJ
Tel: 01304 863000

Seafrance
Whitfield Court
Honeywood Close
Whitfield
Dover Kent CT16 3PX
Tel: 01304 828300

Utilities

Electricité de France (EDF)
(Information)
Tel: +33 0 58 13 70 00
www.edf.fr

Gaz de France
23 rue Philibert Delorme
75840 Paris Cedex 17
Tel: +33 1 47 54 20 20
www.gazdefrance.com

Web Hosting

Financial Systems Limited
www.frenchpropertylinks.com
dfs@financialsystems.co.uk

Sam Mooney
(Web Design)
11220 Riex-en-Val
France
Tel: +33 4 68 24 02 94
www.fortheloveofwork.com

Stickland Web Studio
83 North Trade Road
Battle, East Sussex TN33 0HN
Tel: 01424 775021
www.sticklandweb.co.uk
mike@sticklandweb.co.uk

Turn page for a full details of all the estate agents featured in this guide.

DIRECTORY

Index of Agents

Code	Name and address	Contact details
AMR	Agence Maison René 19 The Yews, Horndean, Portsmouth, PO8 OBH	02392 599 409 www.agencemaisonrene.com, derek@agencemaisonrene.com
AZP	Azur Properties Villa Azur Corniche Supérieure Saut du Loup, 83380 Les Issambres Saint-Maxime	+33 689 15 50 62 www.azurproperties.com, info@azurproperties.com
BRE	Breton Homes 44 Rue Val, 22400 Lamballe	+33 296 50 19 97 www.bretonhomes.com, rendezvous@bretonhomes.com
BUR	Burgundy 4U Martoret 71960	+33 385 33 41 46 www.burgundy4u.com
CHA	Châteaux & Châteaux 54 Rue Taitbout, 75009 Paris	+33 149 95 99 01 www.chateauxetchateaux.com, sbg@chateauxetchateaux.com
CON	Conseil Patrimoine 52 Boulevard Victor Hugo, 06200 Nice	+33 497 03 03 33 www.france-immobilier.com
DAK	David King & Associates International Property Consultants, 76 Gosberton Road, London, SW12 8LQ	0208 673 6800 www.dkassociates.co.uk, web@dkassociates.co.uk
DEM	Demeures de France 41 Rue Barrault, 75013 Paris	+33 144 17 95 40 www.demeures.com, demeures@demeures.com
DEV	Devon International 16 Rue Pasteur, 55700 Stenay	+33 329 80 69 75 www.relocatefrance.com, howa35@aol.com
FPS	The French Property Shop Elwick Club, Church Road, Ashford, TN23 1RD	01233 666 902 www.frenchpropertyshop.com
FRA	Francophiles Ltd Barker Chambers, Barker Road, Maidstone, Kent, ME16 8SF	01622 688 165 www.francophiles.co.uk, sales@francophiles.co.uk
FRO	Immobilier 3 Frontières 18 Avenue Clemençeau, Mulhouse, 68100	+33 389 46 33 60 www.immobilier3frontieres.fr, info@immobilier3frontieres.fr
HDG	Agence Immobilière Herman de Graaf Le Bourg, 24800 Saint-Jean-de-Cole	+33 553 62 38 03 www.immobilier-dordogne.com
HIN	A Home in Normandy	01263 861 760 www.ahin.info, mail@ahin.info

Code	Name and address	Contact details
HRF	Homes in Real France 3 Delgany Villas, Plymouth, Devon, PL6 8AG	01752 771 777 www.hirf.co.uk, sales@hirf.co.uk
JOS	Josselin Immobilier 19 Rue Olivier de Clisson, 56120 Josselin	+33 397 75 64 78 www.frenchpropertysales.com, info@frenchpropertysales.com
KAY	Kay Dream Homes 6 Place St Pierre, Gémozac, Charente-Maritime	+33 681 74 98 46 www.kaydreamhomes.com.fr christopher.kay@wanadoo.fr
LAF	L'Affaire Française 25 Grand Rue, 16200 Jarnac	+33 545 81 76 79 www.french-property-net.com enquiries@french-property-net.com
LAT	Latitudes French Property Agents Grosvenor House, 1 High Street, Edgware, Middlesex, HA8 7TA	0208 951 5155 www.latitudes.co.uk, sale@latitudes.co.uk
LAV	Lavender Homes 25 Derwent Avenue, Kingston Vale, London, SW15 3R	0208 287 2459 www.lavenderhomes.co.uk, info@lavenderhomes.co.uk
PAP	Papillon Properties Woodside Cottage, Catmere End, Saffron Walden, CB11 4XG	01799 527 809 www.papillon-properties.com, samanthalear@papillon-properties.com
ROU	Agence Rousseau Immobilier 22 Rue Baron Quinart, 08000 Charleville-Mézières	+33 324 56 10 10 www.rousseau-immo.com contact@rousseau-immo.com
RUR	Rural Retreats Montpelier House, 99 Montpelier Road, Brighton, BN1 3BE	01273 747 127 www.le-guide.com, ruralretreats@le-guide.com
SIF	Sifex 1 Doneraile Street, London, SW6 6EL	0207 384 1200 www.sifex.co.uk, info@sifex.co.uk
SUC	Success Immobilier 28 Rue d'Hesdin, 62130 Saint-Pol-sur-Ternoise	+33 321 04 58 46 www.successimmobilier.com,
VDR	Agence Vallée des Rois 23 Rue de l'Hôtel de Ville, 49250 Beaufort-en-Vallée	+33 241 45 22 22 www.loireproperty.com, agency@loireproperty.com
VEF	VEF (UK) Ltd 5 Greenwich View Place,Millharbour, London, E14 9NN	0207 515 8660 www.vefuk.com, info@vefuk.com
VIA	Vialex International 47470 Beauville	+33 553 95 46 24 www.vialex.com

Index

Acknowledgements

Brittany

Bob Pearson, Breton Homes,
Tel: +33 2 96 50 19 97

Trudi Williams & Nicola,
Josselin Immobilier,
Tel: +33 2 97 75 64 78

Karine Chaumont,
Francophiles,
Tel: 01622 688 165

Carolyn Cohen & Françoise
Bonner, Latitudes,
Tel: 020 8951 5155

A House in Brittany,
Tel: 01903 202 272

Ian Fowler, Aims
International,
Tel: +33 243 04 26 99

Adam Harrison,
Harrison Stone,
Tel: 01798 342 776

Normandy

Derek Grimshaw,
Agence Maison René,
Tel: 023 9259 9409

Karine Chaumont,
Francophiles,
Tel: 01622 688 165

Carolyn Cohen & Françoise
Bonner, Latitudes,
Tel: 020 8951 5155

Sarah Francis, Sifex,
Tel: 0207 384 1200

Nicholas Stallwood &
Stephen Small,
French Property Shop,
Tel: 01233 666 902

A Home in Normandy,
Tel: 01263 861 760

Nord-pas-de Calais

Karine Chaumont,
Francophiles,
Tel: 01622 688 165

Carolyn Cohen & Françoise
Bonner, Latitudes,
Tel: 020 8951 5155

Sarah Francis, Sifex,
Tel: 0207 384 1200

Nicholas Stallwood &
Stephen Small, French
Property Shop,
Tel: 01233 666 902

Karine Beauvallet,
Demeures de France,
Tel: +33 1 44 17 95 40

Success Immobilier,
Tel: +33 3 21 04 58 46

Île de France

Derek Grimshaw,
Agence Maison René,
Tel: 023 9259 9409

Siegfried Boulard-Gervaise,
Châteaux & Châteaux,
Tel: +33 149 95 99 01

Karine Beauvallet,
Demeures de France,
Tel: +33 1 44 17 95 40

David King, David King &
Associates,
Tel: 020 8673 6800

Sarah Francis, Sifex,
Tel: 0207 384 1200

Nicholas Stallwood &
Stephen Small,
French Property Shop,
Tel: 01233 666 902

Beth Edgell & Paul Owen,

VEF UK,
Tel: 020 7515 8660

Champagne-Ardenne

Nicholas Stallwood &
Stephen Small,
French Property Shop,
Tel: 01233 666 902

Derek Grimshaw,
Agence Maison René,
Tel: 023 9259 9409

Sarah Francis, Sifex,
Tel: 0207 384 1200

Karine Beauvallet,
Demeures de France,
Tel: +33 1 44 17 95 40

Beth Edgell & Paul Owen,
VEF UK,
Tel: 020 7515 8660

Rousseau Immobilier,
Tel: +33 324 56 10 10

David & Marian Howard,
Devon International,
Tel: +33 329 80 69 75

Immo France,
Tel: +33 3 24 33 32 86

Alsace, Lorraine, Franche-Comté

Karine Beauvallet, Demeures
de France,
Tel: +33 1 44 17 95 40

Nicholas Stallwood &
Stephen Small,
French Property Shop, Tel:
01233 666 902

Sarah Francis, Sifex,
Tel: 0207 384 1200

Derek Grimshaw,
Agence Maison René,

Tel: 023 9259 9409

David & Marian Howard,
Devon International,
Tel: +33 329 80 69 75

Immobilier 3 Frontières,
Tel: +33 389 46 33 60

Moret Real Estate,
Tel: +33 384 28 18 73

Sirguey Immobilier,
Tel: +33 389 07 77 17

Corinne, Valencay Immobilier,
Tel: +33 389 46 59 60

Vosges Mountain Properties,
www.vosgesproperties.com

The Loire

Caroline Vroom,
Vallée des Rois,
Tel: +33 241 45 22 22

Carolyn Cohen & Françoise
Bonner,
Latitudes,
Tel: 020 8951 5155

Nicholas Stallwood &
Stephen Small,
French Property Shop,
Tel: 01233 666 902

Sarah Francis, Sifex,
Tel: 0207 384 1200

Burgundy

Benjamen Haas, Burgundy 4 U,
Tel: +33 385 33 41 46

Derek Grimshaw,
Agence Maison René,
Tel: 023 9259 9409

Karine Chaumont,
Francophiles,
Tel: 01622 688 165

COMITE RÉGIONAL DE NORMANDIE

Poitou-Charentes

Samantha Lear,
Papillon Properties,
Tel: 01799 527 809

Nicholas Stallwood &
Stephen Small,
French Property Shop,
Tel: 01233 666 902

Sarah Francis, Sifex,
Tel: 0207 384 1200

Beth Edgell & Paul Owen,
VEF UK,
Tel: 020 7515 8660

Kay Dream Homes,
Tel: +33 6 81 74 98 46

L'Affaire Française,
Tel: +33 545 81 76 79

Limousin & Auvergne

Karine Beauvallet,
Demeures de France,
Tel: +33 1 44 17 95 40

Samantha Lear,
Papillon Properties,
Tel: 01799 527 809

Nicholas Stallwood &
Stephen Small,
French Property Shop,
Tel: 01233 666 902

Karine Chaumont,
Francophiles,
Tel: 01622 688 165

Rhône-Alpes

Nicholas Stallwood &
Stephen Small,
French Property Shop,
Tel: 01233 666 902

Sarah Francis, Sifex,
Tel: 0207 384 1200

Carolyn Cohen &
Françoise Bonner,
Latitudes,
Tel: 020 8951 5155

Aquitaine

Carl Schofield,
Vialex International,
Tel: +33 553 95 46 24

Cate, Agence Herman de
Graaf,
Tel: +33 553 62 38 03

David & Marian Howard,
Devon International,
Tel: +33 329 80 69 75

Karine Chaumont,
Francophiles,
Tel: 01622 688 165

Karine Beauvallet,
Demeures de France,
Tel: +33 1 44 17 95 40

Nicholas Stallwood &
Stephen Small,
French Property Shop,
Tel: 01233 666 902

Sarah Francis,
Sifex,
Tel: 0207 384 1200

Midi-Pyrénées

Carl Schofield, Vialex
International,
Tel: +33 553 95 46 24

Nicholas Stallwood &
Stephen Small,
French Property Shop,
Tel: 01233 666 902

Sarah Francis,
Sifex,
Tel: 0207 384 1200

Karine Chaumont,
Francophiles,
Tel: 01622 688 165

Carolyn Cohen & Françoise
Bonner, Latitudes,
Tel: 020 8951 5155

Action Habitat,
Tel: +33 565 29 74 74

Languedoc-Roussillon

David King,
David King & Associates,
Tel: 020 8673 6800

Karine Chaumont,
Francophiles,
Tel: 01622 688 165

Sarah Francis, Sifex,
Tel: 0207 384 1200

Anna McGee, Lavender
Homes, Tel: 0208 257 2459

Beth Edgell & Paul Owen,
VEF UK, Tel: 020 7515 8660

Nicholas Stallwood & Stephen
Small, French Property Shop,
Tel: 01233 666 902

Abafim,
Tel: +33 562 34 54 54

**Provence, Côte d'Azur,
Corsica**

Bernadette, Azur Properties,
Tel: +33 689 155 5062

David King, David King &
Associates,
Tel: 020 8673 6800

Anna McGee, Lavender
Homes, Tel: 0208 257 2459

Beth Edgell & Paul Owen,
VEF UK,
Tel: 0207 515 8660

Sarah Francis, Sifex,
Tel: 0207 384 1200

Index to advertisers

ADVERTISERS